REINVENTING (WITH) THEORY IN
RHETORIC AND WRITING STUDIES

REINVENTING (WITH) THEORY IN RHETORIC AND WRITING STUDIES

Essays in Honor of Sharon Crowley

EDITED BY
ANDREA ALDEN
KENDALL GERDES
JUDY HOLIDAY
RYAN SKINNELL

UTAH STATE UNIVERSITY PRESS
Logan

© 2019 by University Press of Colorado

Published by Utah State University Press
An imprint of University Press of Colorado
245 Century Circle, Suite 202
Louisville, Colorado 80027

The University Press of Colorado is a proud member of the Association of University Presses.

The University Press of Colorado is a cooperative publishing enterprise supported, in part, by Adams State University, Colorado State University, Fort Lewis College, Metropolitan State University of Denver, University of Colorado, University of Northern Colorado, University of Wyoming, Utah State University, and Western Colorado University.

∞ This paper meets the requirements of the ANSI/NISO Z39.48-1992 (Permanence of Paper).

ISBN: 978-1-60732-891-9 (paperback)
ISBN: 978-1-60732-893-3 (ebook)
DOI: https://doi.org/10.7330/9781607328933

Library of Congress Cataloging-in-Publication Data

Names: Alden, Andrea L., 1977– editor. ǀ Gerdes, Kendall (Kendall Joy), editor. ǀ Holiday, Judy, editor. ǀ Skinnell, Ryan, 1978– editor. ǀ Crowley, Sharon, 1943– honouree.
Title: Reinventing (with) theory in rhetoric and writing studies : essays in honor of Sharon Crowley / edited by Andrea Alden, Kendall Gerdes, Judy Holiday, Ryan Skinnell.
Description: Logan : Utah State University Press, [2018] ǀ Includes bibliographical references and index.
Identifiers: LCCN 2019020503 ǀ ISBN 9781607328919 (pbk.) ǀ ISBN 9781607328933 (ebook)
Subjects: LCSH: English language—Rhetoric. ǀ English language—Rhetoric—Study and teaching (Higher) ǀ Invention (Rhetoric) ǀ Rhetoric.
Classification: LCC PE1408 .R4275 2018 ǀ DDC 808/.0420711—dc23
LC record available at https://lccn.loc.gov/2019020503

Jim Simmerman's "A Blessing" was previously published in Home: Poems (Port Townsend, WA: Dragon Gate Press, 1983), 94–96. Reprinted with the permission of the Estate of Jim Simmerman.

Cover photograph: ruins of ancient theater of Herodion Atticus © elgreko/Shutterstock.

For Sharon

CONTENTS

        Matthew Heard   269

     Afterword: Feeling and Historiography
        Debra Hawhee   279

     Appendix: Sharon Crowley's Publications by Year   287
     Contributors   293
     Index   297

FOREWORD

Bruce Horner

Composition has long had a vexed relationship with "theory." We can account for the vexed character of that relationship in terms of the conditions in which most of those working in composition find themselves. On the one hand, theory can seem simply impractical for a field eminently focused on the practice of writing and its teaching, of no use in helping us figure out how to meet the urgent demands of this Monday's set of classes, or the stack of student essays waiting for us to read. Further, insofar as composition (courses, programs, teachers, and students) have been relegated to basement status in the academy, and insofar as "theory" is identified with those well positioned in the academic realm (theory, it seems, is always "high" and "critical"), invocations of theory have often enough provoked among compositionists a visceral reaction of suspicion. In short, in return for the contempt in which composition teachers (and students) have typically been held by their ostensible colleagues in the academy generally and in "English" in particular, compositionists have been tempted to reject all that reeks of the academic with disdain, "theory" included. And of course, there is the inevitable inadequacy of even the best theory to the fullness of experience: there is an unavoidable difference, as Raymond Williams has put it, between "what is actually being lived, and not only what it is thought is being lived" (1977, 131), that can make any attempt to theorize that experience seem impertinent.

Rhetoric, insofar as it is itself associated with theory, and even heralded by some as the theory by which composition might redeem itself in the eyes of the academy, has therefore likewise been viewed by many in composition with suspicion. And in fact, attempts by those in composition to resuscitate their academic institutional standing by claiming intellectual ancestry with the tradition of (Western) rhetoric have likewise been viewed with suspicion, not entirely unjustifiably. Like claims to having noble ancestry, the strategy of claiming such ancestry can often be shown to be both factually inaccurate and ethically noxious.

DOI: 10.7330/9781607328933.c000a

How then to explain the obvious appeal of theory, rhetoric, and rhetorical theory evinced by the contributions gathered here from folks who (also) identify themselves in some way with composition, or at least "writing studies"? I would submit that the appeal has to do not with the false promise of improving one's academic institutional status by aligning with high theory: it seems achingly clear that those identified with such theory will remain oblivious to what this collection and its contributors have to say. Instead, the appeal has to do with the potential uses of theorizing, drawing and building as need be on theories in traditions of rhetorical study, for both our understanding and practice of writing and teaching writing (broadly defined): theory not as disseminated entity—that is, as noun—but as verb: something we do, even when we don't recognize ourselves as doing it, and even when others fail to acknowledge what we do as theory.

In saying this, I am invoking theory not so much as something that tells us about what we do—theory as explanatory model—but, rather, from a Marxian perspective, as a "process in society" in Stephen Resnick and Richard Wolff's phrase. Hence, as Resnick and Wolff explain, while "at any moment, a theory is a set of concepts, . . . since theory is a process the set of concepts undergoes continuous change" (1987, 2). Moreover, theory is an "*overdetermined* process [whose existence] is determined by each and every other process constituting that society" (2, emphasis added). Theory, then, is a material social practice that goes unrecognized as such because of how theory and its value have predominantly been imagined. As material social practice, theory, like language, requires and is subject to constant reinvention in its dialectical uptake—moment to moment, site to site.

It is in this sense that we can understand an otherwise troubling anecdote in the interview with Sharon Crowley in that section of this collection. In the interview, Crowley, in describing her experience teaching a course in feminist rhetorics, reports that the older women attending the course "were quick . . . All this was just a case of having it articulated for them. They'd never been able to articulate it because they didn't know there was a language." On the one hand, the anecdote can be read as a story of the course gifting the students with the (feminist) theory that made sense of their experience *for* them—previously they "didn't know there was a language." In this reading, the course, and Crowley in particular, gave that language to them, a language that "articulated for them" what they had experienced and yet not known: the forms of articulation previously available to them were inadequate to, and thereby failed to account for or legitimize, their experience.

The appeal of theory in this reading is that it set things right for the students, who now knew what their experience was (just as, in a different setting, a sermon on, say, the fall from Eden would provide a different sense and knowledge of that experience). Theory, then, from this reading, is what sets things right (or so it claims). It is a story of teachers enlightening students who were previously in the dark about their lives. And it is a story teachers (understandably) love to tell ("I saw the light bulbs go on in their heads!").

But (and no one can determine this) it is also possible to read the anecdote as a story not of the students finally being enlightened about their experience by being given the right language with which to name it (e.g., "sexism," "patriarchy," "silencing") but, instead, of the students seeing the possibility of different ways of naming that experience—that is, of theorizing it differently, with different consequences for their lives going forward. That Crowley herself was (presumably) engaged in that theorizing in teaching the course would model that possibility, making it a practice all the more apparently within the students' own reach. This is the only way I have of making sense of Crowley's description of the students as "quick," a term that suggests not passive (if grateful) reception of enlightenment but, rather, the pace of movement—here, the movement of thought, which is assigned a pace—"quick" or "slow," "stuck" or "advancing."

This is not to say that the students would not have taken up specific terms gleaned from the course on feminist rhetorics or feminist rhetorical theory more broadly. In fact, it seems likely they would have, and did. But in so doing, they would have transformed the meaning(s) of what they took up in the specific uses to which they put them, in their own utterances. They were quick, that is, to put the theories presented to them in motion—to mobilize them, as it were—in the service of their own lives, experiences, interests, and thereby (inevitably) in the process to transform the meaning of the terms and what they were applied to. More to the point, those students would see such mobilizations, and reworkings, as something they were in a position to engage in, and that, in fact, they were responsible for engaging.

This is the sense I take of the otherwise ambiguous title of this collection—"Reinventing (with) Theory in Rhetoric and Writing Studies." Theory is, in this phrasing, both the object of reinvention and a means of that reinvention. At least within rhetoric and writing studies, then, this collection argues both that reinvention of theory is inescapable and that theory is a means to reinvention. To theorize is to reinvent, and reinvention requires theorizing. Such an approach to theory is at odds with the conventional notion of theory as providing the model that subsumes what it models in what Bourdieu critiques as a common slip "from the model of reality to the reality of the model" (1977, 29), or what Resnick and Wolff critique as "essentialist" theories (1987, 2–4).

But this collection is not only about theory but also about its reinvention and its role in reinvention, "in Rhetoric and Writing Studies." As I've already suggested, there is a noxious sense within rhetoric and writing studies that conflates rhetoric with theory and, so conflated, heralds rhetorical theory as the antidote to what ails composition, figured as unthinking, atheoretical action—mechanical movement, not mobilization. Refreshingly, as enthusiastic about theory, rhetoric, and rhetorical theory as this collection is, not one of the contributions invokes rhetorical theory in this way. Instead, then, of praising and prescribing theory, or rhetorical theory, theory is imagined as rhetorical: an invention to name and address exigencies, and hence in need of constant reinvention, and hence what we must continually work at as a means of engaging the material social realm as a "process in society": embodied practice.

Put another way, this collection eschews the ostensible exchange value of "theory" within the economy of academic institutional disciplinary value to focus on, and take up, the concrete labor by which specific (rhetorical) use values might be realized from and through theory and theorizing—for example, rethinking reason, institutions, the body, play, and theory itself—not merely for the sake of rethinking these (if one can imagine doing any such thing) but rather to intervene in the material social process: the seemingly endless killing of unarmed black men by police in the United States; institutional power relations; the prevalence of racist, sexist, classist, and homophobic discourse and practices; the ecological doom humans seem bent on pursuing.

The intricacy of this labor precludes my discussion of those specific efforts here. Instead, by way of illustration, I'll refer to the seemingly more matter-of-fact accounts of Crowley's mentoring of various (then novice) scholar-teachers (chapter 4) and her own account (interview in this collection) of her experience of being mentored. The former account, which poses her mentoring as "rhetoric as a theory and practice," describes not so much someone showing novice academics the ropes and helping them steer clear of institutional and career dangers (though there is some of that), nor someone giving them the goods—on institutions, or Derrida, or the Sophists—but, rather, someone positioning them as fellow theorizers: readers and thinkers about, say, Derrida, poststructuralism, the Sophists, even Crowley herself. The former account offers glimpses of the work of such theorizing, though it is not described as work: groups of colleagues gathering regularly to try to make collective, useful sense of some text—Derrida and others. As enthusiastic as Crowley herself appears to have been about what she and her colleagues were reading, in some ways what they were reading is irrelevant, at least from the perspective I'm advancing here. (In her accounting, Crowley observes that "it could have been anything else, really.") What matters instead is the way in which Crowley and her colleagues—established and not so established—seem to have positioned themselves vis-à-vis one another and the texts they were reading. Although the descriptions of these gatherings are brief, they appear not to have been characterized as lectures aimed at listeners; rather they are efforts at "intellectual sharing," which, notably, consisted of participants "scream[ing] and argu[ing] [thei]r way through [Derrida and other deconstructionists]" (see "Beliefs and Passionate Commitments"). Such engagements, while failing to conform to archetypal images of either mentoring or theorizing, rhetorical or otherwise, can nonetheless be usefully characterized as all of these, once we learn to reinvent mentoring and theorizing as involving such collaborative efforts—regardless of any specific conclusions to which such efforts might lead (pointedly, the anecdotes do not mention any conclusions arrived at).

I'm suggesting that this collection shows us how theory is and may be reinvented, and to what potential ends, and that, as inherently rhetorical, theory is in constant need of reinvention, and, further, why it matters how we take up the work of such reinvention. Shorn of its patina of academic respectability (and, concomitantly, irrelevance), theory, or rather (better) *the work of* theory, is both ongoing and necessary, even if often going unrecognized as theory and instead dismissed as just screaming and arguing, or mere learning. Theory's reinvention is ongoing and inevitable, but our reinventive work—our theorizing—has consequences. Reinventing theory as rhetorical, as reinvented and in need of constant reinvention, matters. This collection shows us how, and why.

REFERENCES

Bourdieu, Pierre. 1977. *Outline of a Theory of Practice.* Trans. Richard Nice. Cambridge: Cambridge University Press.

Resnick, Stephen A., and Richard D. Wolff. 1987. *Knowledge and Class: A Marxian Critique of Political Economy.* Chicago: University of Chicago Press.

Williams, Raymond. 1977. *Marxism and Literature.* New York: Oxford University Press.

A BLESSING

Jim Simmerman

As I understand it
Dowdall drove the car

and swapped a pint
of cheap hooch

for a bird
the size of a Hoover.

L.T. held it
in the back seat

and was shat upon
for his trouble.

Fisher got a haircut
and rode shotgun.

Crowley and I
were at the Branding Iron

scarfing omelets
and chicken-fried steak.

Reser was in Missouri
and the train

that hied him off
was already grinding

through cold New England,
sailing a smoky question mark

over maimed fields
of glittering frost.

　　　* * *

As I understand it
the neck was snapped

and pulled apart
as simply as a party favor.

DOI: 10.7330/9781607328933.c000b

The body hung
upside down for a day

to bleed, as far
above the snapping jaws of dogs

as a star, if you believe
that sort of thing,

above a manger.
In the interim,

Fisher was Oregon-bound,
his first family Christmas

in umpteen years.
Crowley caught cold.

The rest of us
huddled in Joe's Place

buying each other time
and beer.

It was the night before Christmas,
as far as it goes;

where we were going
was nowhere quick.

* * *

As I understand it
the goose was named Death,

and this is its carcass
slaughtered for meat.

Death, our collective goose, cooked
and carved

and the smell is sweet.
If we bow our heads now

it is not out of shame
or hunger

for those we miss.
It is not out of some

predilection for rite—
the tinsel of commerce,

the claptrap of church.
If we bow our heads now

it is only to draw
more closely together,

each unto each,
the family

we've made of ourselves
and are,

gathered for now
and what it's worth.

REINVENTING (WITH) THEORY IN
RHETORIC AND WRITING STUDIES

Introduction

METHODICALLY RE/MEMBERING THEORY
Crowleyan Invention(s)

Andrea Alden, Kendall Gerdes, Judy Holiday, and Ryan Skinnell

Any theoretical discourse that is entitled to be called "rhetoric" must at minimum conceive of rhetoric as an art of invention.
— Sharon Crowley,
"Composition Is Not Rhetoric" (2003)

In fall 2007, this collection's four editors enrolled in Sharon Crowley's penultimate graduate seminar, "Rhetorics of American Feminisms," at Arizona State University. Toward the beginning of the semester, as she did in many of her courses, Dr. Crowley introduced us to an etymological understanding of "theory," which derives from the Ancient Greek verb *theorein*: "to observe from afar." As she explained, during officially sanctioned events in the Agora—performances, trials, deliberations—a representative would be sent to the highest row of the theater to observe and record the entire proceedings, including, for instance, attendance patterns, speakers' performances, and audience reactions. The idea was that a more encompassing view of the situation was vital for understanding the event and its potential significance.

Details of that long-ago class have faded, but fortunately Dr. Crowley recorded her thoughts about the importance of the ancient notion of *theorein* in her book *Toward a Civil Discourse: Rhetoric and Fundamentalism.* She writes that in Aristotle's Greece, "A theorist is the spectator who is most distant from the scene being enacted on stage and whose body is thus in one sense the least involved in the production but who nonetheless affects and is affected by it" (2006, 27). For Crowley, the point of introducing her students and readers to the ancient sense of theorein was to encourage us to think about theory in different ways than we may

DOI: 10.7330/9781607328933.c000c

have been accustomed to. If it is common in the contemporary moment to define theory as abstract, detached, elitist, and impractical, the etymology suggests something like the reverse—theory is situated, temporal, quotidian, and performative. Theory is an embodied practice, even if the topmost theater seats are very far from the main event. Moreover, doing theory is a contingent and continual process indispensable for understanding situations and their potential significance—and, perhaps most especially, for discovering the available means of persuasion.

In Crowley's formulation, theory is a basic building block of rhetoric. When introducing the etymology of theory, she writes, "Another way to put this is to say that theories are rhetorical inventions: depictions or assessments produced by and within specific times and locations as a means of opening other ways of believing or acting" (2006, 28). Doing theory is the practice of surveying the common sense of the community (*doxa*) and discovering the available means of persuasion. The ultimate goal of doing theory in this etymological sense is not to prescribe certain actions (it is not *praxis* in the familiar sense). Rather, it is to ascertain what options exist for rhetors to shape the world around them. Theory is a crucial element of the invention work necessary for rhetors to see the world differently, to discover new possibilities for thought and action, and to thereby effect change.

Crowley's capacious sense of theory and its relationship to rhetorical possibility marks her numerous interventions into the field of rhetoric and composition. When she began studying and writing about poststructuralism in the 1970s, for instance, she believed it could help writing teachers confront the "poverty of current-traditional rhetoric" in very real ways (1979, 279). "Of Gorgias and Grammatology," published in 1979 in *College Composition and Communication,* just three years after the publication of Gayatri Spivak's English translation of Jacques Derrida's *Of Grammatology,* represents one of Crowley's earliest efforts to intervene in the pedagogical common sense that pervaded composition at the time. She argued that poststructuralism gave composition teachers a powerful, theoretical justification for trying "to implant in our students a Gorgianic respect for the power and magic of language" and for "imagining the teaching and learning of writing as a fun thing to do" (284). "Of Gorgias and Grammatology" was an attempt to see the world of composition pedagogy differently and intervene productively in the daily practices of writing teachers. It was also one of the earliest attempts to align the insights of poststructuralism more generally with work in rhetoric and composition in order to discover new possibilities for thought and action. She expanded these efforts in her first book,

A Teacher's Introduction to Deconstruction (1989), which was intended as a brief and lucid introduction to poststructuralism for English and language arts teachers at all levels—a marrying of so-called high theory with the daily work of English teachers that exemplifies theory's situated, temporal, quotidian, performative, and embodied possibilities.

A practicable orientation to theory, invention, and rhetoric is a common thread that animated Sharon Crowley's work as a teacher, scholar, mentor, and colleague over her forty-year career in rhetoric and composition across an impossibly diverse set of professional interests. She wrote expertly about poststructuralism, post-Enlightenment rhetorical invention, ancient rhetorical theory, composition history and pedagogy, intellectual labor conditions, abolishing the universal first-year composition requirement, material and bodily rhetorics, classical liberalism, Christian fundamentalism, American politics, and ideology—and that's to name only the major themes in her books. She taught a wide range of students at universities across the country how to be rhetors and rhetoricians, writers, scholars, thinkers, and members of many different communities. For those of us who cared to pay attention, she also taught us how to be better feminists, antiracists, and antiheterosexists. And in her spare time, among other things, she traveled the country, visiting writing teachers in their offices to try to understand the vast array of labor conditions that characterized the profession so that she could petition chairs, deans, and provosts (as well as dominant stakeholders in the field) to make teachers' lives better. In other words, she did theory in real material ways and tried to teach other people what she was learning in the process.

Throughout her books, articles, book chapters, and position statements; her teaching and mentorship; and her wide professional and institutional service, Crowley has consistently forced us to think about what it means to be a teacher, a writer, a rhetorician, a member of the field, a denizen of our local communities, and an able participant in global contexts. Sometimes she has pushed us hard in the face of (our) strong resistance, and doing so has earned her a reputation in the field as a "consistent contrarian" ("CCCC Exemplar Award Winner" 2015) and something of a polemicist—though, as she makes clear in a recent interview, she does not necessarily accept or feel comfortable with these characterizations (Crowley et al. 2017). Yet, her ethos as a critic is due in no small part to her capacity for "observing from afar" in ways that have repeatedly forced people in the field to see the world differently and to act differently in it.

We could go on, but notwithstanding the previous few paragraphs, the goal of this (re)collection is not primarily to sing Sharon Crowley's praises nor to exhaustively catalog her contributions to the field, were it even possible to do so. Rather, it is to take her notion of theory as an invitation and her practice of observing the field from afar as a provocation. As Diane Davis argues, the task of rhetorical theory "is provocation rather than explanation" (2015, 284). Theory's destinations cannot be prescribed in advance, Davis continues, because "theory that is not given the right or the freedom to veer off unexpectedly . . . is no longer active; it becomes applied theory, sleepwalking theory." What Crowley demonstrated throughout her career, and what Davis helps to elucidate (as does Horner in his foreword to this collection), is that theory must be continually refreshed, redirected, and reinvented if it is to continue to allow us to see, think, and act in new and inventive ways.

The field is more vigorous and more varied for Crowley's theoretical contributions, but rhetoric and writing studies still needs the aeration that reinventing (with) theory can provide. In the years since we left Crowley's classes, her etymological understanding of theory has remained critical for the four of us. It is a commonplace to which we have all returned regularly in our own work to try to discover new possibilities across a range of diverse interests. It is a working commonplace that we believe can help teachers and scholars periodically reinvent the field of rhetoric and writing studies "as a means of opening other ways of believing or acting." And it is the common thread that ties the elements of this book together.

In this book, therefore, we invited contributors to take up the practice of theory that informed Crowley's work. Note that this is not a collection of responses or correctives to Sharon Crowley, nor again is it a collection of encomia, nor is it even a collection of studies that explicitly extend her research. Rather, we asked contributors to take up her inventive *methods* by asking them:

> How might we step back productively and see new directions in the field?
> How might theory help rhetoric and/or writing studies veer unexpectedly? What other ways of believing or acting are potentially available?

In other words, without prescribing an end goal beyond opening new paths, we asked our contributors to do theory. The editors and contributors to this volume seek to observe from afar (though still affecting and affected by our scenes) in order to consider how we might see the field differently, discover new possibilities for thought and action, and potentially effect change in the field and beyond. Our contributors addressed an unpredictable assortment of issues and responded in a wide range of styles and tones that we believe illustrate the variety of ways rhetoric and writing scholars (can) engage with theory. This book moves in some unexpected—maybe even uncomfortable—directions. Bearing in mind the goals at hand, we consider that one of its chief merits.

The collection is bookended by a foreword and afterword, written by Bruce Horner and Debra Hawhee, respectively, that help frame the inventive possibilities opened by the work collected here. We have included some other supplementary materials that give shape and sense to the book as a whole, including some original content (described below) and a supplementary (and hopefully comprehensive) bibliography of Crowley's scholarship. The bulk of the book, of course, is the sixteen chapters that seek new inventive means in rhetoric and writing studies.

Based on the contributions we received, we organized the book into five parts. It should be noted that while many of the chapters could readily fit in multiple categories, we tried to arrange them kairotically, creating a space for each inventive contribution to resonate with related work and with readers.

The first part features just two items. The first is a manifesto on "The Remains of Theory" in which Diane Davis contends that theory is a never-ending pursuit of an ever-shifting horizon: theory invents by "destroy[ing] its 'own' borders." The inclusion of this manifesto reinforces some of the notions of theory we discuss in this introduction, and it points us forward by demonstrating the inventive operation that it also describes—it reads as a guided deconstruction and a deconstruction guide. The second item is an interview with Sharon Crowley that illustrates the practice of rhetorical invention—she (re)invents the itinerary of her career and gives readers an insider's look at some of the significant events, texts, and people that helped shape the field with and around her.

The chapters in part II engage ancient rhetorical concepts in some way or another to analyze contemporary rhetorical problems. Dawn Penich-Thacker takes us back to Greece in order to bring us forward. She looks at how ancient philosophical constructions of "reason" (*logos*) are codified in America's founding documents and continue to underwrite institutionally sanctioned racist, sexist, and homophobic violence. Judy Holiday traces the logic of identity to Aristotelian theories of logic (categories vs. predicables) to explain how identity constructs an epistemology that induces violence. Ryan Skinnell examines the long relationship of rhetoric to institutions and charts paths for (re)inventing institutional rhetorics. William B. Lalicker, James C. McDonald, and Susan Wyche conclude this section by theorizing a practice of sophistic mentoring based on what they learned, tacitly and overtly, from their encounters with Sharon Crowley throughout their careers.

Part III brings together chapters that examine the variety of disciplinary forms that rhetoric and writing studies take in contemporary composition programs and practices. Rhetoric and writing's sub/versive court jester, Victor J. Vitanza, plays around at the edges of one of the field's most cherished rhetorical concepts—audience—to imagine its limitations. Joshua Daniel-Wariya taxonomizes various theories of play at work in the field to imagine ways that they might strengthen and inflect what we know about rhetoric and writing theories. Joshua C. Hilst and Rebecca Disrud recall readers to ideological encounters that structure students' attendance in writing centers, where academic knowledge-making and pedagogical practices often confront the non- and extra-academic values students bring to writing centers. Kirsti Cole investigates how university writing programs are compelled to adopt, and also willingly adopt, institutional value systems that systematically exploit "disposable faculty" and exacerbate unethical labor conditions, despite pervasive disciplinary knowledge about the practices at hand.

Part IV includes chapters that speak to the materiality of theory and to theories of materiality. In her chapter, Jennifer Lin LeMesurier reinvents (at) the complex intersections of emotion and feeling, bodily movement, and rhetorical aims as they are enacted through dance training. J. Blake Scott and Catherine C. Gouge argue for theory building as a methodology for studying the rhetoric of health and medicine. Jason Barrett-Fox and Geoffrey Clegg link two posthumanist topoi—bioinformational and ecological—to rethink the ethics of invention. Bre Garrett investigates the rhetorical action of proximal bodies—in her case, through the lenses of disability studies and multimodal composing—as sites of multidimensional invention and rhetorical delivery.

In the fifth and final part, our contributors rework the nexus between futurity and survival. Kendall Gerdes begins the work of building a rhetorical theory of desire, extending the groundbreaking work of queer theorists to imagine what future(s) desire may make available. Picking up on future orientations, David G. Holmes elaborates the radical prophetic work—"not in the mystical sense of foretelling but in the material sense of forthright telling"—of African American rhetors, scholars, and preachers that allows us to imagine a more just, inclusive, and sustainable future. Timothy Oleksiak theorizes "reading someone to filth" and "throwing shade" as queer listening practices, in which queer rhetors and audiences confront each other, and teach each other how to survive, through insult and laughter. And in the closing chapter, Matthew Heard ruminates on the need to make *weaker* theoretical systems that will allow us, as rhetoricians and humans, to encounter other humans more flexibly on their own terms and in relation to their own needs.

We realize and accept that the choices from which this book developed are partial and limited. Or maybe it is better to describe them as situated, temporal, quotidian, and performative. There are many more available means to be discovered, now and in the future. That is, of course, the promise of Crowleyan theory-making—the task never ends. What we hope for this collection is that it spurs new directions in the field—new ways of thinking and acting for rhetoricians and writing teachers, scholars and students and administrators, and practitioners and theorists that help us see and engage an ever-changing set of situated ideological, material, and rhetorical circumstances. If we are successful, we will open new paths for thought and action, and, in so doing, we will honor Sharon Crowley and celebrate her contributions to the field and to the lives of countless people working within it.

REFERENCES

"CCCC Exemplar Award Winner." 2015. In *Conference on College Composition and Communication Convention Program*, 27–28. Urbana: National Council of Teachers of English.

Crowley, Sharon. 1979. "Of Gorgias and Grammatology." *College Composition and Communication* 30 (3): 279–84.

Crowley, Sharon. 1989. *A Teacher's Introduction to Deconstruction*. Urbana: National Council of Teachers of English.

Crowley, Sharon. 2003. "Composition Is Not Rhetoric." *Rhetoric/Composition: Intersections/Impasses/Differends*, ed. Lisa Coleman and Lorien Goodman, n.p. Spec. issue of *Enculturation* 5. Accessed August 30, 2016. http://www.enculturation.net/5_1/crowley.html.

Crowley, Sharon. 2006. *Toward a Civil Discourse: Rhetoric and Fundamentalisms*. Pittsburgh: University of Pittsburgh Press.

Crowley, Sharon, Ryan Skinnell, Judy Holiday, Andrea Alden, and Kendall Gerdes. 2017. "Forty Years and More: Reminiscences with Sharon Crowley." *Composition Forum* 37: n.p. Accessed February 13, 2018. http://compositionforum.com/issue/37/sharon-crowley-interview.php.

Davis, Diane D. 2015. "Fragments from: 'Rhetorical Theory: Questions, Provocations, Futures." In *Rhetoric Across Borders*, ed. Anne Teresa Demo, 283–85. Anderson, SC: Parlor Press.

PART I

1

THE REMAINS OF THEORY
A Manifesto

Diane Davis

Etymologically, theory is associated with the act of viewing, looking at, or beholding; literally and figuratively, it has to do with vision and the light, with the eye—both the organ that sees and the so-called mind's eye that ideates or contemplates. Often opposed to practice and to truth, it tends to connote passivity (thinking is not yet acting) and uncertainty, as in, "it's just a theory." Or more affirmatively, as Sharon Crowley proposes, theory is performative, "a doing, or an act that recalls a constructed set of other performances"; theories, she writes, are "rhetorical inventions: depictions or assessments produced by and within specific times and locations as means of opening other ways of believing or acting" (2006, 28). As rhetorical invention, theory involves illumination, bringing something to light, arresting a subterranean truth so that it can be seen and operationalized as a coherent practice or method or systematic belief.

What I want to propose here, however—for Sharon and in the name of taking her theory-as-invention provocation to the limit—is that the *force* of theory, its motive and motor, is a nocturnal operation: theory operates in the dark, actively (even hyperactively) tracking that which withdraws from presence and so from vision. There is an autoimmunizing force at the heart of theory that works to protect itself from what would, precisely, put an end to it: the certitudes of sight, both sensible and intelligible. Theory in general, I'd like to suggest, is indeed thoroughly rhetorical and *inextricably* tied up with in(ter)vention: it's the name for a self-deconstructive function intrinsic to any specific performance of theory-as-practice that clears a path for, and pledges itself to, a future that cannot be anticipated.

A theory, any system or performance of conceptual generality used to ground or explain something, establishes and puts itself to work through immunizing strategies, drawing and narcissistically protecting boundaries around itself for pedagogical, political, ethical—maybe

DOI: 10.7330/9781607328933.c001

religious—purposes. A theory must be delimited to be teachable, applicable, even preachable. But built in to any discernable theory is a quasi-suicidal drive that darts straight to the edge of the self-protective boundary . . . and jumps. Taking a hit out on itself, theory destroys its "own" borders, charging through "the very thing within it that is supposed to protect it," as Derrida describes it (2005, 123). The task of theory is not to defend what it brings to light but to respond to a call, an address that comes through in the dark from the as-yet-unthinkable; theory's task is to catch traction on the remains of the thinkable.

Any distinguishable theory is inhabited from the start by this auto-immunizing function, a force of weakness, driven to protect itself against its own protection, picking off its own border patrol to expose instead a *threshold*: a limit that joins what it also separates. Like any and every appreciable phenomenon, a theory defines itself, presents and protects itself, only inasmuch as its so-called constitutive outside—its originary contaminants, the border-crossing "not-its" at the heart of its heart—withdraw from what they've rendered possible. And this means, first, that every attempt to pin down or stick to a specific theory—say, a theory of ethos or kairos or "theory"—every attempt to explicate it by isolating it from a putative outside, ends up an attack on that theory itself, on a part of itself that got designated "other." That's the paradox of absolute loyalty. And/but second, it means that every effort to say, practice, or perform what this theory *is* invites all its not-its to loom up within it, to announce themselves again, to put a call out. In each iteration of this or that theory, the remains of some other here and now, some other not-simply-present presence, some other hope promises itself. And to theorize is to respond to that address, to promise oneself to that promise, to attend to the mark of what withdraws, and so to protect the finite opening to an incalculable chance.

Theory's task is to engage—without assured methods, ideological loopholes, or handrails of disavowal—the remains that haunt the performance of any specific theory, even as they displace that theory's horizons of expectation. Playing at the limits, theory puts those limits back in play, compromising the very identity, the self, "the *sui-* or *self*-referentiality," Derrida notes, of the *sui*cide itself. A theory's autoimmune function does not simply destroy itself "in suicidal fashion," in other words, but dissolves the identity that suicide presupposes, robbing "suicide itself of its meaning and supposed integrity" (2005, 45). Theory saves itself by offing itself: it compromises its "self," turns on itself, corrupts itself, *in order to protect itself*—not against praxis or politics—but against the certitudes of sight, which invite the regulation (and so the stifling) of thought by a telos.

The enemy of theory is what Michelle Ballif recently described as the "panicked rhetorical process" of burying the remains (2013, 143), burying them for the sake of some mystified end-goal, already lit up and waiting. Theory and in(ter)vention share this enemy, and they combat it together, Tai Chi style. Which is to say: not through direct opposition but by shifting position so that the "hostile force dissipates on its own," Avital Ronell observes; "this is another syntax of action, which also suspends the presumed difference between activity and passivity" (2010, 33). To theorize is to actively respond to a nocturnal address, to promise or pledge oneself to that which "obliterates the originariness of site," Ronell writes elsewhere, and of *sight*, to that which haunts the here and now without being simply present, visible, or clear (2000, 270). To embrace a real without remains, as if what is real could be condensed into sensible properties—viewed from afar or under a microscope—is to *refuse* to theorize. Theory, as this style of rhetorical in(ter)vention, is not "antirealist," a label certain contemporary proponents of "new realisms" are fond of tossing around, but a passionate and self-sacrificing love affair with the real: call it a realism *of* the remains. No remains, no theory; no theory, no future.

REFERENCES

Ballif, Michelle. 2013. "Historiography as Hauntology: Paranormal Investigations into the History of Rhetoric." In *Theorizing Histories of Rhetoric*, ed. Michelle Ballif, 139–53. Carbondale: Southern Illinois University Press.

Crowley, Sharon. 2006. *Toward a Civil Discourse: Rhetoric and Fundamentalism*. Pittsburgh: University of Pittsburgh Press.

Derrida, Jacques. 2005. *Rogues: Two Essays on Reason*. Trans. Pascale-Anne Brault and Michael Naas. Stanford: Stanford University Press.

Ronell, Avital. 2000. "Confessions of an Anacoluthon: Avital Ronell on Writing, Technology, Pedagogy, Politics." *JAC: Journal of Composition Theory* 20 (2): 243–81.

Ronell, Avital. 2010. *Fighting Theory: Avital Ronell in Conversation with Anne Dufourmantelle*, trans. Catherine Porter. Urbana: University of Illinois Press.

2

BELIEFS AND PASSIONATE COMMITMENTS
An Interview with Sharon Crowley

Andrea Alden, Kendall Gerdes, Judy Holiday, and Ryan Skinnell

In June 2015, the editors of this book traveled to Sharon Crowley's house in Arizona to interview her as a first step in the process. We sent her a series of questions in advance, which she refers to in some of her answers below and which should be fairly self-evident, but knowing that helps to account for some of the less-than-graceful transitions in the discussion. As Lalicker, McDonald, and Wyche's chapter in this book indicates, we were not the only people for whom an interview with Sharon seemed like a logical first step. The two interviews represented in this book were not coordinated, though some of the same issues did arise. There is also a third interview (Crowley et al. 2017), which was taken from the same discussion as this manuscript and published separately. What we have tried to do here is include only what we think are useful parts of the larger discussion with as little repetition among the three as possible so that readers will find distinctive value in encountering each of the texts.

We want to offer one additional caveat before leaving the interview to speak for itself. It will become fairly clear to readers that this discussion took place before the bulk of the 2016 presidential campaign. As we reread this interview in the process of composing the book manuscript, we were struck by how many times it raised issues that seem to demand fresh answers in light of the election results. Those answers aren't here, and we decided redoing the interview in light of what we know now would not serve the larger goals of the book project.

* * *

GERDES: Something that you teach students early in your classes is the Greek origin of theory and theory as a building block for rhetoric. In another interview (Crowley 2008), you mention reading *Of Grammatology* with a group you called the Poststructuralist Luncheon

DOI: 10.7330/9781607328933.c002

Club, and your first book, [A] *Teacher's Introduction to Deconstruction* (1989) was published about a decade after this reading group. How do you think your work helped introduce poststructuralism to the field? Was it significant that *Deconstruction* was the inaugural book in the Teacher's Introduction series? How central was *Pre/Text* or other journals for publishing poststructuralist scholarship and in creating an audience for it?

CROWLEY: Okay. Well I read through my own stuff in the last week, which is really weird after all these years. And I put together a little bit of an itinerary.

The Poststructuralist Luncheon Club began to meet in '77. My friend Bryan Short—whom I seem to mention everywhere—had been back to Yale for a seminar, and he had studied with Derrida. Derrida was at Yale in '76, and that was the year that Spivak finally got *Grammatology* translated into English, and Bryan came back just steeped in this stuff and kept speaking deconstruction. This was a foreign language to the rest of us. Bryan insisted we read Derrida, and we found we couldn't go it alone. So five of us—Jim Fitzmorris, Jay Farness, Mac Malone, Bryan, and me—would meet at one of our homes every Friday afternoon and read something from the *Grammatology*. We started with it and screamed and argued our way through the book. When we got comfortable with that, we started reading other things. We read a lot of stuff out of the journal *Diacritics*. We read Paul de Man and J. Hillis Miller and around in other deconstructive critics.

We would sometimes spend a whole afternoon on a page or two. And that was at the same time I was discovering the Sophists—I started reading all the historians of rhetoric, the traditional ones, when I got to Northern Arizona University (NAU) because I'd never had a chance when I was doing my PhD at Northern Colorado. I took a lot of courses in rhetoric from the speech department, but I wasn't able to take as much as I wanted and still get a degree in English. So I had this huge reading list when I got to NAU, and I immediately embarked on it and just fell in love with—if you can believe it—with Wilbur Samuel Howell. So I gave myself an education reading that stuff, and I got named the editor of the *Arizona English Bulletin*, which was one of the best of the local rags at that time. And through that I met a lot of wonderful people. Between the people at NAU and Arizona State University (ASU) and the University of Arizona (UA), we formed a little intellectual sharing group, and talked on the phone, and met at local conferences.

That's where I was when Bryan came back from Yale, and Derrida just blew our minds. I mean really just blew our minds. Fitzmorris was a Renaissance scholar, Farness was a classical scholar, and Malone was interested in hermeneutics. And me in rhetoric. Bryan was a Melville scholar, so even to speak a language together was hard for us. But we did it, and it was really fruitful—all of us published books out of that group. I also published "Of Gorgias and Grammatology" in 1979. That was my first effort. I gave that as a lecture at the Wyoming conference.

I was scared to death. It was my first big gig. I had new clothes, a new jacket, and I got up to Wyoming and realized everybody dressed very casually. I loved everybody at Wyoming. That was just a wonderful conference. So I get up on stage and give this paper on Gorgias and the *Grammatology*. After I was done, two older gentlemen came up to the lip of the stage and asked to take me to coffee. And as a young woman I thought, "I don't know about this." And then somebody came up and said, "Mr. Corbett, can I have something-or-other," and I realized it was Ed-fucking-Corbett, and it was Jim Kinneavy with him.

They took me to coffee and Ed says, "Send me that paper, to Three C's." Ed made me revise the paper three times, but one wants an editor like that. That was my first publication in poststructuralism. I did another piece in the early '80s called "writing and Writing" (1985), which is a critique of writing instruction. Then I published the *Teacher's Introduction to Deconstruction* in 1989. Michael Spooner, who was then the editor of NCTE and a former student of mine from NAU, said they needed a piece on deconstruction. So that's how it came about.

GERDES: It sounds like there was a lot of interest in the field.

CROWLEY: Yes, yes. Rhetorical study and comp instruction were just arid at the time. It was current traditional rhetoric in comp instruction and new critical approaches to literary study. It was formulaic and dry. I couldn't believe how excited my colleagues in literature were to read Derrida, and I mean it just opened up a whole new way of looking at things. It could have been anything else, really—anything that would have rescued us from where we were would have been great.

HOLIDAY: Did you stay in touch with Bryan Short over the years?

CROWLEY: Yes, yes. Bryan died early—actually while I was here at ASU. He was one of the best friends I ever had. And another friend up there, lifelong friend, Jim Simmerman who was a well-known poet. Jim taught me a lot about writing. I mean Jim was a practicing poet, wrote beautiful stuff. And a great friend. And then he died a couple years after Bryan. Both of those guys died way too young. They're both younger than me. That was really hard.

ALDEN: I don't think you can ever be ready for something like that.

CROWLEY: Right. Until you experience it. In the questions you all sent me, one of you asked about desire. And right next to that, someone asked about psychoanalysis and about the connections. And you know, I'd like for the profession to think desire and grief and other emotions separate from psychoanalysis—which has its own philosophical problems—and start thinking about the forceful rhetorical power of emotion. That's what I was trying to move toward in the Fundamentalism book (2006), but I was exhausted by the time I got to the end of that and couldn't go there. That's what would have come next had I kept writing, but I'm not even sure you can write that.

HOLIDAY: I'd do it with shame. Rhetorical work on shame.

CROWLEY: I wonder if shame isn't one of those emotions that's a little more accessible to—I don't want to use rational thought—but to language. But grief? And hatred? I've been thinking about hatred a lot this week as we all have [in the wake of the 2015 South Carolina shooting]. How can people be so angry and bitter? People thrive on it.

GERDES: I wonder if you could add anything about the *Teacher's Introduction*. What kind of reception did that get?

CROWLEY: You know I have no idea about the reception. The only person that ever talked to me about it was Ross Winterowd, and he wrote the introduction. Of course, he didn't like deconstruction at all, but he wrote a lovely introduction.

HOLIDAY: Did you ever use it with undergraduates or in first-year writing?

CROWLEY: No, but I used *Ancient Rhetorics* (1993; see also Crowley and Hawhee 2011), and the introduction of that is so poststructural. The one I did before Debra Hawhee came on board—it's less clear at the introduction—but it's more poststructural. You know, I could not have written about invention the way I did without Derrida. I could not have done it without feminism, too.

GERDES: Well that can move us into a question perhaps about the relationship between poststructuralism and feminism in your life. What do you see as the relationship between them?

CROWLEY: When I saw that you'd asked that question in the materials you sent me ahead of time, I thought, "Who the hell knows?" You absorb this stuff, and you use it, but you don't know specifically where it came from. When you write, you think, "Oh, I stole this from somebody. Who was it?" So that's what I mean when I say, "Who the hell knows?" I don't know.

I was in the second wave. I was in graduate school in the early '70s, and so I was part of consciousness raising and women becoming friends, which we never had before, and relying on one another, trusting one another in ways that we had never done before. All of that was daily-life kind of stuff before I began to read feminist theory. And there was feminist theory in the early wave, people like Robin Morgan, but not heavy theory like Butler. And that began to appear in the '80s and '90s. So I don't know how to answer your question. Feminism sort of becomes part of one's bones, does it not? And unlike deconstruction, which you have to learn, once you realize there's woman centeredness in the world and there's possibilities about centering yourself on a female identity, it's like "Oh, okay! I'll put this on and I'll never take it off!"

SKINNELL: We came across what we think is your first journal article (1973). It was specifically about feminism, but there's not a lot of other stuff in your work that is explicitly about feminism. It becomes an unmistakable undercurrent, but why wasn't feminism a thing you took up in the explicit way you'd done in that article?

CROWLEY: Because it was in capable hands. By the time I became a serious scholar there was wonderful work in feminist thought, and I wasn't up to snuff enough to compete with people like Elizabeth Minnich and Donna Haraway and Nancy Fraser and folks like that.

ALDEN: But you taught it—you taught all of their work in our "Rhetorics of American Feminisms" class, for example.

CROWLEY: I loved teaching that class. It was just great to teach feminist classes. One of my favorite experiences as a teacher is that I used to teach Feminist Rhetorics on the undergraduate level, which was the same as the class you took, but at the lower level. Which was fine, I wanted to teach the younger students, but some of the heavier duty stuff I had to leave behind. One time I taught the course and there were a lot of older women in the class—women who were returning to school, whom I loved. They work really hard and they were quick, especially in a feminist class. All this was just a case of having it articulated for them. They'd never been able to articulate it because they didn't know there was a language.

HOLIDAY: It was therapeutic to have it articulated.

CROWLEY: Yes. Right. But one day, it was quite a large class, about forty people. And all the older women were sitting in the front row, and all the young ladies were sitting in the back. I don't even remember what we're talking about, and a hand goes up in the back. One of the young ladies says, "Well I'm not gonna let anything like that happen to me." And you should have seen the women in the front. The eye rolling. It was all I could do to keep my face straight. I nearly collapsed of laughter.

ALDEN: Did they all turn around and go, "You just wait"?

CROWLEY: Well they didn't—they were all real polite, you know—but oh my. That's one of my favorite moments in the classroom.

SKINNELL: Well maybe that leads us nicely back to our scripted questions. We were interested in what you see as the promise of theory in general—rhetorical theory more specifically. Like, having feminism articulated, theorized, was really important for the women you're talking about, for example—and we were wondering if you could talk a little bit about that.

CROWLEY: Well that's exactly what I was trying to do. And one of you also made a comment about your understanding of invention in your questions. I said earlier that I couldn't have written about invention without Derrida and deconstruction, but that got me thinking that there isn't an expansive sense of invention out there in the profession. There just isn't.

HOLIDAY: How did you come to this expansive understanding?

CROWLEY: Well, I'm tempted to say it's from reading the Sophists. I mean, one doesn't read the Sophists—we don't have the texts. But I liked the Sophists because they're pre-Platonic. They're not stuck in the metaphysics of presence, and when you hear Heraclitus say you can't put your foot in the stream in the same water ever—if that isn't an antimetaphysical statement, I don't know what is. Lately I had an opportunity to read Epicurus, the Sophist associated with self-gratification. Actually, Epicurus was a very fastidious person. I don't know where this reputation has come from unless somebody tried to smear him like people tried to smear the Sophists. Anyway, Epicurus had notions about existence—he's the one who invented a theory of atoms. He thought everything consisted of atoms, and he was right of course. He was interested in flow and what happens when opposites bang up against one another. You can just get little tidbits of these philosophers because they've been erased from history by the Platonists and early Christians, who didn't want to tolerate that kind of complexity.

I think the same thing happened to the Sophistic notion of invention. Gorgias would get up and give a speech for three hours. He didn't write, he probably wasn't literate, but he could ring changes on commonplaces for three and four hours. Cicero could speak for five hours and never bore anybody. There were rhetoricians in the public square who spoke for entertainment. Crowds would go and listen to see how many changes they could ring on whatever issue was at hand in the politics of the day. And many of them weren't literate. That's invention. And it goes right along with what Derrida has to say about writing and how it's never subject to speech.

Writing is not subject to thought, it's the other way around.

HOLIDAY: Right, and it's material. So how did you help students arrive at this sense of both the theoretical and the embodied?

CROWLEY: I thought those classes went better without me saying, "Here's what the text says."

HOLIDAY: So how did you guide those conversations so students came to see how theory and invention were connected? Were embodied?

CROWLEY: Well, I really can't answer that question. How I did it, I don't know. I would like to say that's the texts I assigned and the students I worked with.

SKINNELL: Maybe we're asking the wrong question or asking it the wrong way. We've read other people in the field, people who are very well respected in the field, who clearly have different notions of invention than you do. We read some of them in your classes. So how did your vision of invention develop in light of the fact that invention was so well trod?

CROWLEY: Well it was because of the reading that I was just talking about—the Sophists and Derrida and feminist theory. First, I don't want to pass by that early period I was talking about without mentioning Jasper Neel's book about Plato and Derrida (1988). Jasper was there, and he had as much difficulty with the reception of that book as the rest of us did with the kind of stuff we were trying to do.

Anyway, honestly I had no idea my notion of invention was that obscure to people. I thought anybody who's read *Ancient Rhetoric for the Contemporary Student* has a sense of how important invention is. The entire book is about invention. We treat arrangement as invention; we teach style as invention. I mean, how can you not get a clue?

HOLIDAY: Maybe this is a good place to ask the next question. Your work really enlarged our understanding of invention. What other canons need enlarging?

CROWLEY: I'm not sure what the present state of scholarship is. I haven't been keeping with the journals, so I really would be fraudulent to try and answer that. But I do think there was a lot of potential in delivery. Barbara Biesecker was interested in that for a while—probably because of her interest in feminism and the use of the body. I think there's probably still a lot of potential there that nobody's even begun to go after.

I used to teach a class called style. I taught it forever at Northern Arizona University and then I taught it here at ASU. Students would write stuff for their other classes and bring it in; we'd put it up on a big screen and they'd say, "I don't like the way this passage goes." So we'd disassemble it and then reassemble it. With computers you can do that really fast and there's several versions, and you pick which ones you like. In the process, the student realizes she hasn't said what she meant to say, that something else emerges, and that's invention coming through style. That was a fun class to teach.

I mean, I'm not sure how useful the canons even are because when you start to think about them seriously, they blend into one another. They are pedagogical devices, the canons are. And unfortunately in the modern period, they get set up as categories. This really happens in early eighteenth-century or nineteenth-century American rhetoric, where they're just unassailable. And that's not helpful to anybody.

ALDEN: Shifting focus a bit, we're taking it over to ideology.

CROWLEY: Good, I feel more comfortable there.

ALDEN: Good. My question comes from "Reflections on an Argument That Won't Go Away, or, A Turn of the Ideological Screw" (1992). In it, you're defending Phillip Wander after the Karlyn Kohrs Campbell / Forbes Hill debate about the role of ideology. You say, "Ideological criticisms make superior claims on our attention because they acknowledge that all criticism is embedded in its practitioners' values and that any criticism must necessarily be contextualized by consideration of its practitioners' positions in the world . . . To claim as I do that intellectual arguments are always underwritten by ethical and or politically motivated warrants is finally to claim that intellectual arguments are always rhetorical" (262–63).

CROWLEY: What a slick move.

ALDEN: It was pretty slick. And I think many of the same tensions exist when we're talking about ideologically oriented criticisms versus what maybe we talk about as more traditional kinds of criticisms. I wouldn't say there's any real Aristotelian criticism going on anymore, but can you comment on how you see ideologically oriented analysis in rhetoric? Or in the world?

CROWLEY: Clearly we've had a wonderful demonstration since that terrible murder at the Emanuel African Methodist Episcopal Church in Charleston [in June 2015]. Nobody can even think racism, right? I don't know if ideology is the right word to use with regard to it, but it is a system of thought and a system of emotions and a system of bodily manifestation. What is it if it isn't an ideology? And we can't even think it. We can't say it. By "we" I mean Americans in public.

And finally—finally—Obama, of all people, talked about it at the funeral. He used the word "racism," and he said we have got to get past it. I don't know if that will go anywhere—it might drop into the ether. But we need that kind of discussion in public. There are some ideologies that we just can't utter on the public stage. I mean I watch discussions on television and black intellectuals are trying to talk to the hosts, trying to get them to see, and the hosts just can't. They can't see it. It's part of being white.

ALDEN: Yes, it is part of being a person of privilege. Certainly.

CROWLEY: Right. I can remember when I first started to see feminists—by that I mean, people who published in feminism—at the Rhetoric Society of America conference, just discovering rhetoric. It was so exciting and so much fun, and they'd go to a panel—I saw one on Fannie Lou Hamer, for example. The feminist scholars have all the feminist takes on Fannie Lou, but they'd go and hear a rhetorician talk about the speech Hamer gave at the Democratic Convention in '64. I could see the looks on their faces, like, "Oh, where has this been all my life?" And the hiddenness of rhetoric—I mean rhetoric in the sense of the stuff we study, and not in the sense that's all around us—is really still there, it sounds like. And that's very sad. But then on the other hand, if the university knew how subversive it was, they might stamp it out. So there you would be too.

But I don't want to leave this ideology thing because I have an actual answer to your questions. I reread this essay you mentioned here (Crowley 1992) and then I reread the Weaverville essay (2001). I read them in succession. Turns out they're the same essay. I never saw it before, but I see it now. What I'm saying is that the problem with all those people who objected to Phillip Wander is that they are metaphysicians or, in Richard Weaver's case, a theologian. They want to erect a truth with a capital "T," and then everything depends on that thing. And you cannot be a rhetorician and a metaphysician at the same time—you just can't.

SKINNELL: What I found really interesting about both of these articles is that they're not in defense of Wander's argument, necessarily. They're also not defending the attacks on his argument. Both are pleas for not dismissing ideological criticism—like, ideology is the place we need to be hanging out. And that to me is a really subversive argument because there's this commonplace that ideology is the worst thing ever.

CROWLEY: Well the thing about metaphysicians is they don't know they are ideologues. And the reason they don't is because they are so privileged. Nobody ever talks back. So, for example, when Ruth Bader Ginsburg, the notorious RBG, says to her fellow Supreme Court justices like Antonin Scalia and Clarence Thomas, "You're the dumbest man I ever ran across . . ."—she never says that literally, but that's what her dissents often say—what she's saying is, "You can't see beyond the end of your nose, and the reason is your male privilege and your class privilege and all the other things." There are still people in our culture who are like that, who believe that there is only one way to see the world.

ALDEN: Do you think people who do ideologically oriented criticism tend to be people who are marginalized in some way? Would you say privileged people tend to not think about it as much?

CROWLEY: Maybe, but there are examples of white males, for instance, who do really good ideological criticism. Then again, I've met men that I really admire intellectually. I admire their work, and then when I meet them and I find out they're raging sexists, it is just such a disappointment.

ALDEN: Maybe we can link this answer to another question. In *Toward a Civil Discourse*, you talk about rhetoric requiring a theory of desire, which is when you touch on Lacan and Freud.

CROWLEY: Well desire—that's all there is.

ALDEN: Can you talk about how you see psychoanalytic theory in rhetorical criticism and why people seem to have kind of a bad reaction to it?

CROWLEY: You know, I'm not sure why that is. I don't know where psychoanalysis gets its bad name. I found Freud, for example, very useful on occasion. His essay on the ego and the id, extremely useful. So I'm not sure why . . . what do you think?

ALDEN: I think because the entire enterprise rests upon a theory of the unconscious, and people are very attached to thinking that everything they do is consciously motivated.

CROWLEY: Okay. It's the same as the metaphysical.

ALDEN: It's a very similar hierarchy where people suggest they must be in rational control of their mind and reason at all times. It's the mind/body dualism. I think it's very much a part of Enlightenment ideology, and to suggest everything we do is being run by something we have no control over is really disconcerting to a lot of people.

CROWLEY: Well, or you could go straight to Derrida and say language is speaking us and there's stuff in language that misspeaks us. You could say it that way if that's less offensive and if you don't want to go to the psychoanalytic vocabulary.

SKINNELL: Is it less offensive?

CROWLEY: I don't know.

GERDES: I think the differences are important to think about, since these two bodies of theory were developed in very different contexts but seem to share a challenge to the capital "T" thing.

ALDEN: So this takes us back to your articles about ideology. For example, you say traditional criticism begins from a set of substantive warrants grounded in Enlightenment assumptions about the nature of inquiry (1992). You also say there can be no correct reading of a text and traditional criticism assumes there is a correct reading. Given that traditional criticism, the way you were talking about it then, has kind of died off, do you think that maybe that has been supplanted by social science research in English and communications?

CROWLEY: That's an excellent question. I don't have an answer, but I'd like to know what you think.

ALDEN: I think yes. The direction in which both English and communication studies are going. Social science research is the thing to do now—it's got numbers, it's got data, it's got quantification. So rhetoric is being kind of shoved out in favor of researchers who do social-scientific work. I feel like that's the new traditional criticism. That that's more valued way to study communication in general.

CROWLEY: That has a long history in speech departments though. Goes back to the '40s.

You talk to somebody like Don Ochs, or somebody of Don's generation in speech, and they would tell you they felt that way, too. Don was a Cicero scholar, and he was not welcome in the Communications Department. That's why he rotated over to the freshman rhetoric class at Iowa because at least he got to teach rhetoric courses and got to teach Cicero.

HOLIDAY: I wonder how political all this is in the capitulation to administrative purposes. I think about assessment in writing studies and the need for empirical results. It seems very political to me.

CROWLEY: You want to talk about politics? Communication studies got its origin in WWII. They studied propaganda. Roosevelt wanted to know how to find out how the enemy was thinking, so that's what they studied. And not only that, they studied how to bring the American people around to support WWII. Walter Schram and other people like that—that was their whole shtick.

HOLIDAY: I guess that sort of leads into my next question, which is that it's no surprise that you prefer to teach some theorists over others but there are some theorists that stand out as really important that we didn't get from you. For example, Kenneth Burke.

CROWLEY: I love this question. I took two courses in Burke. One from Tilly Warnock and one from Jack Selzer. No slouches, right? I tried. I tried really hard. And I found reading back through my stuff that I cite Burke fairly often. So I was reading him and using him. But I just never . . . I think I probably didn't feel I had a good enough grasp of Burke to teach the texts. That's why I didn't do it.

HOLIDAY: Why is that? I mean, I don't find him as more complicated than Derrida, for example.

CROWLEY: No, I'm not saying he was complicated. I mean slippery, I could just never get a hold of anything.

GERDES: I was about to propose an alternate rationale for your not teaching him, which you can embrace backward through history if you want, which was that his emphasis on identification seems not exactly consistent with your work.

CROWLEY: Yes. Unless you twist him—Jack Selzer has a cool way of reading the notion of identification that makes it more postmodern. I'm not going to try to elaborate that for you. But it can be done. But yes, you're right.

HOLIDAY: And how about Weaver? One of the reasons I say this is until I read your piece on Weaver (2001), I hadn't really thought about whether someone should be in or out of the rhetorical canon, but you argue for not including him in the canon. But then, as you say in "Pure Rhetoric," anyone can be a rhetorician (2009). So the question is, why not include Weaver in the canon?

GERDES: I think the canon is the wrong word for what we're trying to ask, in a way. It's really a question of who's doing rhetoric, I think.

CROWLEY: Of course, Weaver's entitled to do rhetoric. I mean, you know, he gave us a big boost back in the '50s when we needed it, and he ran a pretty decent communications program in Chicago. He taught rhetoric pretty decently, and it was an intellectually respectable program, which is more than you could say about a lot of communications programs in the '50s. So you can't discount him, but as I say in that article, he also participated in some pretty harmful ideology and politics. Weaver's really ugly work is in the unpublished papers and in his dissertation. There's really ugly stuff in those texts. Read "This Southern Tradition at Bay," which was his dissertation. It's since been published (Weaver 1989). And he's part of the Southern Agrarians. Robert Penn Warren, Cleanth Brooks—I mean, Cleanth Brooks did more damage to literary history than almost anybody you could name. He was the inventor of New Criticism, the point of which is to ignore politics and ideology and all of that.

I don't know how many of you heard the speech I gave at Rhetoric Society called "What Shall We Do with the White People?" (2012). Well, I prefaced that with a story about when I was fifteen looking at Elizabeth Eckford being harassed as she walked in front of Central High in Little Rock, and what I noticed was her dress. Totally skipped the racism and politics and ideology. I thought her dress was just lovely. And I wasn't the only one.

GERDES: Alright, switching gears again, here come the drugs questions. A few of us have heard you reminisce about your days smoking pot, running rivers, participating in consciousness raising, and I wonder about that in the context of activism and in what I would call in quotes here, a "nonacademic" part of your life.

CROWLEY: Actually when I ran rivers, we ran with sociologists and philosophers and other rhetoricians. It was a heavy academic crowd, although they weren't all. It was people who were friends, a couple bartenders. I don't know where we got this group together, but we were tight friends and we ran rivers together. With our group, the talk was always good. Around the campfire I remember it being very good and very stimulating. Problem is you can't write anything down, you know, because your notebook will get wet.

GERDES: I wonder about whether those relationships maybe led you to other kinds of activist work. Do you see there being anything separate from your scholarship that you would consider activism, and I wonder if not, then why not?

CROWLEY: I was an activist while I was an undergraduate, I was into the Anti-War movement, and when I was teaching high school, I got really involved in Democratic politics. I elected three lefties to the school board down in Port, Iowa. I ran their campaigns. They weren't enough to make a dent, but they helped. I traveled all over Iowa back in those days promoting Gene McCarthy's candidacy for the presidency. I got run out of town a couple times doing that. But that's about the extent of my activism. It was organized political activism.

GERDES: This next question again draws on *Women's Ways of Making It* (Crowley 2008), where you compare your relationship to writing on some projects to an acid trip. You remark on losing track of time, even forgetting to eat and sleep and feed the cats, and you talk about how hard your writing habit was to break. You were writing all the time and felt bad even to take a break on a Saturday afternoon to go for a drive. I really want to hear you talk about this relationship you have to writing. Part of that question for me is: Why write? And also, how has retirement changed your relationship to writing, and maybe: Why *not* write?

CROWLEY: I was hungry to write. I got out of a marriage because I couldn't write. I married in '79. It lasted three years, and I went off to Ohio State to an NEA seminar with Ed Corbett. Ten weeks on Ohio State's campus with twelve other scholars hand-selected by Ed Corbett and this incredible library. Ed made us meet three days a week just like it was a class. And the rest of the time he expected us to be in the library.

It was a great summer, and I came back and I looked at my husband and looked at where he thought we were going—he wanted to stay in Flagstaff and have children. I didn't want children and that was fine with him before we got married, but it wasn't fine after a while. So I divorced him. I laid on the couch for about three weeks and thought about my life and decided to become the person I became. I've never looked back. And part of that was just getting lost in that writing—doing a writing trip. When you're single, don't have any kids, you can do that. You can write whenever you want. I learned that writing under deadline for the first edition of *Ancient Rhetorics for Contemporary Students*. Back in those days I was teaching a heavy load at Northern Arizona University, and I had to have it done in the summertime. So I was doing four-hour writing stints. I just got addicted.

GERDES: I am interested in the figuring of that as a kind of drug and an addiction because I think that there's something even in the rhythm and schedule that exceeds the rhythm and exceeds the schedule. Avital Ronell calls it "tropium." I love that phrase. And to hear you talk about it that way . . .

CROWLEY: You know, I heard Kenneth Burke talk about it that way. Burke was at Wyoming one year. So accessible and so much fun. William Stafford, the Iowa poet, was there, too, and he and Burke were on stage in an evening session. They were supposed to have a dialog: rhetorician and poet. Here's Burke sitting at this little table—just scribbling away while Stafford talked and talked about the process he uses to produce poems. Just went on and on, until finally Tilly Warnock moved the conversation along. So she says, "Professor Burke, would you like to talk?" He sort of sits up a little bit, looks out at us with his piercing blue eyes. He smiles at us and says, "I just wrote a poem." And the lesson, not lost on that audience, was: you don't get writing by talking.

GERDES: That's great because there's this infectiousness to writing. I want to press you on, why write? Because it's addictive, because it's infectious, because it's a drug? It alters your reality?

CROWLEY: I think I wanted to know what I knew. What the people I was reading knew.

GERDES: So it was a way of thinking.

CROWLEY: Yeah, except as a Derridian I can't really make those distinctions. But you're right. I like the way you describe it. It's like a drunkard. You just need more. I get that with reading now. I've been reading about the Civil War, and I'm going through these heavy scholarly works on secession, and I'll go to bed at night and dream about it. When I wake up, I can hardly wait to get back to it. So I think there's something similar there, too.

GERDES: You say that reading is a way of writing (1989). It's another inscription of what you've read.

CROWLEY: Yeah. You know, *Composition in the University* (1998) was a duty write. It had to be done. Somebody had to show what an abomination the universal requirement was, and they had to do it in scholarly terms. So that was a political write. But the last one—*Toward a Civil Discourse*—that was a labor of love. Because I just wanted to figure all that out—and I didn't. I came to, at the end, a kind of aporia. I should have written another book. I should have gone where I couldn't go at the end of that book, which is a rhetoric of emotion—how do we enact desire in rhetoric, use desire, how we manage it if that's even an option.

GERDES: Well this actually could bring us to my next question—which is about the juggernaut force of an institution and where it pulls you. In *Women's Ways* (2008), you talk about the importance for young women scholars, especially, of finding women confidants, which I interpret as finding people both inside and outside of the field who you can trust. I think about that in terms of the need for solidarity in coping with institutional injustice. How do you cope with or live through the violence of the institution that you actually just can't stop? Sometimes you cannot stop yourself from getting run over by the force of the institution. How do you cope with that amount of institutional force?

CROWLEY: Well I expect you to know the answer to that question because you're doing it. Right? But, yes, once you become tenured, and even better, once you become full it becomes a little easier.

You know when I first knew how institutionalized the composition program is? I was WPA—then it was called Comp Director—at Northern Arizona University, and they had used the *Harbrace Handbook* for a thousand years. I finally went around to all the faculty who taught freshman comp in those days. NAU had a 4/4 load. This was way back in the old days—so I went around to all the faculty members that I knew and said, "This sucks, and here's why." I'd take the *Harbrace* with me, and I'd say we need to use something else. I finally realized they weren't going to let me banish a handbook altogether, so I got them to use Ed Corbett's handbook (1977), which is at least rhetorical. And I took that around to people and showed it to them. "Oh, okay. Alright. We can use this." So I ordered the handbook for the thousands of students that were going through the program, and I went on sabbatical for a year. When I came back, I went over to the bookstore and here's this big plat of *Harbrace Handbooks.* So that's when I learned—institutions are so strong.

But when you guys knew me I was a full professor, and I had been a full professor for a long time so don't mistake what's being called—what? fearlessness? (Crowley et al. 2017)—for the way I always was. When you're an assistant professor or a graduate student, there are super constraints and you just can't afford to tell the truth. You just can't. Except with your friends.

You know when you first started the question I thought, well, there's clearly a way to handle it. You just drink beer, is what you do. And run rivers with your friends. But when you see a colleague who's being abused, if you can strike up a friendship, that's something you can do. To help somebody. And the longer you're in an institution, the more you understand how it works, the more you can give to somebody who's new. But when you're young, it's usually just you and your colleagues. I'm sorry I don't have any magic.

GERDES: Sometimes institutional constraints put you in a position to not be able to avail yourself of those friendships because of competition and privileges that accrue to some people and not others for completely unfair reasons.

CROWLEY: That's the point. Departments are being leaned on by some administrator who has a sheet that he or she has to fill out. And it isn't fair. And the thing you have to learn to do is do your work and not let that affect you if you can. I'm sorry.

GERDES: No, I mean. I think that's a shitty reality that is what I wanted to ask you about.

SKINNELL: Speaking of shitty institutional realities, here's the last hard question from me. One of your persistent interests throughout your career was labor in the field. It resulted in the "Wyoming Resolution" and your advocacy for abolishing the first-year requirement. In some of your papers [archived at the National Archives of Composition and Rhetoric] you reflected on the failures of the Wyoming Resolution, and you said, in effect, "We would go into departments and talk and they ran us out. We would try and have discussions at C's or at MLA and we were chased off the stage."

CROWLEY: Actually we did better with deans. We got sent to a deans' meeting someplace in California once, Jim Slevin and I. Jim was a department chair at Georgetown then, so people listened to him. And they were very receptive, and to a person they said, "Talk to department chairs. It's English departments that are the problem." Of course that's probably blame passing, but on the other hand they were right. They were saying, "We're receptive. We like what you're saying. Go talk to the English department chairs." At MLA we would get support. I talked at a chairs' meeting here in Tempe. David Laurence got me invited to that. And they were very receptive—the English chairs. J. Hillis Miller was in the audience, and he stood up and said, "This is the greatest thing since bread. Let's do it!"

SKINNELL: Years ago you told us you were all but exiled after you wrote "How the Professional Lives of WPAs Would Change If FYC Were Elective" (2002).

CROWLEY: Well I never went to the conference, but you know, they had this great list, the WPA-L listserv. Oh, man. I had to stop reading that.

SKINNELL: Were you prepared for that sort of reaction?

CROWLEY: No I wasn't. But it didn't hurt me if that's what you're asking.

SKINNELL: No, I'm asking if you had expected it. To what degree do you still feel compelled to write something like that if you know how hostile the reaction is going to be?

CROWLEY: If you did what I did—I had a sabbatical, and I spent a lot of it traveling. CCCC's gave me some money to do it because I was running the National Committee on Professional Standards in Postsecondary Writing Instruction, and I got some money from universities to visit. People would ask me to come and give a talk, and then I'd really go talk to the part-timers. And the stories I heard would break your heart, you know? It was just awful.

And once you've been through that experience, you don't really care what WPAs think. You really don't.

If you're going to be a WPA, I can understand doing it to further your career and I suspect some of you will have to do that in your lives. And that's good because you can administer the thing as humanely as you can. But I think you'll find when you get in there, that there are a lot of limits on how humanely you can run the program. And it just eats your soul. Just eats your soul.

SKINNELL: So given what you know about the current state of the field, it appears your advocacy did not achieve its ultimate goals. At least in the short term. What do you see as your successes in the labor fights, and what do you think maybe you would have done differently in the fight over academic labor?

CROWLEY: I don't know that we succeeded at all. I predicted back then that things would be exactly like they are now. I couldn't see that there would be any change. As far as I can tell, they're just worse, at least in the freshman program. And I think what's happened is that the model has been now transferred to the undergraduate curriculum as a whole in more disciplines than ours. I read in the *Chronicle* about philosophers and historians now having the same set of issues. And they don't know how to deal with it any better than MLA did back in the day. And they really have less interest in dealing with it until it starts to threaten their own position. I'm sorry I wish I didn't have to say that. I think it's going to get worse before it gets better.

SKINNELL: What do you mean it's going to get worse?

CROWLEY: The first-year requirement looks pretty good to the corporate world. We do business there just like they're used to doing business. So, the first-year program will always be welcome in the corporate university, I think. I think we'll be lucky if philosophy and literary study and history continue to exist, except at the Ivys and a few R1s, in fifty years' time. I've lived a long time and I've read a lot of history, and I think that universities will change back. In other words, the humanities will come back when some rich guy somewhere fifty years from now realizes what harm has been done. And then the humanities will come back, or something like the humanities will come back. But in the meantime, there are going to be two or three generations of Americans who don't read. Or who read engineering and manuals and stuff.

SKINNELL: So given that, was the time you spent advocating for labor time well spent?

CROWLEY: Sure it was. Here and there people got their conditions changed, and surely the Wyoming Resolution raised consciousness. People at least tried for a while to fix conditions. There had to be local and temporary effects. I know there were because I talked to a lot of people. So I'm sorry, I wish I could be more sanguine about the future, but I don't think it was wasted time or wasted work. Not at all. Because there were local and temporary changes.

HOLIDAY: That sort of reminds me of the first wave of feminism—how long it took. So we don't know, right? What that consciousness-raising does.

CROWLEY: The first thing I did when I retired was start reading American history. The first black people, you know, arrived in America in 1619. I'm not good at math but you can figure out how long that's been, and look at the position black people are still in. Women are still treated terribly in a lot of the world, too. Sorry. This is really throwing a wet blanket on things.

GERDES: I think people need to hear this. I think part of what we do when we ask this question is sound a call to wake people up to where we're at, where we want to be, and the gap between those things.

HOLIDAY: What is something that you haven't yet been asked that perhaps we should have asked? Had you been interviewing yourself, what would you have asked?

CROWLEY: Well if I were given a chance to interview Janice Lauer or Victor Vitanza or some other long-term person, I would ask them, "What kept you going? What kept you getting up every day?"

ALDEN: We're running low on time, so now you have to talk about what you hope your legacy is. We know you're really uncomfortable talking about your legacy, but we'd like to ask you to think about it. Personally, professionally, whatever.

CROWLEY: Well anybody who writes—I'm sure that Shakespeare would have said, if indeed Shakespeare actually wrote the plays, that he would want people to remember his work. To like it and celebrate it. I suppose all of us feel that way. All of us who write.

REFERENCES

Corbett, Edward P. J. 1977. *Little Rhetoric and Handbook*. Hoboken, NJ: Wiley.

Crowley, Sharon. 1973. "The Semantics of Sexism." *ETC: A Journal of General Semantics* 23 (4): 407–11.

Crowley, Sharon. 1985. "writing and Writing." In *Writing and Reading Differently: Deconstruction and the Teaching of Composition and Literature*, ed. J. Douglas Atkins and Michael L. Johnson, 93–100. Lawrence: University of Kansas Press.

Crowley, Sharon. 1989. *A Teacher's Introduction to Deconstruction*. Urbana: NCTE.

Crowley, Sharon. 1992. "Reflections on an Argument That Won't Go Away, or, A Turn of the Ideological Screw." *Quarterly Journal of Speech* 78 (4): 450–65.

Crowley, Sharon. 1993. *Ancient Rhetorics for Contemporary Students*. 1st ed. New York: Macmillan.

Crowley, Sharon. 1998. *Composition in the University*. Pittsburgh: University of Pittsburgh Press.

Crowley, Sharon. 2001. "When Ideology Motivates Theory: The Case of the Man from Weaverville." *Rhetoric Review* 20 (1–2): 66–91.

Crowley, Sharon. 2002. "How the Professional Lives of WPAs Would Change If FYC Were Elective." In *The WPA Handbook: A Guide to Reflective Institutional Practice,* ed. Theresa Enos and Stuart Brown, 219–30. Mahwah, NJ: Erlbaum.

Crowley, Sharon. 2006. *Toward a Civil Discourse: Rhetoric and Fundamentalisms.* Pittsburgh: University of Pittsburgh Press.

Crowley, Sharon. 2008. "Sharon Crowley." In *Women's Ways of Making It . . . In Rhetoric and Composition,* ed. Michelle Ballif, Diane Davis, and Roxanne Mountford, 217–32. Mahwah, NJ: Erlbaum.

Crowley, Sharon. 2009. "Pure Rhetoric." In *Renewing Rhetoric's Relations to Composition: Essays in Honor of Theresa Jarnagin Enos,* ed. Shane Borrowman, Stuart Brown, and Thomas P. Miller, 315–28. New York: Routledge.

Crowley, Sharon. 2012. "What Shall We Do with the White People?" In *Concord and Controversy: Proceedings of the Rhetoric Society of America,* ed. Antonio de Velasco and Melody Lehn, 9–22. Long Grove, IL: Waveland Press.

Crowley, Sharon, and Debra Hawhee. 2011. *Ancient Rhetorics for Contemporary Students.* 5th ed. New York: Longman/Pearson.

Crowley, Sharon, Ryan Skinnell, Judy Holiday, Andrea Alden, and Kendall Gerdes. 2017. "Forty Years and More: Reminiscences with Sharon Crowley." *Composition Forum* 37: n.p. Accessed February 13, 2018. http://compositionforum.com/issue/37/sharon-crowley-interview.php.

Neel, Jasper. 1988. *Plato, Derrida, and Writing: Deconstruction, Composition and Influence.* Carbondale: Southern Illinois University Press.

Weaver, Richard M. 1989. *The Southern Tradition at Bay: A History of Postbellum Thought.* Washington D.C.: Regnery.

PART II

3

THE FALLACY OF REASON

Dawn Penich-Thacker

Police shootings, especially in minority communities across the United States, are not new, but their coverage in mainstream media is in a *kairotic* moment. The injustice of police shootings is increasingly under media scrutiny and garners headlines. In many instances, however, after the media attention has faded, judges or juries find the police officers acted with a "reasonable use of force" based upon a legal standard called "objective reasonableness." Given the regularity with which what seems clearly to be injustice is justified by reference to reason, it is important to look carefully at what is actually being asserted. I argue the concept of "reason" has enjoyed an irreproachable position since the days of ancient Greek philosophy. Following the Enlightenment, reason became a fundamental premise of America's founding documents, and it continues to guide US law and law enforcement. I will demonstrate how Sharon Crowley's (2006) theory of "ideologic" explains why reason has repeatedly won what is essentially an intellectual and political survival of the fittest by articulating—being articulated—with deeply held beliefs situated within powerful discourse communities that enjoy privileged access and scope. Put simply, reason (*logos*) has never been properly recognized or treated as belief (*doxa*) because those who forward its definition and authorize its application are, and have always been, institutionalized members of the hegemonic power structure: first philosophers and their wealthy protégés, then elite Western intellectuals and Founding Fathers, and finally Supreme Court justices and law enforcement officers. By capitalizing on ideologic, these communities have ensured that reason in the current moment cannot be dis-entangled from concomitant core beliefs in Christian righteousness, Anglo-dominance, inherent institutional membership, and intellectual objectivity. Reason was invented by an elite white male power structure and remains the purview of the same elite white male power structure.

DOI: 10.7330/9781607328933.c003

This is nowhere more clear than in the numerous police killings of unarmed Black citizens after which police officers go uncharged or acquitted, protected by the Fourth Amendment's "objective reasonableness" standard and the law enforcement policies predicated upon it since at least 1989, when the Supreme Court ruled in *Graham v. Connor* on "use of force." Probably most famously, on August 9, 2014, in Ferguson, Missouri, Officer Darren Wilson fatally shot Michael Brown, an unarmed eighteen-year-old African American. A Saint Louis County grand jury had to "consider the grounds for official use of deadly force, which is legal when an officer 'reasonably believes' that a person 'may otherwise endanger life or inflict serious physical injury' . . . which allows anyone to use deadly force when he or she 'reasonably believes' it is necessary to prevent death or serious injury" (Eckholm and Bosman 2014, A9). In former prosecutor Katherine Goldwasser's recap, she states, "At bottom is their view of the reasonableness of a belief that his own or someone else's life was in jeopardy . . . if you think that it was reasonable, then you don't charge him. If you think it was unreasonable, you charge" (qtd. in Eckholm and Bosman 2014, n.p.). In Wilson's case, the grand jury decided against charging him with any crimes.

Two days before that decision, on November 22, 2014, in Cleveland, Ohio, Officer Timothy Loehmann fatally shot Tamir Rice, a twelve-year-old unarmed African American boy. The Cuyahoga County prosecutor argued, "there was no reason for the officers to know [the child was unarmed], and that the officer who fired, Timothy Loehmann, had a reason to fear for his life . . . no matter how tragic the circumstances involved in Tamir's death, the law gives the benefit of the doubt to officers." The prosecutor offered expert witnesses to testify Loehmann's conduct was "reasonable and justified," stating the child's death was "unfortunate and regrettable. But it was not, by the law that binds us, a crime . . . Officer Loehmann acted reasonably in shooting Tamir." The grand jury agreed, and Loehmann was not charged (Williams and Smith 2015, A1).

Four months later, on April 12, 2015, in Baltimore, Maryland, Officer Brian Rice and five other officers took Freddie Gray, a twenty-five-year-old African American man, into custody. Gray was fatally injured while being transported by officers in a police van wherein he was handcuffed, but not seat-belted, and left unsupervised for hours while the officers made several unrelated stops.

The lawyer for the officers argued Gray caused his own death, and "there was no evidence that the lieutenant had a 'corrupt motive' or expected that to happen . . . 'the state has failed to present a single witness or shred of evidence to suggest what [he] did wasn't reasonable'"

(Bidgood 2016, A13). By July 27, 2016, all six officers indicted in the Gray incident were either acquitted of all charges or had their charges dropped. Again and again, *reason* is the standard by which such actions are judged.

The Fourth Amendment to the Constitution, added in 1789, ensures "the right of the people to be secure in their persons, houses, papers, and effects, against unreasonable searches and seizures." Despite this sole mention of the term, the concept of reasonableness has developed over time to become one of the most ubiquitous legal standards in American law and law enforcement. "Objective Reasonableness" is the standard by which every judge and jury in the United States is obliged to abide; "reason" is literally the difference between innocence and guilt, life and death, even though designating something as reasonable begs the question of what reason really means.

THE BIRTH OF REASON: ANCIENT GREECE AND ROME

The ancient Greek concept *logos* has a complex history, which numerous scholars of rhetoric have documented and analyzed.[1] Here, I offer an accelerated recapitulation of that complex history in order to contextualize my own use of *logos* to mean "reason."

For rhetoricians, definitions beginning with fifth-century-BCE philosophers are most familiar. For Protagoras and Isocrates, *logos* denoted truth, a concept preexisting the artful maneuverings of *rhetorike* (Schiappa 1992, 1). For all their disagreements, sophistic definitions and those of Socrates and Plato largely coalesce. While today, teachers of rhetoric aim to help students distinguish between fact and belief—*logos* and *doxa*—the ancients conceptualized these terms in deeply related ways. Plato follows Socrates in his understanding of *doxa* as both the inevitable end-state of proper reasoning and the fully realized potential of *logos* (Lott 2011, 358).

For Aristotle, *logos* is divine, beyond interrogation, and therefore unquestionably trustworthy—not unlike *doxa* (Richard 1994, 170). In the *Nicomachean Ethics*, Aristotle relies almost entirely on *logos* to describe men's rightful thoughts, desires, and actions (2004, 1149a). Possessing and recognizing "right reason" is crucial, but for Aristotle, more important is the "presence" of logos, which Thomas Pfau interprets to mean *logos* as *praxis*—reason realized in action (2010, 293). I will later show how this circular reasoning ensures a "reasonable" police officer's actions are immediately deemed "reasonable" by virtue of white men in positions of authority already being granted reasonable status.

For the Stoics, logos was universal and unchanging. Seneca writes, "In our eyes, the fact that all men agree upon something is proof of its truth" (qtd. in Richard 1994, 170). This self-edifying function thrives in contemporary American judicial and law enforcement power structures. Likewise, Cicero predicated much of his work about government, law, and persuasion on "divine" albeit "dynamic" origins: "the original and final law is the intelligence of God, who ordains or forbids everything by reason" (1998, Book 2, 7–10). Nevertheless, Cicero subscribed to a tradition that embraced contradiction. *Dissoi logoi* describes discordant ideas or arguments existing in concert with one another.

Ancient rhetorical philosophers' comfort with duality is significant when considering the tremendous influence classical philosophy had on the Western Enlightenment and America's Founding Fathers. Just as logos was the predominant pre-Christian doxa for the ancients, it followed that Christian doxa served as the premise of reason for the Founders: "the founders interwove Christianity and classical philosophy . . . to the founders, reason and tradition need not be opposed" (Richard 1994, 194–95). This comingling of logos and doxa—specifically the invulnerable and irreproachable quality of reason as "divine"—is the problematic core of contemporary law and law enforcement, which continues to adhere to the concept of "objective reasonableness." This conflation allows logos and doxa to function interchangeably in a way that informs American law and exists at the core of untenable legal patterns in contemporary America. Put simply, the root problem of the Fourth Amendment, police shootings of unarmed Black people, and either no charges or jury acquittals is that the state of "being reasonable" is code for "being a member of a privileged class" (which also, incidentally, often implicitly means white men). This code was written by Greek and Roman philosophers, revived and refined by Western intellectuals, and ultimately institutionalized in the founding documents of the United States.

ENLIGHTENMENT AND THE BIRTH OF AMERICA: THE FOUNDING FATHERS ON REASON

Historian Carl Richard outlines how the men who conceived of American government, the Founding Fathers, "turned to the ancients for their models of government, most notably the Greek republics of the fifth and fourth centuries" (1994, 74). Historians have written extensively about how fully the Founding Fathers integrated ancient ideas and values into their personal and professional identities. Rigorous education in Greek and Latin philosophical works began in primary school and remained constant throughout the Founders' formative years and into college. Ancient philosophers were so present in the lives of elite British and American schoolboys that they were considered personal companions and role models. From archival ledgers of fraternal organizations, we know George Washington took on the persona of Cato, John Adams adopted the pseudonym Cicero, and Patrick Henry was known as Demosthenes (Richard 1994, 58–68). Other ancient traditions the Founders relied upon were attitudes toward civic service, patriotism, colonial practices, the proper role of the military, and a strong sense of superiority over nonwhites (Richard 1994, 53–84, 96; Mills 1997). The Founders "formulated an American public philosophy . . . that affirmed the existence of God, the moral (as well as the natural) order of the universe, the accountability of man, and the importance of practicing the Christian virtues" (Meyer 1976, 181). For all of their progressive ideals, their historical training and allegiance to naturalism and Christian virtues provided a premise from which to justify protecting slavery and institutionalizing racism.

Tasked with creating the documents with which to govern a new nation, the Founders "truly believed that ancient history was a source of knowledge which must be utilized in making decisions" (Richard 1994, 84). In the early and mid-eighteenth century, American lawyers and judges were primarily taught Roman law, a formalized offshoot of natural law (182). Following ancient Roman distinctions between the civilized and the barbarians, they "set up a 2-tiered moral code with one set of rules for whites and another for nonwhites" (Mills 1997, 23). This influence is impossible to downplay. Put within the context of their belief in the *un*-natural, *un*-teachable, and *non*-Christian African slave (or any nonwhite person), by connecting these beliefs—practicing Sharon Crowley's process of ideologic—they created a category of "subpersons" (Mills 1997) who would always be excluded from the bounty of their new American republic.

The Founders' other primary source of inspiration was the Western Enlightenment. Jonathan Israel points out the Founding Fathers were proficient in Enlightenment philosophy, and they used its arguments in highly variegated ways (2010, 40–46). Western Enlightenment philosophers insisted on "the need to base institutions, politics, and legislation on pure reason alone" (157). Reason was the preeminent ideal. David Hume wrote of using reason as a "weapon" (Meyer 1976, 169). John Locke resurrected the "man of reason"—following Plato, Aristotle, and Cicero—as an individual "insulated from the influence of embodiment, passions, and social relations" (Shanks 2011, 33). The Founders gained from Locke a clear sense of "natural reason" that echoed the universalist perspective of the ancient philosophers (Locke 1764, 1690).

The Enlightenment had no more astute a student than Thomas Jefferson, the principal author of the Constitution. The American Enlightenment advocated striking a balance between Christian faith and natural reason; subsequently Jefferson's work on the founding documents aimed to "reconcile faith and reason" (Meyer 1976, 166). Unfortunately, Jefferson's take on the Enlightenment's discussions of faith and science included dismissing the tensions between and among those ideas as "mere 'difference of opinion' [which made American citizens] more reluctant to face up to the profounder political, and ultimately moral, implications of their own premises" (174). This failure encapsulates an early failure to interrogate the notion of reason itself vis-à-vis its definition, scope, and function within a liberal democracy. Their dismissal of the need to define terms and interrogate applicability founded the new world on several abstract principles and myopic assumptions. Indeed, *The Federalist Papers*, which were published between 1777 and 1778 to encourage ratification of the Constitution, refrain from "too precise a definition of [reason and rational], assuming that all right-thinking people are in basic agreement" (Meyer 1976, 184). D. H. Meyer also points out that leaving the fundamental vocabulary of the founding documents vague was simultaneously an assumption that everyone (who mattered) held the same opinions and values (185).

Nevertheless, not all Enlightenment thinkers were as pure in their devotion to reason as Locke and Jefferson. Thomas Hobbes "questioned the reliability of reason . . . the infinite variety of interpretations . . . which in different tempers, customs, and doctrines of men are different" (qtd. in Richard 1994, 173). Challenging his contemporaries' devotion to objective reason as naturally superior and empirically self-evident, David Hume cautioned, it is "on opinion only that government is founded . . . the most despotic and most military governments, as well as . . . the most free and most popular" (qtd. in Barrozo 2005, 235). In this sense, Hume's words of warning align with Meyer's observation that American intellectual life during the eighteenth century, among its many progressive leaps forward, "exhibited a certain capacity for moral blindness" (1976, 184).

Contemporary America continues to suffer from the same malady. The 1776 moral blind spot regarding slavery is the 2016 blind spot regarding the mundanity that attaches to the killing of African American men, women, and children and the refusal to charge or convict the

police officers responsible. As Charles Mills argues, "it would be a fundamental error . . . to see racism as anomalous, a mysterious deviation from
European or Enlightenment humanism. Rather, it needs to be realized
that, in keeping with the Roman precedent, European humanism meant
that only Europeans were human" (1997, 26–27). This belief was deeply
engrained and largely unproblematized in the Founders' mentality even
as they crafted language about the equality of all men and the inherent
liberties to which they are entitled.

The nineteenth century was marked by the "view that reason is able
to satisfactorily solve the ontological and causal riddles of social reality,
to imagine ever better models" (Barrozo 2005, 237). The key term is
"imagine." The "reasonable man" of the Constitution and Bill of Rights
is a fantasy, the product of a highly educated, highly privileged, brilliant,
productive, and elite class of powerful white men whose ideas and mandates are shored up by a millennia's worth of philosophers and learned
men. Reason and the mythological reasonable man survived, as much
beyond reproach (by those who matter) in 1776 as in ancient Greece
or contemporary America. It was not just an ideal, but an identity:
"Americans, who are often considered the least ideological of people,
are in a peculiarly American way the most ideological . . . in a land that
lacked indigenous and ancient institutions, ideas were made to the do
the work of institutions in giving people a sense of common purpose
and direction" (Meyer 1976, 180). Then and now, logos is doxa because
the men who matter and the nation they lead continue to define the
terms and rules of engagement.

IDEOLOGIC: SHARON CROWLEY ON ARTICULATING BELIEFS

For postmodern rhetorical theorists, arguments do not exist in isolation.
In *Toward a Civil Discourse*, Sharon Crowley predicates her argument on a
robust body of scholarship on community, belief systems, embodiment,
and rhetoric in order to coin the concept "ideologic." Ideologic refers
to "the connections that can be forged among beliefs within a given
ideology and/or across belief systems" (2006, 75). Drawing on Pierre
Bourdieu, Crowley reminds readers that the *habitus*, the community
within which all discourse and meaning is made and practiced, is "'a
product of history' . . . subjects are formed by embodied habits drawn
from culture" (62). For that reason, "the connections (articulations)
that are typically made between moments in a given belief system are
also specific to that system, and so their 'logics' are also dependent
on the contexts in which they are used" (62). Ideology is a totalizing

belief system that explains everything for its subscribers; indeed ideology authorizes the very ideas and language believers have access to. In Crowley's words, ideology is defined as "the medium within which beliefs are articulated with one another . . . any system within which beliefs, symbols, and images are articulated in such a way that they assemble a more or less coherent depiction of reality and/or establish a hierarchy of values" (64–65).

For Crowley, beliefs comprise rhetorical commonplaces—universalized refrains about gender roles, national identity, appropriate behaviors, or any number of social ideas and behaviors—but beliefs are also social constructs and therefore conjectures (Crowley 2006, 70). In order to make a conjecture, there must be an initial assumption or unit of knowledge as well as a purpose—a reason for wanting to construct deeper meaning. In this way, beliefs are always already participating in other webs of knowing in the relevant ideology. Thus, Crowley explains that in her term "ideologic," "the morpheme–logic is intended to convey that within ideology, beliefs connect, disconnect, and reconnect" (76). Here, I employ "ideologic" as the stringing together of a series of beliefs to build an argument that functions like logic but is nevertheless a self-perpetuating network of beliefs authorized to masquerade as *logos*. Specifically, ideologic helps us track how a belief in "reason" always already connects with white superiority, male authority, the supremacy of power holders, the objectivity of justice, African Americans as animalistic, Black men as predators, Christianity, and the existence of, and ability to determine, the Truth.

When we investigate how the concept of "reason" has managed to survive virtually unchanged for 2,500 years, we come face to face with the stamina of hegemony. Powerful white male elites, the benefactors of wealth and social status, have had an impenetrable intellectual monopoly on "reason" since its inception. When that *intellectual property* is utilized within a government institution, it is controlled only in such a way that serves its masters, but like an institution, ideology is never concerned with just one arena. It is necessarily intermingled with myriad interests. The concept of ideologic gives us a means to understand the "connections made between and among . . . (positions) that occur . . . within ideology. [A person] selects a moment from a plentitude of others occurring in any number of belief systems. He or she can then deploy a familiar ideologic, articulating (in the sense of connecting) this moment with others" (Crowley 1976, 60). In this context, ideologic explains why a police officer can legally kill a Black child in America.

IDEOLOGIC, OBJECTIVE REASONABLENESS, AND INSTITUTIONAL RACISM

In criminal law, there is an extensive historical precedent for deliberately not defining key phrases in order to retain interpretive wiggle room (Lee 2016, 10–14). *Black's Law Dictionary* defines reason as "the faculty of the mind by which it distinguishes truth from falsehood, good from evil, and which enables the possessor to deduce inferences from facts or from propositions." It defines a reasonable person as "an ordinary person who exercises care while avoiding extremes of boldness or carefulness" and a reasonable man as "a person who acts with common sense, with a good mental capacity who is stable" (Black 1994, 1266).

Placing those terms into a law enforcement context, two US Supreme Court cases guide how police officers do their job. The first is *Tennessee v. Garner* (1985), which deals with the case of a police officer who shot a fifteen-year old boy in the back of the head, killing him, in order to stop him from fleeing. The boy was a burglary suspect (he had snatched a neighbor's purse and ten dollars). The US Supreme Court in a 6 to 3 decision determined the use of deadly force to prevent the escape of an unarmed suspect was unconstitutional because it violated the Fourth Amendment's objective reasonableness clause (USSC 83-1035).

The second US Supreme Court case plays a more nuanced role in dictating to law enforcement officers how to execute their duties. In *Graham v. Connor* (1989), Graham was a diabetic man whose hasty entry and exit from a convenience store in search of orange juice to counteract a pending insulin reaction caught the eye of a nearby police officer. Reacting solely to watching Graham enter and exit the store, the officer proceeded to stop Graham, and in addition to ignoring his diabetic reaction, handled him so roughly that Graham incurred multiple body and head injuries before being released from the "investigative stop" after backup officers learned no incident of any kind had occurred in the convenience store. In a decision, wherein six justices concurred and three concurred in part, it was determined the Fourth Amendment's assurance of "reasonableness" applies to the "use of force" by police officers. Nearly thirty years later, American police departments base their local use of force policies on *Graham v. Connor*.

The *Graham v. Connor* decision reads, "the Fourth Amendment provides an explicit textual source of federal constitutional protection against such physically intrusive governmental conduct." The rest of the opinion penned by Chief Justice William Rehnquist brings to light several traditional, problematic premises about reason: "The inquiry as to the officer's 'reasonableness' is an objective one, with the question being whether the officer's actions are objectively reasonable in light of the facts and circumstances confronting the officer, without regard to the officer's underlying intent or motivation. . . . motivations have no bearing on whether a particular seizure of an individual is unreasonable; subjective concepts like 'malice' and 'sadism' have no proper place in the Fourth Amendment" (USSC No. 87-6571) Justice Rehnquist's repetitive insistence on the objectivity of reason is significant because "the distinctions that are most efficacious socially are those which give the appearance of being based on objective differences" (Bourdieu 1991, 120). Reasonableness is repeatedly denoted as an objective, self-evident entity, while "subjective" concepts are labeled—and therefore dismissed—as such: one's motivation, one's intent, one's state of mind. Reason is positioned as the binary opposite of evil, malice, sadism, and unreasonableness. Recall Michel Foucault's suggestion that to understand a concept, we must study it from the position of its opposite (1994, 394). If we apply Foucault's method, we recognize reason—particularly the reasonable actions of a police officer—as the absence or opposite of sadism, evil, and ill will.

However, as an ordained member of the institution of government, how much more accessible are the beliefs and words needed to cast the police officer as a sacrificing public servant than to break with hundreds of years of ideology and see him as the wrongdoer? How familiar is the image of the "Black menace" in American society? Even for Americans who decry racism and bigotry, "while one is in a hegemonic relation, its strictures can seem totalizing, whether or not one subscribes to the hegemonic discourse in question [they are] nonetheless affected" (Crowley 2006, 64). This is why in the American legal system and in the general public, a police officer almost always gets "the benefit of the doubt" and nonwhites, well, they get something else. In order to "understand the long, bloody history of police brutality against blacks in the United States, for example, one has to recognize it not as excesses by individual racists but as an organic part of this political enterprise" (Mills 1997, 84). Patricia Roberts-Miller's description of scapegoating becomes useful here: "scapegoats are wrongfully stereotyped as all sharing the same negative trait, or as singled out for blame, while other major culprits are let off the hook" (Berlet and Lyons qtd. in Roberts-Miller 2005, 464). Kenneth Burke showed us how identification happens in three steps: naming, associating or dissociating based on named qualities, and finally identification or consubstantiation (1969).

Since its founding, America has engaged in a process of identification that portrays nonwhites as inferior, irrational, and predatory, while whiteness is associated with superiority, rationality, and authority. Historically, the ideologic of articulating whiteness with justice and Black bodies with danger is almost impossible to dismantle, because "some discourses and practices achieve a hegemony . . . a powerful, near-exclusive hold on a community's beliefs and actions" (Crowley 2006, 63). This need not be deliberate to be real; as Crowley notes, "an ideology can cohere below the level of consciousness . . . this borrowing and construction happens whether or not people are aware of its workings" (75). That means for the average (white) American, the image of a Black man conjures the possibility of risk, while the image of a cop conjures the likelihood of safety. Extend the ideologic analysis further, and the objective reasonableness of a police officer killing an innocent person of color becomes self-evident: Aristotle observed that "when reason (*logos*) or imagination (*phantasia*) informs somebody that he is being insulted or slighted, temper infers, as it were, that such a person is to be treated as an enemy" (2004, 1149b). Put another way, when we see an image or behavior we can interpret in accordance with an existing belief, we will manufacture the response that validates that belief (Crowley 2006, 84). If a police officer already believes Black men to be irrational and dangerous, any action at all—even a child holding a toy—initiates a deeply rooted "watchfulness for signs of subperson resistance" (Mills 1997, 83) followed by a reaction of genuine fear, and finally a "reasonable" response: stop the threat at any cost. When that officer is due to face legal consequences, most juries have accessed the most readily available narratives and images, ones fashioned by an ideologic of whiteness, power, reason, and the threat of the "other."

As Americans, we want to believe we support freedom, equality, and justice for all. We value facts, yet "something other than knowledge or understanding motivates people . . . ideology, fantasy, and emotion are primary motivators of belief and action" (Crowley 2006, 59). Mills calls this an "epistemology of ignorance," particularly in terms of whites who are blind to the reality that morality is racialized (1997, 93). Paulo Barrozo writes, "in contemporary law and legal culture, there is an ever-present, if often unarticulated, reliance on the belief that the legal and institutional edifices of society rest on a morally defensible (in deontic or evolutionary terms) foundation. This belief is a spell cast on moral and sociological imagination" (2005, 240–41). What we see in the horrific recurrence of police shootings and the lack of legal consequences is a social and legal paradigm saturated by an ideologic that weaves white superiority, reasonable objectivity, and institutional authority together with metanarratives around justice, safety, and equality so densely that alternative arguments are regarded as unpatriotic, incendiary, even treasonous, if they are heard at all.

WHAT'S A RHETORICIAN TO DO?

If there is anything repetitive about Sharon Crowley's contributions to the world, it is her example that to "do rhetoric" is to be political, even polemical. In "Reflections on an Argument That Won't Go Away," she insists, "To the extent that ordinary citizens are unable to articulate or criticize the discursive conditions that cause and maintain unfair and destructive practices, we academic rhetoricians must bear some responsibility for their silence" (Crowley 1992, 464). Her mandate predates social media, but for many communities of color and alternative narratives in this country, the experience of being unheard persists. Social media platforms such as Twitter and the hashtag technique have certainly amplified alternative voices and arguments, but their ability to penetrate the echelon of the power holders has been minimal. A police shooting incident may garner millions of retweets from community members, watchdog organizations, and special interest groups yet go unmentioned by mainstream media and public officials.

Using Crowley's concept of ideologic, we have a chance, however cautious, to "invent means of disarticulating beliefs . . . [expose] untenable connections" in those moments and through those means where even "a small range of persuasive possibilities may remain open in any given case" (Crowley 2006, 77). We can begin this process of reinvention by first asking questions. Where are the cracks in the "Black menace" ideology? Which joints are rusty in the ideologic of dangerous others + reasonable objectivity + white righteousness? Who makes up the most receptive audience for alternative discourse, and how are they reached? Second, we must resist untenable answers.

Strategies for resistance are plentiful: Ernesto Laclau and Chantal Mouffe support antagonistic counterarguments (see Mouffe 2005b), while Kenneth Burke forwarded the idea of identification through "trivial repetition and dull daily reinforcement" (1969, 26)—a means of persuasion that can be deployed against the master narrative as "repetition with alterity" (Butler 1997, 147). There is a challenge in this. What Pierre Bourdieu calls "the monopoly of the professionals" regulates who can speak and with what language (Bourdieu 1991, 172). It will always be easier for authorized members of the power structure to define the terms and construct or reinforce ideologic, but "power ultimately rests with political masses. The stability of legal and political orders over time indeed depends on a sufficient level of consent on the part of the governed" (Barrozo 2005, 235). When consent is withdrawn, the "effective way to challenge power relations [is] not on the mode of an abstract negation but in a properly hegemonic way, through a process of disarticulation of existing practices and creation of new discourses and institutions" (Mouffe 2005a, 33). The Black Lives Matter movement illustrates the process by which subjects claim agency to invent a new narrative that challenges the hegemony in ways material, epistemological, and political. Following the Electoral College's selection of Donald Trump for the presidency, there has been renewed grassroots energy around taking heretofore-academic conversations about whiteness and privilege to the public via organizations such as SafetyPinBox, which fights institutional racism by educating white allies about how to support people of color. Some mainstream media outlets, for example, the *Washington Post,* have added automatic fact-checking features online and placed a greater emphasis on contextualizing or challenging institutional propaganda and fake news. Efforts like these have the potential to disarticulate reason from whiteness, violence from melanin, and invulnerability from authority. And as rhetoricians, we can honor and heed Sharon Crowley's work by studying, teaching, and practicing resistance to the reigning ideologics that serve so few at the expense of so many.

NOTE

1.   See, for example, Aristotle (2007), especially Kennedy's commentary; Haskins (2004); and Schiappa (1992).

REFERENCES

Aristotle. 2004. *Nicomachean Ethics.* Trans. J.A.K. Thomson. London: Penguin Classics.
Aristotle. 2007. *On Rhetoric: A Theory of Civic Discourse,* 2nd ed. Trans. George Kennedy. Oxford: Oxford University Press.
Barrozo, Paulo. 2005. "The Great Alliance: History, Reason, and Will in Modern Law." *Law and Contemporary Problems* 78 (1): 235–70.
Bidgood, Jess. 2016. "Closing Arguments Sound Familiar at 4th Trial in Freddie Gray Case." *New York Times,* July 16, 2016.
Black, Henry C. 1994. *Black's Law Dictionary.* 6th ed. New York: Springer.
Bourdieu, Pierre. 1991. *Language and Symbolic Power.* Cambridge: Harvard University Press.
Burke, Kenneth. 1969. *Rhetoric of Motives.* Berkeley: University of California Press.
Butler, Judith. 1997. *Excitable Speech: A Politics of the Performative.* New York: Routledge.
Cicero. 1998. *The Republic and the Laws.* Trans. Niall Rudd. New York: Oxford University Press.

Crowley, Sharon. 1992. "Reflections on an Argument That Won't Go Away Or, A Turn of the Ideological Screw." *Quarterly Journal of Speech* 78 (4): 450–65.

Crowley, Sharon. 2006. *Toward a Civil Discourse: Rhetoric and Fundamentalism.* Pittsburgh: University of Pittsburgh Press.

Eckholm, Eric, and Julie Bosman. 2014. "For Ferguson Grand Jury, Details and Responsibilities Are Abundant." *New York Times,* November 14, 2014.

Foucault, Michel. 1994. *Power: Essential Works of Foucault 1954–1984.* Ed. James D. Faubion. New York: New Press.

Graham v. Connor et al. Bd., 87 US 6571 (1989).

Haskins, Ekaterina V. 2004. *Logos and Power in Isocrates and Aristotle.* Columbia: University of South Carolina Press.

Israel, Jonathan. 2010. *A Revolution of the Mind: Radical Enlightenment and the Intellectual Origins of Modern Democracy.* Princeton: Princeton University Press.

Lee, Youngjae. 2016. "Reasonable Doubt and Moral Elements." *Journal of Criminal Law and Criminology* 105 (1): 1–37.

Locke, John. 1764. *Second Treatise on Government.* Cambridge: Christ College.

Lott, Toomas. 2011. "Plato on the Rationality of Belief. Theaetetus 184–7." *Trames* 15 (4): 339–64. DOI: 10.3176/tr.2011.4.02.

Meyer, D. H. 1976. "The Uniqueness of the American Enlightenment." *American Quarterly* 28 (2): 165–86.

Mills, Charles W. 1997. *The Racial Contract.* Ithaca: Cornell University Press.

Mouffe, Chantal. 2005a. *On the Political.* New York: Routledge.

Mouffe, Chantal. 2005b. *The Return of the Political.* London: Verso.

Pfau, Thomas. 2010. "The Letter of Judgment: Practical Reason in Aristotle, the Stoics, and Rousseau." *Eighteenth Century* 51 (3): 289–316.

Richard, Carl J. 1994. *The Founders and the Classics: Greece, Rome and the American Enlightenment.* Cambridge: Harvard University Press.

Roberts-Miller, Patricia. 2005. "Democracy, Demagoguery, and Critical Rhetoric." *Rhetoric and Public Affairs* 8 (3): 459–76. DOI: 10.1353.

Schiappa, Edward. 1992. "Rhetorike: What's in a Name? Toward a Revised History of Early Greek Rhetorical Theory." *Quarterly Journal of Speech* 78 (1): 1–15.

Shanks, Torrey. 2011. "Feminine Figures and the 'Fatherland': Rhetoric and Reason in Locke's 'First Treatise of Government.'" *Political Theory* 39 (1): 31–57.

Tennessee v. Garner et al. Bd., 83 US 1035 (1985).

Williams, Timothy, and Mitch Smith. 2015. "Cleveland Officer Will Not Face Charges in Tamir Rice Shooting Death." *New York Times,* December 28, 2015.

4

A BRIEF ETIOLOGY OF VIOLENCE
The Logic of Identity and the Metaphysics of Presence

Judy Holiday

The first act of violence that patriarchy demands of males is not violence toward women. Instead patriarchy demands of all males that they engage in acts of psychic self-mutilation, that they kill off the emotional parts of themselves. If an individual is not successful in emotionally crippling himself, he can count on patriarchal men to enact rituals of power that will assault his self-esteem

—bell hooks, *The Will to Change: Men, Masculinity, and Love*

Poet and 2016 MacArthur Foundation "Genius Grant" recipient, Claudia Rankine, recently spoke at my home university about the ubiquity of racism and racialized aggression in the United States, which is the focus of her book, *Citizen: An American Lyric* (2014). During her talk, Rankine remarked that one of her greatest surprises researching #BlackLivesMatter came when reading the transcripts of interviews with officers who had fatally shot unarmed African American citizens. Rankine asked audience members how they supposed those officers responded to the question "Why did you shoot?" When a number of audience members shouted out, "I was afraid," Rankine nodded, explaining that she had expected the same response and was therefore stunned to read of the number of police officers who answered, "I don't know" to the question of motive. Rankine described this group of officers as "significant" in size, adding that during interviews these officers identified themselves as nonracist and caring Christians who repeatedly expressed remorse and confusion over their own actions.

While Rankine expressed interest in pursuing this conundrum in her future research, I sat in the audience wishing to speak to her about my own theoretical work on the ideological—and thus

DOI: 10.7330/9781607328933.c004

rhetorical—construction of intersubjectivity, which helps explain unjustifiable police shootings and other pervasive forms of violence. The number of instances in which presumably good-willed police officers, who are trained to deal with life-threatening situations, shoot unarmed individuals in nonthreatening postures (e.g., running away or with hands in the air) should not be overlooked as exceptions. While training police officers to shoot at human-shaped targets might serve to explain some of these shootings, training does not explain the much higher incidence of people from traditionally underrepresented and stigmatized groups getting shot (e.g., Black, LatinX, Native American) (Rankine 2014, Ritchie and Mogul 2008). Rather, such profound inequity morally obligates us to figure out the logic(s) operating in such performances and charges us to question the very existence of tragedies like police shootings, and, perhaps more importantly, the existence and continuance of cultures that institutionalize and authorize violence.

Much as Margaret Mead (2017) argued that war is a human invention, in this chapter I argue that virtually all of the human-induced violence we see in our world results from a distinct and learned episteme that, like war, is a human invention. By episteme, I mean a naturalized structuring structure or heuristic of cognition that underwrites "knowing" and that differs from an "ideology" in that ideologies represent specific sets of beliefs (e.g., sexism, racism), whereas epistemes reflect deeper *ways of believing and knowing,* larger cognitive architectures capacious and flexible enough to encompass countless ideologies. As I explain below, this episteme underwrites one of two distinct and oppositional intersubjective orientations that structure social relations in most contemporary societies. I use the term "intersubjective orientation" to describe how humans are rhetorically oriented to *inter*act with others (and themselves). "Interact," however, is laden with the assumption of engagement, whereas the episteme I am demarcating as the cause of violence ironically trains individuals *not* to engage (inter)relationally with others (or themselves) and erupts situationally.

I have felt deeply since childhood that there must be a way to reduce the staggering amount of violence and suffering that take place on this planet, and a possible means toward that end is the focus of this chapter. Since the discussion periodically turns theoretical, I define terms as they surface, and I draw on Sharon Crowley's (1989) discussion of Aristotelian grammar, particularly categories versus predicables, as a metaphor to illustrate the two distinct intersubjective orientations discussed in this chapter. Based upon diametrically opposed philosophies, these two distinct but cooperational intersubjectivities are easily illustrated by Aristotelian logic, which Crowley explains is "based upon the grammar of a simple sentence—categories and predicables, classes of things and the possible relations between things" (3). Essentially, an intersubjective orientation based upon predicables (i.e., "relations between things") is fluid and promotes relationality, cooperation, and growth (with respect to self, other, and community) whereas an orientation based upon categories (i.e., "classes of things") is fixed, rigid, and limiting—a mode of being that calcifies identity, obviates relationality, and authorizes self-directed, other-directed, and communal violence. I ultimately hope to show that most cultures, despite socially just movements and strands within them, took a damagingly wrong turn by basing their metaphysics on categories—on fixedness, rather than on contradiction and change.[1]

OUT, OUT, DAMN EPISTEME

I am unaware of any single rhetorical theory that connects all types of human-induced violence, ranging from self-cutting and social withdrawal to conversion therapy and structural poverty, though the remarkable work of James Gilligan (2001) comes close in many ways to a unifying theory and informs my own. I contend that violence is a consequence of a naturalized episteme (as distinguished from ideology in first end note) because a person can be fully aware of one exploitative ideological system yet blind to or supportive of another, which suggests that an epistemology undergirding all systems of oppression has been largely naturalized. Epistemes frequently operate at the level of perception and serve as "schemas of perception" (Foucault 1994) that, like learning to tell time, structure our daily lives and lived experiences while being flexible enough to accommodate cultural and situational shifts. This chameleonic dimension of epistemes explains their tendency to become so naturalized as to seem intrinsic.

As a mode of perception that structures and determines the very nature of social relations, an epistemic orientation that inhibits relationality obviously presents a serious problem as a foundation *for* relationships. Nevertheless, this episteme is deeply entrenched in most cultures and is acquired at such a young age as to seem natural. Naturalization of the episteme is further compounded by its capacity as an epistemic infrastructure to bypass conscious, critical, and deliberate thought. This insidious capacity enables people to pass immediate judgment upon themselves and others with little or no reflection (again, depending upon the person and circumstances). Social psychologists call the capacity to act without conscious thought "automatic thinking," whereby perceptual practices are integrated into organized bodily movements and habits that become so habitual that the vigorous process of interpretation that should be a vital part of perception "is skipped in an attenuated process of perceptual knowing" (Alcoff 2006, 188). Of course, as Marilyn Cooper so deftly explains, while agency among humans doesn't necessitate conscious volition, deeply habituated practices certainly "can be brought to consciousness" (2011, 434).

Automatic thinking in itself is not a problem in that all sorts of human literacies rely upon and utilize it, from cooking to playing sports, but automatic thinking can and does present a significant threat when it organizes our very sociality, on the macro- and microlevel, particularly with respect to self-perception and other-perception. When automatic thinking is combined with what cognitive psychologists call "labeling,"[2] or what Iris Marion Young (1990) calls the "logic of identity"—judging a person or group based upon rigid categorical, usually stereotypical, knowledge—we end up with a type of intersubjective training and a subsequent intersubjective orientation that not only legitimate social hierarchies but that also potentially justify assessing the *moral* worth of people and other living things without (at its worst) even a modicum of reciprocal and flexible engagement. On the other end of the spectrum, an intersubjective orientation that deems all people (and arguably all life) innately invaluable presents a notable contradistinction and alternative to such a limited and limiting intersubjectivity.[3]

While it may seem obvious at this point that morally ranking the worth of individual human lives and other life forms based upon categorical labeling is untenable if we are to actualize a socially just landscape, it is much less obvious that this dispositioning *writes* and *gives right* to violence—making it rhetorical and therefore, I argue, eradicable, like a disease. Hence my use of "etiology" in the title of this chapter.

I use the term "violence" broadly to refer to human actions and behaviors that inflict any and all types of emotional or physical harm, in contrast to those social psychologists, who define violence as "aggression that is intended to cause harm extreme enough to require medical attention or to cause death" or who "extend this definition to include causing severe emotional harm" (Warburton and Anderson 2015, 373). I prefer a more capacious definition of violence for two reasons. First, because violence can be "minor" yet nevertheless impactful, which is one of Rankine's points in *Citizen*—that racialized microaggressions inflict damaging psychological stress and are reminders of the constant burden people of color are forced to bear. But second, a more extensive definition of violence begins to capture a sense of the much larger cultural disease to which I allude in this chapter. Some social psychologists use "aggression" to refer "only to behavior" and "not to a mindset or an emotional state" (Warburton and Anderson 2015, 373), which I adopt as a means of distinguishing "aggression" as an intrinsically human capacity from "violence" as a learned, rhetorically constructed and cultivated network of cultural practices.

In the remainder of this chapter, I take an epidemiological approach that presents violence as a cultural disease, a disease firmly rooted in intersubjective training. I first address commonplaces to the contrary and then draw upon Iris Marion Young's concept of the "logic of identity" to depict violence as a cross-cultural disease that is rhetorical in nature (i.e., epistemic, symbolic, and performative). I argue that the intersubjective orientation underwritten by the logic of identity is learned via culture, that it teaches hierarchical thinking and fosters rage, shame, alienation, and a host of other asocial affective modalities. I contend that this "logic" is incompatible with social justice. Furthermore, I juxtapose hierarchical dispositioning with an alternative intersubjective orientation—one based upon the notions of the intrinsic worth of all life and of the impossibility of capturing the entirety of one's self or another. While these two embodied "presences" represent two dramatically disparate ways of being and perceiving the world around us, they nevertheless operate dynamically and in tandem, surfacing situationally.

After depicting violence as a complex rhetorical system grounded in perception, I argue that hierarchical dispositioning and the logic of identity work hegemonically to supersede large-scale constructive change. As such, they demarcate a place for rhetorical intervention.

VIOLENCE IS *NOT* AN INTRINSIC DIMENSION OF THE HUMAN

There is a tendency to essentialize violence as an intrinsic component of the human, which is understandable given the ubiquity of violence in the world. Even among rhetoricians, there is a tendency to naturalize violence as physiologically endemic to the human condition or as endemic to language use.[4] I therefore begin my argument by countering these commonplaces.

The idea that human violence is somehow physiologically endemic is complicated by research on aggression. A brief look at psychologists' take on aggression should help clarify what I mean. According to Brad J. Bushman and Craig A. Anderson (2001), the field of psychology often distinguishes between two types of aggression: impulsive (affective) and instrumental (strategic). Notably, the former, as in the case of a temper tantrum, may be purely a response to frustration and may not include intent to harm, whereas the latter (strategically using aggression to achieve one's ends) intends harm but does not necessarily entail affect (e.g., personal antagonism or anger). Bushman and Anderson challenge this dichotomy with several arguments. Because they argue that aggression may serve several simultaneous purposes, they opt for a definition of aggression that focuses on the intent to harm (274). Even though Bushman and Anderson argue for such a definition, the pertinent point here is that acts of aggression do not *necessarily* entail intention to harm—at least among children. Indeed, as social psychology literature demonstrates, healthy childhood development entails human young learning to inhibit their impulses (e.g., aggression, immediate self-gratification) as part of learning to be prosocial ("Executive Function" 2012).

VIOLENCE IS *NOT* INNATE TO LANGUAGE

That language is productive, flexibly accommodating the very epistemic dispositioning this chapter addresses, should not be misconstrued as a sign that language itself is the progenitor of contemporary humanity's disposition to violence. As I discuss below, culture is the true progenitor. I have had many conversations with colleagues who insist that learning to categorize and classify, which *is* inherent to language use, is to blame. Were that true, all human cultures would be rife with the disposition to value some lives over others. Or inversely, all human cultures would consistently devalue life. We have historical witness, however, to indigenous cultures that base and have long based their social, political, and economic organization upon the sanctity and interconnectedness of all life (human and nonhuman), past, present, and future. Were xenophobic in-grouping and the moral ranking of people a dimension of language itself, we wouldn't have the narratives we do about societies organized around the worth of all lives and the dignity of each (see, e.g., Allen 2001, Las Casas 1971, Johansen 1982).

This glimpse at cultural relativity instead indicates a deeply learned intersubjective orientation that I am suggesting destructively serves as a gestalt for most dominant contemporary cultures, one that enables human-induced violence: bullying, self-loathing, eating disorders, incarceration, weapons manufacturing, the daily use of carcinogens (e.g., fossil fuels, pesticides, nuclear plants). Each practice—whether self-directed, other-directed, or collective—is underwritten by the assumption that some lives are more valuable than others. Aggression qua violence redirects us to see aggression as culturally cultivated and sustained—and dehumanization and cruelty as cultured and cultivated human enterprises. Admittedly, most good-willed individuals would cringe at the thought that they were complicit in someone else's suffering and would even refuse to participate in such practices if they knew the names and stories of those who suffered. Nevertheless, the abundance of all types of violence in this world indicates that violence does not sit at the end of words, when communication has failed, but rather as an indication of communicative success, that is, the success of practices and discourses of hierarchy and domination—and thus as a by-product of cultural transference.

VIOLENCE *IS* CULTURAL

While humans are hardwired for both empathy and aggression (De Waal 2013), I contend that the will to harm or not harm others is culturally cultivated. Culture has an integral stake in how children learn to deal with aggression and whether violence becomes a normative enterprise. Developmentally, for instance, a nationwide study of 100,000 Canadian children showed that a third of the children exhibited infrequent physical aggression (PA) as toddlers "and virtually no PA by pre-adolescence" (Coté et al. 2006, 68), which indicates not only the importance of socializing children to control their aggressive impulses but also the possibility of entire cultures doing so.

The study also demonstrates the influence of culture on the development of violent tendencies. "About one sixth of children," the authors note, "mostly boys from disadvantaged families, exhibited an *atypical* developmental pattern reflected in more frequent and stable use of PA" (Coté et al. 2006, 68; emphasis added). These boys' "atypical developmental pattern" provides solid evidence that systematically incorporating advantage and disadvantage into the institutions, discourses, and other systems of culture fosters violence and that socially constructed hierarchies incite it. In summarizing the study, the authors conclude that the "results suggest that most children learned relatively well to inhibit PA by the end of childhood and that a minority failed to do so" (68).[5] Clearly, children can be relatively well-socialized to inhibit aggression, a point that demands we interrogate the cultural conditions that animate it in adults. For instance, the "minority [who] failed" to learn impulse control not only had the misfortune of suffering disadvantage as children, but they also acquired new disadvantages insofar as psychology scholarship roundly demonstrates that children who do not learn to inhibit aggression do not achieve long-term interpersonal or social success (Cole 2010). These "mostly boys" become adolescents and adults who lack self-control, flexibility, and strong executive monitors, rendering them developmentally unprepared for social and professional success (Center on the Developing Child at Harvard University 2016). This is an indication that, culturally speaking, the inhibition of aggression and the fostering and development of self-regulation benefit both individuals and their larger communities. Additional evidence that violence is culturally cultivated emerges when we look at extremely young children, say toddlers, whose aggression doesn't appear to be ideologically motivated at all by normative knowledge. Rather, toddlers' ideology mostly concerns the personal: fulfilling immediate self-gratifying goals or personal needs, such as basal security.

VIOLENCE *IS* IDEOLOGICAL

Instances of aggression among adults, however, speak to the ideological dimension of what I'm distinguishing as violence. Studies on intimate partner violence (IPV), for example, show that "individuals perpetrate IPV because society socializes them to do so" and because those individuals find IPV acceptable (Finkel et al. 2009, 483). The same authors also note that some IPV happens as a result of what they call "self-regulation failures" (483), momentary gut-level lapses in self-control, which should not, I contend, be read as proof positive of an essentialist's argument about violence. Instances do not serve to universalize a thing but may theoretically suggest variety and difference. Or those instances may indicate the importance of context (e.g., the Canadian boys who did not learn to inhibit their aggressive impulses). For instance, we cannot rule out the possibility that "self-regulation failures" might not happen in a world absent of the violence and stressors rife in this one. The only accurate assessment we can make from the study on IPV entails acknowledging the damaging influence of gender socialization as well as the importance of prosocial training that trains people to deal with frustration and stress and that emphasizes relationality and empathy for others.

When we further examine violence outside of an interpersonal frame, we can see that the influence of ideology on structural violence is so widespread as to be inexhaustible in kind. For instance, many US citizens endorse exclusionary immigration and naturalization laws for economic reasons yet consider themselves persons who abhor violence. Such individuals may not consider their actions violent and may feel fully justified in thinking constructively about their own nation-states, for wanting their fellow citizens, say, to have enough food. What their thinking demonstrates, however, is illustrative of the detrimental episteme I am discussing—an episteme that teaches people to accept social inequity and socially constructed hierarchies as "just the way things are." Entailing much, much more than a simplistic in-group/out-group mentality, this episteme structures sociality and the way individuals are perceptually and performatively predisposed by sanctioning practices of exceptionalism, unearned privilege, hypocrisy, and ignorance, as well as by producing a welter of affective modalities, including inferiority, superiority, shame, arrogance, and hate.

Clear-cut cases of group violence, those involving lynch mobs, for example, further illustrate the enormous influence ideology has upon human behavior and decision-making, particularly with respect to how surrendering of self-regulation via deindividuation is rationalized. Roy Baumeister and Kathleen Vohs explain how "group norms inform collective action" and ideologically justify violence in ways that are societally sanctioned (2007, 234). They write, "Most crowds behave orderly and restrained. Even when they loot and pillage and rape, crowds display a considerable amount of organization and structure to their atrocities. Far from blindly pursuing destruction, the crowd is normally propelled by moral beliefs and consensus. Moreover, its violence is not random, but targeted and symbolic of its purposes" (234). If rape, murder, and genocide are organized and orderly enterprises—not anomalies—then we must deduce that violence is ideological and operates epistemically, requiring the participation of community members. Having internalized and naturalized the episteme, members of the crowd take it upon themselves to morally assess the worth of others and inflict violence upon those not deemed worthy. It is an insidious system of violence in which everyone learns to police each other, as judge and jury (even those who refuse but must bear the trauma of witnessing).

Furthermore, if brutal and atrocious violent behavior in crowds is organized and orderly when driven by social norms, then we need to interrogate all of humanity's daily mundane activities that obscure violence, such as global economic systems that ensure poverty. When I first learned of poverty as a child, I remember being astounded that adults allowed it to exist, and I was horrified by its existence—as horrified as I would be now were I to witness a lynching. Yet poverty is an accepted social norm that I've learned to live with. Hunger, suffering, all part of everyone's day. If this weren't bad enough, many cultures compound economic violence by criminalizing poverty, as does the United States, for instance, when undocumented immigrants who flee their home countries in search of better economic and political and less violent social conditions are discriminated against, demeaned, detained, and deported. That millions of human beings are considered "illegal" in the United States alone compels us to question the foundations of cultures that not only sanction such debasing and punitive practice but that actually rely upon such brutality as integral to their functioning (see "Timeline" 2014).

Given that all theory inheres in praxis, what theoretically drives such violence? As the next section explains, violence is an inescapable byproduct of a complex moral system that determines a subject's worth and that is derived from learning the logic of identity (LOI) (Young 1990). As I hope to show, gendered and other hierarchical norms are manifestations of the logic of identity, which demonstrates that LOI serves as a primary principle of social organization, one that undermines cooperation. Logic of identity structures human consciousness in a way that precludes the need for conscious deliberation or interrogation (which explains why violence is often conflated with the absence of rhetoric rather than as a rhetorical product).

THE METAPHYSICS OF PRESENCE AND THE LOGIC OF IDENTITY

In *Toward a Civil Discourse*, Sharon Crowley explains that the "assumption that human beings operate in relation to some medium is characteristic of postmodern thought, whether this medium is called 'discourse' (Foucault), 'writing' (Derrida), 'the symbolic' (Lacan), 'hegemony' (Gramsci) or 'the *habitus*' (Bourdieu)" (2006, 62). The quagmire-like medium in which humans are currently entrenched, I argue, stems from the metastasizing cancer that is the LOI episteme, which is cloaked by and could not function without what Jacques Derrida calls the "metaphysics of presence" (qtd. in Crowley 1989).

Crowley (1989) explains that the metaphysics of presence assumes that language is a neutral technology, a vehicle for the mind's thoughts, rather than a shaper of the mind. Anyone who grows up in such an epistemological medium learns to "look through language, not at it" (5), a pivotal point for my argument, for in the primacy of any given moment it is all too easy to forget that perception is not a direct or accurate apprehension of reality. Certainly, our perceived reality feels real, right? But that feeling is an illusion. Consciousness is derived from culture, not the other way around.[6] As Crowley puts it, "Derrida might argue that traditional metaphysical thought about minds, world, and language has it precisely backwards, or upside down, or inside out. Consciousness does not precede, and give birth to language; rather it is language that makes consciousness possible" (4). Nevertheless, in most contemporary cultures humans learn to conflate reality with their apprehension of it, which explains why addressing an issue as long-standing as human violence becomes difficult even for scholars, especially if language per se is considered the shaper of consciousness. Violence is truly a cold case file, so long cold as to be buried.

In exhuming this file, then, it becomes imperative to explain how an episteme such as one that authorizes violence works. In short, "the metaphysics of presence" plays a significant part in how violence operates. The metaphysics of presence, what Crowley calls Derrida's analysis of *Western* metaphysics (but which I'd argue underwrites *all* patriarchal systems), relies upon "a lived reduction of the opacity of the signifier" (qtd. in Crowley 1989, 5) and enables people to believe that their experiences are a direct apprehension of reality.[7] By privileging "the signified (presence, consciousness, self, mind, reality, truth, reason)" over the signifier (e.g., language), Crowley explains, "metaphysics could become the 'first science'—first in both senses, primary and fundamental—because it could ferret out essences which were uncontaminated by language" (5). The culture (i.e., the medium: think petri dish) generated by such an epistemic orientation produces a sense of self that is constant and projects that same sense of constancy upon others.

Because the metaphysics of presence inculcates a sense of self that sits outside of language and culture (a self who is "real") and socializes individuals to ignore the influence that culture and context exert on the shaping of perception, it provides a perfect backdrop for patriarchal systems whose oppressive and exploitative practices rely upon the naive or not-so-naive performativity of practitioners. Marilyn Cooper explains such performance as a conceptual merging of *kairos* and habituated practice (Bourdieu's *habitus*), as that which isn't possessed "'but something that one is,' something that 'makes it possible to appreciate the meaning of the situation instantly . . . and to produce at once the opportune response'" (2011, 435).

In this fashion, as the world that is learned becomes "real" to children, children have little choice but to learn and perform (or resist) the many ideological systems in which they have been immersed. Much of the immersion children experience, unfortunately, involves narrative, symbolic, and performative systems (e.g., the nexus of militarism, materialism, and race that Martin Luther King Jr. called out) that place subjects in either ordinate or subordinate positions in relation to each other and that are thus inherently oppressive and exploitative. Children subsequently learn to morally assess and (de)value specific identities and, in tandem with the "metaphysics of presence," to perceive those identities as real, comprehensive, and fixed.

Young (1990) calls this moral assessment process the "logic of identity"—a deeply internalized reductive hierarchical assessment system by which people learn to appraise the worth of themselves and others via their group memberships. The LOI relies upon categorical knowledge,[8] and it develops over time to become an epistemic structure. This facility, if it can be called that, derives from specific and enduring intersubjective training that produces and naturalizes hierarchical dispositions by teaching human young to esteem and disesteem the whole of a person based upon certain "characteristics" of that person (e.g., gender + hair color = "blondes are fun-loving but dumb"). To "master" the patriarchal world of hierarchical systems, then, children must learn to disrespect themselves and/or others, and they do so by practicing and embodying LOI via immersion in narrative regimes prior to and during their development of metareflection. Children learn to feel superior or inferior to others situationally (with attendant affective modalities, including shame and arrogance), depending upon the categories involved and the degree to which LOI epistemology becomes a prevailing worldview. Learning LOI relies upon seeing oneself in relation to others, yet doing so is ultimately an ego-centered and competitive endeavor in that children must learn to elevate or deflate themselves in relation to others, a process that fosters arrogance, shame, and extrahumanization or dehumanization of the self and other.

Virtually everyone is trained to internalize norms of assessing themselves and others categorically, resulting in an internalized and imperfectly naturalized assessment system that essentializes humans in order to determine their worth. How and when this hierarchical dispositioning surfaces depends upon each individual and each situation, so much so that an individual who reacts categorically to someone (say, a husband responding misogynistically to his spouse) may react relationally and deliberatively to that same person under similar circumstances at a different time. Clearly any category can serve as an identity and depends upon the larger culture, the individual, and the circumstances. Categorical plasticity as a concept demonstrates its epistemicity. While the categories themselves don't ultimately matter, the automatic thinking that reduces the other (or self) certainly do. I think the opening epigraph makes that clear.

While I agree with bell hooks that patriarchal cultures demand that males learn to "kill off the emotional parts of themselves," my argument is that everyone is required to do so. To varying degrees and in various ways, virtually everyone learns to withdraw and put up walls as part of learning "the world." Logic of identity represents a training that paradoxically constricts the human capacity to engage in modes of reciprocal respect by shoring up the boundaries of the self. Young refers to this practice as "non-overlapping otherness" that "wells from the depths of the Western subject's sense of identity, especially, but not only in the subjectivity of privileged groups" (1990, 170). "Non-overlapping otherness" is certainly not the sole domain of males. Although girls are generally socialized to think more ecologically than boys,[9] and thus generally take in a larger context when making decisions (C. Gilligan 2008), they can and do enact violence against themselves or others. Conceiving violence in the way that I am suggesting, as a situational "sealing of the heart" (Brennan 2004) that produces emotional detachment from oneself or other better captures the widespread raced, classed, gendered, and aged violence that results from systems of oppression.

One of the first means by which children learn LOI is through gender discrimination, and it is important to keep in mind that both dehumanization, extrahumanization (both of which reduce), and outright cruelty are dimensions of this logic. For instance, after her best-selling novel *Strange Fruit* was banned in Boston, Lillian Smith wrote of her notoriety, "You are called bitch and saint, whore and heroine, you are praised for your courage and sneered at for your obscenity; you are made into stereotypes, no one sees you as a person, not even those who admire your book most; you are turned into images which please them or appeal to their feelings of hate or admiration, to their fears and hopes" (Loveland 1986, 72). Smith's analyses and lived experiences trenchantly demonstrate that LOI operates to capture—and dismiss—the Other (which of course can be the self).

A "knowable" subject, then, is an essential component of LOI, which dismisses the rich multiplicity and uncapturable alterity of any person. Even cases of adulation tend "to conceptualize entities in terms of substance rather than process or relation" (Young 1990, 99).

Ironically, the perceptual reduction of self or other thus "represses difference" by reducing the different to a mere categorical opposition (Young 1990, 98). We see, then, how learning the LOI episteme flips what *is* real: Despite the *fact* that difference ontologically underwrites humanity, learning LOI constructs difference as absolute otherness. As Young reminds us, difference cannot entail "absolute otherness, a complete absence of relationship or shared attributes" (99).[10] "The irony of the logic of identity," Young explicates, "is that by seeking to reduce the differently similar to the same, it turns the merely different into the absolutely other" and "inevitably generates dichotomy instead of unity" (99).

It's easy to see here how a hierarchical epistemic orientation is truly diseased as an *intersubjec*tive template. Within the constraints of such an orientation, there is little or no motivation to *inter*act with a subject with whom one has no relation. While it is clear that relatively few people act in such a closed-off fashion much of the time and the majority of people do so more rarely, all told, we are subsequently faced with widespread violence, whether or not the violence is self- or other-directed. It becomes imperative, then, to ensure that our cultures socialize children to default to empathy and respect, rather than to competitive aggression and disrespect.[11]

CATEGORIES:PREDICABLES :: VIOLENCE:SONDER

The experiential knowledge derived from having learned LOI provides us with an avenue for explaining all types of violence, which shut down relations and put up absolute boundaries instead. For example, while I cannot assert that every one of the police officers mentioned in my opening paragraph behaved as they did due to their learning the LOI episteme, LOI does provide us with a tenable theory that explains the raced and gendered disparities we see in police shootings in the United States. Categorical knowledge helps explain, for instance, racial disparities noted in a Florida study of police shootings in which "victim[s] had neither threatened police with a weapon, nor committed a violent crime": Police "were about three times as likely to shoot a black person who was running away (16–5), or who was suspected [of] a minor crime like drug possession or shoplifting (17–6), and four times as likely to shoot a black person in the back (8–2)" (Balko 2017).

If these statistics alone don't convince readers that violence is derived from a learned and naturalized episteme that trains individuals to categorically assess and judge others "intuitively" (i.e., rapidly and reductively), then consider how learning the "logic of identity" justifies and licenses violence when "police" is the category. Despite 900–1,000 people getting fatally shot in the United States each year by on-duty police officers, according to a study by Phillip Stinson of Bowling Green University, only 54 officers have been convicted of fatally shooting someone unjustifiably in more than 11,000 cases of fatal shootings between 2005 and 2015 (Bialik 2015). Clearly, the automatic bias that accompanies the category of "police" licenses a staggering number of fatal shootings. While jury decisions involve many variables not taken into account here, the sheer number of cases in which juries find on behalf of police officers illustrates the categorical biases underwritten by the LOI episteme.

These jury decisions also demonstrate how the LOI trains and authorizes everyone to police and to judge. In Aristotelian logic (categories vs. predicables), Crowley notes, "the basic assumption" of "the law of identity," is that "either a thing is or it is not" (1989, 3). By basing intersubjective training on categories, not predicables, everyone learns to distinguish between "legitimate" and "illegitimate" lives as a function of categorical identity.

Predicables suggest possibilities for reframing our engagements. They deemphasize identity in favor of contradiction—that is, difference. Intersubjective orientations based upon predicables recognize and celebrate change, which epistemically requires practitioners to recognize what we and other forms of life hold in common. With respect to humanity, some commonalities include the limitations and rewards inherent to subject positions (e.g., ignorance, group-specific knowledge) and the understanding that every individual is in development and that learning involves mistake making. Such an orientation could never justify the rapid and automatic moral assessment of a subject but would, rather, inculcate a sense of "sonder." Sonder is a recently coined word that, according to the *Dictionary of Obscure Sorrows*, means: "The realization that each random passerby is living a life as vivid and complex as your own—populated with their own ambitions, friends, routines, worries and inherited craziness—an epic story that continues invisibly around you like an anthill sprawling deep underground, with elaborate passageways to thousands of other lives that you'll never know existed, in which you might appear only once, as an extra sipping coffee in the background, as a blur of traffic passing on the highway, as a lighted window at dusk" (Koenig 2012, n.p.).

Intersubjective orientations based upon predicables, then, honor the ecology of life, the dignity of each life, and the interconnectedness of all. They foster communication, compassion, and flexibility in contradistinction to categories (LOI), which cultivate emotional detachment, impaired communication, excessive emotional rigidity, and the foreclosing of communication in favor of a power differential.

Because there isn't space here for an in-depth look at an epistemology based upon sonder, I have focused my efforts on demarcating a space of intervention to which Audre Lorde famously turned our attention (i.e., "the master's tool") because so many difference scholars have misidentified difference as the primary issue that humans need to address.

Difference itself is not the problem. Rather, the LOI episteme, which is learned, impedes our embrace of difference. My goal in this chapter has been to show that our grounding metaphysics, based upon categories (LOI) instead of predicables, has it backward. Predicables provide us with discourses of interconnectedness rather than separation, cooperation rather than competition, and celebration of difference.

Notably and possibly disastrously, however, despite being grounded in categorical (i.e., hierarchical) dispositioning, dominant cultures in the United States and elsewhere nevertheless capaciously accommodate alternative nonhierarchical discourses that are commensurate with joy, love, sharing, and empathy—which obscures the elephant in the room. Both intersubjective orientations work in tandem to constitute a complex rhetorical social web that is naturalized, despite there being two distinct metaphysics of presence. The problem as I see it is that hierarchical dispositioning forms an overarching "terministic screen" (Burke 1966) that is porous enough to allow for performances of its own dissolution while keeping the screen intact.

Confronting and reconfiguring our relationship to this screen is an important first step in eradicating violence.

According to the American Anthropological Association, "It is a basic tenet of anthropological knowledge that all normal human beings have the capacity to learn any cultural behavior" (1998). I contend that it is high time we consciously engage that capacity in much more positive and constructive ways that will favor all of us, not just the few. The direction that our social evolution takes and perhaps even our continued existence as a viable species may depend upon it.

NOTES

1. The origin of the basing of metaphysics on fixed categories is ultimately unknown, though we see it already codified in the Hebrew Bible and in the writings of Plato and Aristotle.

2. This combination is the way in which legal scholar Ian Haney Lopez (2014) uses the term "automatic thinking."

3. I use the term "intersubjectivity" to denote any relation between subjects (inter + subject)—that is, the individual in relation to the social, in relation to the other, or in relation to the self. Of course, the social, other, and self are merely subject positions in the postmodern sense, fluid and situational.

4. After multiple conference presentations on the topic and much resistance to the idea that violence is an aspect of enculturation, I no longer consider my work obvious even as I know that some readers might see this work as "preaching to the choir."

5. The authors' language illustrates another way cultural practice reinforces the idea that aggression is intrinsically motivated. By suggesting that it was the boys, not the

larger culture, who "failed," the study, purportedly descriptive, places blame on the boys and indirectly on the families, not on structural disadvantage.

6. Some mystics argue that there are perceptual instances in which the Real is directly apprehended, but I'd argue that even those experiences are shaped by medium and context.

7. The West does not own patriarchy, and this essentialist metaphysics undergirds all patriarchal systems.

8. Psychologist Epstein describes categorical thinking as "all-or-none black-and-white thinking" (1998, 208) that tends "to lump things together without making finer distinctions" and "is a major source of prejudice" (77).

9. In *Rethinking Ethos: A Feminist Ecological Approach to Rhetoric*, the editors define ecological thinking as "a habit of mind that takes into consideration the entire ecology of a given rhetorical situation. The rhetor accounts for her subject position relative to others, as well as the shifting material, cultural, and historical situations circulating around rhetorical acts" (Ryan et al. 2016, viii).

10. As Crowley puts it, "the otherness of listeners and readers" is that which "gets us talking and writing after all" (1989, 9).

11. For those concerned about the vulnerability of pacific cultures, keep in mind that in cultures whose intersubjective ground is based upon empathy and the embrace of difference, humans could historicize and remember this terrible epistemic era to retain the ability to call upon aggression if needed (if aggression is indeed hardwired), but doing so would be deliberative, not automatic.

REFERENCES

Alcoff, Linda Martín. 2006. *Visible Identities: Race, Gender, and the Self.* Oxford: Oxford University Press.

Allen, Paula Gunn. 2001. "Kochinnenako in Academe: Three Approaches to Interpreting a Keres Indian Tale." In *Norton Anthology of Theory and Criticism*, ed. Vincent B. Leitch, 2108–25. New York: Norton.

American Anthropological Association. 1998. "AAA Statement on Race."

Balko, Radley. 2017. "Another Survey of Police Shootings Finds Wide Racial Disparities." *Washington Post*, April 7, 2017.

Baumeister, Roy F., and Kathleen D. Vohs. 2007. *Encyclopedia of Social Psychology.* Los Angeles: Sage.

Bialik, Carl. 2015. "An Ex-Cop Keeps the Country's Best Data Set on Police Misconduct." *FiveThirtyEight*, April 22, 2015.

Brennan, Teresa. 2004. *The Transmission of Affect.* Ithaca: Cornell University Press.

Burke, Kenneth. 1966. *Language as Symbolic Action: Essays on Life, Literature and Method.* Berkley: University of California Press.

Bushman, Brad J., and Craig A. Anderson. 2001. "Is It Time to Pull the Plug on the Hostile Versus Instrumental Aggression Dichotomy?" *Psychological Review* 108 (1): 273–79.

Center on the Developing Child at Harvard University. 2016. *Building Core Capabilities for Life: The Science behind the Skills Adults Need to Succeed in Parenting and in the Workplace.* https://developingchild.harvard.edu/resources/building-core-capabilities-for-life/.

Cole, Pamela M. 2010. "Promoting Emotion Regulation in Young Children at Risk for Classroom Behavior Problems." National Head Start Research Conference. https://www.acf.hhs.gov/sites/default/files/opre/cole.pdf.

Cooper, Marilyn M. 2011. "Rhetorical Agency as Emergent and Enacted." *College Composition and Communication* 62 (3): 420–49.

Coté, Sylvana, Tracy Vaillancourt, John C. LeBlanc, Daniel S. Nagin, and Richard E. Tremblay. 2006. "The Development of Physical Aggression from Toddlerhood to Pre-Adolescence: A Nation Wide Longitudinal Study of Canadian Children." *Journal of Abnormal Childhood Psychology* 34 (1): 68–82.

Crowley, Sharon. 1989. *A Teacher's Introduction to Deconstruction*. Urbana: NCTE.

Crowley, Sharon. 2006. *Toward a Civil Discourse: Rhetoric and Fundamentalism*. Pittsburgh: University of Pittsburgh Press.

De Waal, Frans. 2013. *The Bonobo and the Atheist: In Search of Humanism among the Primates*. New York: Norton.

Epstein, Seymour. 1998. *Constructive Thinking: The Key to Emotional Intelligence*. Westport, CT: Praeger Publishers.

"Executive Function and Self-Regulation." 2012. Center on the Developing Child Harvard University. http://developingchild.harvard.edu/science/key-concepts/executive -function/.

Finkel, Eli J., Nathan C. DeWall, Erica B. Slotter, Megan Oaten, and Vangie A. Foshee. 2009. "Self-Regulatory Failure and Intimate Partner Violence Perpetration." *Journal of Personality and Social Psychology* 97 (3): 483–99.

Foucault, Michel. 1994. *The Order of Things: An Archaeology of the Human Sciences*. New York: Vintage Books.

Gilligan, Carol. 2008. "Moral Orientation and Moral Development." In *Feminist Ethical Theory*, ed. Alison Bailey and Chris Cuomo, 467–77. Boston: McGraw Hill.

Gilligan, James. 2001. *Preventing Violence*. New York: Thames and Hudson.

hooks, bell. 2004. *The Will to Change: Men, Masculinity, and Love*. New York: Atria.

Johansen, Bruce E. 1982. *Forgotten Founders: How the American Indian Helped Shape Democracy*. Harvard and Boston: Harvard Common Press.

Koenig, John. 2012. *The Dictionary of Obscure Sorrows*. http://www.dictionaryofobscuresorrows .com/post/23536922667/sonder.

Las Casas, Bartolomé de. 1971. *History of the Indies*. New York: Harper and Row.

Lopez, Ian Haney. 2014. Interview with Bill Moyers. "Ian Haney López on the Dog Whistle Politics of Race (Part One)." *Moyers and Company*. April 28, 2014.

Loveland, Anne C. 1986. *Lillian Smith: A Southerner Confronting the South*. Baton Rouge: Louisiana State University Press.

Mead, Margaret. 2017. "Warfare: An Invention—Not a Biological Necessity." In *Inventing Arguments*, 4th ed., ed. John Mauk and John Metz, 118–23. Boston: Cengage.

Rankine, Claudia. 2014. *Citizen: An American Lyric*. Minneapolis: Graywolf.

Ritchie, Andrea J., and Joey L. Mogul. 2008. "In the Shadows of the War on Terror: Persistent Police Brutality and Abuse of People of Color in the United States." *DePaul Journal for Social Justice* 1 (2): 175–250.

Ryan, Kathleen J., Nancy Myers, and Rebecca Jones. 2016. *Rethinking Ethos: A Feminist Ecological Approach to Rhetoric*. Carbondale: Southern Illinois University Press.

"Timeline of Agricultural Labor." 2014. *National Farm Worker Ministry*. http://nfwm.org/ education-center/farm-worker-issues/timeline-of-agricultural-labor.

Warburton, W. A., and C. A. Anderson. 2015. "Social Psychology of Aggression." In *International Encyclopedia of Social and Behavioral Sciences*, 2nd ed. James D. Wright, vol. 1, 373–80. Oxford: Elsevier.

Young, Iris Marion. 1990. *Justice and the Politics of Difference*. Princeton: Princeton University Press.

5

TOWARD A WORKING THEORY OF INSTITUTIONAL RHETORICS

Ryan Skinnell

It is essential to understand how . . . conformity becomes patterned and routine in society, how persons come to expect certain conduct from each other, and how stable social patterns become established, organized mechanisms. The process by which this happens—the process by which norms come to be routinized, established, and, . . . built into social organization—is what we call institutionalization.

—Leon Mayhew, "Introduction" to *Talcott Parsons: On Institutions and Social Evolution*

On US Interstate 35, heading north from Dallas to Oklahoma City, there is a road sign outside a small farming town that says, "America's Farmers Grow Communities." At the bottom of the sign is an institutional attribution: Monsanto Fund. "America's Farmers Grow Communities" is a donation program that distributes small grants to community nonprofit organizations based on farmers' nominations. Some organization in the small Texas town where the sign resides is apparently a recipient. For anyone suspicious of Monsanto's business practices, it is easy to get caught up in the irony of a multinational agriglomerate adopting the highly localized signifier of "growing community." For rhetoricians, it may even be easier to fall into assessing the rhetorical purpose of something like the Grow Communities fund in terms of its appeals—as, perhaps, a transparent pathetic appeal to small farmers and rural communities or as a broader attempt by Monsanto to counteract pervasive accusations that the company is "evil" by fostering Burkean identification.[1] Maybe it is usefully understood as a visually persuasive appeal or as a material instantiation of rhetorical agency or as a small hub in a sprawling rhetorical network or even as a textbook example of what Ross Beatty calls "windyfoggery" or "bureaucratese" (1982).

DOI: 10.7330/9781607328933.c005

Any or all of these perspectives promise to enlighten the rhetorical work of the road sign. However, though rhetoric specialists are well equipped to read the rhetoric of the "America's Farmers Grow Communities" sign, there are still important institutional elements at work that are hard to understand within our current models of rhetorical action—Monsanto as both cause and effect of the sign, the potential nonhuman/institutional audiences, the site(s) of rhetorical motivation, the effects of such an appeal on *doxa*, and many more. I contend that we have not developed very thoroughgoing models for thinking through the sign as more than a collection of traditional rhetorical appeals. More specifically, I contend that the road sign is a textbook example—one among many—of institutional rhetoric, but it also signals that we are not yet well positioned to examine Monsanto as an institutional rhetor, nor to understand the work of institutional rhetorics more generally. It is a truth often acknowledged by rhetorical scholars that institutions have an outsized influence on public discourse (e.g., Porter et al. 2000), and yet in rhetorical studies we have not developed detailed institutional theories to explain how they get the right to speak, how they exercise that right, how they convey the right to speak to other institutions and individuals, and how institutions shape discourse in powerful and distinct ways.

In this chapter, I argue that rhetoricians would be well served by undertaking such work. As G. Thomas Goodnight points out in his study of strategic maneuvering in the medical field, "Institutions regulate behavior through providing norms that reward 'acceptable' conduct, sanction the 'inappropriate,' and order expectations of exchange" (2008, 360).

Another way to understand Goodnight, though he does not make this connection explicitly, is that institutions are involved in the rhetorical processes of establishing and maintaining what ancient rhetoricians termed *doxa*. As a slight corrective to most contemporary definition of doxa as something like a generalized common sense, Sharon Crowley defines the ancient concept of doxa as "current and local beliefs that circulate communally" (2006, 47).[2] In short, doxa names the common sense(s) shared within a specific community and a specific time based on (relatively) specific discursive conventions. As Goodnight makes clear, institutions help to establish those conventions.

Taking Crowley's definition of doxa, and Goodnight's claims about institutions' effects on establishing norms and expectations, together with sociologist Leon Mayhew's assertion that institutionalization is "the process by which norms come to be routinized, established, and,

. . . built into social organization" (1982, 12), it becomes clear that studying institutions has much to teach rhetoricians about institutional considerations and vice versa—considerations, I might add, that are increasingly important to understand in a progressively multinational, globalizing, corporatizing, post–Citizens United, institutional reality.[3]

Goodnight, and other scholars I discuss below, have taken early steps in that direction, but in this chapter, I make the case that rhetorical theorists need to proceed further in developing theories of institutional rhetorics. I contend that institutions are both central to the work of rhetorical studies and simultaneously understudied by rhetorical theorists, but rhetoricians have largely been content to define institutions contextually. This chapter will attempt (1) to indicate how prominent, but indistinct, institutional considerations currently are in rhetorical studies, (2) to note the beginnings of potentially fruitful theories of institutional rhetorics in rhetorical studies, and (3) to introduce some of the possible directions for developing a more systematic working theory of institutional rhetorics into the field. My goal here is not to develop a theory of institutional rhetorics—that will require the combined efforts of many scholars working from a variety of theoretical perspectives. But I will argue that those combined efforts are worth making.

RHETORIC IN/AND/OF/FOR INSTITUTIONS

In their efforts to build a theory of institutional ethnography for writing studies scholars, Michelle LaFrance and Melissa Nicolas assert, "The field of writing studies is intricately bound up with institutions. Yet, the term *institution* seems significantly absent from the field's journals and ongoing research efforts" (2012, 130). LaFrance and Nicolas are right that writing studies is intricately bound up with institutions, as is its close cousin, rhetorical studies. But their second point—about the absence of the term "institution" in writing and rhetorical studies' scholarship—is somewhat misleading. Institutions are not absent from writing and rhetorical studies, exactly. To the contrary, the term is constantly proffered in every area of the writing and rhetorical studies landscape. If institutions are nowhere, it is only because they are everywhere.

At the risk of stating what is already obvious, "institution" has long been uttered in the same breath as rhetoric. In fact, as Nan Johnson helpfully points out, rhetoric plays an inherently "institutional role" in "inscribing discursive practices" and reinforcing the status quo (2002, 1–2). Johnson is particularly interested in considerations of gender, race, and class in the nineteenth century, but her basic insight is broadly applicable and, I would argue, has been generally accepted dating back to Corax and Tisias. Rhetoric and institutions are, and have always been, intimately intertwined. Rhetoric and institutions may or may not need each other to exist, of course, but the relationship is often—maybe always—symbiotic.

Another way to make this point is to say rhetoricians have been talking about institutions more or less for as long as rhetoric has existed, using a variety of more or less implied meanings. In "Antidosis," for instance, Isocrates casually makes the point that "there is no institution devised by man which the power of speech has not helped us develop" (1992, 253–56). At roughly the same time Aristotle was developing his lecture notes on rhetoric, he was also developing "sound social and political philosophy that encompasses the nature and role of institutions" (Crespo 2016). Quintilian's classic multivolume treatise on rhetoric is, incidentally, called *The Institutes of Oratory*, and according to some rhetorical scholars, his efforts became institutionalized in the Roman Empire (e.g., Sloane 2001, 205).

The common sense of the relationship between institutions and rhetoric might suggest that rhetoricians also have a precise sense of what an institution is, or, as in the case of "rhetoric," at least a bevy of carefully considered definitions to draw from.[4] This is, however, not the case. In fact, even in the examples from antiquity cited above, there are multiple working, but essentially implicit, definitions of institutions: Isocrates indicates that institutions are any man-made [*sic*] civilizing collective, including laws, cities, and the arts. Economist Ricardo Crespo argues that Aristotle's (tacit) theory of institutions was built on slightly more distinct models of political communities, markets, and money (2016, 8). In Quintilian's work, the institutes of his title mean something like the systematic collection of specialized professional knowledge, and to say that his pedagogical theories were institutionalized is to say they were adopted and legitimized by official state organizations. In each of these cases, and in countless others, we can derive the meaning of "institution" from the context, but it should also be clear that institution—as a term and concept—functions as something of a floating signifier. Within certain flexible limits, it can be made to mean what we need it to mean, including everything from (a) a beginning point to (b) a legitimizing force to (c) an oppressive authority to (d) a collection of related resources to (e) a habitual series of actions to (f) a person with a lasting reputation.

The indistinctness of institutions persists into the vast majority of contemporary rhetoric scholarship, so that LaFrance and Nicolas can reasonably note the absence of "institution" as a specific concept even as the word and its multiple meanings appear nearly as regularly in rhetoric and writing scholarship as do other central concepts like deliberation, argument, and writing. The point is further demonstrated by looking at three of the most prominent assemblages of rhetorical studies' disciplinary terminology. While "institution" or some variation of the term appears in use dozens of times each in James Jasinksi's *Sourcebook on Rhetoric* (2001), Thomas O. Sloane's *Encyclopedia of Rhetoric* (2001), and Theresa Enos's *Encyclopedia of Rhetoric and Composition* (2010), none of the compendia of key terms actually has an entry for the concept, nor even a specific in-text definition. Clearly readers know it when they see it.

Likewise, Paul Heilker and Peter Vandenberg's *Keywords in Writing Studies* (2015) makes wide use of the word in a variety of contexts, but the book does not have an entry for "institution" as a keyword. What makes Heilker and Vandenberg's text especially notable, however, is that it is a sequel to their 1996 book, *Keywords in Composition Studies*, in which "institution" does merit an entry, written by Elizabeth Ervin. Ervin, citing multiple sources, argues that "Compositionists have long been sensitive to the ways in which education institutions are both material and discursive formations" and, moreover, that the concept of "*institution* embodies the complex relationships between discursive *and* material constructs" (1996, 124). Undoubtedly true, but not especially precise. Even as Ervin's work helps sketch the prominence of the term in composition scholarship, her chapter also indicates challenges involved in defining the concept. In the work she cites, institutions are "roughly synonymous" with other concepts, or generalized "systems of exclusion and regulation," or material embodiments of abstract sociocultural forces, or "unstable constructs" themselves (124–26). In other words, no one really seems to know exactly what institutions are. Ervin concludes, rightly I think, that institutions are "filled with weaknesses, tensions, contradictions, and possibilities" (126), but she does not ultimately encourage readers to grapple with the term and/or concept going forth. It seems enough to know that institutions exist, that they exert force, and that they might be able to be changed.

Furthermore, Ervin's assertion reinforces a marginally hedged commonplace about the fundamental brokenness of institutions in rhetorical studies. That is, rhetoricians often (maybe even usually) take an oppositional approach to institutional analysis. For one telling instance, James Porter et al. contend that institutional critique is "not interested in simply reporting how evil institutions are" (2000, 613). The implication seems to be that institutions are intrinsically evil, but noting that fact is no longer a sufficient scholarly goal since it is so darn obvious. This anti-institutional attitude is not without some justification, but it nevertheless closes off potential for understanding institutions differently.[5] In this general assessment, Porter et al. and Ervin are joined by a number of other scholars who see institutional change as important work, but who seem nevertheless content to deal obliquely with what institutions are, what they do, and how and why they do it (e.g., Atwill 2002; Lamos 2012; Skinnell 2016).

WHO SPEAKS?

Another example from Monsanto's road sign should suffice to crystalize the potential of studying institutional rhetorics. There are questions raised by the sign, which are less about its persuasive intent—traditional rhetorical appeals—and more about the institution that produced it. I'll limit myself to one: Who speaks when "Monsanto" speaks? As yet, the question about who speaks is rather harder to answer than it might at first seem—not because there are no good answers, but rather because there is an abundance of possible answers. We might say, for instance, that Monsanto speaks, which is indicated by the attribution on the sign. Monsanto is a business with particular goals, and it therefore speaks on its own behalf. This version of the answer suggests, not unreasonably, that institutions are rhetorical and therefore act strategically through language.

The immediate obstacle, of course, is that Monsanto cannot literally speak, having no speaking mouth or typing fingers of its own. Monsanto is not altogether posthuman, so it must borrow language-producing apparatuses from people. So we might say Monsanto is the people it comprises. The people speak. But, of course, not all of them speak for Monsanto. I assume there is a general, and practical, disinclination to assume that the average Monsanto employee can make official pronouncements for the company, for instance. By the same token, neither is there a single person who may stand in for Monsanto. Even very powerful people within the company—the CEO or chairman of the board, for instance—are not solely responsible for Monsanto's speech. We might say there are collectives—the marketing team or the legal team—who do the speaking. Again, however, Monsanto's speech is not reducible to the marketing team or the legal team, and moreover, the lawyers and marketers are not always speaking in Monsanto's stead. And further still, Monsanto is designed to outlast any individual or group of speakers. The road sign, for instance, does not become defunct because the CEO leaves. In other words, if the CEO leaves, she or he does not take the right to speak on behalf of Monsanto with them. The more closely one pulls at the "who speaks" string, the harder it is to come to a definitive answer to who is speaking when Monsanto speaks. The challenge of considering "who speaks" is just one among many when institutional rhetorics are at play.

I am belaboring the point, but not without some cause. Institutions are as ubiquitous and invisible as the air we breathe—cataloging every use of "institution" in rhetorical studies would result in a virtual Borgesian Library of Institutional Babel. The concept is (and institutions are) maddeningly pliable, and yet it is clear that institutions are vitally connected to rhetoric—to language, symbol systems, communicative acts, persuasion, power, norms, expectations, doxa, identity, and more. Still, rhetoricians have yet to build a working theoretical model of institutions such that they continue to be as diversely constituted as powerful organizations that use rhetoric (Lynch 2005), as "rhetorically constructed human designs" (Porter et al. 2000, 611), and as "discursive constructions that shapeshift [sic] according to the particular standpoint of the person interacting with the institution" (LaFrance and Nicolas 131), and that is to cite only scholars writing specifically about institutions.

I am not interested in sloughing off the various definitions of "institution" to find the one, true meaning. Nor am I interested, it should be clear, in declaring that the term is so overused as to be meaningless. As I noted briefly above, "institution" can be variously deployed within certain flexible limits—it does not mean everything—so appraising the (flexible) limits of the concept can help rhetoricians generate a better understanding of the multiple functions of institutional rhetoric and its force in the world. That is, given the ubiquity and complexity of "institution," and given its centrality to the work rhetorical scholars do, we would be well served by developing a more careful and explicit understanding of institutions in, and, of, and for rhetoric in order to consider more precisely how institutions and rhetoric work in, around, and for one another. In calling for a more precise theory of institutional rhetorics, then, I want to extend the long tradition of presupposing rhetoric's interconnection to institutions as a way to help rhetoricians both ask better questions about institutional rhetoric and begin to develop better answers.

INSTITUTIONAL RHETORICS: SOME INITIAL LINES OF FLIGHT

As I have already noted repeatedly, many rhetoric and writing scholars have written about institutions in relation to rhetoric and vice versa. A

much smaller number of rhetorical scholars have written about institutional rhetoric as a theoretical concept worthy of thorough consideration in its own right. In fact, from what I can ascertain, there are
just three rhetoric scholars who have begun this work: David Zarefsky
(2008), G. Thomas Goodnight (2008, 2015), and Mark A. Thompson
(2013, 2016).[6] There is not room in this chapter for a full explication
of their work, but I do want to briefly introduce their arguments here
because they offer us some useful starting points for expanding the
study of institutional rhetorics.

The major distinguishing characteristic of Zarefsky, Goodnight, and
Thompson's work is that they draw explicitly on institutional scholarship from other fields—scholarship that attempts to grapple with the
complexity of institutions. Zarefsky, for instance, offers a working definition of institutions ("formal structures of decision-making, bound by
accepted procedures, norms, and conventions that together define
the parameters of acceptable discourse"), which he situates within
Goodnight's technical sphere of argumentation (2008, 318).[7] Zarefsky's
definition of an institution, wittingly or not, also echoes the work of
a number of twentieth-century sociologists who wrote about institutions, including Max Weber, Thorstein Veblen, Talcott Parsons, Emile
Durkheim, and Anthony Giddens. Zarefsky's goal is to distinguish institutionalization from his main interest, political argumentation, but his
explicit alignment of rhetoric with institutions, and his apparent nod to
eminent institutional theorists are useful for our purposes inasmuch as
they clue us in to more than a century of work that studies and attempts
to unravel institutional matters.

Goodnight refers more intentionally than Zarefsky to the work of
institutional theorists, though he is less interested in classical theories
of institutions, à la Weber and others, and more interested in New
Institutional Theory. According to Goodnight, New Institutional Theory
exchanges a strictly utilitarian, self-interested, cost-benefit classical view
of institutional decision-making with the view that "social actors can
reach reasonable decisions and reach agreement because their training, identity, and allegiance within a field creates a partnership that
transcends particular utility calculations and contractual arrangements"
(2008, 361). Furthermore, "what counts as reasonable thinking and valid
judgment is grounded in the logic of the institution" (361). Within this
view—as expounded by a number of sociologists, economists, political
scientists, institutional theorists, and more—the varying definitions of
"institution" exist in relation to developed sets of institutional logics and
rhetorics. Essentially, human actors establish and formalize particular

logics and rhetorics in institutional frameworks, which then shape possibilities for future actions. Goodnight adopts New Institutional Theory to
explain institutional contexts in which argumentation occurs, a point he
later extends to encourage rhetoricians to develop more sophisticated
understandings of how contemporary economics informs rhetoric and
argumentation (2015).

Perhaps rhetoricians' most thorough engagement with institutional
theories is in the work of Mark A. Thompson. Drawing again on
Weberian definitions of "institution," Thompson thoughtfully unpacks
some of the pervading assumptions about what institutions are and what
they do that is of interest to rhetoricians. He writes: "Though many
critics have linked institutions to coercive power, the subjugation of
individuals, and the maintenance/enforcement of exploitive systems of
dominance . . . , it is not always helpful to approach institutions with this
assumption . . . [A]ny presuppositions about domination and exploitation should be muted until we can demonstrate that such dimensions
are actually in play" (2013, 6–7).

By calling attention to, and then redescribing, the persistent assumptions of coercive institutional power,[8] Thompson is then able to draw
our attention to different ways that discourse circulates in relation to
institutions: "(1) between individuals within institutions; (2) between
individuals representing two or more different institutions; and (3)
between institutions and 'the outside world'" (2013, 7). In keeping
with his specific purposes, this move allows Thompson to focus more
narrowly on what he calls "institutional argument": "the ways in which
claims are asserted and defended in institutional contexts, and the ways
in which institutional practices factor into strengthening or weakening
arguments made" (8; see also Thompson 2016). In the process of nar-
rowing his focus, Thompson begins to chart the expanse of institutional
theories and the ways in which they may enlighten a more robust theory
or theories of institutional rhetorics, and also why it may be worthwhile.
In short, what we think we know intuitively about institutions wraps in an
incredible assortment of cherished, but often overly simplified, assumptions about how they function rhetorically and why.[9]

INSTITUTIONS FOR RHETORIC

Zarefsky, Goodnight, and Thompson introduce an expansive field
of institutional studies. Classical theories of institutions are generally
characterized by macrostructural analyses. Within classical theories,
some of the main objectives have been to try to define institutions in

contrast to organizations, cultures, and other corporate entities and to try to understand how institutions impose continuity, conformity, and constraint (see Scott 2008). Max Weber's and Talcott Parsons's theories provided the baseline for institutional theories for several decades, until the 1980s and 1990s, when New Institutional Theory, or neoinstitutional theory, developed in an effort to account for issues of individual agency, institutional contingency, cultural change, and more (see Powell and DiMaggio 1991).

More recently still, institutional theorists have begun to elaborate what Patricia H. Thornton, William Ocasio, and Michael Lounsbury (2012) call the "Institutional Logics Perspective." Institutional logic, which seems especially promising for rhetoricians, is defined by Thornton, Ocasio, and Lounsbury as "the socially constructed, historical patterns of cultural symbols and material practices, including assumptions, values, and beliefs, by which individuals and organizations provide meaning to their daily activity, organize time and space, and reproduce their lives and experiences" (2). The institutional logics perspective avails rhetoricians of a series of symbolic and material analytic frames—including storytelling, bounded agency, motive, and interinstitutional relations—that have the potential to enlighten the rhetorical work of twenty-first-century institutions.

Take, for instance, an example that has circulated in digital rhetorics scholarship recently. In 2007, Ian Bogost coined the term "procedural rhetoric" to name a "new type of persuasive and expressive practice," which is the "practice of using processes persuasively" (2007, 2–3). Bogost is interested primarily in computational processes and video games, and his work has had much influence on the digital and new materialist turns in the field of rhetorical studies. Bogost's theory of procedural rhetoric has been generative in those areas of inquiry, and for good reason. But a theory of institutional rhetorics suggests that procedural persuasion is considerably older than the kinds of computation Bogost is primarily interested in. One might look, for instance, to the development of forms and bureaucratic procedures to formalize certain institutional "practice(s) of using processes persuasively" that date back centuries.[10] This is not to say Bogost is wrong—far from it. It is only to point out that by setting the two theoretical perspectives next to each other, we potentially stand to enhance both. The same goes for any number of other areas of rhetorical scholarship.

What various forms of institutional theory can teach us is that institutions serve a number of crucial rhetorical functions. Among them, institutions foster—and sometimes betray—trust and dependency (Smith and Freyd 2014); they invent and ossify customs (Gordon 1991); they amplify claims and assertions (Thornton, Ocasio, and Lounsbury 2012); they are—or act as—impersonal, naturalizing arbiters (Friedrich 2008); they maximize rhetorical, processual, and economic efficiency (Yates 1989); they discipline and normalize institutional actors (Wrenn 2013); they attempt to deprioritize individuality in favor of uniformity (Sarangi and Slembrouck 1996); they instantiate, naturalize, and house topoi (Agar 1985); they generate perceptions about widespread assent to goad individuals to identification (Jones 2002, 194); and they serve as arbiters of symbolic value (Ahmed 2016). This is only to scratch the surface of the ways in which institutional characteristics and theories connect to and depart from well-established rhetorical theories of symbolic action. As Thompson (2013) helps us recognize, institutional rhetorics comprise and exceed a "rhetoric of institutions" framework. I contend that by developing more systematic theories of institutional rhetorics, rhetoricians stand to learn a lot about what it means to act rhetorically in a fundamentally institutional world and, by extension, to act institutionally in a fundamentally rhetorical world.

NOTES

1. Even as I was writing this chapter, chemical and pharmaceutical giant Bayer has agreed to purchase Monsanto for $66 billion. Assuming the merger happens (which it has not yet, and may not if federal regulators intervene), it remains to be seen what this will mean for the Grow Communities fund and what it will mean in the long run for understanding an I-35 road sign that gestures to entities that may be vanishing.

2. *Doxa* is not entirely distinct from hegemony (Crowley 2006, 5), though it also does not necessarily imply the exertion of violent force that is often read into Gramsci's version of cultural hegemony.

3. Citizen's United provides an especially rich flashpoint for examining connections between rhetoric and institutions, given the Supreme Court's effective granting of First Amendment political speech rights to corporations. That flashpoint deserves far closer study than I can provide here, but it is an unmistakable point of entry. And, oh yeah, the reality of "President Trump" undoubtedly offers another such entry point.

4. Muckelbauer (2004) ruminates on the many "promiscuous"—even constitutively divergent—definitions of rhetoric.

5. Some of the most trenchant scholarship in rhetoric and writing studies is being done (and has long been done) by labor scholars and activists. Crowley (in)famously had her hand in labor activism, of course (see 1998, 2002), and more recent work by Horner (2016), Kahn et al. (2017), Strickland (2011), Welch and Scott (2016), and others has critically assessed, corrected, and extended the continued work of labor analyses in the field. Much labor scholarship highlights the unrelenting antilabor (and, in some cases, apparently antihuman) biases of contemporary institutions, which make labor and other activism necessary. However, as in other areas

of rhetoric and writing studies, more often than not, institutions are definitionally flexible even as they are constitutionally rigid. See McCloskey (2011), especially chapter 33, for a persuasive argument as to why we need richer thinking than a purely oppositional approach allows.

6. Cleveland's 1971 dissertation appears to be the earliest claim to a theory of "institutional rhetorics," but he was working in the field of sociology, not rhetoric. His work definitely bears on the work in rhetorical studies, but I have opted not to include him here (1) because of his disciplinary affiliation, and (2) because his theory of institutional rhetorics is more or less consonant with the work of the other scholars I focus on.

7. There is also useful work to be done in considering whether institutions are identical to "organizations" in the ways that rhetorical scholars such as Faber (2002, esp. chap. 2) and Leon (2013) use the term. As I point out briefly below, some sociologists and institutional theorists have also considered the terms in comparison, but from what I can ascertain, there aren't any definitive conclusions.

8. This view of institutional power is, of course, perfectly in keeping with Foucault's highly influential body of work. In fact, I would argue that Foucault's largely implicit theories of institution, institutionalization, and institutional power provide the foundation for the vast majority of contemporary rhetoricians' assumptions about what institutions are and do.

9. See Searle (2005) for a similar and compelling case.

10. For a compelling example from rhetorical scholarship, see Yates (1989).

REFERENCES

Agar, Michael. 1985. "Institutional Discourse." *Text* 5 (3): 147–68.

Ahmed, Sara. 2016. "Resignation is a Feminist Issue." *Feminist Killjoys*. https://feministkilljoys.com/2016/08/27/resignation-is-a-feminist-issue/.

Atwill, Janet M. 2002. "Rhetoric and Institutional Critique: Uncertainty in the Postmodern Academy." *JAC* 22 (3): 640–45.

Beatty, Ross. 1982. "Windyfoggery and Bureaucratese." *Rhetoric Society Quarterly* 12 (4): 261–69.

Bogost, Ian. 2007. *Persuasive Games: The Expressive Power of Videogames*. Cambridge, MA: MIT Press.

Cleveland, Charles E. 1971. "Institutional Rhetorics as Universes of Discourse: Institutionalization of Consensual Cues in Social Conversation to Define the Situation." PhD dissertation, Northwestern University, Chicago.

Crespo, Ricardo F. 2016. "Aristotle on Agency, Habits, and Institutions." *Journal of Institutional Economics* 12 (4): 867–84. DOI: 10.1017/S1744137416000059.

Crowley, Sharon. 1998. *Composition in the University: Historical and Polemical Essays*. Pittsburgh: University of Pittsburgh Press.

Crowley, Sharon. 2002. "How the Professional Lives of WPAs Would Change if FYC Were Elective." In *The Writing Program Administrator's Resource: A Guide to Reflective Institutional Practice*, ed. Stuart C. Brown, Theresa Enos, and Catherine Chaput, 219–30. Mahwah, NJ: Lawrence Erlbaum.

Crowley, Sharon. 2006. *Toward a Civil Discourse: Rhetoric and Fundamentalisms*. Pittsburgh: University of Pittsburgh Press.

Enos, Theresa, ed. 2010. *Encyclopedia of Rhetoric and Composition: Communication from Ancient Times to the Information Age*. New York: Routledge.

Ervin, Elizabeth. 1996. "Institution." In *Keywords in Composition Studies*, ed. Paul Heilker and Peter Vandenberg, 124–27. Portsmouth, NH: Boynton/Cook.

Faber, Brenton D. 2002. *Community Action and Organizational Change: Image, Narrative, Identity.* Carbondale: Southern Illinois University Press.

Friedrich, Markus. 2008. "Government and Information-Management in Early Modern Europe: The Case of the Society of Jesus (1540–1773)." *Journal of Early Modern History* 12 (6): 539–63.

Goodnight, G. Thomas. 2008. "Strategic Maneuvering in Direct to Consumer Drug Advertising: A Study in Argumentation Theory and New Institutional Theory." *Argumentation* 22 (3): 359–71.

Goodnight, G. Thomas. 2015. "Rhetoric and Communication: Alternative Worlds of Inquiry." *Quarterly Journal of Speech* 101 (1): 145–50.

Gordon, Colin. 1991. "Governmental Rationality: An Introduction." In *The Foucault Effect: Studies in Governmentality*, ed. Graham Burchell, Colin Gordon, and Peter Miller, 1–52. Chicago: University of Chicago Press.

Heilker, Paul, and Peter Vandenberg, eds. 1996. *Keywords in Composition Studies.* Portsmouth, NH: Boynton/Cook.

Heilker, Paul, and Peter Vandenberg, eds. 2015. *Keywords in Writing Studies.* Logan: Utah State University Press.

Horner, Bruce. 2016. *Rewriting Composition: Terms of Exchange.* Logan: Utah State University Press.

Isocrates. 1992. "Antidosis." In *Isocrates*, vol. 2, trans. George Norlin, 179–366. Cambridge, MA: Harvard University Press.

Jasinski, James, ed. 2001. *Sourcebook on Rhetoric: Key Concepts in Contemporary Rhetorical Studies.* Thousand Oaks, CA: Sage.

Johnson, Nan. 2002. *Gender and Rhetorical Space in American Life, 1866–1910.* Carbondale: Southern Illinois University Press.

Jones, H. S. 2002. *The French State in Question: Public Law and Political Argument in the Third Republic.* Cambridge: Cambridge University Press.

Kahn, Seth, William B. Lalicker, and Amy Lynch-Biniek, eds. 2017. *Contingency, Exploitation, and Solidarity: Labor and Action in English Composition.* Fort Collins and Boulder: WAC Clearinghouse and University Press of Colorado.

LaFrance, Michelle, and Melissa Nicolas. 2012. "Institutional Ethnography as Materialist Framework for Writing Program Research and the Faculty-Staff Work Standpoints Project." *College Composition and Communication* 64 (1): 130–50.

Lamos, Steve. 2012. "Institutional Critique in Composition Studies: Methodological and Ethical Considerations for Researchers." In *Writing Studies Research in Practice: Methods and Methodologies*, ed. Lee Nickoson and Mary P. Sheridan, 158–70. Carbondale: Southern Illinois University Press.

Leon, Kendall. 2013. "*La Hermandad* and Chicanas Organizing: The Community Rhetoric of the *Comisión Femenil Mexicana Nacional.*" *Community Literacy Journal* 7 (2): 1–20.

Lynch, John. 2005. "Institution and Imprimatur: Institutional Rhetoric and the Failure of the Catholic Church's Pastoral Letter on Homosexuality." *Rhetoric and Public Affairs* 8 (3): 383–403.

Mayhew, Leon H. 1982. "Introduction." In *Talcott Parsons: On Institutions and Social Evolution*, ed. Leon H. Mayhew, 1–62. Chicago: University of Chicago Press.

McCloskey, Deirdre N. 2011. *Bourgeois Dignity: Why Economics Can't Explain the Modern World.* Chicago: University of Chicago Press.

Muckelbauer, John. 2004. "Returns of the Question." *Enculturation* 5 (2): n.p. http://enculturation.net/5_2/muckelbauer.html.

Porter, James E., Patricia Sullivan, Stuart Blythe, Jeffrey T. Grabill, and Libby Miles. 2000. "Institutional Critique: A Rhetorical Methodology for Change." *College Composition and Communication* 51 (4): 610–42. http://dx.doi.org/10.2307/358914.

Powell, Walter W., and Paul J. DiMaggio. 1991. *The New Institutionalism in Organizational Analysis.* Chicago: University of Chicago Press.

Sarangi, Srikant, and Stefaan Slembrouck. 1996. *Language, Bureaucracy, and Social Control.* London: Longman.

Scott, W. Richard. 2008. *Institutions and Organizations: Ideas and Interests.* Thousand Oaks, CA: Sage.

Searle, John R. 2005. "What Is an Institution?" *Journal of Institutional Economics* 1 (1): 1–22.

Skinnell, Ryan. 2016. *Conceding Composition: A Crooked History of Composition's Institutional Fortunes.* Logan: Utah State University Press.

Sloane, Thomas O. 2001. *Encyclopedia of Rhetoric.* Oxford: Oxford University Press.

Smith, Carly Parnitzke, and Jennifer J. Freyd. 2014. "Institutional Betrayal." *American Psychologist* 69 (6): 575–87.

Strickland, Donna. 2011. *The Managerial Unconscious in the History of Composition Studies.* Carbondale: Southern Illinois University Press.

Thompson, Mark A. 2013. "Institutional Rhetoric, Argument, and the House Un-American Activities Committee, 1949–1956." PhD dissertation, Carnegie Mellon University, Pittsburgh.

Thompson, Mark A. 2016. "Institutional Argumentation and Institutional Rules: Effects of Interactive Asymmetry on Argumentation in Institutional Contexts." *Argumentation*, 31 (1): 1–21. DOI 10.1007/s10503-016-9395-5.

Thornton, Patricia H., William Ocasio, and Michael Lounsbury. 2012. *The Institutional Logics Perspective: A New Approach to Culture, Structure, and Process.* Oxford: Oxford University Press.

Welch, Nancy, and Tony Scott, eds. 2016. *Composition in the Age of Austerity.* Logan: Utah State University Press.

Wrenn, Mary. 2013. "Fear and Institutions." *Journal of Economic Issues* 47 (2): 383–90.

Yates, JoAnne. 1989. *Control through Communication: The Rise of System in American Management.* Baltimore: Johns Hopkins University Press.

Zarefsky, David. 2008. "Strategic Maneuvering in Political Argumentation." *Argumentation* 22 (3): 317–30.

6

THE SOPHIST AS MENTOR
Sharon Crowley's Rhetoric as a Theory and Practice of Mentoring

William B. Lalicker, James C. McDonald, and Susan Wyche

It is a hot day in Arizona: 116 degrees in the shade. The three of us arrive in Phoenix to visit Sharon Crowley,[1] now retired and living in the Arizona desert. She has been a mentor to each of us since we were young academics, nearly thirty years ago, and we have traveled from Louisiana, Pennsylvania, and Hawaii to reconnect with her and discuss her theory of mentoring.

What we hope to discover is embedded both in her rich body of rhetorical theory and in our own and others' memories and experiences with her. Memory is communal, "associative, global," as Crowley points out: "Composers working from memory may be led down interesting byways as they mentally walk the paths of their carefully organized memories" (1993b, 36).

Stepping into Sharon's living room, which is darkened against the hot Arizona sun, we hope to tread interesting byways to an understanding of how she came to be a cherished mentor in our profession.

As the afternoon wears on and temperatures cool, she invites us to join her at her favorite local cafe, and then to stay at her house for an impromptu overnight. When we return to her home, she turns on the evening news, and we shift seamlessly from talk of rhetoricians we know to talk about the rhetoric of national politics. With Sharon, one never knows where the conversation will go next—institutional politics, Black Lives Matter, the lyrics of Lyle Lovett, the Master of Rome series by Colleen McCullough sitting on her bookshelf, or the latest episode of *Game of Thrones*—it's all grist for the rhetorical mill. It doesn't matter what we talk about, really; it's *how* we talk. Sharon's mentoring may incorporate raucous laughter, pointed comment, cold beer—and then the insightful analysis that you think about, learn from, and remember

DOI: 10.7330/9781607328933.c006

when its power can be applied to the rhetorical and material tasks you confront in your professional life.

* * *

When Crowley began her career, what passed for theory in rhetoric and writing studies was the "current-traditional" stance that approaches each instance of writing (especially student writing) as a noun, not a verb—a limited, fixed, and decontextualized document displaying a surface to be critiqued and corrected by a more knowledgeable reader. In response, she argued that writing instruction should be based on a rhetoric that dovetails at the intersection of feminist theory, deconstruction, and classical rhetoric, especially sophistic rhetoric, challenging a modern liberal rhetoric that privileges reason and the empirical by instead privileging invention, ethos, and subjectivity. Crowley's reading of classical rhetoric changed the focus of student engagement toward invention, the function of a living mind making an argument to an audience in a political-historical context. Her emphasis on invention posits the creative mind of the writer—including the student writer at any level of experience or academic hierarchy—as worthy of consideration. Her rhetorical theory allies itself with a Freirean insistence on student agency: writing teachers, like the sophists, should expect "their students to become active participants in their communities and to conduct their lives in a manner which would afford them an authoritative voice" (1989b, 318). Students are not passive imitators of their betters and of the belles-lettres essay ideal—not passive receptacles of established knowledge—but inventive, powerful, and knowledgeable, and are to be abetted and respected, not merely corrected or shaped, by their teachers.

Until the 1980s, as academics realized that graduate students needed mentoring for the job search and teaching, as well as for research, to compete in the increasingly tough market for tenure-track positions, most universities did not seriously engage in formal mentoring (Ebest 2002, 212–13). Existing mentoring practices, like current-traditional writing instruction, had been shaped by Enlightenment values—of self-reliance, hierarchy, and desire for control—and, according to Jenn Fishman and Andrea Lunsford, Adam Smith's conception of the conscience as "the internal judge or 'impartial spectator'" (2008, 24).[2] This impartiality assumed mentors and mentees were white and male. Faculty were rarely interested in taking on female graduate students as protégés, as Crowley discusses in her oral history on Maxine Hairston, Winifred Bryan Horner, and Lynn Bloom (1988; see also Enos 1997; Fishman and Lunsford 2008).[3] And Gail Y. Okawa (2002) discusses how "colorblind" approaches to mentoring are unable to address the challenges that scholars of color face. The power differential between mentor and mentee in traditional mentoring can easily create "abusive" relationships (Fishman and Lunsford 2008; Ebest 2002). These problems—which may be more acute for rhetoric and writing specialists because of low institutional respect for teaching, administrative work, and rhetoric and writing scholarship—have led writing scholars to rethink and reconstruct academic mentoring.

We argue that applying Sharon Crowley's rhetorical theory to mentoring experiences can push the field's rethinking of mentoring. Much mentoring scholarship is based on practice and experience, of formal mentoring programs and of individual mentors, often at the expense of theory, and rhetoric and writing scholars generally ignore the rhetorical theories of their own field when they do use theory to develop mentoring approaches. Yet mentoring is a rhetorical activity, as mentors act as rhetors, sometimes to protect a mentee and often to open opportunities for them; and sometimes as a rhetorician, modeling and guiding mentees to become more effective scholarly writers and more persuasive speakers and writers in the myriad rhetorical administrative, pedagogical, and other situations in which they operate. The making of knowledge in mentoring needs to be based on a balance of theory and practice.

The approach to mentoring that we develop out of Sharon Crowley's theories and experiences, which we call sophistic mentoring, considers the shifting subjectivities of mentors and mentees and embraces activism, collaboration, and egalitarianism as they work together to develop mentees as scholars, teachers, WPAs, and citizens of the institution. Because teaching for Crowley is not a predictable one-way dissemination of knowledge from teacher to student, but a mutual engagement (1989b, 332–33), her theory suggests, by extension, a rich way of thinking about mentoring when coupled with an examination of her mentoring experiences and practices. Crowley herself avoids writing about her practice: "[I am] reluctant to share with readers what I take to be the relatively intimate relation that obtains between me and my students"; "[I] never . . . figured out how to write with candor about my own pedagogy for a faceless audience" (1989a, 108–9). But because of her transformative mentoring, Crowley's influence is much deeper than her published work alone. By sharing and examining stories from our own experience and from interviews with Sharon and others, we hope to explicate Crowley's practice and theory of mentorship to develop our theory of sophistic mentoring.

One reason to look to Crowley in developing an approach to mentoring is that the changing subjectivities, or *ethoi*, of rhetors and their audiences are crucial to her rhetorical theory, just as the subjectivities of mentor and mentee are central concerns in much of the scholarship on mentoring in rhetoric and writing studies. Cindy Buell captures much of how mentoring approaches construct the subjectivities of mentors and mentees in her four categories of mentoring: the "cloning model," in which "mentors seek to duplicate themselves"; the "apprenticeship" model, in which the mentee "become[s] a valued member of the profession" by learning "through [the mentor's] eyes"; the "nurturing" model, in which the mentor takes on the role of mother or care-giver; and the "collaborative and co-constructed" "friendship" model (Buell, cited in Miles and Burnett 2008, 116). Most rhetoric and writing scholars treat the cloning and apprentice models as a single approach, which they usually reject as hierarchical or patriarchal and incapable of addressing the problems of a woman or person of color in need of mentoring (see, e.g., Enos 1997; Fishman and Lunsford 2008). Rhetoric and writing scholars instead often develop a nurturing model based on an "ethics of care" (Gabor, Neeley, and Leverenz 2008; Lauer 1997; Rickly and Harrington 2002; Trachsel 2002) or a friendship model (Ashe and Ervin 2008; Baake et al. 2008; Fishman and Lunsford 2008; Horner 2008).[4] Some scholars, such as Katherine S. Miles and Rebecca E. Burnett (2008), however, see a role for master/apprentice relationships given the fluid, dynamic, and flexible nature of the subjectivities of mentor and mentee. The relationship between mentor and mentee may not be able to avoid being hierarchical at first, given the hierarchical nature of academic institutions, though that relationship should transform into a more and more equal relationship if the mentoring is effective.

Buell's four models do not exhaust the subjectivities of mentor and mentee in rhetoric and writing scholarship. Because traditional mentoring practices seek to reproduce the status quo in academia, Theresa Enos proposes "maverick" as an alternate term to "mentor" that challenges oppressive and problematic practices, traditions, and attitudes in institutions (1997). Sally Barr Ebest discusses Janet A. Schmidt's "three functions" of the mentor in higher education—"role model, information provider, door opener" (2002, 212)—subjectivities that a mentor may adopt at different times.

Applied to mentoring, Crowley's rhetorical theory would favor approaches to mentoring that encourage dynamic, kairotic relationships in which the roles of the mentor and mentee shift according to their projects and circumstances (a defining characteristic of sophistic rhetoric). In defiance of "a liberal modern assumption that stable rhetorical subjects exist prior to the rhetorical event," Crowley argues that rhetorical encounters and discursive performances "entail or produce the very subjectivity we call 'rhetor'" (2006, 51). "Rhetorical subjects are outcomes" of the rhetorical encounter (51)—rhetor *and* listener, teacher *and* student (and, by extension, mentor *and* mentee)—reconstructed in every rhetorical situation (or *kairotic moment*). This position leads Crowley to insist on Aristotle's definition of rhetoric as an art of invention, "an ability, in each case, to see the available means of persuasion" (qtd. in 2006, 27). But by translating Aristotle's word *dunamis* (ability) as "can-do-ness," Crowley appropriates Foucault's definition of power—where the possibility of power originates in difference—"in inequalities in force relations" (2006, 51). A can-do mentoring approach requires the mentor and mentee to work out the subjectivities that they need in order to face their situation. A Crowleyan mentor (that is, a sophistic mentor) would emphasize a balance of the needs of both community and individual; a collaborative inventiveness; a keen awareness of cultural memory, knowledge, values, and ideology; and a flexible and dynamic subjectivity within the culture. Crowley's example as a mentor complicates and adds to any theoretical description of a sophistic mentor, adding layers of challenge, modeling, and protection of the vulnerable or marginalized through a process of critiquing cultural assumptions, especially within institutional contexts.

A sophistic mentoring approach would eschew a rigid traditional cloning/apprentice model of mentoring as insensitive to competing subjectivities and as particularly frustrating for women, academics of color, and those from the working class—those who do not see themselves mirrored in the profession. A sophistic mentor and mentee largely determine and invent their individual subjectivities and their relationship, though within institutional, disciplinary, and cultural confines. The institutional context of a department or a mentoring program conditions the subjectivities available to a mentor and mentee, just as universities, until recently, had made the position of mentee largely unavailable to women graduate students and faculty because of the culture's "patriarchal assumptions about what women 'are' and could 'do'" (Crowley 2002, 179). Differences in rank between the mentor and mentee—and differences in "force relations" among faculty, administrators, and others that the mentor and mentee deal with (as determined by gender, race, or disciplinary conflicts)—are all enacted as they forge a mentoring relationship, to build the mentee's "intellectual authority" (Crowley 2008, 227). Crowley's insistence on the importance of the word "available" in Aristotle's definition would prevent her from picturing self-invention in mentoring as unlimited;

self-invention in mentoring operates within, while also challenging, these confines.

Crowley's "can-do" concept of invention and ethos implies that mentors and mentees should develop the mentee's confidence, intellectual authority, and sense of activism, working collaboratively and imaginatively to explore the available means of persuasion for changing long-standing and often apparently intractable problems that bedevil and oppress rhetoric and writing faculty, as well as women and people of color. Yet Crowley also recognizes that the rhetorical and institutional situation sometimes shows that taking on an issue is too risky, time consuming, or futile. Crowley acknowledges the importance of recognizing the available means of persuasion when she advises that women in rhetoric and writing cultivate friendships and find a mentor "who's been at that institution for a long time, who knows how the institution runs, and who has been on a lot of committees, and can tell you what committee to get on, and who to cultivate, and how the institution works" (2008, 229).

Applied to a mentoring context, the rhetorical event engages the subjectivity of both the mentor and the mentee, shaping the subjectivity of the mentee as a professional, a scholar, a teacher, or an activist; the mentee's potential in the beginning of the relationship is realized through reflection and action, guided by the experienced rhetor: "Rhetorical power can be activated by people who are equipped to articulate available openings in discourse, in both senses of 'formulating' and 'connecting'" (Crowley 2006, 52). According to Crowley, a rhetor's subjectivity is usually inhabited for a short time and competes with other subjectivities—it is not constant. One moves in and out of these subjectivities, in a flow of sporadic rhetorical acts embedded in quotidian life. Certainly one who has been mentored by Sharon would recognize her power to seize these "openings in discourse" and create connections and meaning, activating moments of learning when least expected. And these openings were specific to contexts of race, gender, and professional status—not as a basis for treatment, but as subjects that Sharon introduced or welcomed if the mentees introduced them. She openly engaged the subject of difference, and specifically *our differences*, without fear or hesitation—a relief at a time when difference was often unspoken by so many of our other teachers and mentors.

Most important for Crowley, rhetors/teachers and, by extension mentors, must be aware of the ethical and political implications of their practices—the relationships that develop between teacher and students, among students, and between writers and readers are always specific to a certain time or place and to the special persons who come together to perform the practice. This is a theme throughout her work. She points out that, because their art was immersed in the adjudication of immediate cultural concerns, Sophists taught their pupils that the practice of rhetoric entailed attention to important ethical, political, historical, and legal questions. As she argues, "Any practice entitled to be called 'rhetoric' must intervene in some way in social and civic discursive networks" (2003). The Sophists expected their students to become active participants in their communities and to conduct their lives in a manner that would afford them an authoritative voice (1989b, 318). This expectation directed Crowley, in her own scholarship, to engage in issues such as reforming institutional labor practices, challenging the freshman English requirement, and analyzing current political discourse. Mentoring, therefore, should actively engage the social and civic contexts in which the mentor and mentee are situated.

MENTORING AS CREATING COMMUNITY

Above, we explicate a theory of sophistic mentorship based on Sharon Crowley's rhetorical theory, and looking more carefully at some specific examples in practice can help illustrate the theory. For us, and for many of Sharon's other "mentees," the mentoring relationship began with an intellectual encounter (at a conference, a job interview, a department meeting, a graduate class meeting, or in one of the interstitial spaces of these events) and resulted in an invitation to join Sharon and others for food, drink, talk. This practice of inviting neophytes into professional community—often after a single encounter in which she became engaged with a conference presentation or other intellectual exchange—originates from an incident in Sharon's own professional development, which she would later pay forward many times over. She tells us that while working as a writing teacher with a budding interest in rhetorical theory, she gave a talk at an early Wyoming Conference, which later developed into her 1979 *College Composition and Communication* article, "Of Gorgias and Grammatology," one of her first publications. Ed Corbett and Jim Kinneavy—two senior scholars in the field at that time—invited her for lunch and talked to her about her presentation. Corbett, then editor of *CCC*, said he wanted to publish it. She notes that she had to revise the article three or four times before it was accepted, but it was eventually published. At the time, she was surprised that Corbett and Kinneavy noticed her and were generous enough to take the time to encourage her, and she attributes their influence to her becoming seriously engaged as a scholar of rhetorical theory (see also Crowley 2007).

Sharon's mentoring is perhaps most noteworthy for her reaching out to graduate students and junior scholars of other institutions, not just her own. This too has precedent in the example of Corbett and Kinneavy, both from major research universities, mentoring Sharon despite her training from the smaller, regional University of Northern Colorado. When she advises women entering the field to develop a far-flung web of support, she addresses both the mentoring needed by individual academics and the mentoring necessary for the development of the relatively small discipline of rhetoric and writing in the shadow of the larger discipline of English. That she has a large number of mentees who were not her own graduate students is testimony to her inclusive and egalitarian style—she walked her talk of creating community across, not only within, institutions.

Victor Villanueva, a leader in rhetoric and writing for his work on racism and discrimination in literary practice, describes his experience with Sharon when he was a junior colleague in her department at Northern Arizona University:

> When I first arrived at Northern Arizona, I was one year from my PhD, two years on the tenure track, one publication, which was co-authored, struggling to find my way through a second publication . . . Sharon Crowley had been my host during the job interview. Very soon after my arrival, Sharon handed me a manuscript of hers for me to read/review/comment on. It became *Methodical Memory*. Felt completely intimidated by it. Never commented . . . I just didn't know what to say to this person who could write of Gorgias and Derrida and, apparently, Cicero as comp history. What I hadn't realized at the time was that Sharon was breaking me into the profession, a very quiet mentoring. (Villanueva 2016)

Although Sharon's mentees have become established teachers, scholars, department chairs, deans, and published writers—leaders and authorities in their own right—many recall that first time when a professor and scholar they looked up to asked for their opinion, not as a performance to be evaluated, but because she genuinely cared to hear what they had to say. It was a lesson many took away from their experience with her and applied to their own careers, and passed on to their own students and mentees. Sharon had a way of doing this that belied the serious intellectual engagement that was at the heart of her relationships. Villanueva, again:

> One special aspect of the camaraderie she inculcated . . . was a Marxist reading group. A small group of us (not all of us academics) would meet at her house on Trail of the Woods (what a lovely name for a street!) having read some agreed upon text, and we would talk. And the talk would range far and wide: me carrying on about racism; Carol [Villanueva] wanting to tie it all to world economics; Sharon noting Marx's presence

in everything she had read of the poststructuralists; our playfully disagreeing at times—I mean disagreeing seriously but able to laugh about it all
rather than get caught up in who's right . . . This was the fantasy of what
academic life would be: our own Bakhtin Circle—the Crowley Crew . . .
Those Wednesday nights provided the foundation for the next quarter
century of books and articles and courses and even casual conversation.
(Villanueva 2016)[5]

For so many of her mentees, Sharon created her own Xenophonic
Symposium—seriousness and playfulness balanced against one
another—enacted over pizza and Miller Lite, and recast in the American West.

As is appropriate in a mentoring relationship that honors the subjectivity of both the mentor and the mentee, Sharon Crowley was also
changed by these encounters. In the "Acknowledgments" of her final
book, Crowley thanks not only the theorists that she cites in the text, but
also Villanueva, "for conversations about racism that I could never get
over," and notes her indebtedness to "the students who participated in a
seminar on the rhetoric of liberalism offered long ago at the University of
Iowa." This is typical of Sharon as a sophistic mentor, seeing students and
junior faculty that she is mentoring as the ones teaching her (2006, xi).

MENTOR AS PROTECTOR AND EMPOWERER

No discussion of Crowley's rhetoric of mentoring would be complete
without addressing her concerns about the politics of everyday life in
the academy, including the influence of gender and race in the academy
and how traditional academic mentoring largely failed to make room
for women and academics of color. The modernist assumption that bodies and personal lives shouldn't matter, that they get in the way of an
objective universal rationality that academe strives for, figures into the
traditional academic mentoring practices in which most of us began our
careers. But to spend time with Sharon Crowley meant engaging and
questioning this division between minds and bodies, both intellectually
and in terms of our own personal narratives and social experiences.

Clearly this is a responsibility that Crowley took to heart. As a member
of the generation of women scholars that followed Winifred Horner,
Lynn Bloom, and Maxine Hairston, Crowley-the-writer defended graduate students, contingent faculty, and junior colleagues who struggled
under hierarchical, racist, or sexist threats in the institution, by examining the assumptions underlying institutional structures. Sharon, as
embodied mentor, championed less-privileged members of her own

departments at several universities, provided leadership on countless hours of national conference committees, and provided counsel and protection to those she adopted as mentees at other institutions.

"Protector" is an important but controversial function for a sophistic mentor to add to Schmidt's three functions of the mentor—role model, information provider, and door opener (Ebest 2002, 212). In her interview for Michelle Ballif, Diane Davis, and Roxanne Mountford, Crowley vividly describes the responsibility she felt to protect graduate students and untenured faculty that she was mentoring in her institutions: "We asked Crowley what she would do if some young woman she was mentoring were being discriminated against or persecuted for her scholarship, and Crowley told us without hesitation that she would 'console her, make sure she's okay, and then I would go beat the shit out of whoever was doing the discriminating or persecuting.' . . . 'I'd just go put a stop to it. Because I have the kind of stature now where I can do that'" (qtd. in Crowley 2008, 231). For Crowley, a sophistic mentor is not only a teacher but a rhetor who should use her tenure, rank, stature, and rhetorical abilities to protect students and untenured faculty, especially from abuse in institutions that she describes as "awful places—bitter, nasty, they bring out the worst in people" (231). But in Donna Strickland's critique of Crowley's work in the Conference on College Composition and Communication (CCCC) to reform the labor conditions of rhetoric and writing teachers, she argues that any attempt "to 'help' and 'protect' can all too easily slip into a kind of paternalism" (2011, 63). She points to Crowley's comment that the CCCC was founded to protect rhetoric and writing teachers as assuming the field's continuing "managerial unconscious" that valorizes rhetorical scholars as dominating managers of an underclass of contingent faculty and graduate students. Similarly, Marcy Taylor and Jennifer L. Holberg describe Crowley's arguments for the Wyoming Resolution as promoting "the representation of graduate assistants as slaves/apprentices," "reinscribing . . . hierarchical divisions among teachers of writing through the traditional machinery of disciplinary 'training'" (1999, 619). Here, Crowley's desire to create structures in the CCCC to protect contingent faculty and graduate students constructs them as an underclass supporting an elite class of rhetoric scholars. Although neither Taylor and Holberg nor Strickland were writing about Crowley's mentoring, their critiques may imply that a mentor who acts as a protector for a graduate student or untenured colleague may unavoidably reinforce paternalistic and exploitative relationships between students and faculty or between junior and senior faculty that are rife in academia. Taylor and Holberg's association of the term "apprentice" with both slavery and "mentoring" (620) echoes feminist condemnations of the master/apprentice model of mentoring in academia and in other literature on mentoring.

Villanueva, however, represents the mentor's protector role as positive and necessary. He describes the "protector" role taken on by Crowley (and other mentors) early in his career in broad terms, explaining how they "assigned him work or spoke on his behalf or leveled the playing field for him at different times" (Okawa 2002, 513). For Villanueva, mentoring "is a process of conscious socialization of the mentee into an alien culture, a process that becomes perceptual and relational" (513). For him, this mentoring meant "being able to enter into an intellectual friendship" (514). In an email exchange with us, Villanueva elaborated on Sharon's protection of the mental and emotional space he needed to find his voice and how she extended respect to him as someone whose voice deserved that space:

> In fact, to this day I don't see her as having been a mentor (certainly not in the way that I have been) but more a protector, watching that I was only minimally exploited (the only person of color in the department of course, new to the profession, eager to please, even if the pleasing worked against me) . . . I was saved from committees, thanks to Sharon; I was saved from assuming the duties of comp director as an assistant prof when the director resigned; I was allowed to teach matters that were of interest to me—the politics of literacy, comp theory (for undergrads), the philosophies of composition. None of that warm, motherly care from Sharon—but I was being quite consciously cared for and by her, behind the scenes. In front of others, she treated me as a colleague, and in so doing I grew to see myself as belonging among these folks, so foreign to me. (Villanueva 2016)

This protection is not paternalistic (nor maternalistic, as Villanueva points out). Although Crowley acknowledges that her rhetorical theory appropriates a classical rhetoric and education that served a highly patriarchal and elitist Greek society (1989b, 319; 1993a, 19–20), she draws heavily on feminist theory to address these limitations of sophistic rhetoric. Sharon avoids paternalism as a mentor because she does not use protection as a way to exert power over her mentee: her feminist and Freirean stance that demands respecting, listening to, and learning from mentees, and her practices to empower and encourage free thinking for mentees, counter paternalistic mentoring practices.

In critiques of the Wyoming Resolution movement, some writers have pointed to the anonymity of the emotional graduate student speaking to the audience at the Wyoming Conference that Crowley and two coauthors described to galvanize support for the resolution (Robertson et al. 1987, 277) as an example of how Crowley-the-writer's protective attitude effaced the student and created a subjectivity of contingent faculty as victims. This is counter to Crowley's theoretical constructs and, unknown to the profession, an example of Sharon-the-mentor shielding the graduate student (identified years later as Susan Wyche, one of the authors of this chapter) so that the student could return to her institution and complete her graduate work without fear of retribution from her department administrators. Sharon anticipated what eventually unfolded, and Susan's own professors advised her to leave her campus and finish her dissertation out of sight to ensure that her involvement with the Wyoming Resolution would not impact the judgment of less sympathetic professors concerning her scholarship. Sharon's assessment of Susan's situation led Crowley-the-writer to put aside her normal inclination to credit the graduate student by name.

From a mentoring perspective, Susan's account of this story in "Reflections on the Wyoming Conference Resolution" (2017) illustrates our definition of sophistic mentoring based on Sharon Crowley's rhetoric and experience. Her mentoring was protective, even though she could not offer direct protection that she could have if Susan and Connie Hale, a second graduate student at Wyoming, were students in her department. Sharon acted as a caregiver—seeing to Susan's immediate emotional needs and advising Susan and Connie about institutional protections. Her mentoring was rhetorical, kairotic, inventive, collaborative, and activist. Sharon, Linda Robertson, and others took Susan's call to do something about the contingent faculty problem seriously and brought Susan and Connie into a conference-wide collaborative process that led to the composing of the Wyoming Resolution and challenged the institutional status quo head on. And the mentoring relationship that Sharon, Susan, and Connie forged changed their subjectivities in multiple ways over the week and after, as all three and others in Laramie came to see themselves as activists who could challenge a national problem, changing the courses of their lives and careers.

Most mentoring scholarship focuses on the role of the mentor in assisting mentees on a path to professional employment, rather than either Villanueva's "conscious socialization" or Crowley's political protection, perhaps because both fall outside the normal institutional roles identified for professors and their students or mentees. Perhaps, too, the protector role often occurs outside the interactions of the mentor and mentee, when the mentor argues on behalf of the mentee with potentially harmful parties. Yet both of these functions played an important part in many of Sharon's mentoring relationships, and as Sharon said of her own mentors, "they showed me the ropes . . . how things worked politically."[6] With new professionals, Sharon pulled back the curtain on privileged behavior that might, intentionally or not, harm mentees' development and eventual success. She was especially cognizant of the intersection of gender and the academic institution, frequently pointing out gender inequities in professional practices, including scholarship, and personally befriending and standing up for female graduate students in her own department and that of other universities, sometimes with some risk to her own position and authority.

MENTORING ACROSS GENERATIONS

Sharon Crowley's approach to mentoring is powerful, in part because she does not view it as something contained by brick-and-mortar boundaries; instead, intellectual engagement moves seamlessly from class or conference room to cafe, barroom, or dance floor, and from generation to generation. Even as Crowley engaged the political issues through her scholarship, Sharon continued to advise and protect, professionally promote, and intellectually engage with the graduate students that she met at Wyoming and other conferences. Indeed, the Wyoming Resolution gave rise not only to many years of collaboration between Crowley and these graduate students, lecturers, and junior faculty who rallied to the cause, but they became, either directly or indirectly, the next generation of standard bearers on professional issues. And like their mentor, they took on this fight in their scholarly writing, in political battles closer to home at their own institutions, and in their influence on their own students and mentees.

Susan Wyche eventually published several pieces on the Wyoming Resolution, but only after obtaining her doctoral degree, and only recently identified herself as the "unnamed graduate student" (Wyche 2017). Bill Lalicker became co-chair of the Council on Basic Writing to champion the most stigmatized students in the academy, argued for contingent faculty conversion to scholarly professionalism in writing programs, and collaborated on the writing and the successful adoption of the Indianapolis Resolution supporting contingent faculty. In 2017 he coedited *Contingency, Exploitation, and Solidarity: Labor and Action in English Composition* (see Kahn et al. 2017). Jim McDonald co-chaired the CCCC Committee on Contingent, Adjunct, and Part-Time Faculty and coauthored an article on the history of the Wyoming Resolution with Eileen Schell (a former student of Connie Hale, whom Sharon mentored with Wyche at the landmark 1986 Wyoming Conference, bringing the story full circle).

The Wyoming Conference provided a unique context for Sharon's style of sophistic mentoring. The Cowboy Bar in Laramie, Wyoming was, for many years, the dive of choice for evening entertainment after conference sessions finished. You might have spent half the night drinking, discoursing, and dancing with Sharon Crowley, but if anyone in the group had an eight-o'clock presentation the next morning, everyone was expected to be present and accounted for at the first session. Whether you were a scholar from a major university with several books under your belt, a lecturer from some rural campus with an unrecognizable name, or a graduate student giving a shaky first talk, the Crowley Crew was there to ensure you were not speaking to an empty room, but were engaged with a community of supportive, rhetorically minded colleagues.

This scenario demonstrates one noteworthy fact about Sharon Crowley: she always showed up. In the years following the publication of the Wyoming Resolution, the leaders of the Wyoming Conference reserved the morning of the last day of the conference for individuals to share problems concerning working conditions at their home institutions. The idea was to help folks move past the problems they described and find solutions in collaboration with the group. Sharon was always there. She sat through years of similar meetings at CCCC, and as chair of the CCCC's National Committee on Professional Standards in Postsecondary Writing Instruction, traveling the country listening to our professional woes (see CCCC Committee 1989). At the time, she shared with a few of us that the repetition of these stories depressed her, primarily because there was little that she and her colleagues could do. She listened respectfully as people for whose benefit she was working sometimes expressed their frustration by launching personal attacks against those who had worked on the Wyoming Resolution and Statement on Professional Standards. Sharon struggled with her own frustration at the limits of her power to effect structural change. Even at her own institutions, where she consistently battled for better conditions for her junior colleagues and graduate students (her efforts often unknown to those on whose behalf she worked), there were limits to what she could accomplish. Nevertheless, she took on these challenges both fearlessly and fiercely. Her mentoring empowered many others in our profession to engage for workplace justice, locally, and nationally; her mentoring argued for a vision of rhetoric and writing studies that addressed political issues, especially the structures that we ourselves inhabit, and we all benefited because she was there as a mentor. In our professional and political moment now, when a deprofessionalized professorial workforce needs the collaborative, protective, and challenging guidance of tenured and powerful mentors more than ever, Crowley's theory-rooted sophistic mentoring model finds its kairos again.

* * *

The next morning, we rouse ourselves to take leave of Sharon's hospitality. Our brief sojourn has renewed our understanding of the influence a powerful mentor can have on young scholars—at least as we experienced it then—and the spirit with which Crowley continues to engage us through her resurrection of sophistic rhetoric and practice.

NOTES

1. Sharon Crowley is referenced in this article in two ways, as "Crowley," the author, and "Sharon," personal friend and mentor. This is a distinction that Sharon made to us in a story about herself and James Berlin, and we adopt the referencing here to distinguish when we are seeing Crowley as a theorist and scholar, through her written work, and when we are talking about her as a mentor, who we know through personal experience.

2. Fishman and Lunsford discuss how Fenélon's *Télémaque*, which was republished as an Enlightenment textbook on mentoring, helped establish mentoring as a "popular phenomenon" in the eighteenth century in interpreting the mythical relationship between Mentor and Telemachus in *The Odyssey* as a lesson in Enlightenment values (2008, 20–27). Sally Barr Ebest discusses the influence of the German research university in constructing graduate student mentoring as an "apprenticeship as junior researchers" (2002, 212). This master/apprentice relationship was "father-like" and "loving," according to Sharon Merriam (cited in Ebest 2002, 211) with women "noticeably absent" (212) in the graduate program conception of the scholar. Ebest uses Jane Tompkins's phrase "antipedagogical indoctrination" to describe the attitude mentors took toward preparing scholars for teaching (213).

3. Crowley writes in admiration of Horner, Bloom, and Hairston for their can-do-ness in forming themselves as pioneering women in rhetoric and writing when the field had no self-conscious history, and held little respect or power in English departments. All three began their careers as part-time teachers; all raised families while they completed their graduate work; and all fought, and won, repeated battles over salary or tenure. Bloom, Horner, and Hairston, Crowley concludes, "had no role models, no mentors. If later generations of professional women have any advantage over them, this advantage lies precisely in the fact that we have foremothers of courage and character" (1988, 206).

4. Fishman and Lunsford (2008) propose replacing the terms "mentor" and "mentee" with "colleague."

5. The Wednesday night reading group described by Villanueva was a continuation of the Poststructuralist Luncheon Club originally organized by Sharon's mentor and department chair, Bryan Short, in 1978. Crowley credits this club as crucial to her understanding of deconstruction and poststructuralist theory and discovering their relevance to sophistic rhetoric (Crowley 2008, 228; see also Crowley 1989c, 50).

This is another example of Sharon's paying forward her own collaborative mentoring experiences to those she mentored.

6.   From a personal conversation with the authors.

REFERENCES

Ashe, Diana, and Elizabeth Ervin. 2008. "Mentoring Friendships and the 'Reweaving of Authority.'" In *Stories of Mentoring: Theory and Praxis*, ed. Michelle F. Eble and Lynée Lewis Gaillet, 83–97. Anderson, SC: Parlor Press.

Baake, Ken, Stephen A. Bernhardt, Eva R. Brumberger, Katherine Durack, Bruce Farmer, Julie Dyke Ford, Thomas Hager, Robert Kramer, Lorelei Ortiz, and Carolyn Vickrey. 2008. "Mentorship, Collegiality, and Friendship: Making Our Mark as Professionals." In *Stories of Mentoring: Theory and Praxis*, ed. Michelle F. Eble and Lynée Lewis Gaillet, 52–66. Anderson, SC: Parlor Press.

Buell, Cindy. 2004. "Models of Mentoring in Communication." *Communication Education* 35 (1): 56–73.

CCCC Committee on Professional Standards for Quality Education. 1989. "CCCC Initiatives on the Wyoming Conference Resolution: A Draft Report." *College Composition and Communication* 40 (1): 61–72.

Crowley, Sharon. 1979. "Of Gorgias and Grammatology." *College Composition and Communication* 30 (3): 279–84.

Crowley, Sharon. 1988. "Three Heroines: An Oral History." *Pre/Text* 9 (2–3): 202–6.

Crowley, Sharon. 1989a. "On Intention in Student Texts." In *Encountering Student Texts: Interpretive Issues in Reading Student Writing*, ed. Bruce Lawson, Susan Sterr Ryan, and W. Ross Winterowd, 99–110. Urbana, IL: NCTE.

Crowley, Sharon. 1989b. "A Plea for the Revival of Sophistry." *Rhetoric Review* 7 (2): 318–34.

Crowley, Sharon. 1989c. *A Teacher's Introduction to Deconstruction.* Urbana, IL: NCTE.

Crowley, Sharon. 1993a. *Ancient Rhetorics for Contemporary Students*, 1st ed. New York: Macmillan.

Crowley, Sharon. 1993b. "Modern Rhetoric and Memory." In *Rhetorical Memory and Delivery: Classical Concepts for Contemporary Composition and Communication*, ed. John Frederick Reynolds, 31–44. Hillsdale, NJ: Lawrence Erlbaum.

Crowley, Sharon. 2002. "Body Studies in Rhetoric and Composition." In *Rhetoric and Composition as Intellectual Work*, ed. Gary A. Olson, 177–87. Carbondale: Southern Illinois University Press.

Crowley, Sharon. 2003. "Composition Is Not Rhetoric." *Enculturation* 5 (1): n.p. http://enculturation.net/5_1/crowley.html.

Crowley, Sharon. 2006. *Toward a Civil Discourse: Rhetoric and Fundamentalism.* Pittsburgh: University of Pittsburgh Press.

Crowley, Sharon. 2007. "Two Gentlemen in Wyoming." In *1977: The Cultural Moment in Composition*, ed. Wendy Sharer, Brent Henze, and Jack Selzer, 65. West Lafayette, IN: Parlor Press.

Crowley, Sharon. 2008. "Sharon Crowley." In *Women's Ways of Making It . . . In Rhetoric and Composition*, ed. Michelle Ballif, Diane Davis, and Roxanne Mountford, 217–32. Mahwah, NJ: Erlbaum.

Ebest, Sally Barr. 2002. "Mentoring: Past, Present, and Future." In *Preparing College Teachers of Writing: Histories, Theories, Programs, Practices*, ed. Betty P. Pytlik and Sarah Liggett, 211–21. New York: Oxford University Press.

Enos, Theresa. 1997. "Mentoring—and (Wo)mentoring—in Composition Studies." In *Academic Advancement in Composition Studies: Scholarship, Publication, Tenure*, ed. Richard C. Gebhardt and Barbara Genelle Smith Gebhardt 137–45. Mahwah, NJ: LEA.

Fishman, Jenn, and Andrea Lunsford. 2008. "Educating Jane." In *Stories of Mentoring: Theory and Praxis*, ed. Michelle F. Eble and Lynée Lewis Gaillet, 18–32. Anderson, SC: Parlor Press.

Gabor, Catherine, Stacia Dunn Neeley, and Carrie Shively Leverenz. 2008. "'Mentor, May I Mother?'" In *Stories of Mentoring: Theory and Praxis*, ed. Michelle F. Eble and Lynée Lewis Gaillet, 98–112. Anderson, SC: Parlor Press.

Horner, Winifred Bryan. 2008. "On Mentoring." In *Stories of Mentoring: Theory and Praxis*, ed. Michelle F. Eble and Lynée Lewis Gaillet, 14–17. Anderson, SC: Parlor Press.

Kahn, Seth, William B. Lalicker, and Amy Lynch-Biniek, eds. 2017. *Contingency, Exploitation, and Solidarity: Labor and Action in English Composition*. WAC Clearinghouse. Boulder: University Press of Colorado.

Lauer, Janice. 1997. "Graduate Students as Active Mentors of the Profession: Some Questions for Mentoring." In *Publishing in Rhetoric and Composition*, ed. Gary A. Olson and Todd W. Taylor, 229–35. Albany, NY: SUNY Press.

Miles, Katherine S., and Rebecca E. Burnett. 2008. "The Minutia of Mentorships: Reflections about Professional Development." In *Stories of Mentoring: Theory and Praxis*, ed. Michelle F. Eble and Lynée Lewis Gaillet, 113–28. Anderson, SC: Parlor Press.

Okawa, Gail Y. 2002. "Diving for Pearls: Mentoring as Cultural and Activist Practice among Academics of Color." *College Composition and Communication* 53 (3): 507–32.

Rickly, Rebecca J., and Susanmarie Harrington. 2002. "Feminist Approaches to Mentoring Teaching Assistants: Conflict, Power, and Collaboration." In *Preparing College Teachers of Writing: Histories, Theories, Programs, Practices*, ed. Betty P. Pytlik and Sarah Liggett, 108–20. New York: Oxford University Press.

Robertson, Linda R., Sharon Crowley, and Frank Lentricchia. 1987. "The Wyoming Conference Resolution Opposing Unfair Salaries and Working Conditions for Post-Secondary Teachers of Writing." *College English* 49 (3): 274–80.

Strickland, Donna. 2011. *The Managerial Unconscious in the History of Composition Studies*. Carbondale: Southern Illinois University Press.

Taylor, Marcy, and Jennifer L. Holberg. 1999. "'Tales of Neglect and Sadism': Disciplinarity and the Figuring of the Graduate Student in Composition." *College Composition and Communication* 50 (4): 607–25.

Trachsel, Mary. 2002. "The Give and Take of Mentoring." In *Against the Grain: A Volume in Honor of Maxine Hairston*, ed. David Jolliffe, Michael Keene, Mary Trachsel, and Ralph Voss, 59–72. Cresskill, NJ: Hampton Press.

Villanueva, Victor. 2016. Message to Susan Wyche. July 28, 2016.

Wyche, Susan. 2017. "Reflections on the Wyoming Conference Resolution." In *Labored: The State(ment) and Future of Work in Composition*, ed. Randall McClure, Dayna V. Goldstein, and Michael A. Pemberton, 3–13. Anderson, SC: Parlor Press.

PART III

7

REFLECTIONS ON BEING "AGAINST AUDIENCE" WITH SHARON AND OTHERS

Victor J. Vitanza

There is one word that I would use to describe my very special relation-ship with you, today. You, the audience. That is the readers. Here and not here. I am against you! Personally, and yet publically, against you! And why, you may ask? Simply put, the ear is uncanny! Our relationship is impossible, whether you are here or not here. Being-here (*Da-sein*) does not make it any easier to hear. And yet, the one word that I would appeal to as a possible re-description of my very special relationship with you here, today, is (yes, yes, yes) "against." To be sure, this word is prob-lematic. That I repeat the word three times, say yes to the audience three times in saying I am against you, saying no to you, is, indeed, problem-atic! This saying *nes* and *yo* desires an explanation. (Please understand: I am not here in this writing to blame you, audience, but to praise you!) This word, this word "against," is for me a Heraclitian word. In this special sense, then, I am perpetually not only contra to (i.e., "against") you, the audience, but also along side you (i.e., standing with you, next to you, against you). In a phrase taken from Nietzsche, I would say, as I have said on occasions before, and some of you have not understood, that you and I share a certain, uncertain "pathos of distance."

Just recently, and yet, years ago, I was on a panel with Sharon Crowley and Linda Brodkey. When the two were introduced, they were likened to Thelma and Louise. Later, after they had read their papers—I had yet to read mine—they started hugging each other, I guess, to celebrate their solidarity on some point of agreement. The chair of the session pointed out how well Thelma and Louise were bonding together. Now, I don't have anything against people hugging each other, but I had not yet read my paper. I sat there wondering whom in the hell I might be . . . in that film . . . on that stage. (This principle of individuation is a dangerous thing!) I quickly dismissed the possibility that I might be one of those

DOI: 10.7330/9781607328933.c007

bad cops chasing Linda and Sharon, or the so-called good cop, and (instead) had a hallucination that I might be the Rastafarian, who was more like a character out of a Cheech and Chong film. I guess *he* was included for a comic spell.

After I was introduced and finally had a chance to read my paper, I was totally ignored. And I mean totally ignored, at least, until I stepped off the stage. Linda's paper was about her plight at UT-Austin, with English 306, and with various journalists (a big deal!). Sharon's paper was a proposal to do away with the universal requirement of freshman composition (wow!). My paper, entitled "teaching-nothing" was about turning the university or multiversity into a perversity; was about dis-inventing the university, tearing it down; was about going on the road (thank you, Jack); and ended with a call to Trotsky, Trotsky, Trotsky from polis to polis, teaching and leaching, like the early Sophists did. When it was time for questions, everyone loved Thelma and Louise, and (as I said) they totally ignored me. Even Linda and Sharon ignored me for the rest of the conference. Although I must say that at the reception, Sharon told one of the bartenders at the cash bar that she wanted to buy a drink for me in my absence, and told the bartender the drink would be given to "that man over there who looks like Marx." The bartender asked, "Who is Marx?" Which gets me to the subject of my paper: You see, I have problems with audiences.

Later, a participant at the conference and a member of the audience told me, that he thought—he was sure, in fact—that I was delirious, that I was hallucinating. Gayatri Spivak, who also read a paper and who was in the audience when I read my paper, was kinder. She just said that she agreed with me. I thought could this be simpatico? Could this be what Kenneth Burke calls consubstantiality? Was I going to get to bond with Spivak? So there we were at the cash bar and I told Gayatri—I could call her Gayatri now and tell her this most intimate story!—that Bob Connors had likened her and me together at one time. I told Gayatri that Bob told me about two years ago that he had written an introduc-tory essay on historiography for graduate students in our field and that Bob said that when I wrote, I wrote the way Gayatri Spivak wrote but on acid.

Having heard this story, Gayatri took out her tobacco tin, took a pinch, and put it in her mouth, and asked, "Who is Bob Connors?" Evidently, I'm not the only who has problems with audiences. I had real empathy for Bob, because I too have felt at times like the man in the American Express commercial.

* * *

Well, all of this has been by way, my way, of an introduction, and I think that now I should get to the im/proper part of my paper; if not, then, I'm only going to sound more and more like no one, reading another one of someone's self-expressive papers. So off to the paper im/proper, hi ho, hi ho, it's off to the paper improper, we go: The paper im/proper should always begin with an orienting meditation. I have two: The first, I call twiddle dee; the next, I call twiddle dum. Are you, the dear audience, catching on to what I'm doing yet? There is method to this delirium, this hallucination. I'm doing something with these names and combinations. Do you have an ear for what I'm saying? Is there an audience in the house? There's an emergency: Is there an audience in the house?

Twiddle dee:

> *On the question of being understandable. One does not only wish to be understood when one writes; one wishes just as surely not to be understood. It is not by any means necessarily an objection to a book when anyone finds it impossible to understand: perhaps that was part of the author's intention—he did not want to be understood by just "anybody." All the nobler spirits and tastes select their audience when they wish to communicate; and choosing that, one at the same time erects barriers against "the others." All the more subtle laws of any style have their origin at this point: they at the same time keep away, create a distance, forbid "entrance," understanding, as said above—while they open the ears of those whose ears are related to ours.*
> —Friedrich Nietzsche, *The Gay Science*

Twiddle dum:

> *To know that one does not write for the other, to know that these things I am going to write will never cause me to be loved by the one I love (the other), to know that writing compensates for nothing, sublimates nothing, that it is precisely there where you are not—this is the beginning of writing.*
> —Roland Barthes, *A Lover's Discourse*

Part I: *"Che vuoi?"* [Lacan's *What do you want?*] "You're telling me that, but what do you want with it, what are you aiming at?"

> *"'I am Saint Blasphemer, and don't forget it,' Jesus replied with a laugh."*
> —Nikos Kazantzakis, *The Last Temptation of Christ*

I will not have shared my fantasies with just "any body." But what I will do here, with a little help from Sharon (my muse), these mornings is to ruminate on three figures or, perhaps better put, three masks. (Some of you, to be sure, might say that they are not masks but fantasies! If so, then so!) The first is a mask of Fredrich Nietzsche; the second, Jesus Christ; and the third, Kenneth Burke. Yes, yes, yes, I'm going to ruminate on Nietzsche, Christ, and KB. Is there no greater blasphemy? I call them (my) three "hysterics." There must be a greater blasphemy! Each of this trinity of hysterics has had problems with audiences. Hysterics, while they can be entertaining for, or even at times attracted and attractive to, audiences, nonetheless have problems with their audiences. (Simply recall Dora with Freud, Freud with Dora, and Freud with himself.) Hysterics often seem to be saying something, whatever that might be, to audiences, but the audiences either don't finally follow what is being said (there is a gap), or audiences give no signs of having understood. At least, no signs are given, from the point of view of the hysteric. (Sometimes hysterics feel totally ignored!) As Slavoj Žižek says: "This gap can best be articulated with the help of the Hegelian couple 'for-the-other'/'for-itself': the [hysteric] is experiencing himself as somebody who is enacting a role for the other, his imaginary identification is his 'being for the other,' and the crucial break that [the audience] must accomplish is to induce him to realize how he is himself this other for whom he is enacting a role, how his being for the other is his being for himself" (1989, 106). (Let us recall the other couples that I have mentioned thus far: Thelma and Louise, the Rastafarian and I, Cheech and Chong, twiddle dee and twiddle dum. The Sophists understood such couples: While they were teaching and leaching, they engaged in *dis logoi* and *dat logoi*. Freud did not understand such couples. Nor did Leslie Fiedler.) But it's all more complicated, for this situation of speaker-as-hysteric confronting an audience can be reversed, and more often than not is, with the audience as a group of hysterics confronting a speaker. An audience—oh, the dear audience—can and does say: "We're demanding this of you, the speaker, we're demanding clarity, we're demanding understanding, we're demanding satisfaction, but what we're really demanding of you is to refute our demands because these are not them" (see Žižek 1989, 111–12). Can you imagine what would happen . . . do we have to imagine? . . . What would happen . . . when a speaker/writer hysteric and an audience of hysterics confront each other along the same line of communication? (I remind you again of the other couple Dora and Freud, the very scene of pedagogy and of writing.)

At one time or another we have all had problems with audiences, even with ourselves as an audience for our *self*. Here today, I'm interested in why Nietzsche, Christ, and Burke have had problems with audiences; I'm not interested, however, in why they (or the audiences) apparently failed to communicate, so that I might, therefore, learn from their so-called mistakes and then suggest to us all how to communicate more effectively. (I'm not an adherent of "philosophical rhetoric"; I'm no follower of I. A. Richards.) Instead, I'm interested in these masks, this trinity of hysterics, because they represent, at least it seems to me, the very epitome of what I would call a social relationship founded—and founded paralogically—on the apparent impossibility and yet the possibility of communication. (I'm not here as a messenger with exclusively bad news, for I think that there is some saving grace for our various projects.)

Nietzsche, Christ, and Burke have not only had their own problems with audiences but also at times have speculated on, or enacted/performed for us, why such problems are inevitable and necessarily tragic. By "necessarily tragic," I mean such problems are not to be corrected/fixed, but are to be viewed in the light of what Nietzsche calls "cheerful pessimism." Heraclitus and Empedocles knew of these problems of the tragic nature of knowledge, these problems with the logos; so did Plato, but look at what he did to solve these problems, changing—as radically as he could, via dialectic, via genus-species analytics—the very nature (*physis*) of the logos. While Heraclitus was a "cheerful pessimists," Plato became "theoretical man." While Heraclitus stood in the very storm of Being, seeing the lightning flash, but flash obscurely, the very essence of logos, Plato drove the storm away. (Hail Sharon, let's boogie in the storm together.) I quote from and interject into Martin Heidegger (1984): Plato organized "all available means for cloud-seeding and storm dispersal in order to have calm in the face of the storm." He guaranteed, for the most part, understanding (or *a-poria*, i.e., easy passage) to and for his audience, his interlocutors. (What a price you, the dear audience, the dear interlocutor, will have had to pay! and what a debt you must finally repay!) Again as Heidegger says: ". . . this calm is no tranquility [no understanding for the audience]. It is only anesthesia; more precisely, the narcotization of [further stupefy the audience's] anxiety in the face of thinking" (78).

Isocrates was no better! Aristotle was no better! Cicero and Quintilian no better! I'm afraid that we will never recover from them. Some of us, however, are nonetheless, hysterics, pharmakonically hysterics, like the presocratics (Heraclitus, Empedocles, and others) were. We, I submit, don't have a problem of having to recover. If you're not a hysteric, not a Heraclitian, you are, then, the one with the problem!

This has been my other im/proper, perhaps impolitic (opening) statement; now, I would like to re/turn to the trinity of hysterics. The mother, the daughter, and the holy material.

* * *

> *"Am I understood? . . . Have I been understood?" . . . "Not at*
> *all, my dear sir"—"Then let us start again, from the beginning."*
> —Nietzsche, *On the Genealogy of Morals*

Part IIA (tu est): Fredrich Nietzsche. Nietzsche, in *Twilight of the idols* calls "Dionysian man"—who he himself identifies with, thinks himself to be ("for-itself")—a "hysteric." Dionysian man (who is non gender specific) "enters into every skin, every emotion; . . . is continually transforming himself" (1988, 73). He is polytropic. He, then, is not one, nor is he two; instead, he is a hysterical, radical many. Interestingly enough, Nietzsche in his last letter to Jacob Burckhardt wrote: "What is disagreeable and offends my modesty is that . . . I am every name in history" (1968, 686). Speaking hysterically and polytropically, addressing Burckhardt, speaking against him (the other), the scholar of Renaissance individualism, Nietzsche is not saying that he is each and everyone of you . . . in the audience . . . (another other); instead, he is saying that he is all that you (the other) could be, but refuse to be, because of unconscious repression, conscious suppression, political oppression. (To this point we will eternally return. After all is said and undone, would you not, my dear audience, agree that the repressed has a way of re/turning?)

And so we have, and have had, problems reading, understanding Nietzsche. He, of course, knew of this before we did. Look at a sampling of what he has said: "The time for me hasn't come yet: some are born posthumously" (1969, 259). "I am no man, I am dynamite" (326). He knew he would be radically misunderstood and misused. (Have you yet read Jacques Derrida's *The Ear of the Other* [1985]?) Ears, indeed, are strange places. What goes on there, in them, we dare not discuss publicly, and yet we must. About ears, Nietzsche wrote: "Always presupposing that there are ears—that there are those capable and worthy of the same pathos, that there is no lack of those to whom one may communicate oneself.—My Zarathustra . . . is still looking for those—alas, it will have to keep looking for a long time yet!" (1969, 265). Sara Kofman (1987, 48), a brilliant audience for Nietzsche, writes: "The correct (harmonious) understanding of a text is not determined by the size of the ear." The ass, after all, has large ears, but can hear nothing when Dionysus speaks. Kofman continues: "It is to Ariadne's small ears that Dionysus speaks. To the intuitive ears of women . . . Women's small ear is this third ear mentioned by Nietzsche, the artistic ear which position[s] itself beyond metaphysical oppositions such as truth and falsehood, good and evil, . . . clarity and obscurity" (48).

Nietzsche more than anyone else, I think, understood that with the death of tragedy came the birth of audience (or as he put it, came "the public of spectators"), with all of its irresolvable problems. (When tragedy died, "there was [a] deep sense of an immense void" [2010, 76].) In tragedy, there was the satyr chorus. All was the chorus; all was community. There was no audience! As Nietzsche has it, however, "Euripides brought the spectator onto the stage"; he brought "the mask of reality onto the stage" (77). Euripides hailed, interpolated the chorus (hail chorus! Hail audience!). Euripides climbed down to the stage, became a thinker on the stage, and as a thinker-spectator, "he confessed to himself that he did not understand his great predecessors" such as Heraclitus and Sophocles (80–81). (Hence the birth of you people, the birth of divided us, the birth of "audience against.") Euripides set aside the satyrs and poets so that he could become a thinker on the stage. He separated poetry, or Sophistic rhetoric, from philosophical rhetoric. Euripides would have nothing, consequently, to do with his ancestors' "cheerful pessimism" (what Nietzsche later calls "la gaya scienza"); instead, Euripides, like the decadent Socrates, became "theoretical man." For him, the drama (like everything), in order to be "beautiful . . . must be intelligible" (83–84), must be "conscious" (86), must be understood by the dear audience.

And the even greater result? Nietzsche writes: "The spectator now actually saw and heard his double on the Euripidean stage, and rejoiced that he could talk so well. But this joy was not all: one could even learn from Euripides how to speak oneself" (2010, 77). (Do we have another mythic account of the origin of rhetoric? I think so. And to boot cum heel, one that tells us what is wrong with "philosophical rhetoric" and the so-called new community that it founds and feeds.) Euripides, and let us not forget Socrates, the disastrous interpellators! The spectator through Euripides begins to believe that he or she should "pass judgment" on, or critique, the drama. This new Euripidean drama creates the conditions for the possibilities of the new subject, which Jacques Lacan calls the subject that presumes to know. Or as we also call it, the subject of authority, the subject of phallo-logo-centric thinking. Euripides, Nietzsche says, "makes it appear as if the older tragic art had always suffered from bad relations with the spectator," or with the public. The subject that presumes to know, therefore, becomes reactionary man and woman, becomes the reactionary audience.

* * *

"Another mask! A second mask!"

—Nietzsche, *Beyond Good and Evil*

"I speak," he murmured, "but to whom?
To the air. I am the only one who listens.
When shall the desert grow ears in order to hear me?"

—Nikos Kazantzakis, *The Last Temptation of Christ*

Part IIB. (To Be) Jesus Christ. When I refer to Christ, it has to be understood, that I'm referring to the Nietzschean interpretation or mask of Christ. (Nietzsche wrote a book entitled *The Anti-Christ* [1988]. He also wrote an autobiography, *Ecce Homo* [1969], which he concludes by asking, "Have I been understood? Dionysus versus the Crucified." [335]) When I refer to Christ, I'm also referring to Nikos Kazantzakis's *The Last Temptation* [1960], which is based on Nietzsche's mask of Christ. Furthermore, I'm referring to Martin Scorsese's cinematic rendition of the novelistic rendition. (We know that Kazantzakis read/studied Nietzsche; he even went on a pilgrimage to all the towns in Germany that Nietzsche ever lived in or even passed through.) And so how are this-cum-these Christs hysterical? This Christ, as Nietzsche states, is Dionysius, the hysterical many, the polytropic one. But if you need a more direct account, interestingly enough, Slavoj Žižek, in his *Sublime Object of Ideology*, says:

> Scorsese's film *The Last Temptation of Jesus Christ* [has as its] theme . . . the hystericization of Jesus Christ himself; it shows us an ordinary, carnal, passionate man discovering gradually, with fascination and horror, that he is the son of God, bearer of the dreadful but magnificent mission to redeem humanity through his sacrifice. The problem is that he cannot come to terms with this interpellation [Hail Jesus!]: the meaning of his "temptations" lies precisely in the hysterical resistance to his mandate, in his doubts about it, in his attempts to evade it even when he is already nailed to the cross. (1989, 114)

If Christ felt at odds, can you imagine how Mary felt (Hail Mary!) when it was announced to her that she would be the virgin mother of the savior! Christ and Mary, I dare say, had problems with audience. Throughout the novel and the film, Christ is confronted with voices, events that hail him. And he asks: Father, what is it that you want? He asks: "Che vuoi?" What do they (these voices/events) really want? (Mary asked the same question.) Christ has a problem with audience: Let us recall Christ, on the cross, crucified between two audiences. He looks at his earthly audience and says to God, "forgive them Father, for they know not what they do." He turns to his heavenly audience, and says, "Why hast Thou forsaken me?" (See Psalm 22, King James Version.) He gets no answer. Without hope, however, he continues.

In the Kazantzakis version of the Nietzschean version, Christ—in his last temptation, while on the cross, in his last hallucination, his delirium (he falls into deliriums from a very early age)—sees himself being represented posthumously by Saul-cum-Paul, St. Paul, his once-upon-a-time audience, addressing/hailing the multitudes, speaking of what he, supposedly Christ, had said. However, whereas Christ speaks of redemption, Paul speaks of resentment, guilt, revenge; Paul speaks of and sows the seeds of the reactionary life, which is not life but death. (Like Judas, Paul speaks from the "spirit of revenge" [see "On Redemption" in Nietzsche 1968, 249–54].) Finally, Christ objects, but Paul says: "Shout all you want. I'm not afraid of you. I don't even need you any more. The wheel you set in motion has gathered momentum: who can control it now? . . . I shall become your apostle whether you like it or not. I shall construct you and your life and your teachings and your crucifixion and resurrection just as I wish. Joseph the Carpenter of Nazareth did not beget you; I begot you—I, Paul the scribe from Tarsus" (Kazantzakis 1960, 477–78).

But lest I mislead you with this conflict between Christ and Paul, a conflict that suggests that Christ's earthly audience is misappropriating him, let us look (again) at the heavenly audience, or representers, as portrayed by Kazantzakis (actually Heraclitus, Nietzsche, and then Kazantzakis). Earlier in the novel, Matthew the evangelist, decides he is going to write down, record, everything that Christ says and does, "where he was born and who his parents and grandparents were, the fourteen generations," etc. What happens, however, "as he began to inscribe the first words on the paper in a beautiful hand, his fingers stiffened. The angel had seized him. He heard wings beat angrily in the air and a voice trumpeted in his ear, 'Not the son of Joseph! What says the prophet Isaiah: 'Behold, a virgin shall conceive and bear a son.' . . . Write: Mary was a virgin. The archangel Gabriel descended to her house before any man had touched her, and said, 'Hail Mary, full of grace, the Lord is with you!' Straight away her bosom bore fruit . . . Do you hear? That's what you're to write. And not in Nazareth; no, he wasn't born in Nazareth. Do not forget the prophet Micah: 'And you, Bethlehem, tiny among the thousands of Judah,'" etc., etc. But Matthew stops writing in order to protest: "It's not true. I don't want to write, and I won't!" Then we are told: "Mocking laughter was heard in the air, and a voice: 'How can you understand what truth is, you handful of dust? Truth has seven levels. On the highest is enthroned the truth of God, which bears not the slightest resemblance to the truth of men. It is this truth, Matthew

Evangelist, that I intone in your ear . . . Write: 'And three Magi, following a large star, came to adore the infant . . .'" Matthew responds: "I won't write! I won't write! he cried, . . . but his hand was running over the page writing" (Kazantzakis 1960, 349–50). Later, Christ wants to see just what Matthew has been scribbling down about him. He reads. He screams out: "Lies! Lies! Lies! . . . I was born in Nazareth, not in Bethlehem." But then, Matthew tells Christ about the angel who visits and dictates to him. Matthew says: "His lips touch my right ear." Christ, befuddled, says, "An angel? [and muses to himself] If what we call truth, God called lies." Then he finally says: "Write whatever the angel dictates" (391–92). (What a wrenching story!)

Reading this novel, like reading the gospels, is for me like standing in the storm of the logos: At the very end of the novel, Christ in his hallucination sees what he thinks might be his disciples and apostles. "[Christ] turned to a hunched-over old man . . . but could not understand who he was . . . When [Christ] searched under the hair, . . . he found a large ear with an age-old broken quill behind it. [We are told, Christ] laughed" (487; cf. Zarathustra in Nietzsche 1968, 250). Allow me now to turn, re/turn, to Kenneth Burke.

* * *

Who would not call men to him—though he felt compelled to
dismiss them when they came, communion residing solely in the
summons?

—Kenneth Burke, *Towards a Better Life*

I am not the mouth for these ears. Must one smash their ears
before they learn to listen with their eyes? Must one clatter like
kettledrums and preachers of repentance? Or do they believe only
the stammerer?

—Friedrich Nietzsche, *The Portable Nietzsche*

Part IIC (To See). KB. Papa Burke refers to his own hysteria, in his letters to Malcolm Cowley. Burke, the hysteric! Burke writes about hysteria in *A Rhetoric of Motives* (1969). Burke, like the Christ I have introduced, is thoroughly Nietzschean. Burke, however, has forgotten how thoroughly Nietzschean he is. He has repressed it, most ironically, in the name of negation. I say "ironically" because though KB has repressed his hysterical excesses, they, nonetheless, eternally return, as he engages in them over and over and over again. Whereas, he says, Nietzsche is in the cult of the primitive positive, he situates himself well within the philosophy of negation (repression, disavowal) (see Burke 1966a, ch. 7). This is how he distinguishes, distances himself ("for-itself"), deflects Nietzsche ("for-the-other"). No wonder KB suffers from headaches.

But Burke is not only suffering from being mysteriously hailed by a phantom Dionysian Nietzsche, Burke not only suffers as a stammerer, he is also suffering from being hailed by particular Apollonian members of the CCCC. They say: Tell us Burke, how can we use you? (Burke hysterizes, Use me?) I have already written about this problem of appropriation in dis/repect to KB. But Burke, like Nietzsche before him and Christ yet before him, is surely uncomfortably, comfortable being misappropriated. Just recall KB's response to us in the journal *CCC*, or recall his response to Wayne Booth in *Critical Inquiry*, a response KB entitles "Dancing with Tears in My Eyes"—which is a line, an image, as I have stated already in print, right out of Nietzsche's *Thus Spake Zarathustra*. KB, too, finds it perhaps impossible to find ears for what he has to say.

After much, much time, ninety-three, almost ninety-four, years, Papa Burke, our father who art in Andover, NJ, has given up, over and over again, on trying to figure out what the audience wants from him. As I suggested earlier and intermittently throughout, however, I am cheerfully pessimistic. In this light (and partial gloom), then, let's go back (briefly), let's hallucinate (kairotically) to the 1989 CCCC—March 17, Friday, 3:25 to 4:40 p.m., in Seattle, Washington. It's the Metropolitan ballroom in the Seattle Sheraton. The session is entitled: "Kenneth Burke Speaking on Language and Power." There are, by my estimate, approximately a thousand people. All three aisles are completely filled. In my further estimation, it's our finest moment, at the CCCC. Ever! Allow me to explain: After introductions, Burke begins to talk. Actually he begins to hallucinate, begins to dis/engage in delirium. My sense is that many in the audience are thinking How sad, the years have affected his ability to speak/think publicly. I, as well as a few other people in the audience, know, however, that this Burke, this ninety-year-old Burke, is typical, vintage Burke. He not only speaks/thinks publicly this way but he also has been writing in this nondiscursive, but appositional manner from the very beginning. All of this is not to say, however, that KB is not concerned with audience. Of course, he is, though differently. In, for example, two pages of *A Rhetoric of Motives*, he intermittently writes: "Just what are we getting at here?" Then, "See what our problem is." And again, "Can we keep our line of thinking clear here for the reader?" And as a follow up and transition, he writes: "By adding one more confusion, we may add the element that can bring clarity" (1969, 9–10). In the same book, he writes and I interject: "'Like most [in an] hysterical seizure, [I] require an audience" (39).

So here's KB on the stage at the CCCC, apparently tripping out in front of a large audience. He's talking about his new project, which is to work on "Constitutions," and he announces that he wants to form an ad hoc committee to assist him on this project. As he continues—and now I get to the representative anecdote, which has been the whole purpose of this paper—KB stops talking in the middle, or muddle, of a sentence. We sit and wait patiently. It eventually becomes obvious after a while that he's looking for a word. And it becomes more, and over and over again, more obvious that he is not going to continue with his thought until he finds the word that he desires. At this point, this marvelous thing happens: the audience begins to call up words, to throw up words to the platform in an effort to help KB. Is it this? No. How about this one? No. Well, this one? No. There we were, an ad hoc committee, all thousand of us, playing word golf, with KB. There we were with Pops "chewing the phatic communion." Did you hear and understand what I said: "There we were with Pops 'chewing the phatic communion.'" Well, I didn't want it to end. I've since reflected on it many, many times, over and over and over again. "Chewing the phatic communion." Somehow or other, a Dionysian KB re/turned, gave birth again, to the attic stage; a Dionysian KB re/turned us all to being a chorus, a community without spectators. Again Dionysius was . . . is . . . alive. Great Pan was . . . is . . . alive. In the theatre of hysteria. At the CCCC.

* * *

At this point in the chapter, the end, it's time to tidy up, to refer to my beginnings. I would rather not. I have recalled three masks, three figures. I will leave them there, above your heads, I hope, with their wings beating above your heads, and with their lips touching your left, far left, ears.

NOTE

A quote that I wanted to work in but could not: "The last philosopher I call myself, for I am the last human being. No one converses with me beside myself and my voice reaches me as the voice of one dying. With thee, beloved voice, with thee, the last remembered breath of all human happiness, let me discourse, even if is only for another hour. Because of thee, I delude myself as to my solitude and lie my way back to multiplicity and love, for my heart shies away from believing that love is dead. It cannot bear the icy shivers of loneliest solitude. It compels me to speak as though I were Two [or some more]" (Nietzsche 1987)

REFERENCES

Barthes, Roland. 1978. *A Lover's Discourse*. Trans. Richard Howard. New York: Hill and Wang.

Burke, Kenneth. 1966a. *Language as Symbolic Action*. Berkeley: University of California Press.

Burke, Kenneth. 1966b. *Towards a Better Life*. Berkeley: University of California Press.

Burke, Kenneth. 1969. *A Rhetoric of Motives*. Berkeley: University of California Press.

Derrida, Jacques. 1985. *The Ear of the Other.* Trans. Peggy Kamuf. Lincoln: University of Nebraska Press.

Heidegger, Martin. 1984. *Early Greek Thinking.* San Francisco: Harper and Harper.

Kazantzakis, Nikos. 1960. *The Last Temptation of Christ.* Trans. P. A. Bien. New York: Simon and Schuster.

Kofman, Sarah. 1987. "Nietzsche and the Obscurity of Heraclitus." *Diacritics* 17 (3): 39–55.

Nietzsche, Friedrich. 1966. *Beyond Good and Evil.* Trans. Walter Kaufmann. New York: Vintage.

Nietzsche, Friedrich. 1968. *The Portable Nietzsche.* Trans. Walter Kaufmann. New York: Penguin.

Nietzsche, Friedrich. 1969. *On the Genealogy of Morals and Ecce Homo.* Trans. Walter Kaufmann. New York: Penguin.

Nietzsche, Friedrich. 1974. *The Gay Science.* Trans. Walter Kaufmann. New York: Vintage.

Nietzsche, Friedrich. 1987. *Philosophy in the Tragic Age of the Greeks.* Trans. Marianne Cowan. Washington, D.C.: Regnery Gateway.

Nietzsche, Friedrich. 1988. *Twilight of the Idols and The Anti-Christ.* Trans. R. J. Hollingdale. New York: Penguin.

Nietzsche, Friedrich. 2010. *The Birth of Tragedy and the Case of Wagner.* Trans. Walter Kaufmann. New York: Vintage.

Žižek, Slavoj. 1989. *The Sublime Object of Ideology.* New York: Verso.

8

LUDIC RHETORICS
Theories of Play in Rhetoric and Writing

Joshua Daniel-Wariya

The call for proposals for this collection was situated in response to Sharon Crowley's description of theory in *Toward a Civil Discourse: Rhetoric and Fundamentalism* (2006). Crowley terms theories "rhetorical inventions" that are created within specific material circumstances and contain the possibility of discovering new ways of thinking, believing, and acting (28). This aligns well with the way theory in rhetoric and writing studies is often described as situational. Susan Miller, for instance, describes theory as "particular discourses that arise in specific intellectual and material circumstances" (1992, 64). Moreover, as Raul Sanchez claims, theories in rhetoric and writing are inexhaustible resources for rhetorical invention, because "the way such work is done—the kinds of questions asked, the particular objects chosen for analysis, requires rigorous and continuous reevaluation" (2012, 237). Theories are invented in specific intellectual and material circumstances to describe the contingencies of particular times. Notably, theories of rhetoric and writing today are often tasked with accounting for the composing practices enabled by a wide range of digital and computational objects—including interfaces, videogames, and software—and considerations of *play* often accompany these types of new media. Scholars indeed mention play as digital media intersects with familiar territory like invention (Newcomb 2009; Ulmer 2002), style (Brooke 2009; Lanham 2007), and arrangement (Dunn 2001; Rouzie 2005). But how is play theorized within the field of rhetoric and writing?

To answer this question, in this chapter I survey three sites where scholars discuss rhetoric in relation to videogames and game-based pedagogies: (1) a 2008 special issue of *Computers and Composition*, (2) a 2010 special issue of *Currents in Electronic Literacy*, and (3) a 2013 edited collection titled *Rhetoric/Composition/Play*. Following Brian Sutton-Smith's landmark study of play rhetorics in *The Ambiguity of Play* (2001), I

DOI: 10.7330/9781607328933.c008

provide a taxonomy of three broad types of play theories that currently exist in the field today: (1) experimental theories that describe play as safe, pleasurable, and productive; (2) experiential theories that describe play as personal, motivating, and reflective; and (3) exploratory theories that describe play as imaginative, transformational, and subversive. I call these theories of play "ludic rhetorics," and, following Crowley's insight that theories are "rhetorical inventions" that open new possibilities for understanding the world, I suggest that the taxonomy of play theories offered in this chapter may be useful in helping to identify and describe specific ways theories of play intersect with the work of rhetoric and writing.

LUDIC RHETORICS AND THE AMBIGUITY OF PLAY

One challenge in describing ludic rhetorics is that play is notoriously difficult to define, and this is a problem play theorists have discussed for some time. For example, in Johan Huizinga's landmark *Homo Ludens* ([1938] 1980), Huizinga discusses terms for play in a variety of different languages and points out that while most languages have a word for play, what is actually referenced by the term varies wildly across cultures. More recently, in *The Ambiguity of Play*, Brian Sutton-Smith illustrates how academic disciplines tend to have their own conceptions of play that are rooted in how that particular discipline conceptualizes and makes knowledge.[1] For example, Sutton-Smith claims that child development researchers often take the connection between play and learning as axiomatic. Children play in order to test their limits and to learn what sorts of behaviors work in different circumstances, such as how a child might learn general problem-solving skills by playing with puzzles. According to Sutton-Smith, however, the belief in this connection does not actually rest on empirical evidence (2001, 24). This "rhetoric of progress" is deployed commonly because it supports the deeply held beliefs of researchers in these areas and helps them justify their truth claims and build arguments.[2]

While Sutton-Smith is not a rhetorical theorist, his approach to making knowledge about play is largely a rhetorical approach, and it squares well with what Crowley says about how rhetorical theory has classically conceived knowledge as a product of language. For example, consider the following passage from *The Methodical Memory*: "In a fundamental sense, knowledge did not exist outside of language for classical rhetoricians. The ancient rhetorician's task was to compare statements about what was known or agreed upon with statements about which there was disagreement. He made this comparison in such a way as to move an audience toward acceptance of the disputed point. Successful invention and arrangement depended on his ability to discern whether his language would affect listeners in the desired fashion. Thus classical rhetoricians treated language as a powerful means of moving people to action" (1990, 3). A major point of discussion in *The Methodical Memory* for Crowley is that modernist thinking has conceived invention as a largely internalized process of knowledge production (5). In other words, unique and individual human minds were best suited to work through complex problems and arrive at previously unconsidered insights. This view of knowledge production is fundamentally at odds with how rhetorical theory has classically understood both language and knowledge as contextually situated within a particular space-time. Similarly, Sutton-Smith's fundamental insight from *The Ambiguity of Play* is that while individual disciplines have tended to understand their own theoretical conceptions of play as scientifically validated or even axiomatic, such play theories are better understood as the rhetorical inventions described by Crowley. Sutton-Smith points out that disciplines studying phenomena as different as the body, behavior, or language "all use the word *play* to for these quite different things" and that their play theories "come to reflect these various diversities" (6). This means that the term "play" comes to stand as a kind of placeholder for the values and presuppositions of particular scholarly disciplines. Therefore, rhetorical study of the things scholars talk about when they talk about play can help us make sense of what those scholarly communities value. In creating a taxonomy of the rhetorical inventions that are the various theories of play in rhetoric and writing, I contend that we can bring our field's values and assumptions into somewhat sharper focus.

For the purposes of the taxonomy of play theories described in the following pages, a few things are worth noting from the above discussion. For one thing, what is meant by the word "play" can be quite different depending on the rhetorical context of its usage. Scholars of rhetoric and writing who use the term to describe different sorts of classroom settings or rhetorical situations may actually be using the term to reference very different things. Understanding this, scholars of rhetoric and writing would do well to consider how what they presume the word to mean in any given context might be rooted in their own disciplinary conceptions of knowledge. In other words, a researcher working with something like workplace genres in professional writing might assume different things to be true about what play is than would a researcher working on rhetorical theories of new media. Once we as researchers are aware that our understanding of play is tied to other ideologies from our research areas, then we may begin to question how and to what extent our assumptions about play help us justify particular truth claims and build arguments. With all of this in mind, the purpose of the taxonomy provided in the following pages is not to arrive at a once-and-for-all correct definition of play, or even to comprehensively account for each and every theory of play that exists in rhetoric and writing. Instead, my hope is that the taxonomy will help researchers stop to pause and consider what they mean by play in any given context, reflect on how what they mean by play is itself a product of their own disciplinary ideologies, and become more critically aware of the rhetorical power their assumptions about play might hold for their work in general.

EXPERIMENTAL PLAY AND THE RHETORICS OF FRIVOLITY AND PROGRESS

Merriam-Webster's Dictionary defines "frivolity" as "lacking in seriousness" and notes that it is "marked by unbecoming levity." Despite claiming frivolity is the most pervasive of the play rhetorics, Sutton-Smith paradoxically devotes fewer than twelve pages to it. This rhetoric is defined by contrast from the serious and positions play as "nonsense" or unproductive waste.

Sutton-Smith says it derives from Puritanical orthodoxy in which "work is obligatory, sober, serious, and not fun, and play is the opposite of these" (2001, 202). Play is a commodity, something afforded only to those who have the resources to *not* work.

Sutton-Smith discusses frivolity only tangentially because it is a popular rhetoric. Academics who study play assume from the outset that it has some value and cannot be dismissed as only waste. However, this rhetoric is still pervasive, and people who study play or games must often justify why the subject is worthy of serious academic inquiry. This pervasiveness is particularly evident in game studies, where many scholars have invested a great deal of time demythologizing the rhetoric of frivolity.

Albert Rouzie, for example, argues, "Educators have inherited deeply entrenched divisions between work and play, seriousness and frivolity, and order and chaos, which ultimately impoverish our culture's view of literacy" (2005, 139). Rouzie is among a group of researchers who have recently brought theoretical attention to play by identifying the work/play split (Alberti 2008; Colby and Colby 2008). In a familiar poststructural move, such research deconstructs that binary and sometimes attempts to reorder the pair's priority.[3] I discuss the rhetoric of frivolity briefly here simply to point out that it impacts every other play rhetoric mentioned in this chapter. In order to discuss play within "serious" academic contexts, scholars start from the position that play has value within the context of rhetoric and writing.

Here, I outline ludic rhetorics that articulate *experimental theories* describing play as safe, pleasurable, and productive. These theories rely on what Sutton-Smith refers to as "rhetorics of progress" derived primarily from evolutionary and biological sciences. The underlying ideology of this theory is that play is a mechanism for learning. Young animals, for example, might play fight when they are young in order to model and practice a type of behavior they will need later in life. Play, whether it is a lion playing and learning how to hunt or fight, or a child playing with blocks and learning the alphabet, functions as a relatively safe training ground that produces real, tangible learning of core skills needed for adult life. Indeed, rhetoric scholars often describe the writing classroom as a training ground where students can practice writing skills in playful ways that emphasize pleasure and fun. By becoming aware of the specific ways this particular theory of play is deployed, teachers and scholars might become more critical of assumptions such as the degree to which play is necessarily safe, or if making writing more fun necessarily leads to better learning.

Scholars who utilize experimental theories may metaphorically describe the classroom as a play space. One example is John Alberti's "The Game of Reading and Writing: How Video Games Reframe Our Understanding of Literacy" (2008). Alberti argues that videogames might be a powerful way to reconceive what scholars mean by "literacy" in terms of new media. In doing so, he suggests that writing instructors could describe the classroom as a play space, suggesting that such a metaphor can help the field reevaluate its assumptions, both about the classroom itself and about play. Alberti believes that pleasure should be returned to the center of writing instruction. One consequence of describing classrooms as play spaces is classrooms can be conceived as utilizing what James Paul Gee describes as "sandbox learning": "Sandboxes in the real world are safe havens for children that still look and feel like the real world. Using the term metaphorically, sandboxes are good for learning if learners are put into a situation that feels like the real thing, but with risks and dangers greatly mitigated, they can learn well and still feel a sense of authenticity and accomplishment" (2007, 39). When writing classrooms are described as sandboxes, they become experimental sites where students can try things out, fail, hit the reset button, try, and fail again with the reduced consequences. For

Alberti and others, this description of play is useful for rhetoric and writing because it helps teachers emphasize the *processes* of learning.

Experimental theories also suggest that both play and learning are pleasurable. Therefore, writing instruction that engages play will tend to generate student learning. Throughout Gee's work on gaming, he argues that learning is biologically pleasurable for humans because it triggers pleasure centers in the brain that reinforce and reward behaviors that help people learn.[4] For example, while describing composing with new media, Andrea Davis and colleagues claim, "Because crafting the slideshow felt like play, I [we] invested more time and more energy, and ended up with a product that is more compelling, and even fun, than an academic essay could ever be" (2007, 189). Arguments like this define pleasure as a central connection between play and learning. Albert Rouzie also articulates this theory of play:

> Once I let myself make a contribution more playful in my own composing, I was hooked. If I felt less alienated, more connected through infusing my work with electronic play, then so could others. But that motivation pales in contrast to my own need for pleasure.
>
> Without it, I had no future in English studies or in the field of rhetoric and composition. I felt pleasure in this eruption of play, and it made me feel hopeful about the vitality of rhetoric and composition studies. (2005, 4)

Ludic rhetorics are often marked by these commonsense pairings of pleasure, play, and learning.

However, the field is already rightly beginning to confront this ideology with skepticism. In "Ludic Snags," for example, Richard Colby and Matthew S.S. Johnson point out several problematic patterns that have emerged in game-based pedagogies. Among them, they suggest, is "what we see to be rather disturbing academic trends, including the (we think false) assumption that more fun equals better learning" (2013, 84). While experimental theories understandably attempt to harness the pleasure and fun-making possibilities of play, the ideological assumption that making an activity more playful or fun necessarily makes it better for learning should be met with skepticism.

Experimental theories also tend to emphasize productive play. One example of this is Rebekah Colby and Richard Colby's essay "A Pedagogy of Play" (2008), in which they offer both general reasoning and concrete examples for how and why teachers might bring online role-playing games like World of Warcraft into the writing classroom. Colby and Colby describe what they term an "emergent theory of learning" rooted in student writing generated by playing games of emergence. Such games of emergence include activities like chess, which have a very small set of rules that open a large possibility space for play. Such games create many different possibilities for how the game might unfold, with no single winning strategy that works every time. In Colby and Colby's view, games of emergence, like Warcraft, present the player with rhetorical choices; through play, gamers have to assemble their resources and make strategic decisions about which course of action will be most effective. Their pedagogy asks students to play Warcraft over the course of the semester and write strategy guides that argue for the effectiveness of particular play styles. Students may also write a proposal to game designers or debate strategy with other gamers in online forums. In any case, their experience of play serves as a research site and training ground; students gather evidence for the textual products they will compose while practicing the same kinds of strategic moves required by writing.

The experimental theories of play discussed in this section describe play as safe, pleasurable, and productive, which opens a variety of possibilities for teachers and researchers in rhetoric and writing. These ludic rhetorics make it possible for scholars to conceive of writing assignments heavily invested with fun, pleasure, and learning through trial and error, in which students can invent a wide variety of rhetorical strategies to complete their assignments effectively. By pointing out what such theories assume to be true about play, however, my hope is that we as researchers might become more aware of the limitations of those assumptions. For example, it is important to remember that games and play do not eliminate risk, nor do they even eliminate danger. That pleasure that can emerge from such forms as sandbox learning or trial and error is, I believe, obviously true and worthy of attention from teachers of writing. However, this does not mean that games and play are equally "safe" or effective as learning strategies for all students. If we are to think of games as a form of literacy in the age of new media, it is important to remember how particular literacy practices can function to favor students of certain backgrounds over others. Just as students from middle-class backgrounds may have advantages over other students because their discourses at home are closer to academic discourse, game-based pedagogies should reflect on ways they can perpetuate inequality. In other words, just because a particular writing pedagogy emphasizes play for the purpose of pleasure and fun does not necessarily mean that it will result in effective learning. Whenever experimental theories of play appear in scholarly conversations of rhetoric and writing, it is useful to question the limitations of the safety suggested by sandbox theories of learning, as well as whether concepts such as fun and pleasure *may or may not* enable learning for students with different backgrounds and experiences.

EXPERIENTIAL THEORIES AND THE RHETORIC OF THE SELF

While the rhetoric of progress expresses one theory of play, another theory is related to what James Berlin terms "subjective theories" of rhetoric that "located truth either within the individual or within the real that is accessible only through the individual's internal apprehension" (1987, 11). Rooted in what Sutton-Smith calls "the rhetoric of the self," here I describe *experiential theories* of play that emphasize individuality, motivation, and self-reflection.

Sutton-Smith claims, "rhetorics of the self focus on play as having its basis in the psychology of the individual player" (2001, 173). Such rhetorics might take the form of a psychoanalyst describing an individual's psychic experience or a neurologist describing the firing of synapses. Sutton-Smith argues that the rhetoric of the self enjoys popularity during periods of romantic ideology because individual expression and the self are highly valued. Composition theory has often been informed by romanticism and many ideas today are still shaped by its powerful zeitgeist, including discussions of plagiarism, authorship, and copyright.

The experiential theory of play expressed by the rhetoric of the self is similarly intertwined with romantic thinking. In some ways, these theories may deliberately articulate romantic ideology, while in other ways they may take play as an opportunity to critique and respond to romantic conceptions of the self. Rouzie, of course, was well aware of this ideological grounding in his groundbreaking work on play. Rouzie argues that poststructural theory, in seeking to create a more nuanced account of the socially constructed self, sometimes dismissed play due to its emphasis on raising political self-consciousness. Rouzie claims that such approaches "appear to have thrown the baby of play out with the bathwater of the romantic subject" (2005, 35). Rouzie does not mean that play is always romantic, but that it has often been assumed as such and subsequently ignored by theory that attempts to either critique or move past Romanticism. Following Rouzie's apt observation, in this section I analyze the experiential theory of play in rhetoric and writing to consider the possibilities it creates.

Experiential theories emphasize play as a powerful way to enable self-motivated student writing.[5] For example, in "Public Writing in Gaming Spaces" (2008), Matthew S.S. Johnson argues that the writing gamers do for gaming communities has a specific audience and purpose and is also capable of causing actual change in those communities. Examining massively multiplayer online games (MMOGs) such as Ultima Online, Johnson argues that virtual environments work as public spaces where players can have real effects on their environment by interacting with other players through their writing and even have a direct influence on game design (2008, 278–280). In this way, Johnson's discussion of play relies on the experiential theories I am describing. Just as Sutton-Smith says the rhetoric of the self involves the internal motivations of individuals, Johnson points to play as an intrinsic motivation for writing: "Gamers, motivated by seemingly simple 'play,' participate in an enormous number of writing activities, creating a diverse body of texts: gamer-authors writing online journals (from both player-characters' and games' perspectives), strategy guides, walkthroughs, fan fiction, and blogs. They also participate in gaming forums and other online discussions and create their own websites" (2008, 271).

Such theories, I contend, illustrate clearly how students may paradoxically claim to dislike writing, but produce vast quantities of it in relation to play. Much like with experimental theories, it may be wise for teachers and researchers to approach the issue of intrinsic motivation with a healthy dose of skepticism, since the writing that emerges in such communities is likely motivated by a wide range of factors. Still, such work does go a long way toward demythologizing commonly held beliefs that young people dislike writing.

Experiential theories also emphasize the ways play can help students both compose and reflect upon individual experience. For example, Zachary Waggoner points to the established tradition in composition textbooks that has students reflect on individual experience as a means to generate writing. He writes: "Through a cultural studies approach students learn to think and write critically about the life texts and practices they are familiar with, thus connecting their educational experiences and their everyday life experiences. In theory, this enables students to more enthusiastically engage in classroom conversations and in their writings on popular culture subjects. It also helps FYC writers consider audience and context for both the popular culture texts they are examining and the students' writings on these texts" (2010, n.p.). Waggoner argues that while composition textbooks often reference media such as television, music, and film, videogames and other objects of play are rarely, if ever, discussed. He outlines a pedagogy that asks students to reflect upon their individual experiences in virtual worlds such as *Morrowind* as a means to help students feel more connected with their writing and to claim ownership of their own writing and experiences.

Experiential theories further emphasize the ways play provides a method for students to critically respond to representations of the self, particularly in new media. One excellent example can be found in Jennifer deWinter and Stephanie Vie's "Press Enter to 'Say': Using

Second Life to Teach Critical Media Literacy" (2008). Following new media scholars who have called for pedagogies to provide students with new media literacies suited for the twenty-first-century learning, deWinter and Vie begin with the premise that "skill-and-drill" multiple choice testing fails to prepare today's students to think about and act critically toward the majority of texts they encounter today. Their argument is that developing critical awareness of one's own subjectivity formation is crucial to new media literacy. They propose that "instructors . . . take a look to *Second Life*, a popular online simulated environment, as a dynamic text to engage students in questions regarding power, ethics, intellectual property, and community" (2008, 313). Following current trends in new media, deWinter and Vie claim that in order to develop literacy for today, students need practice both producing and analyzing new media texts. They argue that participation in online communities provides a means to engage such practice.

An experiential theory of play can be seen clearly through deWinter and Vie's conception of avatars. They ask students to create avatars for Second Life and then critically examine the intersections between their offline and online identities. While deWinter and Vie effectively critique elements of the rhetoric of progress by insisting the online environments are not "safe havens" and admit that discourses of power operate in and through them, they also claim that "avatars operate as projections of one's own self" (2008, 316). The authors ask students to engage in the complex interplay of avatar construction by attempting to compose the self through Second Life's limited player creation mechanic. They then provide a set of heuristics to help students critique the possibilities for identity in the online space. Second Life, for instance, does not allow for the creation of disabled avatars, a reality that severely limits their representational potential for disabled selves.

With their emphasis on motivation and self-reflection, experiential theories of play open a variety of possibilities for teachers and researchers, especially because they challenge teachers to think critically about the types of writing students produce outside of the classroom, as well as their myriad reasons for producing said writing. Due to composition theory's history with Romanticism, the particular ideas in this section of the taxonomy may be the ones most familiar to readers of this collection. While exploring the connections between play and its capacity to produce self-motivated writing can be quite productive, a heightened awareness of the specific ways experiential theories of play are deployed should give writing instructors reason to pause and reflect. As we ask writing students to represent their own experiences in game spaces as sites of critical reflection, we should deeply consider how particular games and play spaces may not only fail to represent people of color, disabled students, women, and transgender students, but may have histories of being overtly hostile toward such people. Whenever experiential theories of play appear in scholarly conversations of rhetoric and writing, we should stop to consider what kinds of selves are actually represented and how.

EXPLORATORY THEORIES AND THE RHETORIC OF THE IMAGINARY

In this section, I describe exploratory theories that depict play as imaginative, transformational, and subversive. These theories articulate what Sutton-Smith refers to as the "rhetoric of the imaginary," which is his most ambitious and ambiguous rhetorical category. He writes: "Gathered here are all who believe that some kind of transformation is the most fundamental characteristic of play. Not surprisingly, therefore, artists of all kinds are here. The heterogeneity of this rhetoric is illustrated by listing many of the concepts relevant to its description: imagination, fancy, phantasmagoria, creativity, art, romanticism, flexibility, metaphor, mythology, serendipity, pretense, deconstruction, heteroglossia, the act of making what is present or absent present, and the play of signifiers. It was not easy to choose a name for this rhetoric, for the very reason that it is not a simple category" (2001, n.p.). Just as Sutton-Smith suggests that the rhetoric of the imaginary was difficult to name because it is not simple, I likewise struggled naming the ludic rhetorics that articulate the theories of play I describe in this section. I settled on "exploratory theories" because these approaches to play, rhetoric, and writing indeed explore the edges of what classrooms invested with and modeled on gameplay actually look like.

Exploratory theories imagine new pathways and possibilities for rhetoricians to make persuasive claims made possible through computational and procedural media. For example, consider Matt King's "*Rhetorical Peaks* and What it Means to Win a Game" (2010). In this article, King discusses his own participation in the development of Rhetorical Peaks, a videogame for rhetoric and writing classes developed at the Digital Writing and Research Lab at the University of Texas. King draws on Ian Bogost's theory of procedural rhetoric, which Bogost describes as the "art of persuasion through rule-based representations and interactions rather than the spoken word, writing, images, or moving pictures" (2010, ix). For Bogost, computational texts such as videogames use procedural rhetorics to make claims about the world through modeling complex systems with code. For example, in a basketball videogame, programmers would need to build a model of what a proper jump shot looks like. How high should the player jump before the ball is released? How far from the basket should the player be to have the best chance of making the shot? Such a model is necessarily rhetorical and embodies claims about how a jump shot works, or how it could or should work.

King's article is representative of exploratory theories of play that attempt to imagine new forms rhetoric might take in sites such as videogames and software applications, as well as how traditional and familiar forms of rhetoric manifest at those sites. While Bogost's theory shows how games in general are always rhetorical, King asks, "To what extent is rhetoric procedural? In other words, could any specific set of processes—and thus, any videogame—describe what it means to do rhetoric?" (2010, n.p.). King points out that one traditional concept students of rhetoric must learn is the need to shift their communicative strategies and approaches based on context. Therefore, if forms of procedural rhetoric such as videogames are to inform rhetoric and writing studies, it is worth asking if those forms are capable of teaching that traditional lesson. King speculates that a videogame such as Rhetorical Peaks might work well for this purpose, if it is designed specifically to model a particular attitude. In other words, the game "demands an ability and willingness to switch between different processes and logics, to seek out the limitations of any particular orientation" in order to reach its end goal (2010, n.p.). In this way, playing a videogame can help students explore both what rhetoric means and what it means to use rhetoric.

Exploratory theories also suggest how play, especially in digital environments, transforms sites of rhetoric and writing that are not necessarily seen as such until they are given closer scrutiny. For example, take Kevin Moberly's "Composition, Computer Games, and the Absence of Writing" (2008), in which he argues that computer games incorporate composition into their gameplay. This facet not only requires gamers to read and make meaning of symbols, but to write and revise their play in response to those symbols (284). While the writing gamers do is typically seen as "play," Moberly claims that videogames can not only teach students the fundamentals of composing and about the sociopolitical contexts in which writing occurs, but also how reading environments influence how texts are written.

In particular, he discusses the adoption of "voice chat" by the popular MMORPG World of Warcraft. While users of the game have traditionally used text interfaces to communicate within the game, Moberly points out that the adoption of voice chat through headsets and secondary interfaces such as Skype has become increasingly common. For the game, the idea behind such a move is twofold: first, it makes the game more accessible; second, it "effaces" writing. In other words, discursive writing in a text chat interface disappears, making it more difficult to recognize the role language plays in shaping the virtual environment of something like World of Warcraft. Through play, something that was once writing is transformed into something no longer recognized as writing, but language is still experienced through that play.

Exploratory theories often gesture toward the subversive nature of play. As an example, consider Justin Hodgson's "Developing and Extending Gaming Pedagogy: Designing a Course as a Game" (2013). While previous approaches I have discussed in this chapter have asked students to play a game in their class, or even take elements of game design to help them structure a class as a play space, Hodgson attempts to push this idea even further by designing a course as a game from the outset. Hodgson's approach makes three main suggestions: (1) design the course as a game, (2) model the course design after a specific game (in this particular case, Hodgson models his course on World of Warcraft), and (3) have students play the actual game concurrently with the course.

Such an approach obviously in many ways utilizes an experimental theory of play that imagines a classroom as a play space. For instance, Hodgson specifically points out that such an approach is "ideal for encouraging students to feel free to make mistakes, to safely fail" (2013, 51). At the same time, I contend that this also embodies a theory of play that tacitly suggests the subversive nature of play. Play theorists in general have tended to highlight this aspect of play, such as Miguel Sicart's recent description of "play as a dance of resistance and appropriation, of creation and destruction of order" (2014, 98). As such, if rhetoric and writing scholars are to seriously invite play into their classrooms, we should expect that such an invitation includes a degree of danger in creating resistance and a certain "destruction of order" to our classrooms.

Hodgson's approach points to one potential way play disrupts his class. Specifically, in modeling his course after World of Warcraft, he had to create a competitive grading system. In order for students to get an "A" in the course, they had to maintain their overall score within 10 percent of the highest score in the class. Students, he says, quickly figured out ways to game the system of his course. He writes: "Students quickly realized that three Cs were better than one A in terms of course points, so they churned out work to get points rather than focusing primarily on the quality of the work, the rhetorical engagement, or the method, the mode, the medium, or the message—that is, they 'played' the system" (2013, 55). In exploring the edges of inviting play into his classroom, Hodgson discovered a potential breaking point. While he wanted students to deeply engage with specific rhetorical tasks, students found ways to play the course in a way that they would play a game. In this way, his approach embodies an exploratory theory of play that illustrates the real ways play can be subversive, even in a classroom setting.

Through their emphasis on exploring new forms of rhetoric and how they might reshape classrooms altogether, the theories in this section pose deep and challenging questions for rhetorical theory and the teaching of writing. These ludic rhetorics ask scholars to reflect upon the forms rhetoric takes in twenty-first-century composing, as well as to consider the consequences and possibilities laid open when the destructive side of play as invited into our classrooms along with the games they inhabit. Just as with the other sections of this taxonomy, however, rhetoric and writing scholars may want to spend considerable time reflecting on the limitations of exploratory theories, particularly as it concerns modeling classrooms on digital spaces. This may be especially true as mobile, augmented reality games such as Pokémon Go become more widespread. Game designers have for some time suggested that social, mobile, and augmented reality gaming (ARG) is the future of gameplay (McGonigal 2011). My own university, for instance, has already incorporated mobile gaming into freshman orientation for new students, such as using Pokémon Go to teach students how to find and locate library resources. No doubt, teachers of rhetoric and writing are likely already in the process of imagining how such forms of play might infuse our writing classrooms, modeling classrooms of the next generation on ARGs in the same way the writing instructors modeled classrooms on MMOGs over the previous decade. What questions, however, do such explorations require instructors to consider about students' own rights to their personal data when playing such games on their mobile devices? What ethical considerations should be taken into account, and how might they appear in the day-to-day work of teaching in things like policy statements, grading scales, and syllabi?

CONCLUSION

In this chapter, I have surveyed three recent publications that contain a variety of essays on videogame rhetorics and game-based pedagogies, reasoning that these are apt sites to examine ideologies of play currently deployed in rhetoric and writing studies. Using Brian Sutton-Smith's model of general play rhetorics, I have identified three broad, theoretical descriptions of play in the field. I have termed them "ludic rhetorics," which is intended to reference the ways rhetoric and writing scholars theorize various types of play as they relate to new media objects such as videogames. Here, I want to briefly mention two caveats regarding my descriptions and then return to Crowley's suggestion that theory should function as a type of rhetorical invention.

First, it is important to note that the rhetorical taxonomy I have set up in this chapter is *rhetorical*. The descriptions are not objectively true, nor are they intended to be stable or unmoving. As a rhetorical invention itself, this model simply intends to provide one particular viewpoint on the field as it currently stands. No doubt, many other theorists would describe the field using different terminology and potentially reach different conclusions. The usefulness of a taxonomy such as this, I contend, rests in how well it helps the field describe and identify the ways play intersects with the work of rhetoric and writing or to imagine ways it might in the future. Second, considerable overlap exists between the categories of ludic rhetorics I have described. This should not be read as a suggestion that any one essay or scholar relies on one theory of play and one alone. Play is a notoriously difficult concept to define—indeed, much like rhetoric—and even Sutton-Smith has suggested that it may be impossible, or even unnecessary, to resolve all these contradictions. As I stated previously, my hope is that it will help researchers who have perhaps not reflected deeply on what is assumed through uses of the word "play" in their work stop to pause and consider what the term means in any given context, reflect on how what they mean by play is itself a product of their own disciplinary ideologies, and become more critically aware of the rhetorical power their assumptions about play might hold for their work in general.

NOTES

1. Although not a scholar of rhetoric, Sutton-Smith's work on play was greatly influenced by the rhetorical theories of Kenneth Burke. Sutton-Smith claims, "The modern use of a rhetorical approach to matters of scholarship and science probably owes the most, ultimately, to two great scholars of rhetoric, Kenneth Burke, whom I had the good fortune to meet, and Ludwig Wittgenstein, whom I did not" (ix).

2. Sutton-Smith defines seven distinct play rhetorics that are deployed in popular culture and in a variety of academic disciplines. He claims, "Rhetorics are narratives that have the intent to persuade because there is some kind of gain for those who are successful in their persuasion" (2001, 16). These rhetorics of play intend to persuade other researchers in the field that a particular scholar's claims are reasonable and valid.

3. Scholars such as Sutton-Smith and Ian Bogost argue that in attempting to "heal" the work/play split, scholars have sometimes ignored work in other disciplines that has already considered the complex relationship between work and play. This includes Johan Huizinga's *Homo Ludens* and even poststructural theory, such as Derrida's "Structure, Sign, and Play."

4. Gee claims, "Pleasure is the basis of learning for humans and learning is, like sex and eating, deeply pleasurable for human beings. Learning is a basic drive for humans" (2005, 4).

5. Games are often characterized as *autotelic*, which means that they are a "self-motivated, self-rewarding activity" (McGonigal 2011, 45).

REFERENCES

Alberti, John. 2008. "The Game of Reading and Writing: How Video Games Reframe Our Understanding of Literacy." *Computers and Composition* 25 (3): 258–69.

Berlin, James. 1987. *Rhetoric and Reality: Writing Instruction in American Colleges, 1900–1985.* Carbondale: Southern Illinois University Press.

Bogost, Ian. 2010. *Persuasive Games: The Expressive Power of Video Games.* Cambridge: The MIT Press.

Brooke, Collin. 2009. *Lingua Fracta: Towards a Rhetoric of New Media.* New Jersey: Hampton Press.

Colby, Rebekah Shultz, and Richard Colby. 2008. "A Pedagogy of Play: Integrating Computer Games into the Writing Classroom." *Computers and Composition* 25 (3): 300–312.

Colby, Richard, and Matthew S.S. Johnson. 2013. "Ludic Snags." In *Rhetoric/Composition/Play: Reshaping Theory and Practice through Video Games,* 82–97. New York: Palgrave Macmillan.

Crowley, Sharon. 1990. *The Methodical Memory: Invention in Current-Traditional Rhetoric.* Carbondale: Southern Illinois University Press.

Crowley, Sharon. 2006. *Toward a Civil Discourse: Rhetoric and Fundamentalism.* Pittsburgh: University of Pittsburgh Press.

Davis, Andrea, Suzanne Webb, Dundee Lackey, and Danielle Nicole DeVoss. 2007. "Remix, Play, and Remediation: Undertheorized Composing Practices." In *Writing and the Digital Generation: Essays on New Media Rhetoric,* 186–97. Jefferson: McFarland and Company.

deWinter, Jennifer, and Stephanie Vie. 2008. "Press Enter to 'Say': Using Second Life to Teach Critical Media Literacy." *Computers and Composition* 25 (3): 313–22.

Dunn, Patricia. 2001. *Talking, Sketching, Moving: Multiple Literacies in the Teaching of Writing.* Portsmouth: Heinemann.

Gee, James Paul. 2005. *Why Video Games Are Good for Your Soul.* New York: Common Ground.

Gee, James Paul. 2007. *Good Video Games and Good Learning: Collected Essays on Video Games, Learning and Literacy.* New York: Peter Lang.

Hodgson, Justin. 2013. "Developing and Extending Gaming Pedagogy: Designing a Course as a Game." In *Rhetoric/Composition/Play: Reshaping Theory and Practice through Video Games,* 45–60. New York: Palgrave Macmillan.

Huizinga, Johan H. (1938) 1980. *Homo Ludens: Study of the Play Element in Culture.* New edition. London; Boston: Routledge.

Johnson, Matthew S.S. 2008. "Public Writing in Gaming Spaces." *Computers and Composition* 25 (3): 270–83.

King, Matt. 2010. "Rhetorical Peaks and What It Means to Win the Game." *Currents in Electronic Literacy* 11 (1): n.p.

Lanham, Richard. 2007. *The Economics of Attention: Style and Substance in the Age of Information.* Chicago: University of Chicago Press.

McGonigal, Jane. 2011. *Reality Is Broken: How Games Make Us Better and How They Can Change the World*. New York: Penguin Books.

Miller, Susan. 1992. "Writing Theory: Theory Writing." In *Methods and Methodology in Composition Research*. Carbondale: Southern Illinois University Press.

Moberly, Kevin. 2008. "Composition, Computer Games, and the Absence of Writing." *Computers and Composition* 25 (3): 284–99.

Newcomb, Matthew. 2009. "Arguing at Play in the Fields of the Lord; Or, Abducting Charles Pierce's Rhetorical Theory in 'A Neglected Argument for the Reality of God." *College Composition and Communication* 61 (1): W45–65.

Rouzie, Albert. 2005. *At Play in The Fields of Writing: A Serio-Ludic Rhetoric*. New Jersey: Hampton Press.

Sanchez, Raul. 2012. "Retheorizing Empiricism and Identity." *College English* 74 (3): 215–33.

Sicart, Miguel. 2014. "Play Matters." *Playful Thinking*. Cambridge: MIT Press.

Sutton-Smith, Brian. 2001. *The Ambiguity of Play*. Cambridge: Harvard University Press.

Ulmer, Gregory. 2002. *Internet Invention: From Literacy to Electracy*. New York: Longman.

Waggoner, Zachary. 2010. "Life in Morrowind: Identity, Video Games, and First-Year Composition." *Currents in Electronic Literacy* 11 (1): n.p.

9

UNHURRIED CONVERSATIONS
Writing Center Models for Ideological Intervention

Joshua C. Hilst and Rebecca Disrud

Composition and the larger academic enterprise often assume that higher education will have a liberalizing effect on students—and it often does. As Sharon Crowley points out in *Toward a Civil Discourse* (2006), however, some students come to higher education with durable conservative or fundamentalist belief systems, including nonreligious ones. Although the values of liberal education—skepticism, open questioning, logical reasoning, and internal consistency—and liberal ideology are often conflated, liberal education will generally admit any ideas that adhere to its logical processes. Nevertheless, Stanley Fish (1994) points out that some arguments lie even beyond the scope of what is recognized as free speech and thus beyond the scope of acceptable arguments in the academy. Although students sometimes raise fundamentalist ideas in classrooms, the power differentials of those contact zones often stymie or modify expression of the most controversial ideas, and the critical mass of students can obscure individual disagreement or resistance to questioning. On the other hand, when students bring fundamentalist claims to the writing center, tutors working within what Crowley calls the "deliberative" (or skeptical academic) paradigm must openly disagree with the students they want to support, and those using non-directive pedagogy (which we discuss below) must help students make objectionable arguments stronger and more eloquent.

Nonetheless, with their individualized, empathetic, and unhurried tutor-student interactions, writing centers harbor enormous potential for developing the thought processes valorized by the academy. Indeed, we argue that writing centers can more fully realize ethical modes of inquiry through the model of invention Sharon Crowley (2006) describes rather than through more traditional tutor roles like the deliberative stance or using nondirective methods to improve an unethical argument. Although our observation that one-to-one interactions can

DOI: 10.7330/9781607328933.c009

uniquely impact student development is not necessarily new, we con-
stellate it within the ambits of both unhurried conversation and several
recent writing center theoretical frameworks, including the "queer
turn" and the writing center as the locus of legible social tensions.

More specifically, we offer the unhurried conversation, particularly
the proximity of the tutorial, as a "queer turn" in writing center practice.
By queering, we are invoking Harry Denny's concept to move beyond
normative lenses in order to analyze "practices that inscribe meaning,
making certain bodies and ways of doing visible and marked and others
illusory, invisible, or unmarked" (2010, 42). That is to say, an unhurried
conversation might fit well within such a set of queering practices by
bringing other bodies, other meanings, and other values into play and
opening up new inventive possibilities. Dovetailing with the concept of
queering as exposing previously invisible practice, Geller et al. (2007)
suggest in *The Everyday Writing Center* that too much writing center scholarship tends to cast centers as spaces of peace and harmony, insulated
from many of the tensions of the university. Following the lead of *The
Everyday Writing Center*, we will not offer here a "scripted" model tutorial
but instead give suggestions "in-the-moment-at-the-point-of-need knowledge producers" need as they work with writers.

Writing center talk has been a focus of scholarship for some years.
Kenneth Bruffee famously focused on conversation when he wrote,
"Reflective thought is public or social *conversation* internalized" (1995,
89; emphasis added). In this way, Bruffee almost presages Sidney
Dobrin's criticism that "composition studies lacks a discourse to talk
about writing as phenomena precursory to the phenomena it writes"
(2011, 25). In the writing center, we understand that individuals are
neither the beginning nor the end of writing. Rather, writing is closer to
a discourse that moves through writers. For writing centers, the writing
begins in talking. As Stephen North (1984) says, the writing center is
here to *talk* to writers.

As Geller et al. point out, however, the conversations that occur
between tutors and students sometimes expose previously invisible tensions, including tensions between deeply held personal or religious con-
victions of students and liberal academic values. Certainly, writers who
offer opinions that fall outside the regimen of phrases for an academic
discipline are not necessarily unlearned. Rather, they are often offering
commonplaces drawn from conversations into which they have entered.
These commonplaces, as Crowley suggests (2006), are not arguments
meant to persuade others, but rather a kind of in-group signal in praise
of that group's virtues, or epideictic rather than deliberative. Because

these students' views are bound up in personal and community identities, the traditional tutor responses—taking a deliberative approach to reason students out of their opinion or using minimalist questioning to nudge a change in argument—are unlikely to encourage students to consider alternative viewpoints. However, using Crowley's ideas of unhurried, value-laden conversations as well as activating the ancient definition of invention—finding all possible arguments—may better help some students open themselves to the skeptical mindset of the liberal academy, even if the content of their arguments ultimately remains unchanged.

To show how writing centers might fulfill Crowley's prescriptions for the creation of a civil discourse, we will first discuss how writing centers became imbricated in traditional conceptions of process and, paralleling Dobrin's evaluation, with the formation and disciplining of student subjects. We will then show how a model of tutoring that focuses less on altering student subjectivities might create a space for both the tutor and the student to affect one another. In doing so, they can create possibilities for persuasion that *can* (though it must be noted, not always *will*) have a lasting effect on developing individuals inclined toward a more open, robust, and skeptical inquiry. These possibilities also expand tutoring techniques beyond the traditional directive-non-directive and deliberative-passive binaries and suggest that subject formation might not be limited to students but, rather crucially, extends to tutors as well.

MINIMALIST TUTORING FOR MODERNIST SUBJECTS

For the last several decades, writing center theory has in many ways reflected developments in rhetoric and composition. As process pedagogy grew to prominence in the larger field of composition studies in the 1960s and 1970s, it left the writing center with the mission of "cleaning up" the messes that students made as they moved through the various stages of a writing process (Pemberton 1992). In 1984, Stephen North rejected the "remediator" label that many had attached to writing centers when he declared that writing centers make "better writers, not better writing" and articulated a clear affinity for process-oriented composition and opposition to current-traditional rhetorics that focused only on outcomes and reworking the writing *post factum*. North's insinuation in his motto "better writers, not better writing," however, is that writing centers are actually in the business of subject formation, of crafting "better subjects" who personify the liberal characteristics attendant to the modern academic paradigm—an implication we will return to shortly.

Jeff Brooks picks up North's thread and aligns "being of service to students" with students' long-term development and, by extension, their process (1995). For Brooks, minimalist tutoring should occur through simple proxemics in a series of steps familiar to almost any writing center tutor. The tutor should sit beside the student in a peer relationship, the paper should be closer to the writer, the student writer should hold the pen and read the paper out loud, and the tutor should pose open-ended questions to the student. Brooks imparts what would become conventional wisdom in the writing center world: "The less we do *to* the paper, the better. Our primary object in the writing center session is not the paper, but the student" (87). With this welcome focus on long-term writing development over short-term grammar drills, however, came an almost dogmatic disciplinary insistence on non-directive, minimalist tutoring methods (NDMTMs) as well as an implicit imperative to form "better" writing subjects.

Indeed, these theoretical shifts, while valuable in some ways, perpetu-ate what Crowley calls the "traditional function of imparting a univer-sal subjectivity" (1998, 9). That is to say, in order to have a universal rhetoric, there must be a subject who is prepared to be persuaded by that rhetoric—a subject who comes prepackaged with certain requisite knowledge. This subject, we argue, is precisely the subject that both the NDMTM and the modernist university imagine: the student assumed to possess ideas or knowledge waiting to be drawn out. Indeed, for some time, the prevalence of NDMTMs obscured the limits of treating stu-dents within the largely modern (as opposed to postmodern) paradigm of higher education. In Crowley's words, modernism "assumes that each person is an integrated, coherent self, and whereas this self undergoes changes as it experiences new situations, it remains relatively stable throughout its lifetime" (1993, 32). In other words, NDMTMs imagine students within a modernist paradigm in which their identities and knowledge bases are coherent and stable; both process and NDMTMs can work within this paradigm because they draw on knowledge that is already there[r2].

In the modernist paradigm, arguments are also seen to reflect the subjects who made them (rather than say, their time, place, or cultural context), and thus by extension, "good" arguments reflect "good" sub-jects. Crowley comments, "Liberal and scientific thinkers located inven-tion in encounters between individuals and nature rather than in the common language of the polity. In modern rhetoric, then, the quality of invention . . . depend[s] upon the quality of the mind that produced it rather than on the quality of the arguments made available by language and culture" (2006, 35). Within this paradigm, then, it seems reasonable to expect tutors to draw out what we understand as *already* within liberal subjects with NDMTMs, presupposing that answers and ideas are latent within "universal" subject-students and merely awaiting activation.

Nancy Grimm (2011) brilliantly critiques this agenda of subject formation in terms of both the racialized assumptions institutional systems make about students and the ways that higher education locates literacy deficiencies in students rather than in the systems that privilege normative patterns of discourse. Grimm's critique, along with Irene Clark and Dave Healy's (1996) point that noninterventionist policies fail to adequately help some students, spurred a move away from pure NDMTMs in some writing centers (although we would argue they still enjoy much currency in writing center praxis). Many practitioners have also begun making their writing centers agents of systemic institutional change, responding to Denny's (2010) and Geller et al.'s (2007) calls to reframe writing center work in postmodern terms. By recognizing that writerly identity is not universal, static, and individual—but rather bound up with social communities and intersectional markers of race, culture, gender, sexuality, age, ability, and many other dimensions—many writing centers are answering Denny's call for "a dialogue that's genuinely transactional, not about banking for any perspective or essentialist way of being, but dialogue that's a genuine exploration of difference and similarity, about same and other" (50).

Yet we still wonder how these dialogues might play out in moments of ideological conflict. Returning for a moment to the motto "better writers, not better writing," and viewing it through the lens of Crowley's notion of rhetorical invention, we see possibilities for negotiating difference, even a kind of queering of literacy and language, as we will discuss in a moment. Read generously, the refrain "better writers, not better writing" could extend to both parties in a tutorial: the student *and* the tutor. Indeed, if the student-tutor relationship is (not unproblematically) construed as a *peer* relationship, the tutorial can potentially change the tutor as much as the student.

In the following paragraphs, we will briefly explore how two writing center authors working from a postmodern perspective, Marilyn Cooper (2008) and Grimm (1999), offer pathways into these conversations before turning to Crowley's and Arabella Lyon's (2013) ideas for engaging with absolutist claims. Cooper and Grimm show us the potential for two-sided development (both tutors and students), even as they criticize the idea that writing centers should be in the business of changing people. Cooper argues that instead of enforcing modernist ideas of what constitutes an academic subjectivity, writing centers should show students how to use writing to explore subjectivities. In her view, the writing tutor can help students not to subdue themselves to already-delineated subject positions but rather "us[e] language to construct subject positions" (339). Grimm, in turn, urges the academy to move toward an examination of its own assumptions about literacy and identity, aligning with Dobrin's call for composition to discipline writing itself rather than subjects. By focusing on an ideological, rather than autonomous, model of literacy, writing centers can help students see the opaque assumptions embedded within the discourses they are exploring.

By way of example, Grimm introduces us to a student, Mary, who arrives at the writing center with a draft of a paper that reflects her conservative religious belief. Grimm writes that in a traditional, autonomous writing center model, "A tutor might suggest that Mary could reconsider the reading in her course anthology, hoping that as she rereads these essays she will come to see the limits of her traditional ways" (1999, 32). Grimm's approach to this scenario, by contrast, is to suggest that the tutor point directly at the way the assignment constructs the student— "as a media-literate, urban, religiously uncommitted liberal person" (32)—and thus shift attention away from any perceived "shortcomings" of Mary as a person. Therefore, in this model the tutor would *tell* the student that the assignment expects Mary to take a point of view with a certain frame of reference, rather than ask her questions. This perspective might be radically different from the one Mary might normally take, but it would show Mary the kinds of writing that fall within academic parameters. However, just as important for our purposes, such an approach also creates the tutorial as public conversation that can then be internalized. That is, the tutorial produces a kind of conversation that can be realized as writing. Such conversations might take on a character closer to the ethical discourse Crowley envisions in which two individuals negotiate radically different notions of what is real or true.

The modernist limitations of NDMTMs are apparent when tutor and student ideologies clash or when students bring ideas that cannot be submitted to academic processes of logical analysis. In these situations, because traditional non-directive writing center doctrines advise against direct intervention, they leave the tutor with the choice to either continue posing ineffective questions or to help the student develop unethical prose in the student's most persuasive voice.[1] The scenario we visit next comes from a particularly conservative student, but the same problems could arise when a student brings a liberal argument to a conservative tutor, which has been the case on occasion in our university.

UNETHICAL DISCOURSE

The student "Mary" in the previous section might be described as making a good-faith effort. That is, she is attempting to compose discourse that would meet with acceptable responses within the academy. In our experience, however, students sometimes attempt to challenge accepted subject positions, and not in the critical, leftist way that Cooper envisions. Particularly in the wake of recent political events, we have seen open expression of opinions that would customarily be anathema to the values of "academic discourse" in its broadest sense, including racist, sexist, homophobic forms of discourse. In such situations, the tutor faces a difficult decision to use NDMTMs and hope that such a line of questioning will either help the student reconsider her or his argument or make the unethical discourse more academic and stylish, or to occupy the deliberative position and directly oppose the student, likely resulting in an abrupt end to the tutorial.

Michael Pemberton addresses this conundrum in a series of columns for the *Writing Lab Newsletter* by sketching scenarios and asking how tutors might respond. One such scenario involves a hypothetical white, male student who had composed a paper about affirmative action. Pemberton writes:

> This student has chosen affirmative action as a topic, and it is clear from the first few minutes of the conference that the student has strong feelings about it. When you ask him to give a brief overview of his paper before you both look at it more closely, he responds by saying that he thinks that "affirmative action is the dumbest thing [he's] ever heard of." He goes on to say that "black people shouldn't be allowed in most colleges anyway since they're almost all criminals or crackheads. Besides," he continues, "if they're too stupid to get into college on their own, why should we make it any easier for them?" He wants you, as a tutor, to look over the paper with him and make sure it's well-organized and supported. (1994b, 8)

Pemberton notes the "inflammatory" language of the paper and the recalcitrance of the student to consider further argument beyond what he has presented and then solicits responses from his readership.

Two responses highlight the more traditional approaches to tutoring, and we argue here that they are equally unhelpful. One respondent writes that she "would make no direct attempt to alter the content of any of these papers" (Pemberton 1994a, 15) and that she would simply declare the opinions expressed to be "repugnant" and then decide whether to allow the tutorial to continue or not. Her reasoning is based on her support for the First Amendment and the implication that the student's freedom of speech is meaningless if that freedom is not upheld. If we take this response as a starting point, two possible outcomes are likely. The first, less likely, outcome is that the student agrees to stay and participate in the tutorial. In this case, the tutor would be required to help make the student's argument stronger and more eloquent—in short, to retain bad speech but make it smarter sounding. The second outcome is that the student will leave, and likely not happily. In this case, the student's right to free speech would be upheld,[2] but he would likely be alienated from another arm of a liberal institution and would lose access to a potentially valuable set of interlocutors.

Pemberton includes a second perspective from a writing center tutor who was quoted anonymously. The tutor stated, "I would suggest to [the student] that they consider alternative ways of viewing the issue so that they might express their strong feelings in a less offensive and hostile manner" (1994a, 15). The tutor continues by recommending that the student "do some more critical thinking about what it is they really want to say, and . . . rework their papers to reflect their own beliefs, regardless of their professors' [opinions]" (15). While the advice is well intentioned, it's also strikingly similar to Grimm's characterization of the advice given to many academically uninitiated students, namely, that the tutor disguise the institutional expectations of liberal argumentation in anodyne advice. Simply telling a student to do more "critical thinking," while it does avoid the potential direct challenge, doesn't help the student develop. Is a student who drafted a paper hostile to ideas of racial equality on his or her own and in the context of a college course likely to "rework their paper to reflect their own beliefs" in a way that is significantly different and more academically acceptable?

THE DELIBERATIVE POSITION AND THE
IDEOLOGICAL FRAMEWORK OF LITERACY

Deliberative discourse—the dominant academic mode of discourse that invites questions, skepticism, and revision—is unlikely to sway members of noncontingent or absolutist communities toward acceptable academic opinions. Yet, as Arabella Lyon, in *Deliberative Acts: Democracy, Rhetoric, and Rights* argues, "Contemporary deliberations . . . often engage members of disparate communities who refuse, counter, or do not attend to the opposing arguments" (2013, 33). The deliberative tradition, which Lyon traces down from Aristotle, depends on the rhetor knowing the audience and perhaps, just as important, the docility of the audience. That is to say, the Aristotelian tradition assumes that the speaker generally understands (and likely shares) the values of the audience. She notes that the enthymeme, with its missing minor or major premise, demonstrates this kind of knowledge best: it doesn't need to be stated—we know it; our audience knows it; everybody knows it. Furthermore, the audience is docile. As she says, the audience listens, is persuaded, and then leaves through the exits (34). More modern conceptions of persuasion require a different means of moving an audience—one in which the speaker might not know the values of an audience, to say nothing of actually sharing them. For these more contemporary rhetorical situations, Lyon observes, "speech is not about coming to consensus and a tautological peace, but rather about worldly action, finding in-betweens, shared interests, and new discursive regimes" (128). Such interests can be found in the deliberative possibilities of the performed self—one that responds to Hannah Arendt's question, "Who are you?" The question, as Lyon states, opens up the possibility of relation in-between two individuals. That is to say, asking the question "takes us to a narratable self that necessarily involves recognizing the other as different and valuable, because to recognize her is to recognize her life as different but worthy of telling" (80). In asking "who are you," a point might emerge between tutor and student, and this point might be a place where both are implicated and exposed. Both tutor and student might emerge with stories to tell and, in that storytelling, may find themselves talking in a different register. In this storytelling that emerges in-between (another queering concept), Crowley's discussion of a civil discourse speaks to Lyon's.

Crowley's work calls for a similar kind of in-between to emerge not through singular arguments, but rather in working through alternatives. Arguments like the one in the male student's hypothetical essay are problematic not necessarily because they are illiberal in content but rather because they grow out of modes of thinking that only permit singular arguments. Crowley claims that "rhetors who posit unities that transcend temporal and local contexts are making bad arguments because the assertion of a noncontingent foundation shuts down the search for available alternatives" (2006, 130). Conversely, Crowley argues that good rhetoric is inventive: it opens avenues that find all possible arguments. For writing centers, Crowley offers a model for the formation of more ethical, inventive writers in the form of both students and tutors. In many ways, noncontingent thinking is exceptionally difficult to counter because as Crowley freely admits, it often relies on authoritarian leadership and strong community identity rather than the liberal ideals of multiplicity and skepticism.

Lyon suggests that deliberation begin with "recognition" and "reciprocity" (2013, 35). Two sides must recognize difference, and then there must be "reciprocal claim upon the other so that they are willing to discuss those differences" (35). But how can people, particularly writing tutors and students, enter into such relations? Crowley offers a path that honors community membership and recognizes that such membership often influences rhetorical style: "Rhetorically speaking, insiders engage chiefly in epideictic discourse, either praising community values or devaluing the beliefs circulating in other communities. Deliberative rhetors, on the other hand, risk becoming outsiders to a community because they must, of necessity, advocate attention to discontinuity or difference" (2006, 196). In other words, the deliberative position threatens the authority of a closed community, making members of such communities likely to avoid it, and therefore a student confronted with deliberative discourse (either in class or in the writing center) is not likely to be persuaded by the deliberative rhetor's rationale.

One such way of resituating these ways of knowing can be found in our earlier writing center scenario, in which the two approaches allowed by NDMTMs put the tutor into a kind of deliberative stance. When the second tutor recommends telling the student-writer to go do some more critical thinking, it challenges the institutional authority and the community identity of the student who believes affirmative action to be a farce. Thus, the tutor moves outside of the student's community by suggesting that he has not done nearly enough critical thinking. The suggestion may well be true, but the student with the paper is not going to see it that way. He may not have done the thinking, but he believes that some authorities in his community certainly have, which should suffice. The alternative tactic, openly declaring disagreement with the student's argument but then continuing with the tutorial for the sake of protecting free speech, also puts the tutor in a deliberative position, which would no doubt prompt a contentious discussion. In Crowley's framework, the student is arguing epideictically (performing for his own community) while writing tutors are acting in the deliberative role they have been traditionally cast in—agents of liberal skepticism, literal questioners.

Grimm suggests another possibility, which is to point out the tacit ideological implications of the assignment and to show how the assignment wants to construct the student. Following Grimm, the tutor could have a conversation with the student about the subject matter and what forms of argument and evidence might be expected in the university setting. The tutor would then be able to align herself or himself more closely with the student as they explored academic identities and liberal assumptions. In this way, Grimm's ideological view of literacy might align itself with another of Crowley's suggestions regarding persuasion: "A second route is to demonstrate the contingency of given values or sets of values by locating them within space and time" (Crowley 2006, 201). Showing the contingency of a set of values, Crowley indicates, could potentially destabilize those values, leading to a shift in mentality. Also, as Denny shows us, "For mainstream society, ways of knowing seem natural, but their very contingency becomes apparent when their assumptions come into proximity to others marked by racial, gender, class, sexual, national and other forms of difference" (2010, 47). Thus, as the tutor and student explore the values that the academy expects of the student, both begin to see how both those liberal, secular positions the academy valorizes and the racist values of the student are contingent. Crowley's suggestion that rhetors follow a more value-laden set of conversations—articulating different values or the contingency of those values—formulates a rhetoric that invokes intervention as unhurried conversation.

Crowley offers a third option in this situation, however, one that might take significant time and patience to implement but that possibly has the greatest ethical potential: using the inventive capacity of ethical discourse. Crowley's definition of ethical discourse looks beyond traditional liberal/conservative and academic/unacademic binaries, and her approach aligns perhaps more closely with the one-to-one dynamics within the writing center than the sometimes-hurried group discussion of traditional classrooms. Regarding ethical discourse, Crowley writes, "The point of ethical rhetorical exchange is never to shut down argumentative possibilities but to generate all the positions that are available and articulable in a given moment and situation. An ethical rhetor can never foreclose the possibility that an opposing argument will open new lines of rhetorical force. Good rhetoric looks for all available arguments, just as Aristotle insisted. Bad rhetoric, on the other hand, is static and univocal" (2006, 56). Crowley's focus on the inventive potential of rhetorical exchange, rather than on its content, suggests a way to defuse ideological encounters by posing questions about the possible rather than the actual. Although these kinds of questions may resemble the global focus of NDMTMs, they can shift the focus from what the student *has written* to what *could be written* about a subject, allowing the tutor and the student to each participate as "ethical rhetors" in the conversation, rather than restricting the tutor to open-ended questions about the paper itself or a deliberative position that the student will likely regard as hostile.

This kind of work is also envisioned by Nancy Welch (1999) from a psychoanalytic perspective as "putting statements into play," or exploring the possible rather than the actual. The excess and pleasure Welch locates in "in play" encounters provide a vivid contrast to the adversarial (and ostensibly unpleasurable) dynamics offered by the deliberative stance. Within the kind of exchange imagined by Welch and Crowley, tutors and students consider possibilities together. In Welch's description, a tutor would not ignore a statement from a student, but she wouldn't necessarily accept it either. Rather, the tutor would bring "the starting statement *into play*" by asking the student to consider a possible relationship between the original statement and a new object (62; emphasis in original). Welch comments that these relationships are crucial for both students and tutors to form "possible connections among the different spheres, activities, and values that make up their lives" (63).

Following Crowley, one way of putting statements into play is for tutors and students to share personal stories with each other. Crowley describes the utterly central role of pathos in persuasion, writing, "A rhetor who wants to alter beliefs has to arouse an affective response—to get attention. A rhetorical appeal to a belief may arouse or intensify an emotional response if it either confirms or denies some element of the targeted belief system" (2006, 199). Indeed, the conversational modus operandi of the writing center may be better able to persuade than the more argumentative "contact zone" of the classroom—marked as it is by, in Mary Pratt's words, "highly asymmetrical relations of power" (1991, 34). Amplifying the impact of stories is the personal connection ("rapport") often formed between tutor and student, even in the short time of a tutorial. Although the aim of ethical tutoring is not necessarily to "persuade" but rather to open new avenues of argumentation, Crowley's insistence on the impact of stories suggests their usefulness in convincing others to consider other experiences and subsequently expand their positions—in short, to invent.

A tutorial modeled on this kind of ethical discourse might proceed as follows. After reading the paper, the tutor might restate her understanding of the student's argument. She might then ask if the student could think of any other arguments that could be made about the topic—not necessarily arguments that the student agrees with, but any possible arguments. In the likely event that the student fails to come up with anything, the tutor might abandon her NDMTMs and tell a personal story that leads into a different interpretation of the topic. She might then tell a second story that leads into another argument entirely, and the conversation might develop from there. The stories might involve a discussion of the time the tutor believed she was judged prejudicially. Perhaps the tutor might discuss a time in which she changed her mind after encountering someone with a completely different background and perspective. Or, she might just relate a story about the basics of some aspect of white privilege and the fact that she is often surrounded by other white people rather than persons of color—the kinds of stories would change with the dynamics of the individual tutor and student.

The main point would be to offer these stories in the hopes that the student across from her would feel inclined to respond, and not in a hostile way. This approach obviously requires a great deal of empathy and patience from both the student and the tutor, but it is also the method that respects both the student's and the tutor's nonstatic subject positions and the one that might be most likely to convince him to engage in multiple viewpoints, one of the hallmarks of academic thinking, even if he doesn't ultimately change his argument. Whichever type of session is employed, as Denny remarks, "Proximity becomes a crucial tipping point for piercing the naturalized; only by queering the conversation does a different sort of learning happen" (2010, 47). The queered learning taking place, we would argue, has much in common with Lyon's concept of "remonstration." Largely developed from the Confucian tradition, remonstration is explained by Lyon thus: "If, in persuading, there is an audience to be induced or moved toward an end, then in remonstration, the onus is on the speaker to perform and to represent a position to an interlocutor who is observing, assessing, judging, and controlling the level of engagement" (2013, 41). The tutor is the one in the position of representing the other (and "othered") positions in an attempt to engage the student. The tutor avoids traditional deliberative argument but also offers a great deal more than anodyne suggestions. What's more, Lyon shows, there is no obligation in remonstration to find consensus. That is to say, we need not ultimately close down possibility nor find the single answer. We understand remonstration as part of a process—one that is a good in and of itself.

CONCLUSION

Naturally, some students who visit the writing center will resist this conversational approach—just as some students who visit the writing center resist many tutor approaches. Other students come to the writing center as a "hospital," solely for feedback on technical aspects of their writing—punctuation, style, mistakes—writing's "diseases." These students will also likely resist or hurry through any kind of global engagement with their writing. However, this approach might initiate students into academic thinking, not through deliberative rhetoric but through invention and the exploration of possibility, and reflexively expand inventive possibilities for tutors as well.

We certainly do not seek to eliminate non-directive methods; like process pedagogy, they have their place. However, following the call of writing center theorists such as Denny and Geller et al., we want to reframe student identity and literacy within the postmodern paradigm and highlight the writing center's great potential for rhetorical invention using unhurried conversations. It is at the impasse between ideological conflict and traditional non-directive methods that the hidden tension between a student's multifaceted identity and the university's modernist paradigm becomes visible. Rather than ignoring that tension, the writing center offers an alternative path to ethical invention—one that implicates both student and peer tutor. This kind of unhurried conversation might be seen as both queering the path of rhetorical invention and creating meaning that "is negotiated among mutually engaged participants" and that "involves the whole person" (Geller et al. 2007, 7).

As Crowley notes, we can't typically "argue" people into changing their mind. Rather, we have to generate a different kind of response. In these situations, we must think through Denny's call to bring other practices into view and possibly use Lyon's concept of remonstration. A conversational technique, par excellence, remonstration doesn't lead to a specific goal, but instead follows an unpredictable path. Naturally, such invention is no panacea for all the "ills" that often attend student thinking. However, as we seek to help students understand the ways various pieces of writing construct them, and to help them understand the modes of thought employed by the academy, we offer to try and slow things down, if only temporarily, so that a student can engage in new networks.

Networked through social media, our cultural milieu is one in which the personal and ideological mingle as we simultaneously post photographs of ourselves and share deeply held principles. Much of what we do seems to call out to others, "Know me." Writing centers are now uniquely positioned to expose and read the tensions that appear when students call out to be known within the probing, skeptical climate of higher education. Moreover, writing centers have the unique potential—and even responsibility—to engage with students who bring unethical arguments to us, both by being open to knowing those students and by putting those arguments into play to expose their contingency and harm. Although the university is built on ideals of open exchange, we know that such exchange is often short-circuited. However, writing centers have long recognized that conversations contain and implicate both parties. The unhurried conversation in the writing center shows ways to know and to be known while also offering hope for altering unethical speech and producing genuine persuasion.

NOTES

1.   Critiques of non-directive tutoring are not scarce in writing center literature, including Grimm's work and Shamoon and Burns's (1996) quintessential piece. Although these critiques exist, however, they are mainly limited to "exceptional" circumstances involving English-language-learning students, first-generation and nonwhite college students, and graduate students, reinforcing the imagined centrality of a majority white, middle-class student body with other groups as the "exception" (see, for example, Matsuda [2006]). A survey of several popular tutor training manuals demonstrates that such critiques exist mainly for writing center administrators and advanced tutors.

2.   It might be worth considering the issue of free speech and whether a more direct intervention is in violation. For Fish (1994)—who has argued that all communities, even liberal communities, restrict speech to some extent and that those restrictions are what allow speech at all—the issue is something of a red herring. In the academy, Fish points out, academics themselves are the ones who determine whether an argument is academic through processes like peer review. He suggests, "[Academic] values, which include the search for truth and the promotion of virtue, are capacious enough to accommodate a diversity of views. But at some point . . . fidelity to the original values will demand acts of extirpation" (103). In this case, for example, there may be possible objections to affirmative action, but they are, most likely, arguments made from economics or other fields. Thus, the student can possibly be steered toward using academic sources to buttress his argument. If no such sources exist, then the matter is settled—the argument lies outside of academic argument. Thus, in Fish's framework, an article in the writing center is not free speech, nor does an attempt to intervene represent its restriction.

REFERENCES

Brooks, Jeff. 1995. "Minimalist Tutoring: Making the Student Do All the Work." In *The St. Martin's Sourcebook for Writing Tutors*, ed. Christina Murphy and Steve Sherwood, 83–87. Boston: St. Martin's.

Bruffee, Kenneth. 1995. "Peer Tutoring and the Conversation of Mankind." In *Landmark Essays on Writing Centers*, ed. Christina Murphy and Joe Law, 87–98. Davis, CA: Hermagoras Press.

Clark, Irene L., and Dave Healy. 1996. "Are Writing Centers Ethical?" *WPA* 20 (1/2): 32–48.

Cooper, Marilyn M. 2008. "Really Useful Knowledge: A Cultural Studies Agenda for Writing Centers." In *Longman Guide to Writing Center Theory and Practice*, ed. Robert W. Barnett and Jacob S. Blumner, 335–49. New York: Pearson Longman.

Crowley, Sharon. 1993. "Modern Rhetoric and Memory." *Rhetorical Memory and Delivery*, ed. John Frederick Reynolds, 31–44. Hillsdale, NJ: Lawrence Erlbaum.

Crowley, Sharon. 1998. *Composition in the University*. Pittsburgh: University of Pittsburgh Press.

Crowley, Sharon. 2006. *Toward a Civil Discourse: Rhetoric and Fundamentalism*. Pittsburgh: University of Pittsburgh Press.

Denny, Harry. 2010. *Facing the Center: Toward an Identity Politics of One-to-One Mentoring.* Logan: Utah State University Press.

Dobrin, Sidney I. 2011. *Postcomposition.* Carbondale: Southern Illinois University Press.

Fish, Stanley. 1994. *There's No Such Thing as Free Speech: And It's a Good Thing Too.* Oxford: Oxford University Press.

Geller, Anne Ellen, Michele Eodice, Frankie Condon, Meg Carroll, and Elizabeth H. Boquet. 2007. *The Everyday Writing Center: A Community of Practice.* Logan: Utah State University Press.

Grimm, Nancy. 1999. *Good Intentions: Writing Center Work for Postmodern Times.* New York: Heinemann.

Grimm, Nancy. 2011. "Retheorizing Writing Center Work to Transform a System of Advantage Based on Race." In *Writing Centers and the New Racism: A Call for Sustainable Dialogue and Change,* ed. Laura Greenfield and Karen Rowan, 75–100. Logan: Utah State University Press.

Lyon, Arabella. 2013. *Deliberative Acts: Democracy, Rhetoric, and Rights.* University Park: Penn State University Press. Rhetoric and Democratic Deliberation. EBSCOhost.

Matsuda, Paul Kei. 2006. "The Myth of Linguistic Homogeneity in U.S. College Composition." *College English* 68 (6): 637–51.

North, Stephen M. 1984. "The Idea of a Writing Center." *College English* 46 (5): 433–46.

Pemberton, Michael A. 1992. "The Prison, the Hospital, and the Madhouse: Redefining Metaphors for the Writing Center." *Writing Lab Newsletter* 17 (1): 11–16.

Pemberton, Michael A. 1994a. "Directive Non-Directiveness: Readers' Responses to Troublesome Scenarios." *Writing Lab Newsletter* 18 (10): 15–16.

Pemberton, Michael A. 1994b. "The Ethics of Intervention: Part II." *Writing Lab Newsletter* 18 (5): 8–9.

Pratt, Mary Louise. 1991. "Arts of the Contact Zone." *Profession* 1991: 33–40.

Shamoon, Linda K., and Deborah H. Burns. 1996. "A Critique of Pure Tutoring." *Writing Center Journal* 16 (2): 94–97.

Welch, Nancy. 1999. "Playing with Reality: Writing Centers after the Mirror Stage." *College Composition and Communication* 51 (1): 51–69.

10

NO BODY IS DISINTERESTED
The Discursive Materiality of Composition in the University

Kirsti Cole

Twenty years after the publication of Sharon Crowley's *Composition in the University*, her work still resonates deeply, not only in her framing of our continued pedagogical innovations, but also because of her understanding of our labor practices: "For most of its history . . . the required first-year composition course has been taught by untenured faculty" (1998, 5). Compositionists are ready to make arguments to administration about the cost benefit of first-year writing, writing across the curriculum, or TA training programs in order to protect, tenuously, teaching-assistant lines, a new hire, or an entire program. Our expertise in theories of rhetoric, in invention, places us in a position to powerfully negotiate the trends around labor and economy. However, our lived experiences gatekeeping the curriculum, maintaining the budgets, and relying on adjunct labor at our institutions hinder us from doing so. These material conditions connect directly to the rhetoric of crisis created by neoliberal policy in higher education. It is no surprise to compositionists, as we have lamented (though done little to improve) one of the clear material conditions of neoliberalism: the ever-increasing reliance on faculty with no job security.[1]

Nancy Welch and Tony Scott's (2016) collection contains a series of critical readings of and responses to the impacts of neoliberalism on education. Our "managerial unconscious" (Strickland 2011), as Welch and Scott argue, leaves us "insufficiently prepared to respond to austerity measures and vulnerable to the new entrepreneurial schemes" (2016, 7). The constraints of austerity demand that we reread Crowley with careful attention to the bodies doing the work. Taking as permission Crowley's use of personal narrative, I foreground my discussion of labor practices in composition with a brief discussion of my own foray into institutionalized writing programs.

When I was hired, it was the first time that my university had two composition and rhetoric scholars on staff. Part of my job was to create a

DOI: 10.7330/9781607328933.c010

series of graduate courses in composition and rhetoric for our teaching associate (TA) population. After launching a series of courses, I started an online program for teachers who want credentials in composition and communication theory and pedagogy. In other words, without thinking through the implications, I contributed to the cycle of justifying my existence as a compositionist by training more people to teach to the universal requirement.

As Crowley argues, "The required first-year course still serves American universities as a border checkpoint, the institutional site wherein students either provide proper identification or retreat to wherever they came from" (1998, 231). In this particular case, she is focusing on students enrolled in first-year composition. Now, however, we must account for students enrolled in credentialing apparatuses in order to *teach* first-year composition. In the same way that composition classrooms were gatekeeping mechanisms for undergraduates in 1998 and before, we can now argue that first-year composition is even more of a gatekeeping mechanism for graduate students and teaching faculty, many of whom are contingent. Crowley locates this contingent phenomenon in the economics of the post-Fordist economy: specialized jobs, emphasis on consumers, and the feminization of the workforce. She argues that the reliance on part time or "disposable faculty" advantages administrations. However, she also claims that tenured faculty are "complicit in their own demise" (254) because as the requirements for tenure become more stringent, they work to maintain the material conditions of the post-Fordist economy.

The recent increase in low-paying, no-benefits, contingent jobs in higher education demonstrates our complacency in the changing material landscape of labor in higher education. As our areas of specialization increase, as we accept more graduate students into our programs (in many cases to fund the program, but not the graduate students, adequately), and train them for research jobs that don't exist, we reinforce the cycle that the post-Fordist or neoliberal university has created for us. In 1998, Crowley was uncertain about whether or not these labor conditions would undercut the power of disciplinarity. In fact, if anything, neoliberalism artificially reinforces disciplinarity, forcing us into an era of constant budget crises to create and defend disciplinary silos, competing with other departments for limited funding instead of working together to do productive and powerful interdisciplinary research and teaching. The most commonly cited definition emphasizes that neoliberalism is both the operation of a market, and an ethic—one that guides action and belief (Treanor 2005). In academic terms this means that activities in higher education are interpreted as market-like and that the market-like activity of higher education creates and guides how we perceive value. Our perception of value, from an administrative standpoint, seems to be focused on cheap labor. In state institutions in particular, the market crisis has resulted in an educational crisis that faculty and academic administrators such as WPAs are directed to find ways around—the usual directive amounts to "be cheaper."

My department can barely keep up with the demand created by our online program. With the addition of the Higher Learning Commission's (HLC; my university's accrediting agency) requirements that any subject-area instructor at the college level must have eighteen credits in a particular subject area to teach in that subject, I almost drowned in incoming requests. At one point in spring 2016, I received almost one hundred emails each day from prospective students desperate to remain teaching in the profession they had been in for years (some of them up to two decades). The HLC has helped create a demand for my program by compelling student need. My students are employable only if they complete eighteen credits in my program, regardless of how many years they have been teaching composition. Crowley addresses the conditions of need for first-year writing, critiquing the interpellation that occurs when teachers implement institutional aspirations: "The requirement has nothing to do with what students need and everything to do with the academy's image of itself as a place where a special language is in use. The discourse of needs positions composition teachers as servants of a student need that is spoken, not by students themselves, but by people speaking for powerful institutions. Like the narrative of progress, the discourse of needs interpellates composition teachers as subjects who implement the regulatory desires of the academy and of the culture at large" (1998, 257). The discourse of need propagated by the HLC has interpellated me, as a subject of the academy, and has turned my program into a hoop through which teachers must jump, a list to check off, in order to avoid termination.

The inherent contradiction in this discourse of need is what makes Crowley's work so important for compositionists in the twenty-first century. When I approached my administration about hiring a full-time tenure-track faculty member for our online program so that we could increase our enrollments (the hook that I used, of course, made me complicit in shoddy labor ethics: if we hire one person on the tenure track we will increase university coffers since online students pay significantly more than face-to-face students), I was flatly refused. My dean told me that if we were reaching capacity, we should just stop accepting students. Baffled, I asked her why in an era during which faculty are *constantly* talked at about recruitment and retention, why when our own university just hired a (white, male) vice president of enrollment management, the administration would not only dismiss this faculty-led, pedagogically sound gift horse, but tell me to cut back on enrollments in my program. The answer: because full-time faculty are a budget deficit and adjunct or "fixed-term" (adjuncts on a three-year contract with healthcare benefits) are cheaper. *My administration considers full-time, tenured faculty to be a budget deficit.* In other words, a highly lucrative graduate program that requires no physical space and is extremely low cost is dismissed because it is not part of the administrative plan for our campus. This resembles Crowley's discussion of the universal requirement of first-year composition. Programs like mine are the new normal for service programs in composition.

ON CROWLEY: REVISITING COMPOSITION IN THE UNIVERSITY

Although there are differences to be noted—such as the shift in conditions noted above—in many ways Crowley's entire book remains pertinent because, as my review will demonstrate, much has remained the same for composition in the university. There are three conditions in particular that Crowley identifies from which we can draw useful perspectives.

Condition 1: *"Composition specialists who have achieved success in the academic terms of promotion and tenure are often reminded . . . that composition is still not widely regarded as a legitimate field of study" (Crowley 1998, 5).*

The label, and accompanying rhetorical baggage, of the service course translates into a service discipline. As Eileen Schell reminds us, part of the Janus-faced reputation of composition as a service-oriented profession signals both the presence of women in the classroom and their absence from positions of power (1992, 55). The feminization of composition seems to be a component of Crowley's insistence that there be no universal requirement for composition. Even when she imagines this, she posits that we might simply trade an "old master" [departments of English] for a new one: "Hence it does nothing to disrupt the unprofessional and unethical practices that are currently associated with required composition instruction such as hasty hiring, low pay, low status, denial of academic freedom, and intellectual coercion of students and teachers" (Crowley 1998, 29). Her focus here, then, becomes the radical possibilities in disrupting our everyday labor practices, and she traces the history of those labor practices: "First-year composition has always been staffed by people identified as teachers rather than scholars—whether this identification is accurate or not" (121–22). Her description here mirrors Sue Ellen Holbrook's, who writes, "[Composition is] saturated by women practitioners, focused on pedagogy" (1991, 211). Crowley outlines this identification—as teachers not scholars—in order to emphasize the power structures of the academy that remain in place now.

When Jason Brennan, the libertarian philosopher who is fond of the phrase "madjuncts," presses his audience to consider possible outcomes for the adjunct justice movement, he holds up as an example the field of composition. In defending his position on the "business ethics" of the modern university he says, "One of the things [co-author Phil Magness] and I [will] explore is how first-year composition classes appear to be ineffective, and are little more than a jobs program for low quality intellectuals" (2016, n.p.). He seems to take aim at compositionists because one of the individuals who critiques his most recent publication on the business ethics of hiring in academic contexts is, according to him, "a former English madjunct and current activist" who "complains that when we say that adjuncts presumably prefer being adjuncts over whatever their next best option is, we thereby assume that academia is a level playing field." Brennan goes on to claim that Magness and he were not arguing that there is a level playing field but rather that "the very fact that adjuncts stay adjuncts, despite the lousy conditions is—if we assume they are not irrational, misinformed, or stupid—evidence that this is what they consider their best option." This position is stunningly obtuse for someone who claims to be an expert on business ethics, but the aim taking at composition was particularly interesting in that it reinforces our status as illegitimate. In other words, compositionists are an easy target—unrecognized as scholars and scorned as teachers.[2]

With such a large number of compositionists in tenured positions, running writing programs, WAC/WID (Writing across the Disciplines / Writing in the Disciplines) programs, and writing centers, it seems like we should have more agency in the larger discourses of academia. Nevertheless, labor conditions persist in composition programs as they have for decades. For Crowley, Jean Foucault provides a possible explanation: "According to Foucault, the power exercised by modern disciplines is invisible. However, that invisible power consists in the ability of discipline's agents to make individuals visible, so that the capacity of each individual may be measured against the (invisible) standards set by the discipline. The examination has the added advantage, from the point of view of agents of the discipline, of putting individual rankings on display, so that the capacity of individuals . . . may be measured against each other or against other groups vis à vis their relation to the discipline" (1998, 69). Crowley locates here the problem with disciplinary agency. The matrix of invisibility and visibility can and does reinforce a hierarchy of power, rendering those who work within the institutional base visible (and in some cases powerful), and those who do not or cannot invisible, or in the case of Jason Brennan, worthy of scorn.

Condition 2: "I fear that [compositionists] may have learned only too well the lessons taught them by their colleagues in literary studies—that required composition provides full-time faculty with a firm institutional base from which to operate an academic empire" (Crowley 1998, 18).

It is no secret that there is money in composition programs. When first-year composition is a required course, the larger the incoming (traditional, nontransfer) first-year class, the more tuition dollars the university collects. Many WPAs and/or English department chairs have used this reality to make arguments to bolster and build wonderful programs, some of which are staffed primarily with tenure and tenure-track faculty. Crowley locates this within a history of the discipline: "It is worthy of note that Freshman English was the only course that remained as a universal requirement throughout the sixty years (1880–1940) during which the American professoriate created a large number of specialized disciplines and expanded their curricula accordingly" (1998, 167). The majority of contemporary composition programs, however, rely on graduate or non-tenure-track faculty to teach first-year composition: "Even though the cultural roles played by universities and by literary studies itself have changed enormously since the instauration of English studies, the lowly functions envisioned for composition instruction by the Harvard overseers still remain in place in American colleges and universities, fulfilled then and ever since by the universal requirement in introductory composition" (253). I do not cite Crowley here to claim that our field does not recognize these labor practices as problematic, nor do I think that these graduate students and contingent faculty are not excellent teachers.

However, I wonder if our budget management and good departmental citizenship might make composition complicit in the more unsavory practices of academic empire building.

Crowley questions this in the context of instruction in a course, but I will paraphrase her in this way: "I doubt whether it is possible to radicalize [a field] that is so thoroughly implicated in the maintenance of cultural and academic hierarchy" (1998, 235). Of course, nothing in my discussion of the material conditions of labor in composition is new. Perhaps that is part of the problem. The discursive reality of labor in the field is so ubiquitous that it is almost boring—background noise. Crowley reminds compositionists of an important fact: "Until 1940 or so, composition classes were taught by full-time teachers, although they generally were the newest members of the permanent faculty" (118). However, after the postwar enrollment boom and the explosion of graduate programs a few decades later, composition became both more embedded in disciplinarity and increasingly staffed by part-time workers. Although this may seem like a contradiction, the increased demand for, and location of, standing composition programs at colleges and universities required a cheap labor solution to fill the need gap created by the enrollment increases. Crowley locates the discourse surrounding part-time labor within colonial theory: "Anyone who is familiar with colonial studies will recognize the metaphors in which composition teachers have been depicted in the discourse of English studies—as children, serfs, prisoners, and slaves—to be part and parcel of the language of imperialism. . . . Composition teachers were also depicted as poverty stricken, a description that was all too accurate in many cases" (127–28). Crowley is concerned not only about poverty-level wages,[3] but also about the ideological and material impacts that can occur when an academic has no academic status.

Condition 3: "For most of its history, then, the required first-year composition course has been taught by untenured faculty" (Crowley 1998, 4).

Given the indefensible conditions in composition programs, Crowley made her modest proposal in 1998 to "abolish the universal requirement" (240). In her list of six reasons for ending *required* first-year composition, two speak to labor issues and the material conditions of teachers. The first is that "the universal requirement exploits teachers of writing, particularly part-time teachers and graduate students" (240). In her own experiences teaching first-year writing, Crowley reflects on a particularly difficult term and a series of bad teaching evaluations that she received. She understood the bad evaluations as having to do at least in part with her gender and her ideological position. For Crowley, a little bit of anger and some reflection were all she needed in order move forward. However, she is explicit about her own privilege as a tenured faculty member: "If the teacher of the first-year course is unranked, untenured, and utterly without academic status, she does not have the luxury of responding angrily to bad evaluations" (226). It's an interesting rhetorical move to think about anger as a luxury, but of course, it isn't just human emotional capital to which contingent faculty have no access.

Crowley problematizes the stalwart of the academy through the lens of academic status: "Academic freedom is, historically, the notion that entitled university faculty to relative security of employment" (1998, 237). However, "the right to academic freedom has never applied, and does not now apply, to the huge corps of teachers who, year in and year out, teach Freshman English" (238). Crowley argues that academic freedom is tied to tenure and security, but "the bulk of Freshman English teachers, the bulk of English faculty, not only never did have tenure, they never will, as long as the universal requirement imposes a prescribed curriculum on them and their students" (238). And if an instructor is not on the tenure track, she cannot have academic freedom—or indeed any freedom, including the ability to show negative emotions. The connection between prescribed curriculum and employment is one that Crowley discusses at some length, but for the purposes of this chapter, prescribed curriculum connects to the idea of the academic empire.

The second reason Crowley gives for ending the requirement is that "the requirement has negative professional effects. Composition studies is far too invested in the universal requirement. We composition professionals have used the requirements to establish a firm institutional base, and hence we are implicated in all of the unsavory institutional practices it entails" (1998, 243). Crowley is not alone in critiquing the sometimes unsavory practices of institutionalized composition, but contemporary critiques of the field and its position in the university must be read through the crisis rhetoric of austerity.

CONTEMPORARY CONTEXTS: CROWLEY'S COMPOSITION IN THE NEOLIBERAL UNIVERSITY

In their introduction, Welch and Scott claim that composition has served as a "canary in a coalmine" for the "wide-scale restructuring of higher education as a whole" (2016, 5). They argue "austerity and a low-frequency sense of crisis are nothing new to the field. The professional lives of compositionists . . . have long been characterized by making do in an institutional borderland" (5). But, Tony Scott writes, "The center is not holding" (2016, 215). He is not the only author to point to the potential demise of the field of rhetoric and composition or writing studies. Ann Larson argues, "For those of us who identify as compositionists, a principled disengagement from the failed politics of respectability and reform may be the only morally defensible choice in the discipline's aftermath" (2016, 163).

The ominous tone struck by Scott and Larson sounds throughout Welch and Scott's collection. The authors posit that the dominant labor practices in higher education were tested in departments and programs responsible for teaching first-year composition. They critique the structures of managerialism implicit in the marketized values of teaching and research. They argue that producing "post-hegemonic" or "post-critical" scholarship "cedes composition teaching to the realm of market algorithms and efficiency imperatives as it imagines a scholarly future for rhetoric blissfully detached from responsibility for and ideological struggle over writing education" (2016, 8). Their collection is bold in both its assessments and accusations of the ways in which first-year writing is positioned politically and rhetorically. Building from the conditions I outlined in the previous section, in this section I outline three contemporary contexts for composition in the university: austerity, "madjuncts," and gender inequality. These contexts function as ways through which to problematize and potentially strategize around the material conditions that shape the role of writing in curriculums at the first-year and graduate levels.

Context 1: Austerity

Welch and Scott define austerity as a set of policies enacted by governments and institutions, including institutions of higher education, to reduce budget deficits and cut programs, especially social programs, during the shock of especially bad economic times. It is an opportunistic ideological strategy that initiates funding cuts in the public sector that then becomes the new normal in policy over time (Welch and Scott 2016, 9). This definition provides an operational foundation from which to understand how economics and policy work together to impact our ideologies in higher education. The new normal of austerity has impacted most American institutions. The equation is relatively simple: as federal and state support for higher education dwindles, tuition goes up, as does administrative desperation for increased funding. Simultaneously, faculty and teachers are characterized as a problem when they push to make a living wage. Since administrators understand themselves as doing the heavy lifting of academic labor (aka—finding and shepherding money), they tend to view their labor as more important than the work educators do. "We as faculty members face shrinking instructional budgets, an increasingly contingent and underpaid faculty, a decline in state funding for higher education, and an increasingly competitive environment for external research funding[;] we are urged to be entrepreneurs, to find new streams of funding [that those who ostensibly exist in the administration to do so—and can't] while our students face rising tuition, fee rates, and soaring loan debt" (Schell 2016, 178). I read this summary as an intensification of the labor conditions Crowley outlined in 1998.

For Deborah Mutnick, Marx's understanding of consciousness and labor is integral to how we might address the impacts of austerity on our working conditions (2016). If the material conditions of labor determine consciousness, then composition must grapple with the ways in which neoliberalism and austerity shape our scholarship, our teaching practices, and our bodies. Mutnick echoes Crowley's proposal in some ways—composition must self-consciously confront the ways in which our labor practices impact our consciousness.

The ways in which compositionists are called upon to address the rhetoric of austerity are multitudinous in Welch and Scott's collection, and all the authors demand that compositionists begin to work in a different way: "We cannot stop at merely identifying the unequal distribution of our own privilege. So we must write and we must speak—we must bear witness to austerity and we must recognize human suffering—including our own suffering" (Bernstein 2016, 103). The bodily discursivity of Susan Bernstein's call to action places the outcome of austerity in sharp focus: the impact of crisis, of contingency on the lives of people doing the labor. If, as Sheri Stenberg argues, "austerity's ideological consequences determine who and what is deemed valuable, who and what counts as a 'good investment'" (2016, 191), then for compositionists, our historic displacement as legitimate academics intensifies. Our positionality as masquerading scholars is an easy stereotype to employ since "austerity is the looming threat of displacement . . . [of] agency, materiality, bodies, and labor" (Brannon 2016, 226). This displacement can happen in a number of ways including the increase in online education that moves away from face-to-face interactions between students and teachers, the increasing demand for course caps that undermine the effectiveness of writing pedagogy, and, perhaps, most significantly, the reliance on faculty who have no job security and are unable to make a living wage while teaching more classes than full-time faculty in the most teaching-intensive institutions.

Context 2: "Madjuncts"

The term "madjuncts" circulates on blogs written, for the most part, by philosophers and economists. It is a term used to dismiss adjunct justice activists, serving as a sort of shorthand for authors who want to claim that activist adjuncts are "crackpots" (Khawaja 2015) who live in an imaginary world of their own. Madjuncts are almost universally constructed as whiny babies who do not have what it takes to make it in higher education. This picture of the reliance on contingent labor in higher education and in composition not only is utterly shameful, but also in no way acknowledges the material conditions that construct and reify contingency, particularly the engineered split between tenure-track and not-tenure-track faculty.

Welch makes clear the binary between tenured labor and part-time labor: "The ranks of tenure-track faculty are increasingly threatened by the backlash against academia while those of poorly compensated, itinerant, contingent faculty and graduate students are multiplying everywhere, making it difficult to respond effectively to the corporate forces reshaping higher education" (2016, 44). And it is not only difficult to respond because of our material conditions; it is difficult to respond because of data. A 2009 study from the Department of Education claimed that over 70 percent of our teachers live on the academic borderland of part-time labor. A survey tool from the National Study of Postsecondary Faculty showed, in its early results, that that number is inaccurate; however, it lost funding in 2003, so the results were inconclusive. The latest data on the contingent labor force is a 2012 report, "A Portrait of Part-Time Faculty Members," published by the Coalition on the Academic Workforce (Coalition 2012), but the number of respondents who self-identified was small. A possible explanation for the lack of data is that adjuncts who speak out are characterized and dismissed as madjuncts, even in their own institutional contexts. Another explanation is that they are just too damn busy trying to survive to do much else.

Although we clearly need better data, we also clearly need to build coalitions in our local contexts around labor practices that writing programs bear witness to, and in some cases, perpetuate. Deborah Mutnick asks: "What might this mean for faculty in writing and rhetoric where post-Fordist labor practices expose glaring contradictions between the use of outcomes assessment to demonstrate academic excellence and reliance on heavily exploited, deprofessionalized faculty, many of whom teach middle- and working-class students whose own prospects for employment are at best unpredictable?" (2016, 45). Her answer is simple: faculty, both full-time and contingent, must work together to confront the values of the neoliberal academy that we do not share with our administrations. She gives the example of artificial assessment reports that in no way account for the complexities of the learning process (45), but there are many sites in which these confrontations might take place. The need for such confrontations indicates a problematic relationship between the material and intellectual: we are more likely to get tenure-track jobs if we are WPAs, but our intellectual work as WPAs has material impact on the lives of those who deploy our curriculum. Larson refers to the Wyoming Resolution to think through the inseparable history of low-wage labor and our status as a field. Instead of demanding justice, we demanded tenure (2016, 166–67). From my perspective, however, the Wyoming Resolution is a locus of power. Although prestige may not have accompanied composition's winning of rank and tenure, we did win it. The field was successful at the majority of institutions in mobilizing to get academic rank for nontraditional configurations of academic work. However, the history of the location of composition within higher education is still as important for us to understand now as it was for Crowley in the late 1990s.

Context 3: Gender Inequality

Many of the feminist scholars in composition and rhetoric have pointed to the domesticity narrative that prevails in discourse surrounding the field and the ways in which that narrative impacts the visibility and value of women's labor. The adjunct position is doubly implicated in the discursive construct of domesticity. The perception of adjunct teaching as a woman's profession is so pervasive that adjuncts are dubbed the housewives (Anokye 1996; Hairston 1985) of higher education (Schell 1998, 110). Stenberg reflects on the implications of adjuncts being defined as housewives: "From [Schell's] perspective we might say that the corporatizing winds blowing through higher education herald nothing new for writing instruction because writing instruction was privatized—consigned to the domestic sphere—long ago" (2016, 192).

If it is true that composition has served as a canary in a coalmine, it is also true that the canary was female. It is, in other words, easy to test out the restructuring of the neoliberal academy in a field long since identified by administrators as service, as domestic, as feminine: "As administrators try to offload the costs of core educational activities, they create bubbles of re-privatized domestic and un-waged labor among a university's profit-oriented centers . . . What we find in these bubbles of re-privatized and re-domesticated labor is the reordering not only of the terms of production but of social *reproduction* and social *provisioning*" (Stenberg 2016, 195–96). Stenberg notes the ways in which neoliberal values replace embodied actors by decontextualizing individuals and occluding attention to embodied subjectivities laboring in complex contexts (192). The New Faculty Majority Foundation notes a trend supporting the idea that individual agency and embodied actors are replaced in the dominant discursive materiality of austerity: "The rise in contingent faculty coincides with the rise of women enrolled in, and graduating from, doctoral-degree programs. There's a similar argument to made about race" (Baker 2015). Just as contemporary feminist theory and activism are productively intersectional (Cho, Crenshaw, and McCall 2013; Lykke 2010), so too must be our understanding of contingency in composition's labor practices.[4]

Intersectionality undergirds the possibilities for the ways in which composition might respond to austerity. The realities of gender, race, sexual orientation, ability, age, and class affect lived situations—the material conditions of difference can be deployed discursively in academic spaces regardless of academic status (Stenberg 2016). Stenberg proposes located agency ("examining valuing and taking responsibility for our locations") as an actionable strategy by which to "counter neoliberalism's coercive and repressive effects" (192). She argues that located agency "takes seriously both the limitations and possibilities that emerge from our material, embodied locations and knowledges, attending to how our geographic and institutional locations shape what is doable at any given moment" (194). Tony Scott offers a series of actions that compositionists can take within, in my reading, Stenberg's paradigm of located agency. He argues that compositionists should avoid dead-end scholarship for its own sake. He proposes an appeal to values shared by the various stakeholders in the academic learning process such as faculty, students, and parents (Scott 2016, 216). Building these kinds of coalitions, however, requires us to be vocal, informed critics. I do not use institutions here, because in many cases scholars and teachers off the tenure track are employed at multiple institutions, and so coalitions must form to account for environments beyond our silos and towers.

The challenges of the contemporary academy are intransigent, but Crowley's work nevertheless opens alternative possibilities for thinking about them. Instead of seeking security for ourselves, we must maintain critical, creative spaces in which alternative futures can be imagined and pursued. It is tempting to emphasize radical action in such a context; however, Crowley herself "[doubts] whether it is possible to radicalize [a field] that is so thoroughly implicated in the maintenance of cultural and academic hierarchy" (1998, 235). Instead of radicalizing, then, perhaps it is more important to simply *act*. Rather than using tenure as a secure platform for entrepreneurial profit-making, we must instead emphasize the embodied experiences of our teachers and students, our creative processes (216). We can begin to raise consciousness in our local contexts in order to build coalitions that can flexibly and strategically respond to our material and ideological conditions.

NOTES

The term "discursive" is used in the broadest possible sense, to refer to a mode of description characterized by awareness of the socially constructed and linguistically mediated nature of human experience. Similarly, the term "material" is extended to embrace any nonreductionist account of physical being that appears compatible with a discursive outlook (Yardley 1996).

1. In 1975, 30.2 percent of faculty were employed part time. By 2005, according to data compiled by Monks for the AAUP from the Integrated Postsecondary Education Data System (IPEDS), part-time faculty represented 48 percent of faculty members in the United States (Monks 2005).

2. My response to Brennan on his blog post: "As one of those 'low quality intellectuals' who runs a composition program, I request that you and your co-author seek out actual data on first-year composition instead of relying on blog comments and *Inside Higher Ed* interviews. There is a lot of peer-reviewed scholarship that people in other disciplines tend to wholesale ignore because they start with the assumption you make here: that composition scholars are low quality, lack rigor, or somehow don't count as academics. One of the books I would recommend you read is 'Composition in the Age of Austerity.' It would be a basic introduction to the field, but it might serve you well. Over fifty years of scholarship in the field is available to you. Obviously by your standards, you'll want to sort through all of that in order to make an educated claim about the relative efficacy of the curriculum. I'm happy to give you some pointers as I regularly educate new teachers of first-year composition on the history of the field, our methods and methodologies, and our labor practices. Of course, all of this may be moot since you're basing your assumption about comp folks on blog comments. If that's your measure of intellectual rigor, you might be at risk for a few assumptions about you." I received no reply.

3. A current study indicates that of the 51 percent of faculty who are adjuncts, 31 percent of them live near or below the poverty line (Brave New Films 2015).

4. The invisibility of labor is an appropriate place to trace these intersections, as women of color are disproportionately affected by the service burden or "cultural taxation" (Evans 2007; Grollman 2015; Matthew 2016).

REFERENCES

Anokye, Akua Duku. 1996. "Housewives and Compositionists." *College Composition and Communication* 47 (1): 101–3.

Baker, Kelly J. 2015. "Contingency and Gender." *Chronicle Vitae* (blog), April 24. https://chroniclevitae.com/news/984-contingency-and-gender.

Bernstein, Susan Naomi. 2016. "Occupy Basic Writing: Pedagogy in the Wake of Austerity." In *Composition in the Age of Austerity*, ed. Nancy Welch and Tony Scott, 92–105. Logan, UT: Utah State University Press.

Brannon, Lil. 2016. "Afterword: Hacking the Body Politic." In *Composition in the Age of Austerity*, ed. Nancy Welch and Tony Scott, 220–28. Logan: Utah State University Press.

Brave New Films and the New Faculty Majority. 2015. *Professors in Poverty.* YouTube from Brave New Films. http://www.bravenewfilms.org/professorsinpoverty.

Brennan, Jason. 2016. "Do Universities Have a Fiduciary Duty to Fire Madjuncts?" *Bleeding Heart Libertarians* (blog), March 18. http://bleedingheartlibertarians.com/2016/03/do-universities-have-a-fiduciary-duty-to-fire-madjuncts/#disqus_thread.

Cho, Sumi, Kimberlé Williams Crenshaw, and Leslie McCall. 2013. "Toward a Field of Intersectionality Studies: Theory, Applications, and Praxis." *Signs* 38 (4): 785–810.

Coalition on the Academic Workforce. 2012. "A Portrait of Part-Time Faculty Members." December 15. http://www.academicworkforce.org/Research_reports.html

Crowley, Sharon. 1998. *Composition in the University: Historical and Polemical Essays.* Pittsburgh: University of Pittsburgh Press.

Evans, Stephanie Y. 2007. "Women of Color in American Higher Education." *Thought and Action* 23 (Fall): 131–38.

Grollman, Eric Anthony. 2015. "Invisible Labor: Exploitation of Scholars of Color in America." *Conditionally Accepted* (blog). December 15. https://conditionallyaccepted.com/2015/12/15/invisible-labor/.

Hairston, Maxine. 1985. "Breaking Our Bonds and Reaffirming Our Connections." *College Composition and Communication* 36 (3): 272–82.

Holbrook, Sue Ellen. 1991. "Women's Work: The Feminizing of Composition." *Rhetoric Review* 9 (2): 201–29.

Khawaja, Irfan. 2015. "Adjuncting: Conversations Worth Having, and Not." *Policy of Truth* (blog). December 13. https://irfankhawajaphilosopher.com/2015/05/06/adjuncting-conversations-worth-having-and-not/.

Larson, Ann. 2016. "Composition's Dead." In *Composition in the Age of Austerity*, ed. Nancy Welch and Tony Scott, 163–76. Logan, UT: Utah State University Press.

Lykke, Nina. 2010. *Feminist Studies: A Guide to Intersectional Theory, Methodology and Writing.* New York: Routledge.

Matthew, Patricia A. 2016. "What Is Faculty Diversity Worth to a University?" *Atlantic.* November 23. http://www.theatlantic.com/education/archive/2016/11/what-is-faculty-diversity-worth-to-a-university/508334/.

Monks, James. 2005. "Who Are the Part-Time Faculty?" *Academe AAUP.* November 27, 2005. https://www.aaup.org/article/who-are-part-time-faculty#.V9b3wZMrKRs.

Mutnick, Deborah. 2016. "Confessions of an Assessment Fellow." In *Composition in the Age of Austerity*, ed. Nancy Welch and Tony Scott, 35–50. Logan, UT: Utah State University Press.

Schell, Eileen. 1992. "The Feminization of Composition: Questioning the Metaphors That Bind Women Teachers." *Composition Studies* 20 (1): 55–61.

Schell, Eileen. 1998. *Gypsy Academics and Mother-Teachers: Gender, Contingent Labor, and Writing Instruction.* Portsmouth: Boyton/Cook Publishers.

Schell, Eileen. 2016. "Austerity, Contingency, and Administrative Bloat: Writing Programs and Universities in an Age of Feast and Famine." In *Composition in the Age of Austerity*, ed. Nancy Welch and Tony Scott, 177–90. Logan: Utah State University Press.

Scott, Tony. 2016. "Animated by the Entrepreneurial Spirit: Austerity, Dispossession, and Composition's Last Living Act." In *Composition in the Age of Austerity*, ed. Nancy Welch and Tony Scott, 205–19. Logan: Utah State University Press.

Stenberg, Sheri. 2016. "Beyond Marketability: Locating Teacher Agency in the Neoliberal University." In *Composition in the Age of Austerity*, ed. Nancy Welch and Tony Scott, 191–204. Logan: Utah State University Press.

Strickland, Donna. 2011. *The Managerial Unconscious in the History of Composition Studies.* Carbondale: Southern Illinois University Press.

Treanor, Paul. 2005. "Neoliberalism: Origins, Theory, Definition." *Political Aspects* (blog), December 2. http://web.inter.nl.net/users/Paul.Treanor/neoliberalism.html.

Welch, Nancy. 2016. "First-Year Writing and the Angels of Austerity: A Re-Domesticated Drama." In *Composition in the Age of Austerity*, ed. Nancy Welch and Tony Scott, 132–46. Logan: Utah State University Press.

Welch, Nancy and Tony Scott, eds. 2016. *Composition in the Age of Austerity*. Logan: Utah State University Press.

Yardley, Lucy. 1996. "Reconciling Discursive and Materialist Perspectives on Health and Illness." *Theory and Psychology* 6 (3): 485–508.

PART IV

11

ONCE MORE WITH FEELING

Jennifer Lin LeMesurier

*Dance is like . . . I can't explain it man, it's like there's something
missing from the world if you're not a dancer. It's, do you know what
I mean? It's something only dancers understand because movement to
us is like, it's so foreign to everybody. Everybody speaks, and everybody
learns to like—it's all part of the system*—but in order to write with
a passion and speak with a passion, you have to feel that in an
emotional way. *And* dance forces you to feel an emotion, *whether you want to or not, you kind of have to because moving your body in
linear—even when you're learning as a beginning dancer, like ballet,
you're making these shapes. You're learning with,* there's some sort
of expression, *maybe that everything else somehow lacks because you're
not using the full body. [emphasis added]*
—Cat Cogliandro, interview with the author

In an interview I conducted with dance choreographer Cat Cogliandro
(2016),[1] I asked her to talk about her experience working with other
dancers. Specifically, I was asking her to discuss how the context of a
movement-focused class might impact the processes of risk taking and
moving outside of one's typical ways of being. After conducting interviews with twenty dance teachers and students, Cogliandro's emphasis
on passion and emotion aligns with a patterned focus on finding a place
of genuine affect, affect that is not merely put on because of the performance context but rather a true emotional state that is simultaneously
connected to the performer's and audience's previous experience. The
process of becoming a mature performer is thus also a process of entering into emotional identification with one's audience through one's
bodily movement. Feeling is not an obstacle to be overcome but a key
mode for communication.

DOI: 10.7330/9781607328933.c011

Although Cogliandro speaks about this emotion as a natural part of the dancing process, my interviews and observations demonstrate that drawing on emotion as an inventional resource in one's movement requires a great deal of pedagogical nuance to engage with this nonintuitive process. The dance teachers I observed and interviewed used a variety of strategies for helping students to experience comfortable feeling, and a key part of this process is engaging the body in critical movement awareness. In examining this crucial link, we can consider the moving body not only in terms of oppressive *discipline* but also as the manifestation of rhetorical *training*. It is not only one's "embodied history" (Bourdieu 1980, 56) that matters but how one is encouraged to use this history to maneuver and parry rhetorical exigencies with one's bodily capacity. Movement-based pedagogies model strategies for accessing the seemingly most personal aspects of bodily feeling and putting them to work toward broader performative goals. Contemporary scholars are now convincingly demonstrating the need to attend to where emotional aspects (Crowley 2006; Micciche 2005), as well as affective systems and responses (Gregg and Seigworth 2009; Pruchnic and Lacey 2011), are just as vital to rhetorical influence as logical argument. I emphasize Cogliandro's points about emotion and feeling not to reaffirm a crude binary between emotion as personal and liberating versus more rigid structural forces but rather as an example of this strain of pedagogical thinking wherein emotion is not an end in itself but centered as a valid means of exploration and invention.

Understanding the range of available rhetorical options at any given time is an intricate process laden with "wicked problems" (Marback 2009, 399). Wicked problems are ones full of competing interests that require continual reiterations, or, while there is not necessarily one best rhetorical response to a situation, there are nonetheless a variety of bad ones. Problems often become wicked through the intermingling of affect, embodiment, and discourse. Classical rhetoricians accounted for this chaos in their understanding of knowledge as "always changing its shape, depending on who was doing the knowing" (Crowley 1990, 162). Such an emphasis was primarily focused on how to deploy this flexibility in speeches and texts. Now, contemporary scholars are exploring the "radical withness" (Micciche 2014, 502) of rhetorical endeavors; writing always emerges in the contact of writers, environments, objects, and moods, which means we need to account for how it is possible to move through these different points of contact. The features of dance pedagogy I wish to highlight directly address these complications and channel them toward performative invention. To this end, I draw on extensive ethnographic research of dance training and demonstrate how those within a body-centric ecology speak of rhetorical potential in their discourse on the development of moving bodies. Specifically, I draw on vocabulary commonly used in dance and performance culture, the language of individual feeling, sensation, and intention, to explicate a theory of agency that accounts for the tension of freedom and constraint—being both an agent with free will and potentially an agent for something else (Trimbur 2000)—in a way that is inventively generative.

The relationship of agency and rhetoric is one that shifts depending on who is speaking. Rhetorical scholars have wrestled with how to position the locus of rhetorical power, with some looking to social frameworks like tradition (Leff 2003) and others looking at disrupting existing disciplinary subject positions (Koerber 2006) or as emergent in the rhetorical performance and reactions of others (Miller 2007). Whatever ideological baggage or philosophical practices the term still bears, agency is, at its base, the "capacity to act, that is, to have the competence to speak or write in a way that will be recognized or heeded in one's community" (Campbell 2005, 3). The recent wave of scholarship on emotions (Micciche 2007), affect (Edbauer 2005), ethnographic research (Senda-Cook 2012), and posthumanism (Boyle 2016), along with other diverse interdisciplinary threads, complicates our understandings of agency and demands to the point that we look toward the influence of the material, the affective, and the nonhuman on even the seemingly most individual endeavors. The body is a key part of all of these theories, moving amidst the roles of rhetorical responder, mediator, and actor. Debra Hawhee emphasizes how ancient rhetoric was formulated within spaces of mind and body that saw each as equals, meaning that one's rhetorical power is always influenced by the shaping of one's body (2004). Defining rhetorical agency through bodily capacity is therefore less about perfecting a "right" body and more about crafting bodily awareness that enables the mover to recognize and respond to circulating rhetorical resources.

Theorist Carrie Noland (2009) claims we need to investigate how agency is expressed through bodily movement, not for the sake of shoring up modernist ideas of the independent human, but to understand how the capacities of movement exceed and accompany discursive identifications. For Noland, one need not reject either the potential for individual agency or the pressures of external social models. Rather, it is by zooming into the interstices where these forces meet and circulate that one is able to catch glimpses of where agency emerges. These collisions of body and other, these "motor challenges to acculturated behaviors are themselves a form of agency, one that arises from the experiences of movement afforded, paradoxically, by acculturation itself" (2009, 2). Therefore, bodily, kairotic choices are where agency emerges in the momentary, the granular. The "kinesthetic, bodily self-reference" that dancers experience while moving "is not just an ever-changing now, but rather the experience of self-continuity in the midst of change" (Dávila 2012, 109). Even as rhetoricians allow for the porous boundaries between the rhetor and others, we also need frameworks that help us identify which bodily resources recur and how to consciously access them. In working through what dance training emphasizes as bodily constants, we develop a more expanded understanding of how to access differing bodily emphases across various rhetorical ecologies.

In dance specifically, teachers draw on discourses that center feeling and emotion as a key part of bodily imitative practices that build bodily agency. Such work is not a simple acceptance of the presence of emotion but rather a honing process of critical engagement with emotion for rhetorically inventive purposes. I analyze how dance teachers encourage experimentation with rhetorical *personae*, critical practice with imitation, and kairotic reflexive awareness to evoke this critical awareness and channel it toward performative ends. Although different in context than a composition classroom, I argue these strategies support an emotionally engaged way of being in one's body that is also critically aware of one's audience.

FINDING FEELING

In dance, the difficulty of finding feelings that are both authentic to the mover and that communicate persuasively to the audience is set up as an idealized goal, prompting the mover to explore her or his full range of bodily resources. This process is incredibly difficult, but that difficulty of creatively imagining focused possibilities based on previous movement experience is a key theme found in dance teachers' discourse. In the following interview excerpt, dance professor and choreographer Christy McNeil discusses how she prompts students to analyze and enact the emotional range of a movement combination. Choreographers will often describe their work in relation to their own experience, and McNeil explicitly addresses how she teaches her students to respond to this information.

> You probably haven't had that exact experience, so how can you take an experience that is something close to that or that same feeling or that same type of emotion and make sure that your intent is what I'm looking

for within this piece? So I ask them to really think about that as far as facial performance and energetics of the performance and dynamics of the performance. So if I'm asking them to go into a more angry place, like I want to see, I want to see not just an "angry face." I want to see more of a sharp, fast, hitting dynamic than some flowy, like who's angry like that? No one. Like how could you, at least stereotypically use, what most of us consider to be angry dynamics? So that, their intent is a big part of that. (2016)

Here, McNeil offers a version of performance and agency that encompasses what Karlyn Kohrs Campbell refers to as the "personae," "the shifting but central character of the roles that we assume in the plays in which we participate" (2005, 5). We must continually reinvent and perform personae that simultaneously fit cultural understandings of what rhetorical eloquence or, in this case, the appropriate demonstration of anger is, in order to be granted the power of agency. While Campbell focuses on how the personae emerges in textual work, we can see McNeil prompting her students to experiment with this on a bodily level by asking them to tack between individual feeling, grounded in their personal previous experience, and cultural standards of emotion as seen in one's movement patterns. A successful performance goes beyond the putting on of a certain facial expression but instead is more akin to a "citation that appropriates and alters" (Campbell 2005, 7), a series of bodily references that are recognizable launching points for individual exploration. Similar to the goals of an in-class freewrite, it is not about finding a perfectly equal alignment between the mover's (writer's) intent and the audience's perception but rather about finding a mode of expression that feels genuine to both the rhetor and audience.

Los Angeles–based choreographer and teacher Rafael Quintas attempts to help his students find this productive level of feeling through explicitly narrative direction.

I always tell my students right away when you start learning the combo to start thinking of how does this make you feel? Does it make you feel funny? And I always say everything is information for you to move a different way. If it makes you feel weird, maybe commit to being weird and be like "I don't know how I feel about this" [*while talking, he shrinks head down to his chest and shrugs shoulders to his ears*]. Or if you think it's funny, maybe you can even tickle yourself, because that's how free I want you to feel in my class and maybe explore and create different things, go home and create your own choreography. (2016)

As we can see here, feeling is not the desired end but rather a prompt for deep exploration and creative invention. The student is meant to critically experience how abstract feelings of "owning" the movement or "feeling funny" emerge in one's movement qualities. A successful exploration of feeling in the movement exceeds the single performance; Rafael's exhortation to draw on these feelings as the basis for new choreography, new movement, exemplifies the tacit assumption that engaging with feelings in motion invents further creative permutations. The full range of bodily sensation, from feeling weird to being tickled, can be triggers for chaos, but these teachers instead frame these feelings as inventive prompts, focusing attention on the connection between the bodily task and surrounding context.

Crowley points out that the desires that motivate political action are rooted in the body. The body "is both the site and the mechanism that allows human being to represent itself in language and behavior. Desire is expressed through the body. Speech and gesture, writing and dance and painting and so on, are bodily expressions of desire" (2006, 93). These bodily desires are often triggered by collective fantasies, such as myths about historical events (2006, 97–100). Maintaining one's place in these collective identifications requires bodily practices that align with the broader ideological commitments. What the above dance teachers are describing is a critically engaged practice of how it is possible to perform identification through individual exploration of feeling. The mover is positioned not in terms of reaction but invention.

TRAINING AS RHETORICAL PRESSURE

In dance class, teachers have a range of opportunities to try and evoke this emotional exploration. Dance teaching is structured around short exercises reminiscent of the ancient *progymnasmata*. Typically, the teacher will choreograph a short (thirty seconds to three minutes) exercise, demonstrate it, and have the students work through the exercise on their own. The students will then perform it one to three times, depending on class time constraints, the purpose of the exercise, and the teacher's judgment. This process is repeated in most classes, with students taking three to five times per week. Within this structure, the rhetorical principle of imitation is clearly at play. Michael Leff states, "*Imitatio* functions as a hermeneutical rhetoric that circulates influence between past and present. As the *embodied utterances of the past are interpreted for current application, their ideas and modes of articulation are reembodied*, and old voices are recovered for use in new circumstances" (1997, 203; emphasis added). Leff notes how this process of imitation revises the original situations even as the original values are revitalized. Although Leff is focused on political rhetoric, his framework is useful for understanding how bodily movement functions in rhetorical ways, particularly how bodily imitation—bodily training—offers new ways for considering the relationships existing among rhetorical agents and audience members. Crowley points out, "the interestedness of boundary-drawing and distinction-making" (1999, 363) between bodies creates material impact. Categorizing bodies in discourse creates real pressure on how those bodies are physically able to interact. The process of bodily imitation, of collectively moving together toward similar-enough goals, creates opportunities for new potential identifications by fostering bodily practices found outside the norm.

In any space, the various bodies moving and interacting create flows of pressure and counterpressure with varying levels of emphasis and duration. These flows cause certain aggregations of people and materials to feel like a natural end even as they shunt oxygen away from other potential alignments. Noland argues that the link between what is perceived as someone's natural tendencies and cultural knowledge is found within one's bodily training; "kinesthetic experience, produced by acts of embodied gesturing, places *pressure on the conditioning a body receives*, encouraging variations in performance that account for larger innovations in cultural practice that cannot otherwise be explained" (Noland 2009, 2–3; emphasis added). Taking up the metaphor of pressure helps us appreciate how rhetorical events can be jumpstarted by a shift in movement practices. The choreographer Cogliandro places emphasis on dancers "using the whole body" as a desired goal, which is easily contrasted with "typical" postures that only require certain quadrants of the body. Training the body to create these moving counterpressures to dominant habits is formative experimentation with what mixture of affect and movement might be appropriate for the situation at hand or might rewrite the situation entirely.

In the following instance from an intermediate modern dance class at a university, the professor, George, and his students are negotiating pressure and counterpressure as they emerge in the difficult task of working through choreography. Finding feelings that will be productive in working through this combination requires a full engagement with the bodily experience of iteratively performing it amidst the other students.

> The rest of the combo is largely initiated and led by the head movements—at one point they are facing the back, and he tells them to feel the "back of the head" to take them around to face the front again . . . A student says that she's "losing momentum" in one part and can't figure out where her head goes next. She goes to the place in the combo where she gets stuck. Before George can say anything, another student says that it's like someone pulling "the ponytail" on the back of her head. Yet another student

smiles and takes a hold of the one who asked the question, grabbing her ponytail, and guides the other student's head through space. A few other students take hold of their own ponytails and go through the movements pulling on their own hair. (Cogliandro 2016)

The movement that prompts this interaction is a difficult one. After spiraling in one direction and pausing, the students are then supposed to initiate a counterspiral, leading the movement with the back of the head and neck. To successfully perform the movement, the students must be highly aware of where their body is in space and which parts of the body to activate at any given time in the combination. Ultimately, the students need to move through the combination, discovering where their movement affinities make moving easy and where there are initiation points that feel less familiar. The taking hold of each other's hair (reminiscent of the forelock of *Kairos*) is an action that exemplifies the high level of comfort the students in this class had with each other. More than that, it is also an inventive move that centers feeling in the individual body even as it draws students together in temporary multiperson assemblages. Such bodily cooperation demonstrates what it might look like if "rhetorical agency can be remodeled as communicative labor, a form of life-affirming constitutive power that embodies creativity and co-operation" (Greene 2004, 201). Defining rhetorical agency in terms of "life-affirming" labor inclines us toward asking how this labor is enacted between individuals and to what end. In this case, the students are imitating the teacher's model of haptic correction as a way into bodily feeling. The strain on the hair is a rupture that, in this case, serves to trigger enough counterpressure to how one normally carries the head so that the dancer can perform the movement successfully. In another situation, pulling on someone's hair would be an annoyance or assault, but in the context of movement pedagogy such an action is instead an inventive collaboration that emerges from the need to heighten bodily feeling.

In this class, the dancers are imitating the common pedagogical tactic of using touch to redirect student movement. It is not the act of touching that is itself important but what touch within the dance classroom models, a reflexive way of being proximal with other bodies in a pedagogical space. As Noland discusses in relation to Maurice Merleau-Ponty, reflexes are not just unconscious reactions but "are 'interpretations' of an environment, 'proto-significations' rather than purely indexical, automatic responses" (2009, 57). The heightened reflexivity that Noland describes becomes rhetorical with training; movers need instruction in how to transition this process of bodily imitation from "mere" response to a critical, self-reflexive platform from which to judge and act. In the dance classroom, dance teachers present iterative tasks that demand a thoughtful bodily immersion, multiplying access points to the knowledge present in one's body that can be used in future performances. They also often use haptic correction as a means of concentrating attention on one aspect of movement, which means that students iteratively practice how to be directed bodily. In thinking about transference to the composition classroom, the mode of touch is not as important as the continual imitative practice of how to be affected. More than that, this demonstrates how there must also be examples of how being affected is not the end in itself. Rather, the awareness of one's affect should be positioned as a springboard to the range of communicative options such awareness offers in rhetorical situations.

"MAKE IT YOUR OWN"

There are direct links between the emphasis on using emotions and sensations as inventive tools and classical rhetorical pedagogies of imitation; both expect that the repeated bodily performance of a movement combination or political speech will alter the rhetor's ability to inhabit different positions, increasing the range of available identifications. In ancient rhetorical practices and their descendants, there is deep belief in the power of bodily habit as what "draws out the virtuous actions that nature makes one tend toward, bringing them to completion (*teleioumenois*), perfecting them through repetitive practice" (Hawhee 2004, 95) and creating "capacities, flexible bodies of work" (87). It is worth noting that for the ancients, processes of bodily imitation were both rhetorical and moral heuristics. Learning to evoke emotion with one's bodily action is a potentially tenuous ethical area; placing of one's body in a state that greatly differs from one's natural tendencies can create discomfort, perhaps even withdrawal, but such boundary pushing also enables experimentation with occupying different subject positions. What is needed is guidance to channel this agentive potential in ways that are inventive rather than destructive.

A contemporary rhetoric that moves is one that acknowledges this substantial impact of literally moving through alternate states of being in the process of learning, arguing, or influencing. In dance, we see acceptance of imitation as primary to finding a capacity to act, a level of agency, in the explicit discussions of the varied potentials the imitation-based exercises contain. Rather than having to choose which side we are "moral entrepreneurs" for (Greene 2004, 203), a moving rhetoric focuses on the rhetorical potentials found in the feelings that emerge both from individual intent and surrounding bodies, the reflexivity inherent in any situation. Students do not always have to operate from a unified "I" but are presented with opportunities to move with the personae of others.

Without being deterministic, this emphasis on identification as manifested in movement lays bridges between the rhetor and audience. What is rhetorically notable is how dance teachers use this tension as a prompt to spur students onto bodily experimentation and invention. In the following observation of an advanced ballet class at an R-1 University, the professor focuses her comments on the idea of individual ownership to try and prompt the student to both find greater capacity in the movement and search for greater connections with external viewers.

> After a difficult developpé exercise [slow extensions of the leg in all directions], Patricia goes to a student who has not progressed much throughout the term. She tells her to work with counterbalance during a front leg extension, using the lean of her body to counteract the weight of the leg. The student tries it on both sides, losing her balance a little on the 2nd side. Patricia then tells her "you have to own it," that as she stands there watching the student, she can tell from looking in her eyes that the student isn't really "feeling it." Patricia clarifies that she isn't judging the student, that if she has questions she can ask, but that she needs to "take ownership, to explore what works" in her body for that movement. (Cogliandro 2016)

At first glance, Patricia's comments are rather technical. Yet her ultimate landing point is not an abstract marker of technical achievement; the student does not "succeed" if she reaches a certain angle with her leg that mimics the teacher. Instead, Patricia keeps urging the student to personalize this extremely technical exercise for her body. There are physiological aspects to this personalization, dependent on the dancer's particular anatomical structure. Yet Patricia progresses from more anatomical- and position-based terminology—counterbalance, weight—to discourse that focuses on the student's agency in the midst of performing the movement. Although it might be tempting to critique such comments as being too heavily focused on the individual and too little focused on the assemblages of other objects and bodies, such a critique would miss the emphasis on affective expression as a cornerstone of rhetorical dexterity. The lack or presence of feeling is a performative concern in terms of the audience being able to sense what the mover is feeling, but Patricia's emphasis also indicates that what makes bodily work more than mere imitation is an intimate processing of the knowledge gained that can then be sensed in the moment of performance.

Performative success is therefore a rhetorical expression found through combining imitative practice and individual intention. This combination is not alone enough, however. The mover must develop ways of explicitly communicating theirs to an external viewer. In the interview with professor and choreographer Christy McNeil, she addresses how finding ways into making imitative movement align with one's individual aims is indicative of broader epistemological and performative achievements than the singular moment.

> So, I guess in jazz especially what I'm really trying to do is tell them to "yes, imitate me," but also understand what it is that I'm doing so that you're not just—I feel like imitation can sometimes become kind of rote learning, of like, I learn it, I do my test, and then [pfffffbt noise] it's gone. It's like, do you know it, or do you KNOW it? Can you replicate it? Can you, can you then modify it and *make it your own?* And if you can't, then I think you're just imitating. (2016; emphasis added)

The phrase "make it your own" is a curious one in the dance world. Christy's comment clearly suggests that to make it your own is to push past imitation into a higher realm, but these four words do not fully encapsulate the kinesthetic, affective process that goes into such work. Making the combination or movements one's own involves a tricky balance of mastery, openness, and risk-taking, all the while being responsive to those watching and moving around one's self. From these repeated imitations, it is expected that the dancer is then able to transport aspects of those experiences into other contexts. What makes this process of imitation more than a bodily plagiarism is the ongoing, necessary coaction of several bodily and environmental processes. As Anna Gibbs summarizes, the operation of the mirror neuron system means "when we see an action performed, the same neural networks that would be involved if we were to perform it ourselves are activated. In fact we may actually experience something of what it *feels* like to perform the action, as when we watch someone and feel our own body strain toward the movement" (2010, 198–99). Neurologically, every individual develops through this process of mimesis, synchronizing one's behavior to the movements and modes of others. Such mimesis is a "cross-model translation" (196) channeled not only through visual modes but also through eyes, ears, nerves, movements, and words.

Rafael Quintas points out the rhetorical tension found in this cross-modal work of movement imitation. Although he does not use the particular phrase "make it your own" in his teaching, his response illuminates the power found in the exchange between verbal instruction focused on the individual and bodily responses to such an emphasis. "I don't really think I say the actual words maybe 'make it your own.' I like to say like 'let go,' 'be honest.' 'Make it your own' is really hard, depending on the class because I've been to classes where they say make it your own, but they want you, they actually mean make it look really good on your body."

In dance, students are supposed to exceed a base-level mimetic process and instead critically emulate their teachers and choreographers, manifesting their bodily interpretations in on-the-spot performances of the movement combinations. As Rafael speaks about the nuance found in the phrase "make it your own," he is also pointing toward how it is possible to find a critical form of imitation, a process more reminiscent of Gibbs's theorizing of it as "an image in which figure and ground can always be reversed, so that sometimes subjectivity is in focus, while at other times it recedes into the background, leaving something new to appear in its place" (187). This undulation between self and other that necessarily occurs during mimetic activity is a series of kairotic judgments of bodily difference and similarity, and movers negotiate these competing factors by relying on individual feeling and sensation. Dance historian Susan Leigh Foster investigates this bodily resonance via the concept of "empathy," best defined as "a changing sense of physicality that in turn, influence[s] how one fe[els] another's feelings" (2010, 11). For Rafael, "being honest" is a way into negotiating the competing visual and bodily information one must continually traverse—how a combination looks on someone else versus one's own body, how that relates to previous combinations and their associated feelings—while remaining centered enough to make choices in how one deploys movement. The word "honest" is not a marker of sentimental naivete but rather is meant as a trigger to deploy systems of critical judgment in which one is aware of the audience's expectations but also committed to one's bodily experiences as an equally important standard.

Within a feeling-based rubric, a mover's performance success is found through not merely feeling bodily emotion and sensation but through an explicit immersion in the various pathways these feelings provoke. Finding models of movement to repeatedly imitate is a way of both developing productive habits that can be kairotically deployed and also acknowledging the explosive richness of bodily invention. Agency, as the power to move through the full set of available pathways, unconstrained by others' biases or politics, is not something to be grasped but something to feel.

TENDING TO FEELING

Although the editors of this collection remind us that the term "theory" is from the Ancient Greek verb *theorein*, which means "to observe from afar" (Crowley 2006, 27), my research demonstrates another path for theorizing rhetorical work and impact, a path that begins in the close, sometimes sweaty intimacy of bodily movement. I argue that through considering a body-centric pedagogy such as dance, rhetoric is better prepared to reconsider some of the paradigms that have been primarily developed in concert with textual work. The keen focus on emotional feelings in dance teachers' discourse immerses students in the interplay between discourse and bodies by explicitly teasing out how such affective histories are always emergent in one's movement, modeling the use of personal experience in critical, audience-aware ways. In such a framework, rhetorical invention is located within movement itself, a wending between points of realization, refining iterations as the realizations recur and reveal their complexity.

As rhetoric continues to explore moving bodies as texts, processes, and articulations that are worth studying and theorizing, the field needs to also attend to training, the metasystems already in place that guide and constrain our bodies. Dance pedagogies demonstrate how it is possible to foster emotional awareness that serves larger projects of rhetorical invention. A theory of rhetoric that expands focus to the moving, feeling body defines rhetorical success less in terms of finding the singular point to debate and more about finding multiple points for expansion in ongoing debates, living, and collisions—places for rhetorical bodies to inhabit, if only temporarily. Such work means directly grappling with the relation of emotion, bodies, and rhetoric. Crowley articulates how "emotions affect belief, and beliefs arouse emotion. Belief is stimulated, supported, or changed by emotional responses to an environment. Emotions can be stimulated, in turn, by appeals to beliefs already in place" (Crowley 2006, 87). The "visceral pull" (88) of these emotional appeals is not merely a crude version of higher-order logic but rather a recursive interchange of feelings and values that gain rhetorical force through habitual practice. The strategies in this chapter offer further clarity about how to speak of and channel emotions that are not solely reinforcing but that also offer opportunities for rhetorically inclined reconsideration.

NOTE

1. Participants listed by only their first name have been given pseudonyms. All others are referred to by their professional names.

REFERENCES

Bourdieu, Pierre. 1992. *The Logic of Practice*. Stanford: Stanford University Press.

Boyle, Casey. 2016. "Writing and Rhetoric and/as Posthuman Practice." *College English* 78 (6): 532–54.

Campbell, Karlyn Kohrs. 2005. "Agency, Promiscuous and Protean." *Communication and Critical/Cultural Studies* 2 (1): 1–19.

Cogliandro, Cat. 2016. Interview. July 22.

Crowley, Sharon. 1990. *The Methodical Memory: Invention in Current-Traditional Rhetoric*. Carbondale: Southern Illinois University Press.

Crowley, Sharon. 1999. "Afterword: The Material of Rhetoric." In *Rhetorical Bodies*, ed. Jack Selzer and Sharon Crowley, 357–66. Madison: University of Wisconsin Press.

Crowley, Sharon. 2006. *Toward a Civil Discourse: Rhetoric and Fundamentalism*. Pittsburgh: University of Pittsburgh Press.

Dávila, Mónica E. Alarcón. 2012. "Body Memory and Dance." In *Body Memory, Metaphor, and Movement*, ed. Sabine C. Koch, Thomas Fuchs, Michela Summa, and Cornelia Müller, 105–14. Philadelphia: John Benjamins Publishing.

Edbauer, Jennifer H. 2005. "(Meta)physical Graffiti: 'Getting Up' as Affective Writing Model." *JAC* 25 (1): 131–59.

Foster, Susan Leigh. 2011. *Choreographing Empathy: Kinesthesia in Performance*. New York: Routledge.

Gibbs, Anna. 2010. "After Affect: Sympathy, Synchrony, and Mimetic Communication." In *The Affect Theory Reader*, ed. Melissa Gregg and Greg Seigworth, 186–205. Durham: Duke University Press.

Gregg, Melissa, and Seigworth, Greg. 2010. *The Affect Theory Reader*. Durham: Duke University Press.

Greene, Ronald W. 2004. "Rhetoric and Capitalism: Rhetorical Agency as Communicative Labor." *Philosophy and Rhetoric* 37 (3): 188–206.

Hawhee, Debra. 2004. *Bodily Arts: Rhetoric and Athletics in Ancient Greece*. Austin: University of Texas Press.

Leff, Michael. 1997. "Hermeneutical Rhetoric." In *Rhetoric and Hermeneutics in Our Time*, ed. Walter Jost and Michael J. Hyde, 196–214. New Haven: Yale University Press.

Leff, Michael. 2003. "Tradition and Agency in Humanistic Rhetoric." *Philosophy and Rhetoric* 36 (2): 135–47.

Koerber, Amy. 2006. "Rhetorical Agency, Resistance, and the Disciplinary Rhetorics of Breastfeeding." *Technical Communication Quarterly* 15 (1): 87–101.

Marback, Richard. 2009. "Embracing Wicked Problems: The Turn to Design in Composition Studies." *College Composition and Communication* 61 (2): 397–419.

McNeil, Christy. 2016. Interview. July 21.

Micciche, Laura R. 2005. "Emotion, Ethics, and Rhetorical Action." *JAC* 25 (1): 161–84.

Micciche, Laura R. 2007. *Doing Emotion: Rhetoric, Writing, Teaching*. Portsmouth, NH: Heinemann.

Micciche, Laura R. 2014. "Writing Material." *College English* 76 (6): 488–505.

Miller, Carolyn. 2007. "What Can Automation Tell Us about Agency?" *Rhetoric Society Quarterly* 37 (2): 137–57.

Noland, Carrie. 2009. *Agency and Embodiment: Performing Gestures / Producing Culture*. Cambridge: Harvard University Press.

Pruchnic, Jeff, and Kim Lacey. 2011. "The Future of Forgetting: Rhetoric, Memory, Affect." *Rhetoric Society Quarterly* 41 (5): 472–94.

Rafael Quintas. 2016. Interview. July 21.

Senda-Cook, Samantha. 2012. "Rugged Practices: Embodying Authenticity in Outdoor Recreation." *Quarterly Journal of Speech* 98 (2): 129–52.

Trimbur, John. 2000. "Agency and the Death of the Author: A Partial Defense of Modernism." *JAC* 20 (2): 283–98.

12

THEORY BUILDING IN THE RHETORIC OF HEALTH AND MEDICINE

J. Blake Scott and Catherine C. Gouge

In asserting that theories are rhetorical inventions—"depictions or assessments produced by and within specific times and locations as a means of opening other ways of believing or acting" (28)—Sharon Crowley (2006) points to their ideological and performative dimensions. Theories can constitute and support ideologies, or networks of values, that shape what we believe and how we make judgments and otherwise act. In addition to being products of rhetorical performances themselves, theories can motivate such performances and interventions through the understanding, belief, judgment, and exigency that they enable. In this chapter, we want to extend the consideration of these dimensions to the critical and creative act of theory building, which we similarly consider to be inventive, contextualized, and value-driven methodological performance. We use the phrasing "theory building" here to call attention to the act of creating, extending, or adapting theory as an inventional practice and as a key contribution of rhetorical inquiry. Although "theorizing" can be thought of as the process of working through an issue and "theory building" as consciously developing the tools and approaches for *how* to do such work, in this chapter we seek to draw attention to what they have in common, to understanding both as situated modes of inquiry. By extension, "theory" can also be conceptualized as a process, but we might distinguish it from theorizing and theory building as a particular articulation of a theorizing process, one that can travel and be adapted in new contexts.

As an elaboration on this understanding of theory building as an important mode of rhetorical inquiry in itself, we consider how it functions as a methodology or approach to studying and interpreting the rhetoric of health and medicine (RHM). RHM is an emergent and quickly growing scholarly area that draws on rhetorical theory to study the persuasive practices in and around health and medicine (see Scott

DOI: 10.7330/9781607328933.c012

and Meloncon 2018 for a useful discussion of RHM's distinguishing characteristics in methodological terms). We hope this chapter both makes a particular case for valuing theory building in RHM *and* unpacks, through the case of RHM, the broader argument for moving from viewing theory as informing methodology to the act of theory building as itself a methodology. The rhetoric of health and medicine has increasingly focused on building knowledge through mixed method and empirical studies, raising questions about the role of theory building and theorizing in projects that are often explicitly about solving practical problems in health and medicine. The high stakes of RHM and of the phenomena it studies create a heightened need for carefully inventing (with) theory and even approaching theory building as an act of care.

Drawing extensively on feminist science studies scholars, we offer an extended definition of theory, then discuss how theory building functions as a methodology, and explore why the attuned theory building we encourage is important to RHM and rhetorical studies more broadly.

WHAT CAN THEORIZING AND THEORY DO?

One way to define something is to bring its energy and presence into relief by considering what it is not, and that is where we begin our discussion of the nature and functions of theory. We are not working with a notion of theory as a comprehensive, coherent conceptual scheme for exhaustively explaining, generalizing, or predicting phenomena (see Kaplan 1964; Kerlinger 1973); nor do we understand theory building as the practice of discovering generalizations that constitute the fixed frameworks of theories.[1] Instead, we share Crowley's understanding of both as highly contextualized. Although the classical Greek term *theorein* can be translated as studying "from afar," Crowley interprets this to mean the engaged and embedded, rather than detached or removed, study of a production or performance from a critical perspective that is both affected by and affecting the performance (2006, 27–28). If theorizing is a situated inventive act, as Crowley argues, then it cannot be context agnostic; theory's interestedness comes from its entanglements with material-discursive practices, including embodied ones. Karen Barad's theory of agential realism accounts for the ways that "theorizing, like experimenting, is a material practice" (2007, 55). "To theorize," Barad argues, "is not to leave the material world behind" (55); rather, "Theories are living, breathing reconfigurations of the world" (2012b, 207). It follows, then, that theory need not be deterministic, the predictable consequence of a fixed screen. Rather than predicting, theory and theorizing might be most useful when they facilitate attunements and orientations by sensitizing, adapting, and reconfiguring. A specific theory's "strength," Annemarie Mol proposes, "is not in its coherence and predictability, but in . . . its adaptability and sensitivity" (2008, 262).

Theorizing and theory building, as we are defining them, are ideologically and contextually situated modes of inquiry that can help us pose questions, critically interpret enactments and impacts, and provisionally make sense of practices, means, and goals. They are epideictic projects that are about "accounting for how practices matter" (Barad 2007, 90) and crafting affirmative politics and ethical strategies that can be used as "navigational tools" to support a "robust praxis of collective engagements with the specific conditions of our time" (Braidotti 2011, 18). This understanding of theorizing as a rhetorical practice of making sense of what matters is informed by scholars who foreground theory's invention and intervention in intimate time-space entanglements. Paula Treichler points towards this connective rather than distancing role in her claim that theory, ultimately, "is another word for *intelligence*, that is, for a thoughtful and engaged dialectic between the brain, the body, and the world that . . . [they] inhabit" (1999, 2).

Beyond the more familiar approach to defining theory in either/or terms about what it is and what it is not, we want to discuss the functions of theory and theorizing, including attuning and setting a course for our attention as RHM scholars. What are we doing when we enact theories, when we theorize, and when we build theories, and what do our theoretical enactments "do"? According to rhetoricians studying health and medical practices and phenomena, theories can do many things. They can "explain" and "elucidate" (Fountain 2014, 21, 23). They can, according to Treichler, "help us understand the complex relation between language and reality, between meanings and definitions—and how those relations help us understand [specific conditions] and develop interventions that are more culturally informed and socially responsible" (4). They can help to "tell cases, draw contrasts, articulate silent layers, turn questions upside down, focus on the unexpected, add to one's sensitivities, propose new terms, and shift stories from one context to another" (Mol et al. 2010, 262). A theory of multiple ontologies, S. Scott Graham and Carl Herndl write, can "reduce agonism" and "make cooperation possible" (2013, 115). Theories can even constitute forms of caring, as we will later discuss.

We prefer thinking about both theories and theorizing as practices that energize trajectories of thought in the sense that the ideas and practices that emerge are directed—they have an energy behind them.

Theories can be valuable for orienting, energizing, and even disputing trajectories of thought, facilitating new and alternative attunements to situations. As Mol describes it, theory can be "disrupting, attending to surprises, uncovering, conditioning one's sensitivities, enabling attunement, more than offering an exhaustive explanation, determinist scheme" (2008, 261).

Crowley offers an example of theory (and theory building) that highlights its functions to connect and disturb. Drawing from the cultural studies notion of articulation, Crowley defines ideologic as "connections made between and among moments (positions) that occur or are taken up within ideology" (2006, 60). "The morpheme–logic," she further explains, "is intended to convey that, within ideology, beliefs connect, disconnect, and reconnect with regularities that can be traced" (76). Crowley points to the ideology of neoliberalism as a case in point, stating that it "illustrates how beliefs in hegemonic values and practices may be rearticulated" in a way that "legitimates free-market capitalism and globalization by associating them with democracy and traditional liberal values" (e.g., freedom, progress) (77). Rhetoricians can trace such realignments across cultural discourses in specific moments. Philippa Spoel et al. (2014) offer an example of neoliberal ideologic in their study of people's reactions to government "healthy citizenship" campaigns in Canada and the UK. In addition to explaining how these campaigns co-opt liberal notions of personal health management and empowerment in order to shift the responsibility of healthcare from the government to individuals, their study found that the interviewees used a "logic of disassociation" to discern discrepancies between government messages about and its material support of healthy living (131). Crowley explains that identifying ideologic can help "invent means of disarticulating beliefs that circulate within a given ideology, and exposure of untenable connections might assist with the project of disarticulating systems of belief" (77), as she does with rhetorics of religious fundamentalism, and as the citizens that Spoel et al. (2014) engaged did with healthy citizenship campaigns.

We hope our discussion and these examples extend Crowley's observation of theorizing as rhetorical invention to illuminate some specific ways it is rhetorical. In addition to being contextually embedded and performed, theorizing, like rhetoric, is an enactment that is partial and provisional, inventive and receptive, connective and adaptable, provocative and transformative. It is knowledge generating but also modes of action, or, following Barad, modes of intra-action. Theorizing, like rhetoric, is about directing attention to and helping attune to what is possible and desirable. Next, we turn to a fuller discussion of what it means to build theory, and how we might consider this activity to be a methodology worth unpacking and vital to the inventive and interventive potential of RHM.

WHAT DOES IT MEAN TO BUILD THEORY?

Because sense making and theoretical orientations are fluid / in flux and feed back into looking (again, only differently) as new ideas, awarenesses, attunements, practices, (and, yes) theories become a part of what we propose we might think of as a theoretical trajectory, a trajectory that as it moves through the world and engages with different phenomena is both transforming and transformed. Barad and Donna Haraway (1997) have both characterized this process of transformation as diffractive—a transformation for which ideas and other phenomena work through one another to produce something new for each thread or trajectory.

Mol proposes that the value of theorizing and theory building is that it offers those who engage with it a kind of adaptable attunement: "a 'theory' is something that helps scholars to attune to the world, to see and hear and feel and taste it. Indeed, to appreciate it . . . a 'theory' is a repository of terms and modes of engaging with [and interpreting] the world, a set of contrary methodological reflexes" (2008, 262). Theory building is interested and invested in these kinds of becoming because to do such work is to care about how and why things matter, "to tell the stories of what happens to them as they flow, mix, mutate" (Ingold 2011, 30). To engage in theory building is to develop and enact a sensitivity and response-ability to unfolding phenomena that matter, to "be lured by curiosity, surprise, and wonder" about the unfolding phenomena that matter (Barad 2012b, 207). Crafting ways of making sense of the world with theory might be thought as a kind of wayfaring (cf. Ingold 2011, 143) to account for the way that knowledge is transformed and transforming as it moves through the world.

In discussing theory building as a methodology, we draw on Sandra Harding's notion of methodology as a "theory and analysis of how research does or should proceed" (1987, 3), which she distinguishes from method as a "technique for . . . gathering" and analyzing phenomena (2). Methodology involves research methods or techniques, but it also encompasses more, including the ideological lens underpinning the approach and its assumptions, the specific contextual enactments and adaptations of techniques, and a metatheoretical analysis of why and how the research approach should be enacted (see also Sullivan and Porter 1997). Thus, theory is an important part of any methodology, from its exigency to its ideological and epistemological framework to its enactment and rationale. But we want to elaborate on this to consider the ways that theory building can be considered a distinct type of methodology whose goals and approaches primarily revolve around the development and transformative adaptation of theory as a form of sense making. Like other types of methodologies, theory building makes an argument (sometimes implicit) about why and how to engage in research, both through methods but also contextualized practices.

Our proposition also draws on Haraway's and Barad's discussions of diffraction as a way of understanding methodology and theory building more specifically. Haraway argues that diffraction, or "the production of difference patterns," across a history of interactions in the world (1997, 34) is a critical practice that works "to make a difference in the world, to cast our lot for some ways of life and not others," adding that to do this "one must be in the action, be finite and dirty, not transcendent and clean" (36). This provocation moves us away from theorizing and theory building as analytical processes characterized by ontological and epistemological separation and distance between ideas and phenomena, theories and praxis.

Barad extends Haraway's distinction between diffraction and reflexivity in proposing a diffractive methodology that is "respectful of the entanglement of ideas and other materials in ways that reflexive methodologies are not" (2007, 29). For her, this respectfulness and response-ability entail turning our methodological "apparatuses . . . to the particularities of the entanglements at hand" (74), "marking differences [or diffraction patterns] from within as part of an entangled state" (89), and remaining "rigorously attentive" to the specific and nuanced details of such differences and arguments about them (93). "Diffractive readings," Barad explains, "bring inventive provocations; they are good to think [and we would add, feel and otherwise experience] with. They are respectful, detailed, ethical engagements" (2012a, 50).

HOW CAN THEORY BUILDING BE ENACTED IN THE RHM?

Haraway's and Barad's methodologies for diffractive reading suggest some specific exigencies for and approaches to theory building in RHM, some of which overlap with the theory building moves discussed by Karen Schriver (1989) in her review of empirical rhetoric and composition research. We think elements of both discussions can be useful in recognizing the various ways RHM scholars have built and can build theory, whether or not their research had empirical elements.

Working from the premise that theory building, like theorizing, is about engaging, provoking, and provisionally speculating rather than solidifying, cohering, or exhaustively explaining, we want to outline, borrowing and adapting from Schriver and Barad, some "inventional points of departure" for theory building (Schriver 1989, 280). Theory building in the RHM (and rhetorical studies more generally) can develop from the following scholarly moves, among others:[2]

- *Studying how entangled health and medical practices "intra-act" to produce certain meanings, material entities, and boundaries over others* (Barad 2007, 33). Such study does not assume predetermined agents or causal relationships (279). As Barad suggests, this theory building approach can generate insights about how the coagents of health and medicine comaterialize and also matter, in the sense of producing meanings, through phenomena. It can also help us pay attention to the changing reconfigurations and inter-animations of such coagents that include various forms of embodiment—including the researcher's—and a range of nonhuman entities (technologies, medicines, clinical environments, disease agents and conditions, etc.). For example, in her study of intra-actions involving new mothers in neonatal intensive care units, Kristin Bivens's (2018) attention to her participants' changing embodied responses to her own embodied presence as a researcher enabled her to notice particular ways they signaled what she calls "microwithdrawals of consent"—a new concept for attuning and responding to people's changing needs and desire to participate in RHM research. For another example, we point to Christa Teston's (2016) study of how intra-actions among patients, providers, assistive technologies, and other entities in healthcare settings make possible particular understandings of and professional practices around human dignity.

- *"Making speculations based on existing theory"* (Schriver 280) *with new research (e.g., new sites of entangled healthcare practices, new forms of engagement and analysis) that extends or disrupts the existing theory.* Because theorizing is an embedded act, such a move always requires theory's attunement to the practices at hand. Scott (2003) offers an example of this in his rhetorical study of HIV testing practices, examining how they discipline, in a Foucauldian sense, testing's subjects; in doing so, this study extends theorizing about disciplinary power to specific forms of disciplinary rhetorics (e.g., the knowledge enthymeme and scales topos) and their counterproductive effects on healthcare.

- *Fleshing out additional nuances or contingencies of an existing concept or theory with new research.* Like the previous move, this inventional point of departure takes seriously the idea that theory should be contextually attuned. Kimberly Emmons, in her study of gendered depression discourse and women's possible responses to it, offers an adaptation of biopower with her concept of "rhetorical care of the self," which entails a critical questioning of gendered messages and cultural-medical responses to illness (2010, 17). In his historical study of how protein became a central concept in dietary health discourse, Nathan Johnson (2018) develops two concepts—republication and translation—for identifying the functions of background, infrastructural knowledge work, thereby advancing rhetorical infrastructure theory and method.

- *Attentively reading ideas and "insights through [rather than against] one another in ways that help illuminate [fine-grained] differences" and relationships; such a reading avoids starting with one set of ideas as a "fixed frame of reference"* (Barad 2007, 30). A good example of this move is Graham's study of pain medicine research and policy making. Resisting the move of making either rhetorical theory or ontology a foil for the other and pointing to the "theoretical symmetry" in rhetoric's and STS's turn to new materialisms (2015, x), Graham develops a taxonomy of rhetorical-ontological "calibrations" used by multidisciplinary pain science scholars.

- *Reexamining a theoretical framework and its assumptions after "noticing an incongruity in the way an interpretive community conceptualizes" the framework* (Schriver 1989, 281). Heather Zoller (2005) demonstrates this move in comparing theoretical concepts for and approaches to studying activist communication and health activism, before discussing how a critical-interpretative orientation focused on various dimensions of power can broaden health communication research.

- *Noticing and responding to interpretive gaps or "blind spots" of an existing theoretical framework.* Among other reasons, gaps can form from not paying attention to specific embodied experiences and perspectives that matter. In their study of a rural community's skeptical responses to a school-based vaccination effort, Heidi Lawrence et al. respond to discourse-centered, flat, and generalizing notions of medical (antivaccination) publics to offer an alternative account of local publics that make decisions based on shared beliefs and psychosocial experiences (2014, 112). Through addressing a limitation of some rhetorical public theory, these scholars offer physicians and parents more attuned understandings of one another's situated perspectives (113).

- *Exploring alternative explanations of material-discursive practices through different or modified theories, and perhaps conducting research "designed to discriminate among the theories"* (Schriver 1989, 281). In her field study of the day-to-day social-rhetorical interactions of people with chronic mental illnesses at an outpatient facility, Catherine Molloy also offers an alternative explanation of patient agency. She identifies and explains three specific ways mental health patients rhetorically and agilely recover credibility—a "recuperative ethos"—in their day-to-day social interactions at the facility (2015, especially 144).

- *"Theorizing by analogy or metaphor" in order to understand practices in a new way* (Schriver 1989, 281). Although Barad moves away from such theorizing in her work, we still view it as potentially useful and provocative but think, like other forms of theorizing, it should take care to attend to detail and nuance. Treichler provides an example of this move in her call for a "epidemiology of signification—a comprehensive mapping and analysis" of the multiple, contradictory meanings around AIDS (1999, 39). Rather than a loosely applied metaphor for approaching cultural-rhetorical analysis, this concept and methodology were generated from a systematic and nuanced exploration of how biomedical (including epidemiological) and other cultural discourses and meanings travel, inflect one another, and shape people's experiences with the disease.

As a scholarly area that engages a range of theoretical and methodological traditions as well as a range of discursive-material practices, the RHM has by and large taken its methodological ethic seriously, avoiding simple, imprecise, removed, and mimetic analysis. The high stakes of health and medical practices create urgent exigencies for becoming better attuned to, creating better understandings of, and provoking better responses to the ways agencies do and should emerge from them. Health and medical practices are punctuated by what we might call "wicked problems"—that is, complex and ill-defined problems that resist transferrable and sustained solutions (see Conklin 2005)—requiring an embedded, contextually attuned approach to theorizing. In addition, as patients, consumers, and other types of embodied health subjects, RHM scholars are always already entangled in the practices we study, and we therefore bring personal exigency and responsibility to engaging in what Treichler describes as a "thoughtful and engaged dialectic between the brain, the body, and the world that the brain and the body inhabit" (2). For Treichler, "how to have theory in an epidemic [of AIDS]" is a pressing and necessary question. This is because theory is "about people's lives" (3), a lens for discerning, interpreting, and ethically responding to meanings but also lived, embodied experiences around health and illness. In the context of her research, Treichler discusses the challenge of "learn[ing] to live with" and theorize the "disjunction" that AIDS is both culturally constructed and "a real source of illness" (40).

To further illustrate how the RHM has opened up trajectories of theorizing and developed alternative interpretive lenses, we turn now to two clusters of theory building, one around rhetorical ecologies and the other around rhetorical agency.

Extending work on rhetorical ecologies into historical research, Robin Jensen's "percolation model" traces how "ideas, assumptions, and arguments of particular historically distinct moments" percolate up in familiar and new ways in different time periods (2015, 524). Jensen's research illustrates such diachronic connections and repurposings in linking science-based arguments of Progressive Era social hygiene discourse to those of contemporary sex education discourse. Another example extends theorizing of rhetorical health ecologies not across historical time periods but infrastructures for sociocultural circulation. Through his study of women's "social hygiene" lectures in the early 1900s, Dan Ehrenfeld (2018, 45) develops the concept of "ecological investment" to capture how the "constituent parts of complex ecologies [including specific people] 'invest' in the maintenance of circulation infrastructures" (45) supporting the circulation of medical rhetoric, thereby altering these infrastructures. Ehrenfeld explains that one exigency for developing this concept was incongruity among the ways existing understandings of rhetorical ecologies account (or fail to account) for the contributions and impact of individual rhetors.

Others have built theories in health and medicine by thinking about the orientations and assumptions about agency at work in different health/medicine-related rhetorical practices. Kim Hensley Owens's (2015) study of women's experiences writing and enacting their birth plans examines the specific contexts and ways in which these experiences both constrain women's rhetorical agency and open up new forms of rhetorical possibility. Amy Koerber's (2013) study of breastfeeding rhetorics and practices similarly emphasizes the ambiguity of rhetorical-embodied agency in the face of regulatory disciplinary power, arguing that breastfeeding women can potentially disrupt dominant norms by making their embodied practices visible. Both scholars advance nuanced, contingent, and intercontextual understanding of rhetorical agency. Catherine C. Gouge's body of work about compliance frameworks attempts to amplify the compliance logics that impact rhetorical practices and processes in health and medicine. In one project, for example, she brings together rhetorical theory (e.g., from Burke, Hawhee) and the concept of "desire paths" (from urban design and landscape architecture) in order to propose a new approach to paying attention to and valuing patients' divergent texts and practices associated with clinical encounters, drug-approval processes, and large-scale clinical trials (Gouge 2018). To do this work, Gouge reaches outside of the disciplinary boundaries of conventional rhetorical scholarship to connect and reinterpret ideas from different fields (including feminist and disability studies, philosophy of the body, and narrative medicine) through one another, carefully noting the particular contributions of each. In addition to reading insights through one another and using an analogy or metaphor (e.g., desire paths) to differently understand a phenomenon, Gouge's work responds to an interpretive blind spot and proposes an alternative explanation. In contrast to rhetorical theorizing that interprets noncompliance as a rhetorical failure to be fixed, Gouge foregrounds how revaluing divergent acts and seeing them as productive contributions to an ongoing negotiation might afford more emergent and empowering forms of care.

TOWARD THEORY BUILDING AS A FORM OF CARE

Although he doesn't reference theory building explicitly, Jay Dolmage considers theorizing as itself a form of care; "to care about the body is to care about how we make meaning," he writes, suggesting less a disjunction than a mutually conditioning entanglement (2013, 4). In engaging the question "Why do we care?" Treichler asserts that theory is "about people's lives" (3), a mode of discerning, interpreting, and ethically responding to meanings but also lived, embodied experiences around health and illness. In this sense, theory building emerges as a means and form of making provisions for the health or welfare of others, to invoke a common definition of care. All of the functions of enacting theory that we've been describing—attuning, engaging, adjusting, responding, energizing, provoking—can be shaped by values and acts of caring—caring for our research practices, the phenomena of which they are a part, and the embodied stakeholders that participate in both.

Just as theory needs care, care needs theory. In their introduction to *Care in Practice*, Mol et al. propose that care practices need to be thoughtfully "attended to"—they need theory—because "such articulation work may help to make the specificities of care practices travel" (2010, 10) and, moreover, can make specific care practices "easier to defend in public spaces where it is currently at risk of being squeezed" (10).

Key ethical considerations for theorizing and theory building, as those studying rhetorical practices of health and medicine often observe, are praxis oriented: They are about finding ways to make provisions for those with the most at stake, about accounting for the asymmetrical power dynamics of caring, about acknowledging influences and priorities, about making "guarded claims and qualified conclusions" (Schriver 1989, 274). In their discussion of the "Politics of Care in Technoscience," feminist STS scholars Aryn Martin et al. call attention to "the privileged position of the caring subject" which requires a care ethic of response-ability, characterized not by a "prescription" for caring but "a researcher's *capacity and willingness* to be moved, in both the affective and kinesthetic senses" of that word, toward an ameliorative response (11). They go on to encourage researchers to hover in the moments of *potential* movement, to "expose and to question the self-evidences that would otherwise prescribe its proper objects, as well as its seemingly necessary directions, temporalities, intensities, and forms of action" (11). We similarly propose that rhetoricians attend to our response-ability, asking, "who or what tends to get designated the proper or improper objects of care" (12) and who determines whether and how theory building is ameliorative, for whom, and based on what criteria.

The approach to theory building we propose—one that values the attunement of systems of care to collectives and individuals—enables a material ethics and helps us trace the material effects of knowing and understanding. It helps with the project of making sense of what our material-discursive entanglement in the world discloses to us about ethical practice. Barad terms this an "ethico-onto-epistemological" project to recognize the "intertwining of ethics, knowing, and being" (2007, 185). Rosi Braidotti argues that in a world where "quantitative differences for the sake of commodification and profit" (2011, 17) often take priority, "theoretical care," "conceptual creativity," and "ethical courage" are needed to support a "qualitative shift of perspective" (9, 17).

Such an ethics is not content with theorizing from afar, or the loose adaptation, hybridization, or creation of theory for theory's sake. It offers more than a reflexive, critical takedown. "Critical" enactments of theory building are most powerful and productive, we posit, when they do more than offer what Braidotti has called "a sterile opposition" (2011, 6). When it is not about opposition or exclusion, critique can be a creative and generative "engagement of the conceptual imagination in the task of producing sustainable alternatives . . . creative efforts aimed at activating the positivity of differences as affirmative praxis" (6).

Theorizing and theory building can generate "useful knowledge" that can help scholars and other stakeholders better understand unarticulated goals, relationships, functions, and effects of health rhetorics and practices (Segal 2005, 4). In this vein, Judy Segal proposes using rhetorical theory "heuristically, as probes" (16) for investigating problems in health and medicine. As an example of this type of contribution, Segal points to Scott's (2003) work on theorizing the disciplinary rhetorics of HIV testing. Beyond disarticulating the dominant ideologic by which testing's material-discursive practices diagnose subjects according to risk in order to protect some and guard against others, Scott seeks to rearticulate an alternative "ethic of responsiveness" that, among other things, is attuned to the interdependency of testing's stakeholders (234).

In other cases, theorizing and theory building can generate insights that can be taken up more directly to improve health experiences. We can see this in Mol's (2008) rearticulation of a logic of choice into a logic of care; in addition to showing how the dominant "logic of choice" figures patient agency around what is available to consumers or as a kind of exercise of citizenship (both of which prefigure the individualized, ethical role of the patient as one premised on making the right choices), Mol opens up an alternative logic of care that can "meticulously attend to the unpredictabilities of bodies" and experiences of patients (14), attend to "facts and values jointly" (53), carefully adapt and "fine-tune" biomedical research and technology (99), create collective spaces for healthcare storytelling and experimentation (102), and "doctor patiently" (108). "Because . . . caring itself is a moral activity," Mol explains, "there is no such thing as an (argumentative) ethics that can be disentangled from (practical) doctoring" (91). A more specific instantiation of a logic of care, Gouge's (2018) work on desire lines offers another example of (potentially) applied RHM research that provides an alternative way to understand, value, and learn from—rather than jump to fix—divergent practices, such as when people do not take medications as prescribed, when people who smoke are diagnosed with cancer and continue to smoke, or when Alzheimer's patients leave care facilities attempting to return to a home that is no longer theirs.

Practices in health and medicine ought to take seriously the importance of fit in care practices; they ought to value attunement to the unstable relationships among actors and environments, documents and bodies, and acknowledge the ongoing, fluid co-construction of knowledges, agencies, and meaning. And doing this requires both theorizing and theory building as value-laden acts of responsiveness and invention. We hope that scholars in RHM continue this work, engaging with other fields of inquiry (e.g., bioethics, medical anthropology and sociology, disability studies, feminist science studies, and philosophy of the body) that share similar perspectives on the value of theory. Recognizing the inventive and methodological nature of theory building can help us carefully consider the orientations that move us to study in different ways, those that can teach us how to productively "learn to be affected by" the world (Mol 2008, 262). We hope that RHM and rhetorical studies more broadly continue to motivate, open, and expand trajectories of theorizing as forms of care and that those trajectories support the rhetorical practices necessary to attune, engage, provoke, and invent.

NOTES

1. Kerlinger's (1973) definition of theory continues to be cited frequently in behavioral and scientific research. Scientific (e.g., from the U.S. National Academy of Sciences) and dictionary definitions of theory continue to emphasize its comprehensive explanatory and even predictive power. In his classic and also widely cited *The Conduct of Inquiry*, philosopher Kaplan characterizes theory as a "device for interpreting, critiquing, and unifying established laws . . . guiding the enterprise of discovering new and more powerful generalizations" (1964, 295).

2. See Scott and Meloncon (2018) for a similar discussion of theory building in RHM.

REFERENCES

Barad, Karen. 2007. *Meeting the Universe Halfway: Quantum Physics and the Entanglement of Matter and Meaning*. Durham: Duke University Press.

Barad, Karen. 2012a. "'Matter Feels, Converses, Suffers, Desires, Yearns, and Remembers': Interview with Karen Barad." In *New Materialism: Interviews and Cartographies*, ed. Rick Dolphijn and Iris Van der Tuin, 48–70. London: Open Humanities Press.

Barad, Karen. 2012b. "On Touching—The Inhuman That Therefore I Am." *Differences* 23 (3): 206–23.

Bivens, Kristin Marie. 2018. "Rhetorically Listening for Microwithdrawals of Consent in Research Practice." In *Methodologies for the Rhetoric of Health and Medicine*, ed. Lisa Meloncon and J. Blake Scott, 138–56. New York: Routledge.

Braidotti, Rosi. 2011. *Nomadic Subjects: Embodiment and Sexual Difference in Contemporary Feminist Theory*. New York: Columbia University Press.

Conklin, Jeff. 2005. *Dialogue Mapping: Building Shared Understanding of Wicked Problems*. Hoboken, NJ: Wiley.

Crowley, Sharon. 2006. *Toward a Civil Discourse: Rhetoric and Fundamentalism*. Pittsburgh: University of Pittsburgh Press.

Dolmage, Jay Timothy. 2013. *Disability Rhetoric*. Syracuse: Syracuse University Press.

Ehrenfeld, Dan. 2018. "Ecological Investments and the Circulation of Rhetoric: Studying the 'Saving Knowledge' of Dr. Emma Walker's Social Hygiene Lectures." In *Methodologies for the Rhetoric of Health and Medicine*, ed. Lisa Meloncon and J. Blake Scott, 41–60. New York: Routledge.

Emmons, Kimberly K. 2010. *Black Dogs and Blue Words: Depression and Gender in the Age of Self-Care*. New Brunswick: Rutgers University Press.

Fountain, T. Kenny. 2014. *Rhetoric in the Flesh: Trained Vision, Technical Expertise, and the Gross Anatomy Lab*. London: ATTW/Routledge.

Gouge, Catherine C. 2018. "'No Single Path': Desire Lines and Divergent Pathographies in Health and Medicine." In *Methodologies for the Rhetoric of Health and Medicine*, ed. Lisa Meloncon and J. Blake Scott, 115–37. New York: Routledge.

Graham, S. Scott. 2015. *The Politics of Pain Medicine: A Rhetorical-Ontological Inquiry*. Chicago: University of Chicago Press.

Graham, S. Scott, and Carl Herndl. 2013. "Multiple Ontologies in Pain Management: Toward a Postplural Rhetoric of Science." *Technical Communication Quarterly* 22 (2): 103–25.

Haraway, Donna J. 1997. *Modest_Witness@Second_Millennium.FemaleMan_Meets_Onco Mouse: Feminism and Technoscience*. New York: Routledge.

Harding, Sandra. 1987. "Introduction: Is There a Feminist Method?" In *Feminism and Methodology*, ed. Sandra Harding, 1–14. Bloomington: Indiana University Press.

Ingold, Tim. 2011. *Being Alive: Essays on Movement, Knowledge and Description*. New York: Routledge.

Jensen, Robin E. 2015. "An Ecological Turn in Rhetoric of Health Scholarship: Attending to the Historical Flow and Percolation of Ideas, Assumptions, and Arguments." *Communication Quarterly* 63 (5): 522–26.

Johnson, Nathan R. 2018. "Infrastructural Methodology: A Case in Protein as Public Health." In *Methodologies for the Rhetoric of Health and Medicine*, ed. Lisa Meloncon and J. Blake Scott, 61–78. New York: Routledge.

Kaplan, Abraham. 1964. *The Conduct of Inquiry: Methodology for Behavioral Science.* Piscataway, NJ: Transaction Publishers.

Kerlinger, Fred N. 1973. Foundations of Behavioral Research. 2nd ed. New York: Holt, Rinehart, and Winston.

Koerber, Amy. 2013. *Breast or Bottle? Contemporary Controversies in Infant-Feeding Policy and Practice.* Columbia: University of South Carolina Press.

Lawrence, Heidi Y., Bernice L. Hausman, and Clare J. Dannenberg. 2014. "Reframing Medicine's Publics: The Local as a Public of Vaccine Refusal." *Journal of Medical Humanities* 35 (2): 111–29.

Martin, Aryn, Natasha Myers, and Ana Viseu. 2015. "The Politics of Care in Technoscience." *Social Studies of Science* 45 (2): 1–17.

Mol, Annemarie. 2008. *The Logic of Care: Health and the Problem of Patient Choice.* New York: Routledge.

Mol, Annemarie, Ingunn Moser, and Jeannette Pols. 2010. "Care: Putting Practice into Theory." In *Care in Practice: On Tinkering in Clinics, Homes and Farms*, ed. Annemarie Mol, Ingunn Moser, and Jeanette Pols, 7–27. Bielefeld: Transaction-Verlag.

Molloy, Catherine. 2015. "Recuperative Ethos and Agile Epistemologies: Toward a Vernacular Engagement with Mental Illness Ontologies." *Rhetoric Society Quarterly* 45 (2): 138–63.

Owens, Kim Hensley. 2015. *Writing Childbirth: Women's Rhetorical Agency in Labor and Online.* Carbondale: Southern Illinois University Press.

Schriver, Karen A. 1989. "Theory Building in Rhetoric and Composition: The Role of Empirical Scholarship." *Rhetoric Review* 7 (2): 272–88.

Scott, J. Blake. 2003. *Risky Rhetoric: AIDS and the Cultural Practices of HIV Testing.* Carbondale: Southern Illinois University Press.

Scott, J. Blake, and Lisa Meloncon. 2018. "Manifesting Methodologies for the Rhetoric of Health and Medicine." In *Methodologies for the Rhetoric of Health and Medicine*, ed. Lisa Meloncon and J. Blake Scott, 1–23. New York: Routledge.

Segal, Judy Z. 2005. *Health and the Rhetoric of Medicine.* Carbondale: Southern Illinois University Press.

Spoel, Philippa, Roma Harris, and Flis Henwood. 2014. "Rhetorics of Health Citizenship: Exploring Vernacular Critiques of Government's Role in Supporting Healthy Living." *Journal of Medical Humanities* 25 (2): 131–47.

Sullivan, Patricia, and James E. Porter. 1997. *Opening Spaces: Writing Technologies and Critical Research Practices.* Westport, CT: Ablex.

Teston, Christa. 2016. "Dignity and the Posthuman Patient." Paper presented at the Rhetoric Society of America Biennial Conference. Atlanta.

Treichler, Paula A. 1999. *How to Have Theory in an Epidemic: Cultural Chronicles of AIDS.* Durham: Duke University Press.

Zoller, Heather M. 2005. "Health Activism: Communication Theory and Action for Social Change." *Communication Theory* 15 (4): 341–64.

13

VICTIMLESS LEATHER
Toward a New Materialist Ethics of Invention

Jason Barrett-Fox and Geoffrey Clegg

(UN)COMMON TOPICS

Victimless Leather, a controversial bioart project created by Oron Catts and Ionat Zurr, consists of a small polymer base lined with mouse stem cells and human bone cells that, when placed in a bioreactor and fed by the autodrip of a perfusion pump, grows on its own. As the original polymer degrades, the cells replenish and what remains is a quasi-living organism in the shape of a tiny, stitchless jacket. This miniscule semi-living blazer—meant more to complicate the traditional binaries of human/nonhuman, subject/object, wear-er/wear-ee, than to serve as a viable replacement for those who would like to wear leather without the guilt of killing animals—is but one of several recent cultural emergences that make clear the need for a revamped theory of invention and a more capacious understanding of rhetoric, one that incorporates the material as well as the discursive facets of agency, one that opens a channel for hearing how matter speaks to us. Such an intervention complicates traditional humanist notions of inventional agency as something possessed and wrought by individual human agents. In what follows, we offer a provisional take on what the ethics of invention might look like in a posthuman rhetoric influenced by what Scott Barnett and Casey Boyle call "rhetorical ontology," the study of "how various material elements—human and nonhuman alike—interact suasively and agentially in rhetorical situations and ecologies" (2016, 2). In doing so, we piggyback on Sharon Crowley's Aristotelian understanding of rhetorical invention to investigate two important onto-*topoi* in posthumanist rhetoric, two important avenues for exploring matter's voices: the bioinformational and the ecological. What follows is not a set of steps for how to be an environmentalist, nor is it a study of rhetoric rooted in language. Rather, it is an exploration of the possibilities for invention at the point humans become implicated in nature's

DOI: 10.7330/9781607328933.c013

extrahuman emergences, meant to evoke a sense of being-with and being-through rhetoric.

Sharon Crowley has elaborated that any rhetorical investigation must begin by regarding rhetoric "at minimum" as "an art of invention" (2003, n.p.), an art, she explains, that begins when "a writer or speaker" searches for arguments "because some situation needs to be addressed" (2002, 231). At its simplest, Crowley explains, invention incorporates different "methods" for discovering arguments, from Aristotle's *topoi* to Burke's dramatistic pentad and beyond, all of which help "writers analyze the complex relationships always at work in any situation or problem" (233). For Crowley, "Theories are rhetorical inventions: depictions or assessments produced by and within specific times and locations as means of opening other ways of believing or acting" (2006, 28).

Crowley's sense of the timeliness and locality—dare we say materiality— of rhetorical theory provides ingress into rhetorical ontology, calling into question not just the material practices of rhetoric and rhetorical theory but the very vocality and agency of matter itself, its ability to permeate and reshape rhetorical worlds. So just as Crowley leads us to understand rhetoric as an art of invention, *we assert that rhetoric itself is something that matter is inventing upon.* Such an insight demonstrates the urgency for rethinking how to act, how to invent, in a world in which the subject/object distinction is eroded, where we are closer to the stuff we used to think we had conquered, so close as to feel the suasion into which we have been incorporated. One such urgency, for instance, has been articulated by scientists suggesting that humans may not last another century on Earth due to habitat exploitation to global warming to climate change. As suggested above, matter has indeed begun to insert itself into the traditional rhetorical situation, toppling rhetoric's reliance on human discursivity in the political sphere and inaugurating a more capacious understanding of agency, invention, and rhetorical force, not to mention a new ethics of the connectedness of human and nonhuman actors. Hence, rhetorical scholars find ourselves at a kairotic moment—in our field *and* in the Anthropocene—in which material has come to voice, has inserted itself into our conversations, challenging not just the humanist notion that agency is possessed only within discursive subjects but the more complicated notion that "the human agent [even] exceeds the subject as it is constituted by most poststructuralist theory" (Smith 1988, xxx). Karen Barad argues that this moment is defined by our slow waking to matter's vitality, its ability to "make itself felt" (2012, 59). "Materiality itself," she argues, "is always already a desiring dynamism, a reiterative, reconfiguring, energized and energizing, enlivened and enlivening," and such a recognition, in its timely delivery, helps to define an emergent rhetorical situation, framed by the new materialism, in which human discourse has always been co-constituted by materiality (59).

So, the kairotic disciplinary impulse to rethink the ethics of invention must, we argue, enlarge its scope beyond discursive subjects, incorporating the macroscopic view that "matter feels, converses, suffers, desires, yearns, and remembers" (Barad 2012, 59), must "stretch agency away from its traditional seat in subjects to a full consideration of action as *material, affective, ecological,* and *emergent*" (Rickert 2013, 129). In a word, matter has beckoned us to revisit our ethics of invention, newly infused with topoi entangled with ontological urgencies. Such topoi move beyond Aristotle's common topics into what he called *idioi topoi*, which belong "to a particular study like physics or politics" (Kennedy 1963, 100). The questions driving Barnett and Boyle's rhetorical ontology (we prefer the term "onto-rhetoric") push beyond even Christa Olson's sophisticated notion of "embodiable topoi," a trying-on of "persuasive force within bodily performances" (2010, 301). From the ecological urgencies of climate change, such as rising sea levels to micro-beads in our water to islands of plastic in the Pacific, we invent—and are invented by—topics that are forcefully emergent in our consciousness, as if, in an almost Hegelian way, the world is awakening to itself through us. Such topoi pre-enlist human agencies, rhetorically and otherwise: we become part of nature's enthymeme. Onto-topoi function as enthymemes that are (to borrow a phrase from Kennedy), not rhetorical, per se, but metarhetorical: less are they interested in discursive persuasion and more are they interested in the suasion inherent in rhetoric's material entanglements.

Such an ontological recognition is kairotic in another special sense, one that acknowledges but moves us past the traditional scholarship on kairos that understands it as the opportune time for speech and action. Without a doubt, the melting polar ice caps, for example, demand an appropriate and timely response, but an emphasis only on timeliness elides an important element of kairos's original use: its spatiality, its embeddedness in matter. Thomas Rickert explains,

> Yet another shade of meaning for *kairos* stems from weaving. Showing up in works by Homer, Hesychius, Aeschylus, Pindar, and others, *kairos* can refer to the workings of a loom. As one weaves, there is an opening in the warp through which the shuttle must pass; the space lasts only a moment, so the time to make the "shot" through the warp is brief . . . The sense of critical time is clear, no doubt. But just as important, the opening through which the shot must pass is quite clearly a *place* . . . [P]lace here emerges

as an ensemble of material elements that create patterns of open space necessary for action. (2013, 78–79)

The multidimensionality of kairos, its operation in time *and* place, serves as the basis for our investigation of a posthuman ethics of invention, an ethics of invention that invests in the radical connectivity of persons and their embodied realities, environments, and material ecosystems. An ethics of invention in this space requires a commitment to the reinvestment not only in the arguments available in a given situation but the material entanglements that underlie urgencies such as those found *Victimless Leather*: urgencies that call for a reconsideration of the primacy of human discourse and agency, urgencies that foreground bodily, environmental, and biological negotiations. An ethics of radical connectivity must foreground the notion that "agency is not held, it is not a property of persons or things; rather, agency is an enactment, a matter of possibilities for reconfiguring entanglements. So agency is not about choice in any liberal humanist sense; rather, it is about the possibilities of accountability entailed in reconfiguring material-discursive apparatuses of bodily production, including the boundary articulations and exclusions that are marked by those practices" (Barad 2012, 54). A posthuman ethics of invention, then, expands the "field of forces" with which we are connected and to which we attend (55), widening the scope of the rhetorical situation well beyond discourse, beyond individuated human agents, positioning us as "semiaware nodal point[s]," as Rickert calls us, "conduit[s] for a wide, complex array of forces" (2013, 128). Here, the effort is not just in directing our attention but looking for the arguments always-already at work in the material entanglements in which we are enmeshed. Such an insight demands a rhetoric reinvested in an ethics of radical connectivity and disinvested in humanism's unintentionally tyrannical residues.

In 2008, *Victimless Leather* joined other similar exhibits at *sk-interfaces*, an installation at the Foundation for Art and Creative Technology, arranged by face-transplant surgeon Peter Butler. Butler, of the Royal Free Hospital in London, "suggested that using the techniques of bioscience to create works of art allows us to 'dream about possibilities'" and negotiate new ethical entanglements (Rees 2008, 891). Other works in *sk-interfaces* include jars filled with Marion Laval-Jeantet and Benoit Mangin's epidermal cells, "which have been grafted onto pig derma and then tattooed with images of endangered species"; the artists suggest that "to be appreciated," a collector "may choose to have it xenotransplanted onto his or her own skin" (891). Another artist, Orlan, created a living Harlequin coat "from a mixture of her own cells, animal cells, and most controversially, cells from a 12-week-old human fetus of African origin, purchased over the Internet" (891). Yet another artist, Serlac, shows a video of a surgery in which he has an ear-shaped prosthesis made of silicon and stem cells grafted "onto his left forearm," into which he hopes to place a Bluetooth interface so that his new appendage would become "an 'Internet organ' for the body" (891). Such challenges to artistic invention complicate not only the binaries between life and art, subject and object, but also highlight the need to adapt our sense of agency to situations that require dispersing the very stuff of the human in every direction, from transgenic tissues to mediational technologies. Frances Stacey argues for the importance of resituating such work outside the aesthetic and focus on their "bioethical" implications (2009, 496).

More conservative critics, Stacey explains, warn that such inventional strategies belie deeply disconcerting ethical boundary-crossing, calling it "a new 'artful' eugenic movement," or the "aesthetic indulgence in 'carnivalesque sadism'" (2009, 497). Rather than such backhanded rebukes, Stacey argues, these artists should be understood as "thoughtful, crucial interventionists," though "not without some uncertainties and ambivalences" (497). All the aforementioned cases of bio-art call into question the need for a rejuvenated ethics of invention, both inside and outside aesthetic parameters. In each case, from Eduardo Kac's *GFP Bunny*, in which an albino rabbit is transgenically infused with a green fluorescent protein and glows when "illuminated with a blue light," to Kathy High's work recuperating former transgenic laboratory rats that express "HLA-B27, a human class I major histocompatibility molecule" and are used for "research into Crohn's disease"—from which High herself suffers—these aesthetic experiments also function as rhetorical in(ter)ventions, drawing the audience into new kinds of onto-enthymematic spaces, implicating the audience in new ethical contingencies that challenge our notion of the human/nonhuman divide (499). Such invented entanglements draw the audience into an enthymematic space of ethical response, grafting them to a rhetoric that is onto-affective, one in which and to which they can, even must, respond.

ECOLOGICAL TOPOI, OR, (RE)PLACING RHETORIC

Posthuman rhetorical invention allows for a second reading of topoi that draws from a less well-known facet of Aristotle's use of the expression. Before Aristotle offered topoi in rhetorical terms as "ethical or political premises on which an argument can be built" or other "logical strategies, such as arguing from cause to effect" (Kennedy 1994,

5), topos was sometimes "used to denote the underlying extension . . . of the whole universe, or of all things" (Algra 1995, 36). Indeed, in his *Physics*, Aristotle argues that "there are four candidates for the identification of *topos*: (1) form, (2) matter, (3) the *extension between the limits of the body*, or (4) the limits themselves" (Algra 1995, 125). It is the extension between things that drives this use of topos for new materialist rhetoric. Ontologically speaking, topos "is subsumed under a non-substantial category," meaning that one of its base definitional functions is relationality (128); the meaning of *topos*, in this sense, then, is engendered by means of its interactions, its nodal extensions, that both frame and connect.

Such an understanding of topos underscores a fundamental problem of traditional topoi for a rhetoric imbued with an ethic of connectedness. Most rhetorical theory, even in recent ecology-minded incarnations, runs into problems. Byron Hawk, for instance, argues that Dobrin and Weisser's (2012) book, though "clearly on the right track," holds back "from pushing the concept of ecology to its limits by continuing to rely on forms of social-epistemic rhetoric and social construction," those dual handmaidens of humanism (Hawk 2007, 223). Such reliance on social-epistemic rhetorical orientations, Hawk explains, probably occurs "because there is no other completely articulated and accepted paradigm beyond expressivism and social-epistemic rhetoric in which to place their work"; consequently, their pedagogical interventions still rely upon "public action through discourse, on discourse determining and changing material contexts" (223).

A topos of ontological relationality, what we have called before radical connectivity, allows for space for discursive action, but it reasserts rhetoric as acted upon by materiality, a rhetoric shaped by material entanglements, not vice versa. Hawk himself doesn't even push the notion of ecology far enough, arguing that ecology's function should be to "move discussions of writing, rhetoric, and invention beyond the standard inventional heuristics and social categories toward models that integrate environments into writing and inventional processes" (223). The last assertion, that we integrate models of environments into writing and inventional processes, forecloses upon insights that environments, their urgencies, have already incorporated—and cracked the calcifications beneath—such models. The proof of this is simple: urgencies inherent in humankind's contemporary ecological crises extend beyond the parameters of what humanist discourse and action can change or even mitigate. Rather than fatalistic, such a view is ontologically challenging, as it forces us to reconsider futures unimaginable in traditional humanist paradigms.

Our environment offers us constant reminders that the human-nonhuman dam has broken (if it ever existed) and that we are already awash in the complications of messy agentive dispersions and incursions. Climate scientists are nearly univocal about such phenomena. Naomi Oreskes, for instance, examined the abstracts of 928 global warming papers published in peer-reviewed journals between 1993 and 2003 and "found that not a single one fought to refute the 'consensus' among scientists 'over the reality of human-induced climate change'" (Chakrabarty 2009, 200). Such findings also coincide with the 2007 Fourth Assessment Report of the Intergovernmental Panel on Climate Change of the United Nations and virtually all other scientific data produced on that subject in the last twenty years. Arguments that continue "to justify the separation of human from nature history" (Chakrabarty 2009, 204), ensconced in humanism, are losing their force, and for good reason. Bruno Latour puts it this way: "Politics does not fall neatly on one side of a divide and nature on the other. From the time the term 'politics' was invented, every type of politics has been defined by its relation to nature, whose every feature, property, and function depends on the polemical will to limit, reform, establish, short-circuit, or enlighten public life" (2004, 1). Both Chakrabarty and Latour call for a similar dissolution of the fabricated divide between humans and nature. And while such a call is useful in complicating the nature/cultural binary, it obscures the more pressing necessity to recognize that not only does the current relation between humans and nature need to be dissolved, but a new relation needs to be provisionally reconstituted, remediated, *reinvented*. Such entanglements, though dynamic, need to be rearticulated with a sense of agentive distribution and pervasive affectability that acknowledges the radical connectivity between humans and our world (perhaps better: the world and its humans), one in which meaning is constituted through the multiplicity of factors that channel agency in and through humans, channels that help us articulate ourselves-in-becoming and locate ourselves after the fact as we begin to recognize our radical connectedness.

Such a radical connectedness led Nobel–winning chemist Paul J. Crutzen and marine scientist Eugene F. Stoermer to posit the Anthropocene in 2000. In a short piece in *Nature* in 2002, Crutzen argues, that "for the past three centuries, the effects of humans on the global environment have escalated. Because of these anthropogenic emissions of carbon dioxide, global climate may depart significantly from natural behavior for many millennia to come" (Crutzen and Stoermer 2000, 23). The codification of the Anthropocene indicates the formal moment when human and natural histories melt into each other, where human agency and the agencies of nature collide, entangle, and produce urgencies.

To qualify, this speaking-through, this multidimensional clearing of channels *does not determine content but neither does it foreclose upon our awareness of the discursive valences that came before.* Rather, posthuman rhetorical invention pays primary attention to the modalities of entanglement (which simply means articulating being or being-articulated, from Gutenberg's galaxy to DNA's helix to the biome in your bellybutton) in, through, among, and beyond humans. Its primary investment is a suasion not *without people but without individuated agents,* a suasion that is always-already ontically emergent and in need of ontological articulation, one that enthymematically incorporates the audience into an ethics of inventing-being (and being-invented). Indeed, to recapitulate Latour's notion that our understanding of nature is our biggest impediment to an effective ecology, *posthuman rhetoric argues that our understanding of the agency-possessing, individuated rhetor is perhaps the biggest obstacle we face in actualizing rhetoric's capacious power and realizing more accurately humans' place in the manifold.*

THE PRAXIS OF POSTHUMAN ETHICAL INVENTION

Latour, who extends his critique of ecology in a posthuman direction, offers a networked rhetorical situation in which "both humans and non-humans have agency within networks of distributed power" (Pflugfelder 2015, 117), networks that constantly bring their various nodes (actors, actants, assemblages) in and out of relationship and in doing make them speak, or, at least, open them up to being "heard." Nathan Stormer, in a fascinating explication of rhetorical *taxis,* aptly calls such posthuman arrangements "articulations," a kind of posthuman "performative" (2004, 259); Latour calls them "perturbations" (Harmon 2009, 158), and Jane Bennett, in some of her earliest new materialist work, calls this phenomenon "thing-power materialism," her attempt to explain "the ways in which human being and thinghood overlap" (2004, 349) and are articulated.

We find in Crowley's history of writing analogous calls for questioning our discipline's conservative enframement, calls that function as means of exploring and expanding invention on the ground, in the writing classroom. Quite frequently the field gets stuck within ruts of formalism, determinism, or conservatism, all of which bury innovation under the guise of correctness. These pedagogies, in effect, limit complexity in favor of unity and surveillance (Crowley 1995, 229). Crowley provides her groundwork for this perspective in her 2001 disputation of Richard Weaver's definition of rhetoric, wherein she states, "I vigorously resist his insistence that rhetorical invention is an avenue to truth, particularly the exclusive notion of truth adumbrated in Weaver's ideology. Rhetoricians and teachers of composition desperately need a rhetoric that features a rich theory of invention and a panoply of invention strategies on a par with those adumbrated in ancient rhetorics" (2001, 85).

Crowley follows this with reminding us with that our theories need "to be developed within an ideological context that is aware and suspicious of the racism, masculinism, and narcissism" in order to analyze our work effectively (2001, 85). Such calls are not unique in Crowley's oeuvre. Others, specifically Janet Atwill, have asserted our need to break past the humanist constraints of invention in order to open the doors to new discourses. Atwill, in her unpublished dissertation, argues that humanism's suppression of techne in favor of consistency has altered our own ability to suss out subjects, which in turn limits the addition of new inventional techniques (1990). Atwill expands this argument in her book and ties techne and invention together. She offers that "techne marks a domain of human intervention and invention," and "it is often associated with the transgression of an existing boundary—a desire for 'more' that challenges or refines relations of power" (2009, 7). Within the spectrum of techne, we find a kindred spirit to Crowley in that "techne is knowledge as production, not product; intervention and articulation, rather than representation" (7). Crowley's and Atwill's emphases on breaking away from a strictly traditional view of rhetoric and expanding our scope of invention should be our clarion call to continue to back away from humanist strictures of the rhetorical self in order to expand our topoi of writing, expand our invention, and refine our sense of the unique "oughts" and "shoulds" of a radically connected ethics.

Posthuman invention becomes a parallax entanglement of spaces, ideologies, and nodal points converging into a sharpened kairotic action that is not mediated by a simple apocalyptic urgency; rather, it is reconfigured to the unmitigated *whole* of emerging agencies of human-nonhuman actors converging to offer a fuller view of the onto-ecologies around us. In a sense, posthuman invention emerges from the before-now-after without regard to linear or chronological necessities of the moment as they are not regulatory matters for its enactment, nor does it restrict itself to ethical arguments solely bound upon the natural state of the world; instead, we argue for a supranatural invention unfolding beyond the limits of the rhetor unconstrained by the axioms of the past and limitless in its ability to invent itself.

Changing our dispositions means changing our institutions, and in writing studies we still struggle with the complex nature of writing and the role of the actor within the networks we create, not to mention their embeddedness in the corporate neoliberal university. How do we foster invention through these actors, actants, and assemblages? Marilyn Cooper, in her exploration of the complexity theory in composition studies, writes, "We have for a long time understood an agent as one who through conscious intention or free will causes changes in the world. But I suggest that neither conscious intention nor free will—at least as we commonly think of them—is involved in acting or bringing about change: though the world changes in response to individual action, agents are very often not aware of their intentions, they do not directly cause changes, and the choices they make are not free from influence from their inheritance, past experiences, or their surroundings" (2011, 421). Cooper is correct that agents are often unaware of their role within change, a point she goes on to describe as positioning an actor's change as "aris[ing] from [more than] conscious mental acts" (421). However, our goal should be to rethink the nature of disciplinary change to account for the unbounded ethical implications of attunement to human-nonhuman assemblages and their urgencies. In order to fully realize Cooper's vision for complexity within discursive spaces, we must also follow through on adding to these environments by including actors that exist in nonrational roles: bombs primed for the destruction of all environs, viral loads (electronic or molecular), invisible economic imprints that affect us all, and artificial intelligence. This means an expression of our world well beyond the Kantian finitude of our own or even collective, complex experiences.

As *Victimless Leather* offers, our knowledge of bioinscription complicates conversations by challenging grounded biopolitical conversations of the self in relation to the supercomplex material entanglements in which we find our future. Such questions reflect Cooper's want for a "pedagogy of responsibility" that extends past the self and affords all of us a "rhetoric" which "can contribute to the effort to construct a good common world" (2011, 443). While Cooper wishes for us to help students understand that their rhetorics have effects applicable to the larger networked world instead of "affirmations of absolute truth," we must extend our engagements radically in every direction.

Of course, many factors complicate theoretical attempts at complex invention. For instance, Slavoj Žižek's apocalyptic turns toward the inescapable entrapment of capitalism and nature (2011), among others, threaten to stall realistic movement toward Cooper's pedagogy of responsibility and block Crowley's want for new variation of invention. Unlike Žižek, however, Paul Lynch offers that "ironically, the easiest part of writing about the end of the world is finding a place to begin" where the apocalyptic can and is able to be linked into a networked invention (2012, 460). Citing the Horizon/BP spill, Japan's tsunami, global warming, and other ecological disasters, Lynch challenges Žižek's nihilism by reminding us that we have a breadth of ways to view and connect critical ecological questions that extend beyond the body.

Lynch finds no problem with asking us to utilize the Latourian notion of "mak[ing] composition messier and baggier, less prone to clarity and critique, more open to complexity and even confusion," a strategy we have implemented in this essay (2012, 465). Confusion may not be part of Crowley's ideal sense of invention as art, techne, and complex connector, but within Lynch's reading of Latour we have the "chemical reactions and political reaction" (qtd. on 466) needed to expand our posthumanist invention. An ethic of open confusion, then, may be just the place to begin.

Lynch finds within Latourian composition perhaps one of the critical aspects of our work by reminding us that "our job—and ultimately our students' job—would be to give their worlds the capacity to write or to speak" (2012, 468). These are not actions of apocalyptic unveilings or specialized critiques without end; rather, Latourian composition repurposes rhetoric to "recognize the student as a deadly serious realist who wants to enter our academic Thing, and has brought a companion to speak with us" (473). That companion will be the new arguments brought to fore from the students' own complex, nuanced, and networked knowledges that emerge from their questioning events, exploring connective tissues between themselves and nature, experiences, and other nontraditional routes that are still resisted in the composition classroom.

The needs for a more tactile, corporeal sensitivity in composition finds an advocate in Shari J. Stenberg, who borrows from Anna Feigenbaum's work on the fantasy spaces of neoliberal education. Stenberg's effective critique of dismantled classrooms, distance education, and the transaction-based rhetoric of teaching offers a similar critique to Crowley's illusion of sameness within the academy. Whereas Crowley reminds us that the difference between San Jose Community College and Yale surrounds the "very different relations of governmentality" (Crowley 1998, 221) inherent in their students' social and economic backgrounds, Stenberg proffers that similar, current neoliberal forces, operating through legislation such as the No Child Left Behind Act of 2001 and accreditation agencies, not to mention academe's incredible administrative bloat, sell students on the idea that their education is no different than their peers at other universities, where instructors "deliver prepackaged, standardized knowledge much as a Starbucks barista delivers a uniform latte, no matter where she, or the store, is located" (Stenberg 2015, 101). This sanitization of education, which is limited to such constraints and downplays or ignores class difference and ecological difference, ultimately means that the student's agency allows for him or her to find freedom in this space. From this neoliberal fantasy of autonomy comes the belief that "individuals are best served by acclimation to a more standard mode of being and doing," leading to norms that stress this to be "the only 'rational' option" (Stenberg 2015, 102). Much like the past humanist rejection of nonhuman agencies, the agencies of those within our classrooms, whether instructor or students, are ultimately shut out in order to provide a static model of knowledge creation and dissemination.

The politics of the university—and indeed the politics of composition—found in Crowley and Stenberg challenge the corporate monotony and argue for offering students radical inventional connectedness. Where others such as Lynch ask for us to expand and welcome the student wanting to explore their world, Stenberg reminds us of the neoliberal-humanist constraints imposed by forces outside the English Department. Our hope is that composition scholars should help invent the expansion and complication of knowledge and disrupt conservative bureaucratic formations of ontological questions. The incorporation of posthuman invention free from the constraints of disciplinary and institutional constraints should help expand these spaces from such tyranny, though as Ryan Skinnell points out, "the notion that disciplinary specialists could make that decision unilaterally is impossible to maintain" (2016, 138). Likewise, from Skinnell's reading of the last century's attempts at changing composition's relationship in the university, we can only see that "the more information in the hands of institutional decision-makers does not guarantee more composition-friendly decisions" (143). To enact such change, however, we must recode our relationship with the university, knowledge making, and ethical positions to fight against such impossible odds so as to cement a firmer sense that we can invite students into the larger conversations that directly affect them.

SOME FINAL ETHICAL REENTANGLEMENTS

The first and probably the toughest part of reinventing ourselves as rhetors and teachers of a provisional posthuman ethics is attunement, the initial adjustment of our affective features to all the ontological channels open to us. How can we, as Rickert encourages us, think and act with greater levels of affectability to the manifold and in so doing become with it as it becomes through us? How can we pay attention to the ambient features of our assemblages (2013, 9)?

The first steps toward a posthuman ethics of invention may be as simple as throwing off the imaginary barriers of isolated, individuated, humanism, the buttresses of an agency possessed, and pay stricter attention to the agencies sprouting around us—organic or inorganic, mechanical or biological, human or nonhuman—not only their existence but their varying and emergent forms of mediality. Attention to such bioinscriptions surprised Paola Antonelli, the curator of *Victimless Leather*, when she discovered that the tiny living jacket had grown at a rate so rapid that it clogged its own incubation tube, forcing her to pull the exhibit's plug, "killing" it. The tendrils of agency unfurled in that moment, and her entanglement in *Victimless Leather*'s radical ontological invention—its fundamental explosion of a previously compartmentalized materiosemiotics—implicated her as a coagent, counteragent, and in her retelling, an agent of transmission. For Antonelli, and for us, the ethics of invention are born out of emergent situations, situations that demand continual renegotiations of the very boundaries of our own humanity. "I've always been pro-choice," she explains of her attunement, "and all of a sudden I'm here not sleeping at night about killing a coat" (Lapworth 2015, 96).

REFERENCES

Algra, Keimpe. 1995. *Concepts of Space in Greek Thought.* New York: Brill.
Atwill, Janet. 1990. "Refiguring Rhetoric as Art: Aristotle's Concept of Techne and the Humanist Paradigm." PhD dissertation, Purdue University, West Lafayette, IN.
Atwill, Janet. 2009. *Rhetoric Reclaimed: Aristotle and the Liberal Arts Tradition.* Ithaca, NY: Cornell University Press.
Barad, Karen. 2012. "Matter Feels, Converses, Suffers, Desires, Yearns and Remembers." In *New Materialism: Interviews and Cartographies,* ed. Rick Dolpijn and Iris van der Tuin, 48–70. Ann Arbor: Open Humanities Press.
Barnett, Scot, and Casey Boyle, eds. 2016. *Rhetoric, through Everyday Things.* Tuscaloosa: University of Alabama Press.
Bennett, Jane. 2004. "The Force of Things: Steps toward an Ecology of Matter." *Political Theory* 32 (3): 347–72.
Chakrabarty, Dipesh. 2009. "The Climate of History: Four Theses." *Critical Inquiry* 35 (2): 197–222.

Cooper, Marilyn. 2011. "Rhetorical Agency as Emergent and Enacted." *College Composition and Communication* 15 (1): 420–49.

Crowley, Sharon. 1995. "Composition's Ethic of Service, the Universal Requirement, and the Discourse of Student Need." *JAC* 15 (2): 227–39.

Crowley, Sharon. 1998. *Composition in the University*. Pittsburgh: University of Pittsburgh Press.

Crowley, Sharon. 2001. "When Ideology Motivates Theory: The Case of the Man from Weaverville." *Rhetoric Review* 20 (1–2): 66–93.

Crowley, Sharon. 2002. "Teaching Invention." *Strategies for Teaching First-Year Composition*, ed. Duane Roen, Veronica Pantoja, Lauren Yena, Susan K. Miller, and Eric Waggoner, 231–34. Urbana: NCTE.

Crowley, Sharon. 2003. "Composition Is Not Rhetoric." *Enculturation* 5 (1): n.p.

Crowley, Sharon. 2006. *Toward a Civil Discourse*. Pittsburgh: University of Pittsburgh Press.

Crutzen, Paul J., and Eugene F. Stoermer. 2000. "Global Change Newsletter." *Anthropocene* 41: 17–18.

Dobrin, Sidney J., and Christian R. Weisser. 2012. *Natural Discourse: Toward Ecocomposition*. New York: SUNY Press.

Harmon, Graham. 2009. *Bruno Latour: Prince of Networks*. Victoria, Australia: re.press.

Hawk, Byron. 2007. *A Counter-History of Composition: Toward Methodologies of Complexity*. Pittsburgh: University of Pittsburgh Press.

Kennedy, George. 1963. *The Art of Persuasion in Ancient Greece*. Princeton: Princeton University Press.

Kennedy, George. 1994. *A New History of Classical Rhetoric*. Princeton: Princeton University Press.

Lapworth, Andrew. 2015. "Habit, Art, and the Plasticity of the Subject: The Ontogenetic Shock of the Bioart Encounter." *cultural geographies* 22 (1): 85–102.

Latour, Bruno. 2004. *The Politics of Nature*. Cambridge: Harvard University Press.

Lynch, Paul. 2012. "Composition's New Thing: Bruno Latour and the Apocalyptic Turn." *College English* 74 (5): 458–76.

Olson, Christa J. 2010. "Performing Embodiable Topoi: Strategic Indigeneity and the Incorporation of Ecuadorian National Identity." *Quarterly Journal of Speech* 96 (3): 300–23.

Pflugfelder, Ehren Helmut. 2015. "No One at the Wheel? Nonhuman Agency and Agentive Movement." In *Thinking with Bruno Latour in Rhetoric and Composition*, ed. Paul Lynch and Nathaniel Rivers, 115–30. Carbondale: Southern Illinois University Press.

Rees, Jane. 2008. "Cultures in the Capital." *Nature* 451 (February): 891.

Rickert, Thomas. 2013. *Ambient Rhetoric: The Attunements of Rhetorical Being*. Pittsburgh: University of Pittsburgh Press.

Skinnell, Ryan. 2016. *Conceding Composition: A Crooked History of Composition's Institutional Fortunes*. Logan: Utah State University Press.

Smith, Paul. 1988. *Discerning the Subject*. Minneapolis: Minnesota University Press.

Stacey, Frances. 2009. "Bio-Art: The Ethics behind the Aesthetics." *Molecular Cell Biology* 10: 496–500.

Stenberg, Shari. 2015. *Repurposing Composition: Feminist Interventions in a Neoliberal Age*. Logan: Utah State University Press.

Stormer, Nathan. 2004. "Articulation: A Working Paper on Rhetoric and Taxis." *Quarterly Journal of Speech* 90 (3): 257–84.

Žižek, Slavoj. 2011. *Living in the End Times*. New York: Verso.

14

CORPOREAL RHETORIC AS EMBODIED ACTION
Composing in/through Bodily Motion

Bre Garrett

Rhetoricians are being urged to look at the human body and the mate-
rial conditions and practices associated with it.

—Sharon Crowley, "Afterword:
The Material of Rhetoric"

What grabs me, again and again, lies beyond the words. My
moment of connection tends to happen in the warmth of this
hand in mine. It occurs in the material connection that seems
to well up between these gray eyes and my own deep gaze. I can
feel the skin change its electric tonus as I am listening to the
uncoiling account. There's a timbre in the voice that I follow,
even as I lose the words. In the moment of verbal disclosure,
physical intimacy changes the time and space of encounter.

—Petra Kuppers, "your darkness also /
rich and beyond fear"

Embodied agency . . . opens the door to embodied action through
corporeal rhetoric.

—Kristie Fleckenstein, *Vision, Rhetoric, and Social*
Action in the Composition Classroom

At the turn of the twenty-first century, scholars from rhetorical history
and theory, disability studies, composition pedagogy, and computers and
composition legitimized a study of bodies through essential recovery
work. Sharon Crowley was one of the early voices in rhetoric and writing
studies to reclaim bodies as subjects of rhetorical consideration. Human
bodies are the materials of rhetoric, she argued, and "rhetoricians are
being urged to look" (1999, 357). Three years later, she named "Body
Studies in Rhetoric and Composition" as an emerging new area of study

DOI: 10.7330/9781607328933.c014

(2002). Within a few short years, bodies swiftly moved from a realm of "unmentioned" to the heart of intellectual rhetorical inquiry (178).

Crowley charged the field to reconceptualize the subject position based on a posthumanist rather than liberal modernist construction of self and other and, as a result, to rethink the relationship between speaker and audience as well as the nature of knowledge making (2002, 178). Writing at the same moment, Kristie S. Fleckenstein called for an embodied discourse that acknowledged the "somatic mind," or mind and body as "permeable, intertextual territory that is continually made and remade" (1999, 281). Both Fleckenstein and Crowley, citing Susan Bordo, advocated the study of situated bodies as a rejection of the *view from nowhere* that is so often perpetuated in rhetoric and writing scholarship. Crowley specifically called out composition scholars, illustrating, "the 'writing body' is little noticed in composition studies, yet compositionists anxiously and repeatedly write a phantasmic student body into their scholarship" (2002, 178). Through the declaration of body studies, Crowley heralded a reembodying of research methods, theories, and pedagogies.

Bodies, then, have provided a particular place of/for invention, or reinvention—a *topos*—for scholars in the field to investigate the nuances and complexities of rhetorical situations. Any rhetorical action consists of multiple nodes at which bodies must access knowledge and respond back to the world using an abundance of available composing materials. Putting bodies back in rhetoric and writing activity, whether through historical recovery work (Dolmage 2009; Hawhee 2004; Wilson and Lewiecki-Wilson 2001), rewriting delivery and performance (Fishman et al. 2005; Porter 2009), new locations for composition history and theory (Hawk 2007), or embodied pedagogies (Fleckenstein 2010; Lewiecki-Wilson and Brueggemann 2008); through composing with multiple media and modes (Wysocki 2002, 2004), or via new media production and the queering of composing spaces (Alexander and Rhodes 2008, 2010), between 2001 and 2010—a vast number of scholars turned to physical bodies as *topoi*, or places of departure for discovering and creating new knowledges about writing and rhetoric. Redounding from Crowley's initial call, we witness a collective rewriting of rhetoric to include critical spaces for bodies as rhetorical materials.

In this chapter, I propose an embodied theory of rhetorical invention that draws from the intersection of rhetorical theory, disability studies, and multimodal, embodied pedagogies to extend the arguments that bodies perform as topoi, or sites of multidimensional invention, to include considerations of delivery. I draw from person-based research:

In the summer of 2010, I was invited to participate in a workshop series from Petra Kuppers's Olimpias Performance Research Projects (see Kuppers 2000a, 2000b). Olimpias is an artist collective that produces highly embodied performance-based, open-access workshops. The collective consists of larger research projects, and each project consists of a series of workshops, or situated investigative sessions through which participants convene to explore, in radical ways, dynamic embodied communication capabilities. Kuppers's workshops explore the very nature of how humans communicate in a variety of means and expressions—kinesthetic, aural, oral, and linguistic modes—and she invited me to attend a workshop from a new project series, *Feminism/ Disability/Poetry/Embodiment/Performance* (Olimpias 2010). Afterward, I conducted a series of interviews with Kuppers.

I provide an analysis of differently abled bodily topoi as they emerged in the workshop and discuss how they become available means for a corporeal rhetoric. Through a collective interplay of different bodies engaged in varied and fluid movement, invention and delivery collide, creating moments of interdependent, embodied action. To give readers a sense of intercorporeal invention and the lived experience of bodily kairos in real time, I detail an embodied composing scene, which I engaged with as a participant-observer in this Olimpias Performance Research Project workshop. I provide a thick description of Kuppers's performance research methods and draw from a combination of interview data and rhetorical analysis. I also place my analysis in conversation with personal interview footage collected from Kuppers and document Kuppers's spoken, on-the-spot words as a metaanalytical frame.

IMPROVISATORY PERFORMANCE—ACCESS AND ACTION, INVENTION/DELIVERY

> *Enter your body as a stage . . . Make your body a theatre for this word*
> —Petra Kuppers, interview with author

On the afternoon of Sunday, August 8, 2010, I arrived at the Subterranean Arthouse, a small, community-arts venue nestled on Bancroft Way in Berkeley, CA.[1] With a total of six people present, Kuppers initiated the workshop with formal introductions: Neil Marcus, Amber DiPietra, and Eleni Stecopoulos were regular Olimpias participants at the time, working both independently and together in the broad area of embodied poetics. Jina Kim, a PhD student just beginning work at the University of Michigan in disability studies, and I were both guest participants. As part of my introduction, I guide the group through an embodied activity. I rely on the body itself as technology, or as Kuppers names, as "resonance chamber." I direct: *Let's close our eyes. Listen to your body. Feel your bodily presence. If you have any pain, any tensions, acknowledge these feelings, visualize that location in your body. Inhale deeply and exhale.* I proceed to take the group through what I call, when working with teachers, a "center and plant" exercise. *As you continue breathing, select a place on your body from where you can root yourself. The root location may be the bottom of your feet; you may want to select your hand, your back, your mouth. Allow the roots to anchor the ground and feel yourself both lift and sink at the same time. Your body grounds, anchors, but is not stuck, and you have free-flow.*

As we engage in this informal, centering exercise, I pose a series of prompts. I speak slowly, with time to focus on each one: how do you compose, communicate, and/or write through your body? What is your preferred method of composing, of writing? When have you felt disembodied as a writer? Recall this moment. Pause here and think of an image, a metaphor, or a concept that captures your memory. Our conversation focused on writing practices and on embodied means, personal habits, and situated encounters with material and cultural dimensions of composing. Jina talked about multitasking, having "4–5 documents" open at a time, "flipping between projects" as a method of invention. Jina humorously added how she "loves to eat small white candy mints" as she writes, having some repetitious "motion such as hand to mouth in between hands to keyboard." Kuppers spoke of writing as "a ring" that surrounds her body, a circling "in and in and in around retention and delay." Eleni talked about *The Poetics of Healing*, a collaborative program of study that she designed and directed that actively explored alternative kinds of medicine and healing, using somatic exercises and embodied poetics as methods and modes of creative re-production.

Memories about writing, about learning and schooling, don't always elicit positive experiences. Amber selected "a clenched fist" as an image or metaphor that captured a moment when she felt disembodied as a writer. Amber talked about being in pain, a deep bone-pain that emanates from her "inside out" and that radiates from her "spine, through her limbs." Amber uses a motorized wheelchair for mobility, but she often experiences additional pain from sitting upright for an extended period of time. She feels the least degree of pain when lying down, suspended from muscular constraint, stretching and extending her body, and when activity does not necessitate overt attention to physical mobility. The participants' accounts suggest that academic environments, public modes of writing, and writing with computers tend to reinforce certain, normative bodily postures and exclude others.

Writing, as a physical act, suggests particular motions for bodies: hands and fingers typically engage in a primary position, doing most of the movement; wrists and arms cooperate to brace the hands.[2] Bodies typically posture in a sitting-up position, backs, torso, neck, and head up right, top-heavy, hunched-over, and eyes looking toward the screen or the page. The standard motions and corporeal means that I describe here capture a possibility for how bodies produce writing, certainly not the only physical, embodied means. But what I describe encompasses the normative idea and most commonly available practice in terms of cultural and material means—what is most available in cultural memory and practice for bodies and how bodies become inscribed as writers or not.

Writing centers attention back to the page/screen, to the articulation and description of the word. Kuppers admits to feeling removed from writing, literally an "inability to be moved by language," and expresses a desire to become moved again, re-moved, by language, to revitalize what has come to feel dull and calloused. The inability to be moved by language, Kuppers attests, stems from encounters with a language that is not one's own. Language, even a given word, has "a heritage."

EMBODIED RESPONSE: A FORM OF INTERPRETATION

Kuppers transitions us into a group activity that she often implements in her classes as a means of teaching close-reading and textual analysis. She refers to the activity as a method of embodied response, a form of interpretation and critical reading that she turns to as a result of "not wanting to teach argument solely as word." She explains that words can create distance between an individual and meaning, between one another. One can experience "alienation from language and estrangement from a given word." Teachers of writing, reading, and analysis in particular must maintain an acknowledgment that a word, that language, has heritages that may or may not capture a given individual's experience.

Kuppers orients us to the three-part scaffolding of the workshop. She will first lead us through an oral reading of an unfamiliar text, asking that we each focus on a word/concept from the text, or something present in our consciousness. Then, we will move to a combination of voice work and vocal play intermixed with somatic exercises, incorporating movement and touch—a version of what Kuppers calls "contact improvisation." We will explore how we use our bodies to analyze language that is not our own, and we will explore how our bodies, working together, can open possibilities for forging new meanings and new, emergent ways of reading and interpreting a difficult text.

Kuppers begins by reading aloud "Parodos," a poem from Eleni's newly released collection, *Armies of Compassion* (Stecopoulos 2010). She asks that we close our eyes and listen to the words, to the sounds around the words. A few lines into the poem, Kuppers reads: "She beat time in his throat / trying to heal talking." Kuppers poses a broader, collective inquiry for our exploration: "Can words have a transfiguring energy"? She asks us to select a word or concept, something concrete from the poem, or something present in our consciousness. Transitioning us from listening to the poem read aloud to embodied interpretation, Kuppers speaks the following directions in a slow-pace melody: *Enter your body as a stage. What is the chorus of your body? Whatever your word is decline it through your senses. The word trips over the stage; make your body a theater for this word.*

SONORICITY OF LANGUAGE

Kuppers leads us through an intense and slow vocal exploration of our selected words. She asks us to speak the word slowly, focusing on each syllable. She directs that we also play with different variations of breath and volume: whispering, emphasizing different syllables and tones. As each person individually recites her own selected word, I experiment with mine.[3] Go: a guttural 'g' = 'ga' 'gah,' 'gawh,' more lightly stated, 'ga,' 'kah.' When I emphasize the 'o,' I discover an entirely different sound, 'gow,' 'owww,' 'ohhhh,' 'ohwa.' The pronunciation alters depending on the in-and-out rhythm of breath and vocal vibration, which together generate a particular audible sound. It is difficult to capture alphabetically the variations of breath, the time and duration of breath patterns, the extended flow of long, sustained inhalations and exhalations—a limitation of the print modality. I can feel, through the slow articulation, the movement of the utterance through various places of my body. With quick utterances, I can feel short, jaunts of air on the back of my throat. With longer, slower-motion breath, my stomach and diaphragm contract and rise as I inhale and exhale; my chest rounds and drops, in and out, pushing up the breath, a wave of wind that delivers a particular sound. I allow an uninterrupted stream-of-consciousness to make free-flowing associations. I return attention to my body. I frame a definition: *"go"* connotes forward motion, action—moving, going, doing. I return attention to my body, my breath, to the (go)ose bumps on my skin.

In this short portion of the workshop, we explore oral delivery and sound. We invent, in small and local ways, new meanings by making renewed associations—taking a word and altering its structure and context, its audibility, how it streams from our bodies, and how other bodies reingest and understand the new sound. At some points, through the interwhispers, I hear not so much particular words, but I hear communication, jumbled sound effects that come to the ear as an aural atmosphere of harmonies, tones, rhythms, both stunts and flows, and intermittent silence. Our practice seems individual, but we actually work collectively through the multiple sounds, rhythms, and vibrations that circulate. We each release a word, through a complex embodied process, out into the open, shared space; a passerby would hear an ensemble, a plethora of voices, tones, sounds, a rich articulation of some newly discovered creative production that emerged from a collective, embodied rereading of an unfamiliar text. Kuppers refers to the practice I describe above as an exploration of the "sonoricity of language." She says, we forget or, rather, we often neglect to acknowledge, how "language is a medium that vibrates." Language is a medium of sound as much as a linguistic medium. As I explored in the Olimpias workshop, movement, touch, and sound, in combination, unveil a complexity of language and rely directly on different embodied means for linguistic analysis and interpretation.

IMPROVISATORY MOVEMENT AND CONTACT

Kuppers shifts the workshop space slightly from the verbal to the non-verbal, layering spontaneous movement and touch within our verbal play and oral delivery. For Kuppers, such moves belong together, and performance provides a rhetorical space for multimodal, intercorporeal communication. As we continue vocalizing our selected word, Kuppers guides us through free-flowing movements. Already positioned on the floor, she directs us to allow the vibrations in the room to move through our bodies. I move from a sitting position to a flat position, lying on the floor. My right arm rounds from my shoulder to my hip. I imagine that my body takes the shape of a lower case "g" and I contort and shift, invert my legs, curl my knees outward, until I feel the two curves of the "g" take form. I open outward, breaking away from my own "kinesphere" (Kuppers 2003, 121). Others in the room simultaneously engage in spontaneous motions, following their desires in the ways that their bodies enable. The sounds still echo, the wordplay still active, but we deliberately embellish the verbal with physical motion. Kuppers edges us toward "improvisatory contact," a dance technique that "relies on balance and weight transference rather than fixed body patterns or cleanly articulated lines" (120). She directs us toward "the weight of others," to engage other "energy flows" and move with the "vibrations of sound" in order to capture the otherwise "uncapturable," discovering "ways to move with the other."

As we physically inch closer toward one another, I more clearly hear the whispers of others' words. I make out the word "oleander," a term from the poem. I slide on the floor, curved and bent. I stretch out and elongate my arms; in my reach, my back rises and slightly arcs off the ground. I feel the muscles between my ribs, a part of my body often unacknowledged. My elbow touches someone. I redirect my attention; I ease the pressure of my push, so our contact results in more of a brushing than a nudging or slamming. At this point, the moment of touch, we both make choices about whether to embrace more deeply or continue in motion. Our tensions work together, pulling us closer toward one another. I pivot to the right; she turns to the left. Our faces meet—a barely tangible embrace. We rest for a split second and make eye contact—hers, a deep brown. I feel a hesitation: do I stay here, further entangle with this other body, looping arms, making firmer contact, or do I move again, in a different direction, turning away from this body? What is appropriate? Who am I in this moment? And, to echo a question posed by Neil Marcus about different forms of media, "What information is communicated in this way?" We lean further into one another, and the boundaries between self and other further diminish.

Cultural codes about personal space surface through explicitly embodied methods that blend vocality, language, touch, and movement. Movement, in this context, becomes a material means for reflection on spontaneity and restraint, difference and surprise, "wide" and "narrow" movements, terms Kuppers provided in her workshop directions. In "Moving Bodies," Kuppers states that spontaneous movement and tactile interaction provoke "a different sensibility" and different ideas about both social and phenomenological ways of being (2003, 122).

Improvisatory motion is not haphazard motion, motion without method. Rather, in the words of Byron Hawk, the Olimpias workshop facilitates emergent methods that "begin in embodiment" (2007, 105). During the performance of corporeal rhetoric, boundaries blur between invention and delivery and between self and other. Embodied agencies emerge from the instantiated making of collaborative embodied action, from intercorporeal encounters when bodies come together and, in the words of Margrit Shildrick, "enter into a new relationality with themselves and the world" (2002, 36). Distinction from one body to another becomes less productive than the assemblage, linkage, and overlap among/between different bodies, and the physical inter-action that results from collective bodies in motion and from contact across corporeal differences. I observe interaction as the very moment of slippage between invention and delivery—"inventiondelivery"—that takes places through embodied praxis, a slippage also between self and other as intercorporeal, inter-agents.

CORPOREAL RHETORIC AS EMBODIED ACTION

Drawing from this participatory research, I have developed a definition of corporeal rhetoric as embodied action. Corporeal rhetoric means that bodies perform as multimodal places or sites of inter-action. Bodies engage in a range of middle, micromoves that take place among a multiplicity of intercorporeal motions. Corporeal rhetoric grounds knowledge-discovery and creation in the body (Fleckenstein 2010). Although Aristotle lists quite a few bodily dimensions as *topoi*, they are always nondisabled, ideal masculine bodies, for example, strength, health, and speed (Dolmage 2009; Hawhee 2004; Wilson and Lewiecki-Wilson 2001). Corporeal rhetoric, in contrast, attends to the available means of difference, advocating that a range of bodily capabilities should be considered among the available means.

Through a study of Kuppers's Olimpias workshop methods, I conclude that rhetorical activities such as invention, access, and action can be understood as interrelated embodied knowledges, or ways of knowing, located and made available for use via the situated affordances of particular bodies in collaboration with other situated bodies. In performances or enactments of corporeal rhetoric, invention and delivery fold in a bidirectional relationship so the two are, at times, difficult to distinguish. The process resembles a fusion of two otherwise split acts. In the teaching of writing, we too often present invention as preproject work, as a beginning process of collection and discovery that abruptly subsides as one prepares for delivery. Such treatment of invention tends to position delivery as a predetermined knowledge, a mere packaging and sending-forth process rather than a process implicated in the means by which one invents. Such approaches, in writing and in classroom learning, forfeit the creative, social, and embodied aspects of both invention and delivery, what Collin Gifford Brooke (2009) refers to as the "performative" aspects of delivery. In many composing situations, choices regarding both invention and delivery are nonnegotiable or already predetermined by cultural means, what has, through repeated occurrence, become deemed as standard practice. The particular composing technologies and modalities available have become standard for particular use(s). For example, composing in US college classrooms presumes familiarity and facility with word-processing programs and keyboards, perhaps causing bodily discomfort or inaccessibility for a student without normative hands or limbs, or an impoverished student who does not have a history of using computers. Even the invitation to write in handwritten journals or to type on a discussion forum assumes normative embodiment.

For Kuppers, the physical corporeal body functions as a site of rhetorical action at the very location of difference. She curates, through her workshops, communication spaces that break down the separation between speaker and audience and that invite participants to explore the larger question of how to respond in situated encounters. Bodies conjoin as a shared, participatory source of invention for everyone present. In the remainder of this chapter, I analyze what such a method looks like in practice, and I return to a synthesis of how corporeal rhetoric as embodied action reinvents (with) theory in ways meaningful for pedagogical application.

CHOREOGRAPHY AS INTERCORPOREAL RHETORIC

Writing from my cultural perspective has always been really important
—Petra Kuppers, Personal interview with author

Olimpias workshops provide an inventive space for Kuppers and participants to explore the possibilities of embodied composing and communication capabilities. Working within a radical feminist-disability studies tradition, Kuppers's Olimpias Projects take as its primary inquiry an interactive investigation into the politics of bodies and communication, exploring how different bodies are able to communicate and how bodies communicate with one another across significant difference (2010). In Olimpias work, Kuppers directs collaborative performance projects that reinvent open-access communicative spaces through deliberate modes of embodied composing, or writing with bodies' multimodal capabilities. Methods include extemporaneous action and invention in which individuals locate rhetorical presence through collective discovery and motion.

In addition, Olimpias projects reconfigure the traditional author/ audience dynamic as an intercorporeal interaction rather than a transaction in which one individual, a facilitator or teacher, as an authority, imparts meaning to another, situated as a learner. Kuppers operates within an epistemology for which "binaries between us and them, me and you, dissolve into multiple differences between one and the other" (2003, 121). In our interview, Kuppers urged, "There are no external positions . . . Olimpias work addresses its audiences directly." Olimpias performers embody dual positionalities as composer and audience, exhibiting a reflexivity that fluctuates between internal and external channels. Being in the moment is about letting go of one's self, the seeming solidarity of one's own kinesthetic reality, what Kuppers calls "kinespheres" (121). Individual bodies perform as permeable, expandable, and adaptable spaces. Bodies, together, absorb and release collective energy through improvisatory, on-the-spot movement, touch, sound, and deep linguistic analysis. Attention shifts from one's own body, as central and unified, to diffused and intersecting kinespheres. Multiple parts from different bodies produce the potential for a new assemblage—an embodied action that emerges from collaborative spaces of corporeal rhetoric. In such intercorporeal spaces, the impetus remains on "multiple sensations and different loci of connection and flow," which, Kuppers argues, opens the potential for "new forms of community and communication" (120–21).

The work typical of Olimpias is often "so small and tiny," or localized via the workshop experience, Kuppers explains, that the group must consistently ask, "How do you reach outside your own community?" Kuppers's question about how to reach beyond one's own community addresses the twofold rhetorical aim of all Olimpias work: to query the politics of how humans communicate with one another, and to deliberately create alternative spaces for making contact across significant difference (Kuppers 2010). In our interview Kuppers explained, "Most Olimpias people, including myself, deal with fatigue and pain issues, and we can't commit to conventional rehearsals." In Olimpias projects, time and space organize around instantiations of "real time," a prominent concept in disability communities that signals attention to individual lived experience and actual movement through the world. Real-time takes into consideration that any given individual may, at unanticipated points, encounter pain, fatigue, or other embodied dispositions that particularize motivation and action—for instance, constrain forward movement and make it necessary to invent sideways or going-around strategies. Real-time thus takes into account individual differences of bodies, differences in style, and the sudden, unforeseen need for fluctuating schedules. In line with real-time ontology, Kuppers explains, "We do not work on stages" or with a mainstream production mentality based on strenuous attendance, which, across history, has only been accessible to normative or even exceptionally fit bodies.

Real-time is not about calendar time, or *chronos*, but captures what Debra Hawhee calls a nuance of "rhetoric's time," or "the ancient conception of time that attends to degrees of propitiousness" (2002, 18). Hawhee further identifies "bodily kairos" as a physical quickness and strength through which bodies respond with flexibility and adaptability "to the immediate situation" (2004, 71). Hawhee's explication draws from classical Greek gymnastics education, but as Jay Dolmage rereads, Hawhee's account perpetuates the idea that it is the normative rhetor with a masculine, muscular, fit body, who has access to the affordances of bodily action (2006, 271). The concept of real-time helps us rethink rhetorical notions of bodily kairos and also basic assumptions of classroom management and pedagogical design. Real-time repurposes that instead of taking place before composing, for example, research occurs synchronously with invention and delivery; real-time constitutes an active discovery that takes place in face-to-face, collective encounters.

Kuppers refers to Olimpias workshops as new media spaces that create experiences that travel beyond the physical presence, materializing a form of distance learning and accessible participation for those unable to attend. For Kuppers, new media functions in "an installation sense," meaning that the live performances become available in multiple renditions and in a hybrid "environment" that directly engages audiences (2010). Through video and photography, audience participation extends to different realities of real-time—a notion that Kuppers refers to as "non-present presence," a standpoint that anticipates some will be missing but that this absence need not equate noninvolvement. New media, in Kuppers work, locates means of technologies to cast a wider net for audience participation, a function that relates to Anne Frances Wysocki's definition of new media based on "a range of materialities" and possibilities for "human involvement" (2004, 15, 19). Olimpias workshops remain attentive to invention, and process focuses on "the encounter itself" as opposed to the final outcome or product (Hawhee 2004, 16). Accommodation often entails making changes for one individual, but the deeper concept of bodily kairos and real-time suggests that teachers should go further than occasionally accommodating the body that does not fit easily into classroom routines. Rather, teachers should redesign course contexts and spaces so that questions of access become the very topic of invention.[4]

CORPOREAL RHETORIC AS EMBODIED PEDAGOGICAL ACTION

I have been using the phrase "bodies-in-motion" to capture the kinesthetic, physical, spatial body, situated in time, engaged in composing practice, exploring how the corporeal body performs as rhetorical topoi. Bodies-in-motion refers to a body's intricate and personalized material interaction with other composing bodies. Bodies-in-motion also characterizes composing practice that takes place in composing time, in which layered microprocesses swirl forward, composing momentum from invention to delivery. I collect here a series of key principles for embodied composing that derive from my study of Olimpias:

- Embodied composing acknowledges corporeal engagements in writing, moments in which bodies are called to action.
- Embodied composing examines the bodily affordances available in situated composing practice.
- Embodied composing actively considers the situated embodiment of audiences, aiming to cast the widest net for "human involvement" (Wysocki 2004).
- Embodied composing operates according to real-time as opposed to scheduled, chronos (Hawhee 2002; Kuppers 2010).
- Embodied composing experiences the rhetorical canons as interdependent Bodies, situated within use and space, similar to other composing media, "deploy certain affordances," certain capabilities and tendencies that in turn open certain possibilities for creating and delivering meaning (Bailie 2010).

In opening certain capabilities, a question of affordance also necessarily warrants a grappling with both availabilities and constraints or limitations. Affordances, then, are never "neutral," Cindy Selfe insists, or bound solely to the objects/tools that they characterize (Bailie 2010). Rather, cultural practices and norms allocate affordances according to what becomes deemed normative, appropriate use. A theory of bodies as rhetorical "topoi" necessarily foregrounds bodies as places by which and through which one encounters in/access. A study of embodied composing and pedagogy of bodies in motion must maintain an effort toward accessibility, again, a philosophy that impacts rhetorical presence. Embodied composing must always begin with situated bodies located in situated times, places, and contexts. In Olimpias workshops, the bodies present are primarily situated by the context of the workshop tasks. Kuppers's workshop tactics, however, can transfer to classroom environments. Different bodies read and write the world through variations of means. Bodies have different capacities for multimodal means of communication, and human communication in any form—speaking, writing, gesturing, performing—happens by a particular body in a given time, location, and space, most often in complex interaction with technologies, materials, and additional bodies.

Bodily movement and tactile methods—as communicative channels and as physical, tangible ways of knowing and accessing knowledges—may seem far removed from writing, disconnected from how one works with language. However, the need for adjustment in communication may be subtle or abrupt. Fine-tuning awareness of different audiences and ways of adapting to them is a rhetorical exercise. Performance-based methods can help prepare us not only for an array of on-the-spot higher-stakes delivery occasions that demand instantaneous invention, but also attune our bodies to rhetorical possibilities. In a classroom, writers often draw from intercorporeal and kinesthetic modes as methods of embodied invention through the uncharted, behind-the-scenes composing moves of a bodily kairos in real-time. As a modality, kinesthetic elements bridge phenomenological and spatial ways of knowing, both the sensational means by which one understands being and the physical means by which one accesses space (Ahmed 2006; Grosz 1994). Through choreographing words, voices, bodies, and motion—orchestrating movements and transitions of modes and the pauses in between that necessitate reflection, reiteration, and analysis—teachers and writers alike rhetorically arrange performative composing spaces and times. Paying attention to the kairotic body in action can expand rhetorical literacies concerning the overlap between and emergence of invention-delivery as experienced in real-time. Writers can come to understand their own bodies as multimodal means that negotiate the many material and sociocultural elements of communication, including other bodies.

Some students—perhaps students with disabilities, students of color, nontraditional students in term of age or sexuality—may not welcome unsolicited attention to their bodies. As teachers, we may not feel comfortable with placing our own bodies further on display. Another way to phrase the question: what would students lose, what would be the risk, to leave out the body? Many writers and teachers of writing don't always recognize a body's place in communication unless, or *until,* a body "demands acknowledgement" (Lindgren 2008, 146). The unconscious displacement of the body, having the freedom to place the body aside or simply forget or suspend the body's existence, indicates a location of sociocultural privilege. One may overlook the body because one is easily able to access the social world, easily able to participate in public arenas with little alteration or accommodation. For others, a body remains in the foreground as a constant signifier of difference.

Disability studies scholars such as Kristin Lindgren (2008) and others argue that a body is most recognized when difference becomes amplified and measured against representations of what is culturally constituted as normative embodiment. A body is most recognized when a body makes uncontrollable noises, when a body displays some "disfigurement," a visible scar, disproportionate or unsymmetrical body parts, when a body becomes ill, or when a body requires some accommodation to what appears as typical mobility, typical being, and typical communication, such as when a body uses a wheelchair, or walks with a cane or a guide dog, when a body uses a screen reader, or needs an interpreter/signer, when a spoken voice sounds significantly different.

At the opening of this chapter, I argued that embodied agency emerges from the making of collaborative embodied action. Through interaction with other bodies, bodies as composing materials "enter into a new relationality with themselves and the world" (Shildrick 2002, 36).

Intercorporeality is a concept about interfacial colliding, in which bodies as places open to redefined porous boundaries. Distinction from one body to another becomes less productive than the assemblage, linkage, and overlap among/between different bodies, and the physical inter-action that results from contact across corporeal differences. Intercorporeality does not erase individual difference, or mean that two different bodies become one common body, but suggests a suspended moment in real-time in which bodies are between identities, in-between spaces of embodied invention, which folds back into a moment of delivery or action.

At the turn of the twenty-first century, the field observed a resurgence of physical bodies as rhetorical materials. Crowley's interest in what she termed "body studies" and "rhetorical bodies" (2002) ran parallel to a second rising area in the field: disability studies. Scholars integrating disability studies and rhetoric and composition also identified bodies as central to rhetorical study and composing practices. However, disability studies added a necessary critical dimension to "body studies" that emphasized careful attention to bodily differences. For James Wilson and Cynthia Lewiecki-Wilson, "disability studies contribute to an understanding of postmodern rhetoric as an embodied rhetoric of difference" (2001, 18). Disability studies engaged a whole new set of questions about the affordances of differently positioned bodies in the context of composition pedagogy and rhetorical theory. In combination, body studies launched a reinvention of rhetorical theories that emerged from the intersections of materiality and difference.

In the Olimpias Performance workshop, I met individuals who live with differing degrees of pain and fatigue, bodies with different corporealities, abilities, and means by which to move through the world. Kuppers designs workshops, specifically, for differently shaped bodies,

bodies that significantly differ from one another, hands with fewer than five fingers, for example. The direction is not about a correct or standard method but about creating method through bodily means, communicating through the means by which one is able.

As writing teachers, we get caught up in certain ideas of what a text does—its arrangement and style on the page or screen. We lose traction with physical composing bodies—an unintentional exclusion and norming in which we replace situated bodies with a collective "student body," that phantasmic student body that Crowley warns against. This universal, ideal body resembles the myth of normativity (Lorde 1984), which results from erasing bodily differences. Kuppers argues for pedagogies that open access to fuller-bodied participation. A fuller-bodied pedagogy accounts for the dynamic ways that bodies physically and materially come into existence in classroom learning, in writing practice, and in rhetorical activity. Composing styles and spaces differ, and how a body interacts with composing spaces, how a body is able to compose, differs across time. Embodied composing foregrounds differences as spaces of productivity, locating key moments for invention, or reinvention, through unforeseen circumstances. Theories and pedagogies designed around embodied difference address what we can do, as scholars and teachers, to can make accessible the available means of differently positioned bodies, bodies that use multiple literacies for composing and for accessing a wider range of rhetorical choices/moves.

NOTES

1. In the summer of 2010, Kuppers invited me to attend a workshop from a new project series, Feminism/Disability/Poetry/Embodiment/Performance.

2. The act of typing key-by-key or scribing letter-by-letter materializes through a body's interaction with particular composing technologies: paper and pen, computer. Such configurations are culturally prescribed, to some extent, through repeated practice and what becomes deemed as convention; this is particularly the case with school writing and academic conventions.

3. I select the word "GO" —a short utterance to experiment with vocality, sound, breath, and linguistic variation, and a word that had personal resonance with me at the time: foremost, I was working through the personal, family trauma of unexpectedly losing my father. But also, reverberating in my memory, I selected this exact word years earlier, as an MA student in a feminist rhetorics class when I was asked to consider an image and a word that captured Audre Lorde's rhetoric in her famous speech, "The Transformation of Silence into Language and Action" (1984). I include this brief context in order to support Kuppers's claim that *words have heritages*, personal resonances.

4. In the classroom, such pedagogical practices as dance, oral experimentation of the sonoricity of language, and kinesthetic and performative movements, together, touching, exploring the brink of access—such practices call upon the body in literal

and provocative ways. We can design classroom space to resemble more of a studio or workshop space, a space that highlights microprocesses as opposed to finished, polished work. Bringing the behind-the-scenes work into the classroom as collaborative inquiry and investigation, teachers can design studio pedagogies—carving out deliberate space to make room for varied bodily engagements and styles.

REFERENCES

Ahmed, Sara. 2006. *Queer Phenomenology: Orientations, Objects, Others.* Durham: Duke University Press.

Alexander, Jonathan, and Jacqueline Rhodes. 2008. "Multimediat[ed] [E]visceration." Conference presentation, Thomas R. Watson Conference, Louisville.

Alexander, Jonathan, and Jacqueline Rhodes. 2010. Interview. August 6.

Aristotle. 2007. *On Rhetoric: A Theory of Civic Discourse.* 2nd ed. Trans. George Kennedy. Oxford: Oxford University Press.

Bailie, Brian. 2010. "'If You Don't Believe That You're Doing Some Good with the Work That You Do, Then You Shouldn't Be Doing It': An Interview with Cindy Selfe." *Composition Forum* 21: n.p. http://compositionforum.com/issue/21/cindy-selfe-interview.php.

Brooke, Collin Gifford. 2009. *Lingua Fracta: Towards a Rhetoric of New Media.* Cresskill: Hampton Press.

Crowley, Sharon. 1999. "Afterword: The Material of Rhetoric." *Rhetorical Bodies,* ed. Jack Selzer and Sharon Crowley, 357–66. Madison: University of Wisconsin Press.

Crowley, Sharon. 2002. "Body Studies in Rhetoric and Composition." In *Rhetoric and Composition as Intellectual Work,* ed. Gary A. Olson, 177–86. Carbondale: Southern Illinois University Press.

Dolmage, Jay. 2006. "Review Essay: The Teacher, The Body." *College Composition and Communication* 58 (2): 267–77.

Dolmage, Jay. 2009. "Metis, Mêtis, Mestiza, Medusa: Rhetorical Bodies across Rhetorical Traditions." *Rhetoric Review* 28 (1): 1–28.

Fishman, Jenn, Andrea Lunsford, Beth McGregor, and Mark Otuteye. 2005. "Performing Writing, Performing Literacy." *College Composition and Communication* 57 (2): 224–52.

Fleckenstein, Kristie S. 1999. "Writing Bodies: Somatic Mind in Composition Studies." *College English* 61 (3): 281–306.

Fleckenstein, Kristie S. 2010. *Vision, Rhetoric, and Social Action in the Composition Classroom.* Carbondale: Southern Illinois University Press.

Grosz, Elizabeth. 1994. *Volatile Bodies: Towards a Corporeal Feminism.* Bloomington: Indiana University Press.

Hawhee, Debra. 2002. "Kairotic Encounters." In *Perspectives on Rhetorical Invention,* ed. Janet M. Atwill and Janice M. Lauer, 16–35. Knoxville: University of Tennessee Press.

Hawhee, Debra. 2004. *Bodily Arts: Rhetoric and Athletics in Ancient Greece.* Austin: University of Texas Press.

Hawk, Byron. 2007. *A Counter-History of Composition: Toward Methodologies of Complexity.* Pittsburgh: University of Pittsburgh Press.

Kuppers, Petra. 2000a. "Dancing Silence: Traces." *The Olimpias Performance Research Projects.* Accessed September 6, 2010. http://www-personal.umich.edu/~petra/pet8.htm.

Kuppers, Petra. 2000b. *The Olimpias Performance Research Projects.* Accessed September 6, 2010. http://www-personal.umich.edu/~petra/.

Kuppers, Petra. 2003. "Moving Bodies." In *The Teacher's Body: Embodiment, Authority, and Identity in the Academy,* ed. Martha Stoddard-Holmes and Diane Freedman, 119–22. Albany: SUNY Press.

Kuppers, Petra. 2009. "'your darkness also / rich and beyond fear': Community Performance, Somatic Poetics, and the Vessels of Self and Other." *M/C Journal* 12 (5): n.p. Accessed January 20, 2011. http://journal.media-culture.org.au/index.php/mcjournal/article/view/203.

Kuppers, Petra. 2010. Interview. August 9.

Lewiecki-Wilson, Cynthia, and Brenda Jo Brueggemann. 2008. "Introduction." In *Disability and the Teaching of Writing: A Critical Sourcebook*, ed. Cynthia Lewiecki-Wilson and Brenda Jo Brueggemann, 1–10. Boston: Bedford's / St. Martin's.

Lindgren, Kristin. 2008. "Body Language: Disability Narratives and the Act of Writing." In *Disability and the Teaching of Writing: A Critical Sourcebook*, ed. Cynthia Lewiecki-Wilson and Brenda Jo Brueggemann, 96–108. Boston: Bedford's / St. Martin's.

Lorde, Audre. 1984. "The Transformation of Silence into Language and Action." *Sister Outsider: Essays and Speeches*, 40–44. Berkeley: Crossing.

Olimpias Performance Research Projects, The. 2010. "Feminism/Disability/Poetry/Embodiment/ Performance." Subterranean Arthouse, Berkeley, CA. August 8.

Porter, James E. 2009. "Recovering Delivery for Digital Rhetoric." *Computers and Composition* 26 (4): 207–24.

Shildrick, Margrit. 2002. *Embodying the Monster: Encounters with the Vulnerable Self.* London: Sage.

Stecopoulos, Eleni. 2010. *Armies of Compassion.* Berkeley: Palm Press.

Wilson, James C., and Cynthia Lewiecki-Wilson. 2001. *Embodied Rhetorics: Disability in Language and Culture.* Carbondale: Southern Illinois University Press.

Wysocki, Anne Frances. 2002. "A Bookling Monument." *Kairos* 7 (3): n.p. http://english.ttu.edu/kairos/7.3/.

Wysocki, Anne Frances. 2004. "Opening New Media to Writing: Openings and Justifications." In *Writing New Media: Theory and Applications for Expanding the Teaching of Composition*, ed. Anne Frances Wysocki, Johndan Johnson-Eilola, Cynthia L. Selfe, and Geoffrey Sirc, 1–42. Logan: Utah State University Press.

PART V

15

RHETORICAL FUTURITY, OR DESIRING THEORY

Kendall Gerdes

The future is queerness's domain.
—José Esteban Muñoz, *Cruising Utopia*

RHETORICAL INVENTION AND AVAILABILITY

In *Toward a Civil Discourse*, Sharon Crowley remarks with wonder on "how rhetoricians can do without a theory of desire" (2006, 92). She continues, "People engage in rhetoric, after all, because they *want* something" (92). In this formulation, desire is central to the practice of rhetoric—wanting something is a condition that impels rhetorical practice. In the discussion that follows her remark, Crowley draws on psychoanalytic theory to explain the persuasive and ideological functions of fantasy. But the connection between a theory of desire and rhetoric that I explore in this chapter is less about persuasive strategy and more about desire's relationship to rhetoric as invention.

Crowley accepts Aristotle's (2007) definition of rhetoric as "an ability, in each case, to see the available means of persuasion" because it makes invention central to the art of rhetoric. It "ties rhetoric to culture," Crowley argues, because "the arguments generated by rhetorical invention must be conceived as produced and circulated within a network of social and civic discourse, practices, images, and events" (2006, 27). In other words, the ideological networks of a society or culture constrain the availability of arguments. Invention, or discovering the means of persuasion, is limited by something we may call availability, following Aristotle.

Crowley gives us a sense of "the relative availability of arguments as lying along a range or spectrum" whose "endpoints designate arguments that can be imagined or desired but that cannot be constructed in a

DOI: 10.7330/9781607328933.c015

given cultural time and place" (2006, 49). Closer to the center of the range, we would find "arguments that can be generated by a few but not yet widely grasped" and nearer still "arguments that can be generated by many but not yet heard by institutions such as the media" (49). Arguments that are "repeatedly articulated" on "widely discussed or controversial issues" would flank the center, at which lie commonplaces, or "argumentative canards" (50) so thoroughly a part of the common sense of the community that they can be difficult to challenge. Crowley does not suggest that this spectrum can measure progress: only that "the relative availability of arguments changes over time" (50). Changes in availability produce new matrices of intelligibility, which is to say they make some arguments more hearable (and others less). Such changes create lines of force that may be exploited by canny rhetors looking to wield rhetorical power.

Crowley's abstraction to a spectrum elides somewhat the multiplicity of argumentative communities that may be party to single issue or a shared set of issues. Some arguments may be highly available in a small or marginalized community, and so arguments central in their spectrum of availability may lie at the very edge of availability for the wider culture. Some arguments, beliefs, or rhetorical possibilities lie just beyond the horizon, out of reach of the rhetorical perception in general, but since there is no single culture (or context or audience), but always multiple local and specific ones, relative availability is itself relative. Crowley writes that some "ways of seeing, knowing, and believing" may be "readily available in a given context, while others are simply glimmers on an epistemological horizon" (2006, 56).

My contention is that desire has a relationship to availability, and that rhetoricians can explore this relationship by studying the debate in queer theory over antisociality and utopianism. Utopia, of course, is a sixteenth-century coinage from the Greek for "no place" ("utopia, n." 2017; see also Hutchinson 1987). From a rhetorician's perspective, "no place" may simply mean outside the bounds of the available: maybe glimmering on the horizon, but maybe not yet possible for many to hear. In the introduction to their anthology of women's rhetorics, Joy Ritchie and Kate Ronald write, "The discovery of the available means was for Aristotle an act of invention that always assumed the right to speak in the first place and, even prior to that, assumed the right to personhood and self-representation, rights that have not long been available to women" (2001, xvii). Access to these rhetorical rights for women was once utopian—aspirational, but also unheard of: "no place." Of course, women are hardly alone in their exclusion from these rights that condition their ability to be heard. Women are joined in their sec-ondarization by immigrants, people of color, people with disabilities, people of non-Christian religions, incarcerated people, refugees, and queer, transgender, and gender nonconforming people, to enumerate a still incomplete list.

When politics is dominated by beliefs and arguments that oppress these groups and construe them as outsiders, we who populate them must look beyond the available means of persuasion in order to make ourselves heard. When the available means are insufficient, we have to make more arguments available; we have to widen the scope of the pos-sible. Our politics become inevitably utopian: we have to look beyond what is given, to another possible world. Rhetoricians should look to queer theory for a theory of desire that connects wanting something else with a utopian crossing of the limits of the rhetorically available.

At least since the time of Plato's *Gorgias*, rhetoric has had a conten-tious relationship to self-definition. Queer theory, too, seems to name a field marked by the failure to define its central term.[1] Contests over defining these fields (and their objects of study) have enlivened them both and made room for diverse, and at times conflicting and even contradictory, works. Even the term queer, like rhetorike, has under-gone a reclamation project, with somewhat mixed results: neither term has won wide acceptance beyond those who identify with them as self-descriptions. Some in each field have even questioned the continued utility of these central terms, suggesting that the signifying force they once held has been exhausted (Dobrin 2011; Warner 2012). A *queer* desire is, at its roots, a way of wanting something that's not available. Queer theory can teach us about how desire gets formed, mediated, mitigated, and adulterated, and how it can change its own conditions and expand beyond its originary constraints.

In the last decade or so, several major figures in queer theory have litigated a debate over the role of utopianism, futurity, and even politics in queer theory. Lee Edelman (2004) argues that futurity always entails a heteroreproductive imperative and that queerness is always defined by its otherness to that reproductive future. Desire, in his view, is organized and constrained by a political fantasy that privileges heterosexual repro-duction and excludes queer sexuality. This theoretical position, known as the antisocial thesis, provoked an array of respondents who recoiled from the hermeneutical suspicion of Edelman's critique of "the social" as a body constituted by its exclusion or expulsion of queerness.[2]

In a compelling rejoinder to the antisocial thesis, José Esteban Muñoz contends that queerness is not simply the categorical name for excluded excess, but specifically "a structuring and educated mode of desiring that allows us to see and feel beyond the quagmire of the present" (2009, 1). For Muñoz, queerness names not only wanting, but wanting something *else*, something other than what is given. Desiring, for Muñoz, is not only a route of access to the constitutive outside that exceeds the present; it is also a performative way of calling that excess into the realm of possibility, what we might phrase in rhetorical terms as making more arguments available—or rhetorical invention.

My argument is that queer futurity is already rhetorical by virtue of the performative force of its desiring. Rhetoricians can learn about the inventive force of utopianism from this debate and develop a rhetorical theory of desire. In our introduction to this collection, my coeditors and I argue that theories are *inventions*—specific to the times, places, and ideological ecology that fostered them—as well as *inventive*—a way of increasing the supply of available means. A rhetorical theory of desire would thus give an account, not simply of desire's causes or effects (as if that were simple), but of the performativity of desire, of how desire aids the rhetorical work not only of finding all the available means of persuasion, but of making more means and different means available: a theory of *how* (and not just what) desire makes possible.

I want to make my argument by setting up a commentary track alongside two select moments in the debate over the antisocial thesis. I want to start with a reading of Edelman's introduction to *No Future* (2004), in order to present his sophisticated treatment of the relationship between sociality, politics, and futurity through the lens of Lacanian psychoanalysis. I want to show how Edelman's theory poses a challenge to the inherent future-orientation of the field of rhetoric. Then I want to offer a reading of Muñoz's introduction and invocation to *Cruising Utopia* (2009). Muñoz gives a full-throated defense of utopian futurity, linking queer desire to rhetoric in so many words through his exposition of queer performativity. Drawing on Lacanian scholar Shoshana Felman, Muñoz explains and exposes the instantiating power and persistence through time of queer desire. Muñoz's stirring salvo demonstrates the effectivity of the paracritical style Eve Kosofsky Sedgwick (2003) dubbed "reparative reading," in which scholarship engages in world making.

Rhetoric, like utopianism, demands futurity. As rhetorician Erin Rand (2014) has argued, every exercise of rhetorical agency generates a queer remainder, a desiring otherwise and doing something *else* that sends us toward the utopian, toward a no-place that never fully arrives, or whose arrival is always deferred. Rhetoric necessarily opens the space of futurity, even when dominant powers that profit from the status quo may wish the space of futurity to appear closed. To engage in rhetoric is to want something more than what is given, something else than what is given: to engage in rhetoric is to want a future.

THE ANTISOCIAL THESIS: AGAINST FUTURITY

In a forum on "The Antisocial Thesis in Queer Theory" published in *PMLA* in 2006, Robert L. Caserio traces the development of the antisocial thesis back to the publication of Leo Bersani's *Homos* in 1995. Caserio characterizes *Homos* as "expressing a gay skepticism that has dogged every upsurge of gay politics" (2006, 819). For Bersani, "homo-ness . . . necessitates a massive redefining of relationality"—homosexuality could be a force that mandates "the politically unacceptable and politically indispensable choice of an outlaw existence" (1995, 76). It's easy to see the echo in Edelman, who shifts terminology from homosexuality or "homo-ness" to queerness as a structural position: "queerness can never define an identity; it can only ever disturb one" (2004, 17). For Edelman, the defining characteristic of queerness is its outsider status. "Queer" signifies something close to the total alienation from sociality that many of us felt, in our childhoods, would be our ultimate destiny. In fact, the "child," Edelman argues, figures everything from which the "queer" is and will always be excluded: namely, the reproduction of social order through orientation toward the future.

For Edelman, the culturally specific values and identifications stockpiled in the figure of the child animate not just a particular stripe of politics, but all politics as such. Edelman writes, "the fantasy subtending the image of the Child invariably shapes the logic within which the political itself must be thought" (2004, 2). In his view, the respectability politics of the gay marriage movement (and their dominance over queer justice or liberation projects) are a sign of politics' inherent conservatism. Queer (that is, nonreproductive) sexuality exposes the unruly desiring machine, more properly named the death drive in Lacanian terms. Against the "presupposition that the body politic must survive," Edelman stakes out queerness as the categorical opposition to every norm and category. Perhaps an impossible project, Edelman's goal is to resist the temptation to reinvest in making a better future and, instead, to expose the abjection of jouissance by the social order. Queerness is a way of exposing the fantasies that suture together the meaning assigned to the social order over the meaninglessness of (again, Lacanian) Real(ity).

To really grok the contours of Edelman's attack on futurity, some familiarity with Lacanian psychoanalysis is required. The order of the

Symbolic (produced by figuration, as through the figure of the child) is supported by the Imaginary, wherein fantasies work to attach meaning and to cover up the unmoored reality of the Real.[3] To the extent that gay people are absorbed into the center of the fantasy staged by reproductive futurism (say, by accessing the right of civil marriage, or to have their parentage of children recognized by the state), Edelman might allow that their political and social recognition trades off with queerness.[4]

The questions Edelman's work poses in queer theory, and their challenges for rhetoric, are these: Is there a way to have a future without buying into the political fantasy of reproductive futurism? Can there be another kind of futurism—a future that does not eliminate or malign the queerness that it also produces? A futurism not structured by a straight social order and a queer outside? Are there other figures that, though they would present us with different fantasies, would realign our cultural values and identifications with futurity?[5] Can there ever be a different futurity?

QUEER FUTURITY AND THE INVENTIVENESS OF HOPE

José Esteban Muñoz was the architect of this other futurity. Even just the first page of *Cruising Utopia*'s introduction is a stirring invocation of queerness I would call Gorgianic in its alchemical force. In a clear rejection of the antisocial thesis, Muñoz argues that "the future is queerness's domain" (1). Queerness appears here as more than the structural outside of the normal, or the social: "Queerness is a structured and educated mode of desiring that allows us to see and feel beyond the quagmire of the present" (1). Queerness is a way of *wanting* that reaches beyond what is given. After Muñoz's death in December 2013, his readers inscribed lines that immediately follow this passage on the walls of public bathrooms around the country:

> The here and now is a prison house. We must strive, in the face of the here and now's totalizing rendering of reality, to think and feel a *then and there*. Some will say that all we have are the pleasures of this moment, but we must never settle for that minimal transport; we must dream and enact new and better worlds.

For Muñoz, queerness is not (only) a position, quality, or characteristic: it is instead a kind of utopian faculty: "Queerness is that thing that lets us feel that this world is not enough, that indeed something is missing" (1). This definition of queerness echoes the alienation that's so central to Edelman's approach to the term, but in Muñoz's version it opens onto the wide horizon of a *non*-reproductive futurism—not a futurity without reproduction, specifically, but rather a futurity staked on the difference introduced by and into every repetition (see Felman 2003, 33–34, 57; and Muñoz 2009, 154). Something is missing: the available means are insufficient. A queer feeling tells us that what is given is not enough. What rhetoricians may be wont to call the "invention" of queer futurity, Muñoz here names "performativity." He writes, "Queerness is also a performative because it is not simply a being but a doing for and toward the future" (1). Not simply a being, not only a description, but a doing: the enactment of the future as a rupture in the here and now. The connection between queerness and futurity is not incidental; it is integral: "Queerness is essentially about the rejection of a here and now and an insistence on potentiality or concrete possibility for another world" (1). Every queer rejection of the here and now is impelled by an inventive rhetorical energy—by wanting something more.

Performativity links Muñoz's vision of queer desire to rhetoric. Although Muñoz is a performance studies scholar (and chaired the Performance Studies Department at NYU), his use of "performativity" in *Cruising Utopia* is framed (at least at first) in terms borrowed from speech act theorist J. L. Austin, whose influential *How to Do Things with Words* (1976) attempted to define and separate performative language—words that do things—from constative language—words restricted to their referential function. Austin's classifying terms proliferate and tend to break down, and he very nearly replaces the constative measure of truth/falsity with his measure of the success of performatives, felicity/infelicity. Muñoz explains the distinction in a passage on "the eventual disappointment of hope," which he calls "nonetheless essential," Austin "maps out . . . all the things that eventually go wrong" even with felicitous (or I want to say, happy) performatives, as well as "the failure or infelicity that is built into the speech act" (2009, 9–10).

For Muñoz, as perhaps for Austin, performativity is indissociable from futurity. A performative is by definition an attempt (at the very least) to instantiate a future, to call it from potentiality into actuality, to beckon it with not only words and not only actions but even with dreams and feelings. Even in the case of an infelicitous performative, or what we might more commonly call a failure, Muñoz argues that "something else is done" (2009, 154). In a chapter on the suicide of dancer Fred Herko, Muñoz makes the case that this *something else* is inventive; that Herko's dance performance "provide[s] an idea of another way of being in the world that was not allowed within an antiutopian hermeneutic" (165): it was an incarnation of the possibility of living (and moving) otherwise.

Cognizant of the risk of seeming to romanticize queer suicide, Muñoz shows the tense relation between the mere negation of the present, and the unhappiness that ends hope, and the radical negativity that exceeds this simple rejection of the present, negating negativity, and saying no to the present as a way of saying yes to an/other future.[6] Where adherents of the antisocial thesis embrace negativity, Muñoz rejects the binarism that opposes this negativity to sunny optimism. A more *radical* negativity exposes, in words Muñoz borrows from Lacanian performative theorist Shoshana Felman, "the scandal of their nonopposition" (Muñoz 2009, 13; Felman 2003, 104). The futurity of even a radically negative performative depends, I hazard, on some kind of persistence, not self-identical but in other ways durable through time. Performatives join the moment of their enunciation or enactment to the future they anticipate and instantiate. To write that queerness is a performative is to claim that queerness has an insurgent rhetorical force.

Even at the level of methodology, Muñoz parts from the suspicious hermeneutics of the antisocial thesis. Oblique to the stringent interpretive critique practiced by Edelman, where the penetrating rationality of the critic exposes meanings submerged in a given text, Muñoz proposes to take "hope as a critical methodology" (2009, 4). It's not enough to expose utopian feeling. Hoping for queer futurity is not simply awaiting, but *cruising* as a queer mode of searching, a longing way of pursuing that defies the presumed impartiality of the critic or scholar and instead fully implicates the subject in a desiring-seeking that brings the things sought for into being. Cruising as a methodology is aligned with Sedgwick's reparative reading. Sedgwick argues that in the face of ongoing "spectacular, pointedly addressed" violence, hermeneutical exegesis of this violence is not enough to sustain those who it targets. Reparative reading refuses what Muñoz calls "the stultifying temporal logic of a broken-down present" (12); stultify: to cause to appear or be stupid, foolish, or absurdly illogical; to have a dulling or inhibiting effect on ("stultify, v." 2017). Instead of acceding to the alienation of queers from social life, instead of spurning utopianism as foolish or illogical and so inhibiting the imagination of a more vital futurity, the reparative reader turns to "a project of survival" that takes its resources from whatever is available, even from a culture bent on queer exclusion and destruction (Sedgwick 2003, 150–51). Reparative reading is a performative invention of queer utopia. Wanting, hoping, cruising—these are ways of inventing. A rhetorical theory of desire need not begin by defining desire or analyzing its origins; it can start by observing desire's rhetorical effectivity, its capacity or potential to open new rhetorical pathways, generate new lines of force, and make not only new arguments, but even new worlds, become available.

DESIRE AT THE LIMITS OF AVAILABILITY

What I am aiming to show though this (re)reading of Muñoz is that his utopianism is both a theory *of* desire—of the futurity that desire opens performatively—and a theory *that* desires, a theory that itself performs, in the scholarly and critical mode of reparative reading, Muñoz's "doing for and toward the future" (1). This is a *queer* theory, a theory that cruises, that both seeks and produces a utopia. Of course, articulating one's utopian vision does not guarantee the advent of queer utopia—Muñoz tells us it is always on the horizon, yet to come. "Queerness is not yet here," Muñoz warns us in his opening line (1). Utopians will always be wanting; it is the performativity of this desire for a *different* future, and not simply the reproduction of the status quo, that generates a futurity not committed, as Edelman charged, to the maintenance of a permanently exclusive social order.

So here at last is the modest argument I have been hoping to make: utopianism is not *political*, in the sense of providing feasible answers to the question of what is to be done. Instead, utopianism is rhetorical, or more specifically rhetorically *inventive*, and its political work is always the result of the new lines of force it generates and the new arguments and opportunities for argument that it makes available. From this perspective, Edelman's insistence that queerness is always oppositional can be seen to be in some ways consonant with Muñoz's insistence that queerness is not yet here, because the utopian is forever outside or just at the edge of rhetorical availability, lodged in "other ways of seeing, knowing, and believing" that Crowley calls "glimmers on an epistemological horizon" (2006, 56).

Rhetoricians can learn from the debate over the antisocial thesis in queer theory. We can see how the availability of arguments constrains the possibilities for invention, but that this limit nevertheless joins what it also separates. At the edges of availability, new possibilities glimmer. Rhetoric, broadly construed as addressed language, depends not just on sociality but on futurity, too. One example of the work that Muñoz makes possible for rhetoricians is Rand's *Reclaiming Queer: Activist and Academic Rhetorics of Resistance*. Rand argues that queerness names a fund of excess, or a remainder excluded from each exercise of rhetorical agency. Acting or speaking, she argues, always "defers temporarily the possibility of acting or speaking *otherwise*" (2014, 164; emphasis added).

The persistence of this queer remainder, of the potentiality for otherwiseness, marks agency in such a way that the "founding exclusion" of queerness doesn't simply detach from agency but "always inhabits and troubles" it (168). Following Muñoz, Rand positions queerness as a deferred utopian impulse at the heart of every rhetorical act. The Derridean temporality of deferral in this view of queerness lends credence to Muñoz's claim that "queerness is not yet here" (1), but always on the horizon, always in futurity. Desire, in Rand's rhetorical theory, is not just an unmarked generality, innocuous enough (and presumably heterosexual). Desire is markedly queer.

The queer desire that animates rhetorical practice ought to be an object of rhetorical study, but a rhetorical theory of desire need not confine itself to giving an account of the causes or origins of desire, nor to explaining in specific cases what certain desires have made possible in a given instance. A rhetorical theory of desire must also give an account of *how* desire makes things possible, or of *how to do things with desire*. I think Muñoz comes quite near to giving such an account in *Cruising Utopia*. For rhetoricians, studying queer utopianism may teach us about the performativity and rhetoricality of desire, about the inventive power of desire, and about how desire can aid an argument in crossing the given limits of availability. I hope that the time is coming when rhetoricians will take up the queerness of rhetoric's own commitment to futurity, and look to queer desire to teach us about the movement of the unavailable from somewhere near the margins to the center of availability. That would be a rhetorical theory of desire. It's already glimmering on the horizon.

NOTES

1. One scholar writing in the journal of *Utopian Studies* adds her own field to this list: "Rhetoric, like utopian studies, is a discipline with perpetual disagreement over the basic definition of its subject" (Portolano 2012, 114).

2. Edelman is not the only spokesperson for the antisocial thesis; he follows Leo Bersani, Michel Foucault, and Guy Hocquenghem. But I focus here on Edelman because of his express attack on futurity, and because of the responses his polemic spurred.

3. For more on Lacan's work from rhetorical perspectives, see Gunn (2004a) on the relation of the subject to the symbolic, Gunn (2004b) on the imaginary, and Lundberg (2004) on the symbolic.

4. Perhaps what Edelman's analysis most suffers from is the lack of a critique of whiteness. When he identifies the Child as "the common stake in the militant right's opposition to abortion and to the practice of queer sexualities" (2004, 15), Edelman nevertheless overlooks the investment of this (today even more) militant right in securing a white future through reproduction, and through the policy

agenda designed to keep people of color ill and in poverty, and to demonize and censure their parentage of children whenever possible. It is (still) whiteness that distributes the accolades for reproduction—which would mean that queerness is not the only (structural) outside.

5. Other major respondents to Edelman's provocation in queer theory include Halberstam's *The Queer Art of Failure* (2011), which looks at alternative socialities in children's films; Freeman's *Time Binds* (2010), a historiography of queer time; and Love's *Feeling Backward* (2009), an exploration of negative affect, queer attachment, and failed sociality.

6. For a probing and singular examination of these issues, see Page and Schulman (2017).

REFERENCES

Aristotle. 2007. *On Rhetoric: A Theory of Civic Discourse.* 2nd ed. Trans. George A. Kennedy. Oxford: Oxford University Press.

Austin, J. L. 1976. *How to Do Things with Words.* 2nd ed. Ed. J.O. Urmson and Marina Sbisá. Oxford: Oxford University Press.

Bersani, Leo. 1995. *Homos.* Cambridge: Harvard University Press.

Caserio, Robert L. 2006. "The Antisocial Thesis in Queer Theory." *PMLA* 121 (3): 819–28.

Crowley, Sharon. 2006. *Toward a Civil Discourse: Rhetoric and Fundamentalism.* Pittsburgh: University of Pittsburgh Press.

Dobrin, Sidney. 2011. *Postcomposition.* Carbondale: Southern Illinois University Press.

Edelman, Lee. 2004. *No Future: Queer Theory and the Death Drive.* Durham: Duke University Press.

Felman, Shoshana. 2003. *The Scandal of the Speaking Body: Don Juan with J. L. Austin, or Seduction in Two Languages.* Trans. Catherine Porter. Stanford: Stanford University Press.

Freeman, Elizabeth. 2010. *Time Binds: Queer Temporalities, Queer Histories.* Durham: Duke University Press.

Gunn, Joshua. 2004a. "On Dead Subjects: A Rejoinder to Lundberg on (a) Psychoanalytic Rhetoric." *Quarterly Journal of Speech* 90 (4): 501–51.

Gunn, Joshua. 2004b. "Refitting Fantasy: Psychoanalysis, Subjectivity, and Talking to the Dead." *Quarterly Journal of Speech* 90(1): 1–23.

Halberstam, J. 2011. *The Queer Art of Failure.* Durham: Duke University Press.

Hutchinson, Steven. 1987. "Mapping Utopias." *Modern Philology* 85 (2): 170–85.

Love, Heather. 2009. *Feeling Backward: Loss and the Politics of Queer History.* Cambridge: Harvard University Press.

Lundberg, Christian. 2004. "The Royal Road Not Taken: Joshua Gunn's 'Refitting Fantasy: Psychoanalysis, Subjectivity and Talking to the Dead' and Lacan's Symbolic Order." *Quarterly Journal of Speech* 90 (4): 495–500.

Muñoz, José Esteban. 2009. *Cruising Utopia: The Then and There of Queer Futurity.* New York: New York University Press.

Page, Morgan M., and Sarah Schulman. 2017. "Queer Suicidality, Conflict, and Repair." *QED: A Journal in GLTBQ Worldmaking* 4 (1): 68–99.

Portolano, Marlana. 2012. "The Rhetorical Function of Utopia: An Exploration of the Concept of Utopia in Rhetorical Theory." *Utopian Studies* 23 (1): 113–41.

Rand, Erin J. 2014. *Reclaiming Queer: Activist and Academic Rhetorics of Resistance.* Tuscaloosa: University of Alabama Press.

Ritchie, Joy, and Kate Ronald. 2001. *Available Means: An Anthology of Women's Rhetoric(s).* Pittsburgh: University of Pittsburgh Press.

Sedgwick, Eve Kosofsky. 2003. *Touching Feeling: Affect, Pedagogy, Performativity.* Durham: Duke University Press.

"stultify, v." 2017. *Merriam-Webster.com.* Merriam-Webster, Inc. Accessed January 29, 2018. http://www.merriam-webster.com/dictionary/stultify.

"utopia, n." 2017. *OED Online,* Oxford University Press. Accessed January 29, 2018. http://www.oed.com/view/Entry/220784.

Warner, Michael. 2012. "Queer and Then? The End of Queer Theory?" *The Chronicle of Higher Education.* January 1, 2012.

16

BLACK RELIGION MATTERS
African American Prophecy as a Theoretical Frame for Rhetorical Interpretation, Invention, and Critique

David G. Holmes

In *Toward a Civil Discourse: Rhetoric and Fundamentalism* (2006), Sharon Crowley offers a robust critique of the Religious Right's rhetoric of the apocalypse or end times. She concedes that while often exclusive and bigoted, apocalyptic rhetoric has been successful because it taps into pathos better than has the rhetoric of classical liberalism. As a premiere rhetorician and an atheist, Crowley is the quintessential outsider when it comes to Christian fundamentalist rhetoric. Still, she captures the core of why this rhetorical approach works: in some sites or situations, untutored, bias, or bigoted emotion trumps logic—pun intended. Yet there are other delineations of prophetic rhetoric that are decidedly more redeemable for the public sphere than is the apocalyptic.

Untangling prophecy from its sanctimonious etymology, prescribed rhetorical formulations, and dogmatic politics is an undertaking not to be taken lightly. Preaching and prophesying have been used interchangeably as a way of describing stuck-up diatribes designed to put down anyone and anything that does not fit within a myopic definition of what the religious rhetor deems moral. Although these negative associations between and about prophecy and preaching can be accurate, the links are hardly comprehensive or conclusive. As with the church more broadly discussed, it is rather difficult to disentangle prophetic discourse from the negative sociopolitical notions that the phrase conjures up. However, there are a number of scholars, only a few of whom with religious affiliations or investments, who consider making the effort worth the risk.[1]

Thinkers across disciplines have shown how prophetic discourses, while rooted in religion, possess sociopolitical and communicative potential beyond the walls of churches, temples, or mosques. They argue that prophecy divorced from dogma provides a set of fertile resources

DOI: 10.7330/9781607328933.c016

for democratic deliberations as well as social critique of institutional injustices, including those perpetuated by organized religion. More significantly, a range of composition and rhetoric scholars including Geneva Smitherman, Jacqueline Jones-Royster, Shirley Wilson Logan, Keith Gilyard, Beverly J. Moss, Bradford Stull, and, more recently, Adam J. Banks, Carmen Kynard, and Rhea Estelle Lathan have demonstrated how the rhetorical practices enacted in the Black church are indispensable for anyone serious about analyzing, engaging, and, perhaps, mobilizing African American culture. Such deployment of these religiously inflected rhetorical practices—I contend—is prophetic, not in the mystical sense of foretelling but in the material sense of forthright telling. Nevertheless, marginalized truth spoken to mainstream power often portends deliberative or political changes. Consider the predictions in Martin Luther King's mountaintop speech and Barack Obama's acceptance speech following the 2008 election, for instance.

According to Keith Gilyard, the Afro-American jeremiad represents one fertile source of African American "rhetorical practices" (2011). The material struggle of African Americans for humanity adapted the New England Puritans' prophetic calls for religious freedom. Arguably, the prophet Jeremiah (from whom the term "jeremiad" was coined) would have been more alarmed by racist disdain for human dignity than affirming of the transcontinental pursuit for doctrinal liberty. African American inflections of the jeremiad (as prophecy) emphasized speaking truth to power. Future-oriented matters such as the afterworld only mattered insofar as they could offer inspiration for a collective Black agency that could fight for earthly survival, justice, and equality. Historically, African American prophetic rhetoric was rarely about just reaching heaven; it was mostly about renouncing the hell on earth that Black folk encountered. Over the years Blacks—enslaved and segregated—interpreted their struggle through their racial and cultural experiences, and mined those experiences into discursive strategies that would liberate them from their struggles but also accent the beauty and brilliance of Black ways of knowing and being. This is why Gilyard argues that Nommo—an African belief in the profound power of language—when properly understood, functions as more than the Afrocentric power and spiritual energy of the word (2004). Rather, Nommo can and should inhabit spaces in which techniques for interpreting and strategies for critiquing injustice are being cultivated. In other words, Nommo—theoretically and rhetorically—functions as "hermeneutic" and "heuristic." If African American prophetic discourse is one manifestation of Nommo, it too carries the promise for interpretation and invention, not just (or even primarily) prediction. I wish to build upon Gilyard's incisive observations about the Afro-jeremiad and Nommo and, thereby, contribute to conversations that will mine the notion of Black religious discourse broadly and Black prophecy particularly as hermeneutic and heuristic. African American prophecy can provide vistas for interpreting and interrogating American foundationalism, including conservative readings of prophetic discourses, and can evoke commonplaces and communicative modes for creating democratically sustainable and inclusive rhetorics, politics, and pedagogies.

POLITICAL THEORY AS A FRAME FOR RECONSIDERING AFRICAN AMERICAN PROPHECY AS RHETORIC, HERMENEUTICS, AND HEURISTIC

Given Crowley's interests in the antagonistic alliance between the rhetorics of politics and religion, I weave my argument using threads from political theorist George Shulman's (2008) observations about prophetic discourse. I have chosen his work for at least three reasons. First, his book suggests ways of linking prophecy to African American rhetorics, histories, aesthetics, and politics. Second, he draws his argument from the civil rights movement, which remains one of the richest reservoirs for understanding how prophecy can transform the public sphere. Third, Shulman's explication of Black prophetic language can be retrieved and repackaged in the works of composition the rhetoric scholars Keith Gilyard, Adam Banks, Carmen Kynard, Rhea Lathan, and others. While Schulman does not claim to be a rhetorician, his project illuminates how prophecy is discursively malleable enough to crisscross disciplines in much the same way that Steven Mailloux (2006) envisions rhetoric broadly.

George Shulman situates prophecy within the context of political theory. Shulman argues that prophecy is not necessarily restricted to religious codes or regulated by religious people. Among the examples he uses to buttress this point is James Baldwin. A celebrated author of novels, essays, and plays, Baldwin was a formidable voice during the civil rights movement. As a renowned writer, he could speak from a perch and with an ethos that would not be accessible to most preachers. To be sure, Baldwin had mastered the rhetoric and poetics of the Black church as a teenage preacher. But as Shulman reminds us, Baldwin felt that he needed to leave the church to truly preach. He was openly and proudly gay at a time when not only mainstream society and the Black church frowned upon this lifestyle, but also the emerging militants within the Black freedom struggle—some of whom derisively called Baldwin "Martin Luther Queen" (Shulman 2008, 160). But Baldwin's prophetic stance could not be compromised by the restrictive dogmas of racism or homophobia any more than could his style as a creative artist. As a prophet of humanism, he largely rooted his critiques of American society in a raw, demanding, socially conscious, and ethically responsible definition and practice of love, which was not explicitly religious. Conceptually elusive but a reality for all Americans to come to grips with, Baldwin (1963) preaches that we should dispense with any concept of God that does not make us more loving.

For Shulman, prophecy is endemic to and pervasive within American culture. In fact, he refers to prophecy as a "social practice," a global phenomenon that has captured the imagination of a number of cultures and is part and parcel of various religious rituals (2008, 1). Shulman finds the notion so dominant within the American imagination that he conceptualizes prophecy as a "genre" of American politics (6). Perfectly aware of the denotative and connotative perceptions of prophecy as religiously inflected and socially restrictive, Shulman uses political theory and political theology to carve out an alternative reading. While readily acknowledging that prophecy can be employed to dominate, discriminate, and inhibit (he offers the Puritans and Jerry Falwell as examples), prophetic discourse can conversely be deployed to critique oppressive politics and social practices. The principal target of this alternative brand of prophecy is white supremacy. And prophets, from various occupations and communicating in a variety of genres, adapt the language of prophecy to critique white supremacy. Shulman mentions not only Baldwin, but also Martin Luther King, Henry David Thoreau, and Toni Morrison. Prophecy, then, becomes a master trope that cuts across and potentially inhabits other genres of expression, particularly those that possess the promise of liberation.

Put another way, prophecy at its pragmatic best is largely about politics but ultimately about persuasion. Even within Old Testament narratives, prophets had to endure extraordinary odds to critique the powers that were. For the most part, these prophets were about as displaced from the individuals and institutions they criticized as enslaved Blacks were from reaping the benefits of the antebellum economy or segregated Blacks were from fully participating in Southern politics. Still, I realize that asserting that prophetic discourse can be used rhetorically within secular public arenas carries its own drawbacks, which are not easy to untangle from how that form of rhetoric is associated with top-down dictating, rather than one-to-one deliberation. True, Shulman argues that the war against white supremacy, including the battles that King waged, salvaged prophecy from being exclusively oppressive. However, one could view even this brand of prophecy as inhibiting the free flow of grassroots democracy, as some members of the Student Nonviolent Coordinating Committee accused King of doing.

Shulman is obviously aware of this problem. This is why he both recognizes prophecy as a genre of American politics and how it has functioned as "cadences of speech," "registers of feeling," "tropes," "narrative forms," and "tones of voice" (2008, 6). Understanding vernacular as prophecy exposes the rhetorical potential of linguistic terms applied to the prophetic. Hence, while Shulman claims that prophecy can be deployed to combat white supremacy, hence sucking some of the antidemocratic venom from the word, the body politic should be on guard lest the poison of oppression begins circulating in other forms, the overt sexism and covert homophobia that functioned within the civil rights movement, for instance. Shulman opts to describe politically viable prophecy as vernacular because, like language, such a description affords the users with more sociopolitical flexibility. No one party or denomination would, in theory at least, own this kind of prophetic speech. For example, although Shulman considers both King and Baldwin to be prophets, he claims that they viewed America's past differently. Similar to the New England Jeremiads, King viewed America's past as a promise yet to be fulfilled for Black Americans. Baldwin, on the other hand, eyed America's past as a horror to be faced and acknowledged.

Like all forms of language use, adopting prophecy as vernacular is not without its own limitations, as Shulman well knows. But prophecy as vernacular has afforded African Americans greater rhetorical range to revise political discourses than liberal rationalism alone. For Shulman, aesthetics signified by the terms genre, vernacular, idiom, and so on not only describe how prophecy functions politically, but also afford oppressed groups more linguistic breadth to advance their cause. This is why Shulman views vernacular prophecy as being more allied with rhetoric than with philosophy. I would add that any approach to Black politics that stalls at debates but never demonstrates, that *thinks* about without *being* about progress, constitutes a static form of language, regardless of subject matter, a static approach that remains confined to the classroom and restricted within church walls. As Baldwin could not abide an art-for-art's-sake approach to his writings about Black life—indeed themes of affirmation and liberation ooze out of his fiction and nonfiction—Martin Luther King's theology was political, even before that term gained traction in the works of thinkers such as James Cone.[2]

One way Shulman explains vernacular prophecy, therefore, is by describing what prophets do. Borrowing from biblical terminology, Shulman describes political prophets as occupying an "office." A prophet is a "messenger," "witness," "watchman," and "singer" (2008, 5). As messengers, prophets "announce" or declare the unpleasant truths often left unsaid. These announcements carry authority, Shulman contends, not necessarily because of theism but because of the "kind" or quality of claims they are. And if politics generally represent a taboo topic, then those who speak aloud about white supremacy or other institutionalized practices of subordination completely violate mainstream mores. But prophets do more than speak against societal wrongs; they "bear witness" against those who do wrong and on behalf of the wronged, or as Shulman says, borrowing from Morrison, the "disremembered and unaccounted for" (8). I think of those who either do not have access to the political process, lack the literacy or access to participate, or will be ignored by those who control the process.

Ultimately Shulman acknowledges the rhetorical potential of prophecy as a viable political option for African Americans seeking and promoting freedom and equality. Shulman borrows from political theory to interpret how African Americans have invoked a number of genres (mostly artistic) to craft prophecy as an encompassing genre and vernacular with idiomatic accessibility and rhetorical force. Shulman offer a critical conceptual framework for appreciating, interpreting, and explaining the historical and contemporary efficacy of prophecy as social justice discourse.

CROWLEY'S LEGACY, COMPOSITION RHETORIC STUDIES, AND THE BLACK PROPHETIC

In light of the sustained racial injustices articulated by the Black Lives Matter movement and persistent decline of political discourse illustrated by the current election cycle, Crowley's *Toward a Civil Discourse* remains significant. Crowley's deft analysis exposes the deliberative and civic limitations of liberal rationality and religious dogma. Still, she envisions rhetoric—rightly conceived and applied—as a way of addressing this divide. Obviously, I contend that Black prophetic discourses provide one bridge over the troubled waters that Crowley wishes to navigate. One link between Crowley's claim and African American prophecy is *doxa*. For Crowley, exposition of doxa as merely opinion misses the essential rhetorical efficacy of that term. Rather, doxa emphasizes opinion within a "temporal" and "communal" context.[3] Similarly, Black prophetic discourses have routinely operated within spaces—usually though hardly solely churches, temples, and mosques—that inhabit critical moments and community. Consider the civil rights mass meetings and the freedom schools. Both were indispensable venues for promoting critical sociopolitical opinions designed ultimately to influence the entire American body politic. To interpret either the civil rights mass meetings or freedom schools as exclusively Black revivalist spaces bent on espousing fundamentalist ideology is to miss both their political and pedagogical utility.

This is not to say that Black churches, or the civil rights movement that sprang from it, did not perpetuate the sexism, classicism, and homophobia traditionally associated with broader American evangelical culture. Few historians and cultural critics would deny this. In rhetorical studies, Vorris L. Nunley (2011) has cogently argued that the church might not constitute the safe or generative space for radically liberating discourses that venues such as Black barbershops might serve for men and Black beauty shops might for women. The Black church has been and remains a space imbued with the same "isms" as larger society. This is why Black prophetic discourses must be explored in terms of diverse rhetorical histories, methodologies, practices, and places.

African American prophecy has been a viable, but sometimes tacit and undertheorized, theme within rhetoric-composition. For one thing, the vast body of research that has been done on writing instruction that is more inclusive of and rooted in the linguistic and rhetorical traditions of African American culture grows directly out of the liberal discourses of the civil rights movement. The works of Geneva Smitherman and Keith Gilyard, to name a couple of senior scholars, have explored these connections for decades. Within the past decade other voices that see emancipatory composition instruction and practices as the direct legacy of the civil rights movement include Elaine Richardson, Gwen Pough, Adam Banks, and Carmen Kynard, but we can also begin to extract a more prophetic rhetoric from the focus on liberation in their work.

For the remainder of this chapter, I will review these connections in works by Gilyard, Lathan, Kynard, and Banks. Gilyard's monumental body of work is arguably prophetic in its own right. From his first book *Voices of the Self* (1991), to several other volumes and countless essays, he has spanned a number of genres to critique status quo assumptions about language, literature, literacy, and rhetoric. His scholarly corpus has done more than significantly expand our knowledge in these areas; his writings have radically challenged the way American society ignores, dismisses, and denigrates the voices of students of color. Gilyard has questioned the arbitrary and often hindering divides among genres of discourses. Knowledge across communicative modes, he contends, should address the task of liberating its marginalized subjects, students, or readers.

Gilyard's writings on John Oliver Killens are particularly germane to this essay. Best known for novels and poetry, Killens, like many others during the Black Arts Movement, including the recently departed intellectual giant Amiri Baraka, believed that African American sociopolitical advancement and artistic expression were indivisible; Gilyard's first book on Killens even carries the subtitle *The Rhetoric and Poetics* (2003). This fusing of rhetoric and poetics recalls Shulman's claim about aesthetics being one of the most effective modes to couch and advance prophetic discourse. Gilyard's analysis of Killens's aesthetics enriches the critique of the static divide between art and politics. One overriding theme in Gilyard's work is the emancipatory potential of all expression, particularly as that expression speaks to and ultimately becomes a political tool for the marginalized. In a substantive sense, Gilyard's and Shulman's respective analyses hearken back to how poetry was widely perceived before Socrates. Then poetry represented more than style; poetry substantively encompassed the search for and expression of knowledge.

Rhea Estelle Lathan (2015) echoes Shulman's sentiments about the politically liberating power of Black religious language. Lathan explicates the network of connections between African American church rituals, rhetoric, and literacy practices. Lathan introduces the ritual of call and response as one example. More than an improvisational give and take between preacher and congregation, call and response is both dialogical and dialectical. It is dialogical in that the preacher has a word from the Lord to deliver to the congregation, for which she wants feedback; it is dialectical in that often the preacher's content is altered by the force and frequency of the audience's response. Lathan contends that as the call-and-response ritual was used to disseminate the Bible, it was and can still be used to appropriate and analyze other texts. In her words, it is an "intellectual principle of literacy acquisition and use" (Lathan 2015, ch. 3). Hence, call and response is a heuristic for practicing literacy.

Another form of prophetic rhetoric that Lathan explores is "bearing witness." Shulman sees bearing witness as a biblical trope that infuses the aesthetic imagination of James Baldwin and Toni Morrison, as well as the theological sensibilities of Martin Luther King. Because of the cognitive and affective impulse to bear witness, their voices could not remain sequestered in their relative disciplinary spaces. Instead bearing witnesses called upon Morrison and Baldwin to transcend and critique the arbitrary age-old debate regarding art for art's sake versus art as propaganda. King's inflection of bearing witnesses could not permit him to realistically embrace the separation of church and state, if by that was meant oppressed people in a church could not speak against oppressors ruling the state. When Lathan discusses "bearing witness," (see 2015, ch. 4) she invokes the church practice of parishioners confessing their struggles and professing their victories—that is telling their story. The autobiographical nature of bearing witness stretches its significance beyond church walls and the sacred domain more broadly conceived. For Lathan, bearing witness, like call and response (and I would argue other discursive strategies in Black church) blurs the boundaries between sacred and secular, exposing instead a "continuum" between the two (see ch. 1). Also, as is the case with call and response, bearing witness could be appropriated to shape the practice and politics of literacy. The recurring act of bearing witness attests to the "historical case of African American curriculum and instructional methods" (ch. 4). In short, the rhetoric and rituals of the Black church, and often the physical edifice itself, empowered African Americans to experiment with radically creative approaches to literacy acquisition and practice—one prominent example being the Freedom schools housed in churches. These schools prepared Southern Blacks to vote en mass and ideally against the political, economic, and educational apartheid that they had experienced for decades.[4]

Carmen Kynard's book *Vernacular Insurrections* (2013) rings loudly with prophetic tones. In it, she retraces the history of debate about linguistic equity. Kynard's project accentuates the significance of an already monumental, pioneering document within rhetoric and composition: "The Students' Right to Their Own Language." Written in 1974, this document laid the foundation for progressive scholarship, teaching, and educational policy that recognized how integral students' native vernaculars are to the pedagogical process. For the most part, the claims forwarded in "The Students' Right to Their Own Language" are widely accepted among English, linguistics, and literacy scholars. Much like the expanding of the literary canon to include multicultural texts, which also spans the 1960s and 1970s, most objections to linguistic equity have come from nonacademics.

What makes Kynard's book so arresting is the way in which she interweaves this narrative of inclusive literacy practices within the larger story of civil rights and Black power. Similar to Gwen Pough (2002), Kynard views organizations such as the Black Panther Party as having a vested interested in the politics of Black literacy. Black Nationalist groups, so Kynard's argument goes, were not just interested in political agency and a degree of cultural affirmation; their sociopolitical revelation emerged from a linguistic revolution. To put the matter differently, African Vernacular English framed the narrative for the struggle. In most cases, the poetics and politics of Black liberation were indistinguishable from one another. This is a widely known proposition, proclaimed by the giants of the Black Arts Movement, including Amiri Baraka and Larry Neal. Kynard enriches this narrative by fleshing out the connection between politics, poetics, and pedagogy, Afro-centric language, liberation, and learning. The pedagogical approaches that Kynard showcases in her book can best be described as prophetic, and no genre is off limits. As rhetorical and literary educators have recognized for approximately three decades, Kynard demonstrates how the use of hip-hop music can be indispensable to cultivating an emancipatory sensibility within students. While Shulman envisions prophecy as operating as a vernacular within American politics, with all the ideological and practical range that term affords, Kynard underscores more precisely how vernacular inhabits political, cultural, and pedagogical spaces within the Black experiences. Further, for Kynard, it is the failure to see the critical link to and outcome of rhetoric, poetics, and politics of vernacular to pedagogy that constitutes the weightier problem. In other words, exposing how prophecy as vernacular foregrounds an argument that politically values Black rhetoric and poetics as epistemic—in some cases more than Eurocentric logic—is a significant move, to Shulman's credit. But if communicating, expressing, and knowing are not distilled into how people of color teach and are being taught, then these critical gestures remain politically inconsequential.

Adam Banks's scholarship (2006, 2011) also makes significant contributions to the idea of prophetic pedagogy. In both books, Banks steeps his claims about racial disenfranchisement and empowerment within social media in fresh analyses of the civil rights movement. For example, Banks (2006) revisits the conflicting—but eventually complementary—Black cultural icons: Martin Luther King and Malcolm X. Banks calls upon us to reread the twentieth-century television and film documentary images of these men through the twenty-first-century lens of digital media studies. Doing so would allow twenty-first-century audiences to recognize their respective "digital ethos" which, in turn, would result in reinterpreting, recycling, and revising their liberatory messages. A digital media analysis resists confining these men or calcifying their messages to one moment of history that we have moved on from—happily-ever-after style.

Indeed, just as Shulman envisions American social political prophet as a "messenger," "witness," "watchman," and "singer," Banks's notion of digital ethos allows for an ever expanding range of roles and stances, limited only by the practically limitless terrain of online spaces. No longer need prophets or their prophecy be confined to religious (or academic for that matter) credentials and contexts.

In a related vein, Banks (2011) invokes the Western African Griot, who was a storyteller, chronicler of traditions, and guardian of truth. Banks envisions the Black DJ as an heir to the Griot, and as such offers the Black community more than entertainment. The DJ exemplifies how African Americans can "remix" various ways of knowing and modes of communication to suit larger material purposes. This eclectic sensibility is what enabled Africans to adapt the Westernized Christianity used to oppress them and reapply it to support their doctrinal, devotional, educational, social, and political needs. This concept of remixing, therefore, is crucial to Banks's project. With it, he demonstrates how African American rhetorics not only crisscross genres and communicative modes but also encompasses multiple ends and accommodates numerous narratives simultaneously. One way Banks explores the variegated yet syncretic nature of African American rhetoric, broadly conceived, is through a discussion of Black Liberation Theology and the African American sermon. Black Theology allows for the blending of a number of rhetorical narratives, principally those pertaining to civil rights integrationism and Black Nationalism. Black Theology, and the church discursive strategies that informed and are informed by it, can foster an open conversation between "Back in the Day" and "Hip Hop" approaches to Black liberation, empowerment, and agency (see Banks 2011, chs. 3, 4). In other words, millennials need not abandon tradition, and baby boomers need not fear innovation. In fact DJs—before and after the rise of social media—model for us an indispensable truth about African American discursive strategies: they must be rooted in old school tradition but could and must sprout into an infinite number of new school directions. The topoi, commonplaces, or critical stances derivable from Banks's books are particular generative at a moment when online spaces are being co-opted to fabricate and perpetuate patently false stories, masquerading as news feeds. Calling upon the African American oral tradition to digitally reexamine and remix any topic, anywhere and advanced by anyone, invites us to seek out perches of dialectical questioning, critical engagement, and substantive critique.

Gilyard, Lathan, Kynard, and Banks, among other rhetoric composition scholars, suggest the hermeneutical and heuristic nature of

African American prophecy. African American prophetic discourses are confined neither to genre nor geography. Black prophetic critique has circulated within sermons; sacred and secular songs; strikes marches on Washington, on Wall Street, and in Watts; print journalism' and social media.[5] Similar to Baldwin's rhetoric, the Black Lives Matter movement leaders' fierce messages promoting Black humanity represent what Shulman calls the "secularizing" of prophecy (Schulman 2008, 135). Similar to Aristotelian invention, African American prophecy latches onto multiple categories, commonplaces, and stances, but in order to convey truth to power, to expose injustices, and to champion marginalized epistemologies and ontologies. Given the social unrest and political uncertainty that inhabit the globe, Crowley's appeal that we use rhetoric to talk to (rather than past) each other remains a pressing undertaking. Drawing upon, expanding, and applying the cross-disciplinary work of African American prophecy may redeem and enrich conservations not only with the Religious Right but with fundamentalists all over the world.

One of Shulman's chapters closes by describing Martin Luther King's liberating view of prophetic discourse. This description echoes both Crowley's critique of religious rhetoric and my sentiments about the generative potential of Black inflections of that rhetoric: "Then a political response to the Christian New Right should be, not a rigid defense of liberal distinctions between sacred as private and secular as public, but an effort to rework pervasive religious language to foreground its democratic features and challenge its theocratic interpreters. The problem therefore is not religiosity as such but fundamentalism as a practice and the failure to generate countervailing power by contrasting visions" (2008, 130). Black religion matters when it's made (and remade) to matter—prophetically—for all people.

NOTES

This essay contains selections from chapter one of *Where the Sacred and Secular Harmonize: Birmingham Mass Meeting Rhetoric and the Prophetic Legacy of the Civil Rights Movement* by David G. Holmes. Used by permission of Wipf and Stock Publishers.

1. In chapter 1 of my book, I sample a range of thinkers across disciplines who argue for the theoretical, political, and existential viability of African American prophecy. These include, but are not restricted to, George Shulman (political theory), David Chappell (history), and Cornel West (religion, philosophy, and African American expressive culture) (see Holmes 2017). Taken together, these thinkers deem prophetic discourses as indispensable to promoting an evolving culture of American political critique. Significantly, they all argue—with relative degrees of intensity—how prophecy can critique institutional biases and bigotries even within religious institutions.

2. James Cone is one of the pioneering thinkers in the field of Black Theology. See references.
3. See Crowley (2006, ch. 2), for her argument about doxa.
4. For a most provocative study on the freedom schools and the rhetoric and politics of literacy, see Schneider (2014).
5. Shulman considers the lunch counter sit-ins as an example of how "prophecy is an embodied form of symbolic action" (2008, 6). Marches and other physical demonstrations for social justice should fit into this category (see 2008, 6).

REFERENCES

Baldwin, James. 1963. *The Fire Next Time*. New York: Dial Press.

Banks, Adam J. 2006. *Race, Rhetoric, and Technology: Searching for Higher Ground*. Urbana: NCTE.

Banks, Adam J. 2011. *Digital Griots: African American Rhetorics in a Multimedia Age*. Carbondale: Southern Illinois University Press.

Cone, James. 1986. *A Black Theology of Liberation*. Maryknoll, NY: Orbis Press.

Cone, James. 1992. *Martin & Malcolm & America: A Dream or a Nightmare*. Maryknoll, NY: Orbis Press.

Cone, James. 1992. *The Spirituals and the Blues: An Interpretation*. 2nd rev. ed. Maryknoll, NY: Orbis Press.

Cone, James. 1997. *Black Theology and Black Power*. Maryknoll, NY: Orbis Press.

Crowley, Sharon. 2006. *Toward a Civil Discourse: Rhetoric and Fundamentalism*. Pittsburgh: University of Pittsburgh Press.

Gilyard, Keith. 1991. *Voices of the Self: A Study in Language Competence*. Detroit: Wayne State University Press.

Gilyard, Keith. 2003. *Liberation Memories: The Rhetoric and Poetics of John Oliver Killens*. Detroit: Wayne State University Press.

Gilyard, Keith. 2004. "Aspects of African American Rhetoric as a Field." In *African American Rhetoric(s): Interdisciplinary Perspectives*, ed. Elaine Richardson and Ronald Jackson II, 1–18. Carbondale: Southern Illinois University Press.

Gilyard, Keith. 2011. "African American Contributions to Composition Studies." Rpt. in *True to the Language Game: African American Discourse, Cultural Politics, and Pedagogy*, ed. Keith Gilyard, 61–76. New York: Routledge.

Holmes, David G. 2017. *Where the Sacred and Secular Harmonize: Birmingham Mass Meeting Rhetoric and the Prophetic Legacy of the Civil Rights Movement*. Eugene: Cascade Press.

Kynard, Carmen. 2013. *Vernacular Insurrections: Race, Protest, and the New Century in Composition-Literacies Studies*. Albany: SUNY Press.

Lathan, Rhea Estelle. 2015. *Freedom Writing: African American Civil Rights Literacy Activism, 1955–1967*. Urbana: CCCC/NCTE.

Mailloux, Steven. 2006. *Disciplinary Identities: Rhetorical Paths of English, Speech, and Composition*. New York: MLA.

Nunley, Vorris. 2011. *Keepin' It Hushed: The Barbershop and African American Hush Harbor Rhetoric*. Detroit: Wayne State University Press.

Pough, Gwen. 2002. "Empowering Rhetoric: Black Students Writing Black Panthers." *College Composition and Communication* 53 (3): 466–86.

Schneider, Stephen. 2014. *You Can't Padlock an Idea: Rhetorical Education at the Highlander Folk School, 1932–1961*. Columbia: University of South Carolina Press.

Shulman, George. 2008. *American Prophecy: Race and Redemption in American Culture*. Minneapolis: University of Minnesota Press.

17
WHEN QUEERS LISTEN

Timothy Oleksiak

There are sound reasons why rhetoric and composition holds tightly to the promise of change. Queer rhetorical praxis, disability studies, critical feminist theories of composition, and Critical Race theories, for example, share a deep commitment to identifying structural and systemic inequality and finding alternatives for the oppressed and disenfranchised. We want to change oppressive systems and the beliefs and values that circulate within those systems so that our communities are more just. Compositionists study pedagogical strategies that help our students understand the way writing works, and many seek to help teachers increase the likelihood that our ideas will transfer beyond the shared time we have. We want to change the way writing is understood and the teaching that emerges from that understanding.

And yet a necessary precondition for change is an openness to it. Openness, or "the willingness to consider new ways of being and thinking in the world," is necessary for the development of "habits of mind" that equip students with the requisite tools needed for success in and beyond the university (Council 2011, 4). Although important, developing the habit of openness is no easy task. In his famous "Argument as Emergence, Rhetoric as Love," Jim Corder suggests that the terror of "genuinely contending counter narratives" (1985, 21) must be understood before we can ever hope to compose across differences. The terror of confronting such narratives makes it difficult for individuals to remain open to what rhetors offer to audiences. I highlight Corder's point to suggest that openness haunts rhetoric and composition. On one hand, rhetorical negotiation and success in composing seem to require openness as a necessary precondition. On the other hand, some systems of belief refuse to hear disconfirming narratives and, thus, remain staunchly closed to rhetorical negotiations.

One approach the field has taken to the challenge of change and the presumption of openness is an exploration of listening as a rhetorical

DOI: 10.7330/9781607328933.c017

act. Those theorizing listening as a rhetorical act demonstrate how the discourses of others shape and impact the way we compose. Listening is not merely waiting our turn to compose. Rather, it is a blurring of the production/reception binary to the extent that the strategies developed with listening in mind reveal how reliant production and reception are upon each other during cross-cultural exchanges over meaningful differences. Demonstrating how this happens has been a crucial focus for listening since Jacqueline Jones Royster (1996) invited all of us to consider how we might transform listening into fitting responses.

And yet listening fails. While it is certain that listening cannot guarantee rhetorical success, scholars associated with listening as a rhetorical act frequently stop at the recognition of these failures. It is not possible to force others to listen. It is not possible to listen to what you cannot hear. We may place our focus so intently elsewhere that we cannot hear others calling us in to different ways of understanding and persuasion. In these instances, responding to listening's failures requires more than a request to remain open to contending counternarratives. What rhetorical resources, then, are available for those who wish to negotiate beyond these limits? In this chapter, I locate the failures of listening within its reliance on openness. Such work in rhetorical theory is necessary, in part, because much scholarship on listening as a rhetorical act provides few strategies necessary for dealing with moments where listening meets its limits. By tending to queer rhetorical practices, we can expand listening as a rhetorical act and provide a means for responding to the problem of openness haunting listening.

On our way to a queer listening practice, I explore the ways Krista Ratcliffe and Sharon Crowley articulate the challenge of change and openness. Both scholars, I argue, are interested in forms of rhetorical negotiation across differences and work within listening frames that blur the boundaries of production/reception. One meaningful difference between their approaches, however, rests on their assumptions about openness and the starting positions of interlocutors. For Ratcliffe (2005), rhetors are negotiating already in good faith and when they do not, rhetorical negotiations break down. Crowley (2006) makes no such assumptions about faith. She suggests that before any exchange, it is advisable to assess the degree to which the person or people we seek to negotiate with are open. Crowley names this process of assessment "ideologic." It would be false to choose between rhetorical listening or ideologic as a means for understanding listening in rhetorical theory. Rather, a more capacious theory of listening is possible when we integrate ideologic into the structure of rhetorical listening that Ratcliffe advances. After showing how ideologic enlarges listening as a rhetorical act, I then show how the queer practices of "reading" and "throwing shade" function as a form of queer listening that further complicate listening as a rhetorical act. This chapter, then, contributes to rhetorical invention generally and listening as a rhetorical act specifically by providing a conceptual vocabulary and stylized responses that help rhetoricians think through the challenge of change and the haunting of openness in listening.

But first, a request. In contrast to "paranoid reading" strategies, Eve Kosofsky Sedgwick suggests that reparative readings focus on the "performative effect rather than on any claims to truth" (2003, 129). That is, what does the work under consideration *do*? Moreover, a reparative impulse in queer analysis is "additive and accretive" (149). Rather than expose flaws in the thinking about the subject at hand, reparative strategies extend analysis in various directions. My orientation toward this work is and always will be as a generous accomplice with the scholars under consideration. As I seek to be generous to those who influence my thinking, I also seek to receive generous readings of what the ideas within this short chapter might do for those of us who regard listening and queer rhetorical practices with playful seriousness.

WHAT LISTENING MAY DO AND HOW
LISTENING CAN DO DIFFERENTLY

Rhetorical Listening does invite us to consider listening more carefully and does make a compelling ethical claim that providing strategies for others that encounter cross-cultural differences is just. In more concrete terms, rhetorical listening complicates the "reception/production opposition" by focusing on rhetorical invention (Ratcliffe 2005, 46). As I affirm rhetorical listening's project, however, I also want to point to what I see as spaces that can allow rhetorical theorists and teachers to approach rhetorical listening differently. Ratcliffe writes, "as a trope for interpretive invention, *rhetorical listening* signifies a stance of openness that a person may choose to assume in relation to *any* person, text, or culture" whose purpose it is to "negotiate troubled identification in order to facilitate cross-cultural communication about any topic" (10). Locating troubled identifications such as those who adopt racist or sexist attitudes and courses of action based on those attitudes requires that individuals seek out "exiled excess and contemplate its relation to our culture and ourselves" in ways that are nuanced (25). The result of such contemplation can lead composers to invent new forms of cross-cultural communication. Ratcliffe names this space of contemplation "non-identification." Non-identification exists as the space between identification and disidentification,[1] where judgments are withheld and resisted. Non-identification is a theoretical place of personal agency where rhetors may hold themselves open to the discourses of others. This place is crucial for resisting logics of mastery and superiority that keep us within a divided logos in which listening is withheld from speaking/writing. According to Ratcliffe, individuals engaging in rhetorical listening interact with persons, texts, or cultures by

1. Promoting an *understanding* of self and other
2. Proceeding within an *accountability* logic
3. Locating identifications across commonalities and differences
4. Analyzing claims as well as the cultural logics within which these claims function. (26)

All four modes of engagement are necessary if rhetorical listening is to happen, and, as a practice of rhetorical invention, each requires an openness to engaging as rhetorical listeners. Because the *presumption* of openness animates rhetorical listening, there is no need to provide resources for responding to the challenge of openness.

Rhetorical listening is a valuable intellectual project. From the start, it is clear that rhetorical listening is not a universal method for cross-cultural communication. Ratcliffe notes "sometimes rhetorical listening will fail" (2005, 27). In this case, failure is akin to "not useful" or "it doesn't work" as when a person responds but is unable to find a *fitting* response. Although failure in these terms is an appropriate definition for illustrating the limits of rhetorical listening, queer failure (see Halberstam 2001) complicates the process and concepts structuring rhetorical listening. Considering queer failure—particularly low theory's penchant for delighting in incivility—leads to different insights into listening's possibilities.

Rhetorical listening faces the challenge of openness through an exploration of the cultural logics animating claims. For Ratcliffe, "a cultural logic is a belief system or shared way of reasoning within which a claim may function" (2005, 149). Although beliefs are a part of cultural logics, *Rhetorical Listening* often engages cultural logics as a form of reasoning. Recognition of multiple cultural logics at play in the signification of various claims "enable listeners when appropriate, to appreciate the *reasoning* powers of others, even when disagreeing with their assertions" (33). Cultural logics, as such, may recognize beliefs, for example, but the concept is a difficult resource for understanding the extent to which individuals are open to persuasion. The integration of Sharon Crowley's "ideologic" is intended to "confer plenitude" (see Sedgwick 2003, 149) on rhetorical listening by offering resources that can help rhetorical listening respond to those critical values, beliefs, fantasies, or what-have-you's that are vital to an individual's identifications.

In her analysis of religious rhetorics, Crowley suggests that reason alone does not help us make sense of the articulations among beliefs, myths, and fantasies that animate particular positions. Central to understanding Crowley's perspective is the distinction between reason's reliance on perception and observation and ideologic's use of belief, fantasy, desires, values, and so forth, to animate its circulation (2006, 61). When considering a person's position on homosexuality, for example, it might very well be the case that arguments against homosexuals are animated through the *belief* that homosexuality is a sin, unconscious *fantasies* that homosexuality is contagious, and a *rational* (albeit stereotypical) understanding of homosexuals as sexually promiscuous. The concept of cultural logic attempts to get at each of these things, but privileges observation and perception as tools for the task. Ideologic analysis attends to the ways in which emotion, logic, history, and a range of other forces impact an individual's stance toward others.

Ideologic also helps us think through the density of a position and the costs associated with letting those positions go. According to Crowley "[Ideologic] 'explains everything,' and so its disarticulation is very costly to a believer. Many other beliefs must be given up, and others rearranged in order to abandon one . . . For these reasons beliefs that threaten the integrity of a belief system must be highly resonant as well" (2006, 61). Ideologic analysis raises the stakes of cross-cultural communication, allowing rhetors to understand the degree to which an individual is open to change in the first place. When thought through the framework of listening as a rhetorical act, ideologic analysis functions as both a process of understanding the openness of others and a means to trouble the identifications of those who remain closed to persuasion.

Ideologic is a more capacious concept than cultural logics and thus expands our response to listening's limits. As such, it may also help us think through why strategies for rhetorical listening aren't always successful and, with that understanding, invent new strategies. As Crowley explains, "Analysis of ideologic can nonetheless assist invention insofar as it may reveal whether a rhetorical appeal concerning a specific issue can be persuasive to someone whose belief system affects potential *receptivity* to arguments concerning it. If subscription to a given belief system forecasts and limits the ways in which new events and information can be read, it follows minimally that a small range of persuasive possibilities may remain open in any given case" (2006, 77; emphasis added).

The inclusion of ideologic into theories of listening removes the assumption of openness and the suggestion that a person is either open or not. If listening is a stance of openness one takes prior to rhetorical negotiation, ideologic analysis precedes rhetorical listening.

And Yet . . .

What happens when ideologic analysis leads rhetors to conclude that others are tightly closed off? Although ideologic enlarges rhetorical listening, neither Ratcliffe nor Crowley provide the resources for engaging with those who remain closed. Now is the moment to turn queer. The time has come for us to consider the listening queer, specifically.

QUEER LISTENING AND THE LISTENING QUEER

Exploring queer listening practices may find us thinking similar thoughts to those strategies articulated in *Rhetorical Listening* but tuned to different frequencies that allow those interested in listening as a rhetorical act to amplify the range of possibilities for rhetorical invention.[2] And so my goal here is to show a different kind of listening that moves us without taking us very far from the originating goals of rhetorical listening as a project on invention. That is, the temporalities, rhythms, and intensities of queer listening practices might not provide a radical transformation of listening as a rhetorical act, but such queer performatives—citations of queer practices that extend over time to become recognized *as* queer—have resonance for rhetorical listening writ large.

Reading and *throwing shade* are queer stylistic responses that have roots in the African American tradition of "playing the dozens" and a history shared by straight Black women, Black gay men, and queer people of color. This history should not suggest that it is only a rhetorical strategy unique to Black people, nor should it indicate an uncomplicated use by White gay men and White queers.[3] The differences between reading and throwing shade may not always be sharply articulated; however, a delicious illustration of reading and throwing shade comes from the legendary drag mother, Dorian Corey, during an interview in *Paris Is Burning* (1990). Mother Corey teaches us:

> That's a part of shade; that's the idea; knock 'em out if you can; hit 'em below the belt . . . Shade comes from reading. Reading came first. Reading is the real art form of insult . . . you get in a smart crack, everyone laughs and kikis[,][4] because you found a flaw and exaggerated it, then you have a good read going . . . if it's happened between the gay world and the

straight world it's not really a read it's more of an insult: a vicious slur fight. But it's how they develop a sense of how to read. They may call you a faggot or a drag queen, you find something to call them. But then when you are all of the same thing, then you have to go to the fine point. In other words, if I'm a black queen and you're a black queen, we can't call each other black queens cuz we both black queens that's not a read, that's just a fact. So then we talk about your ridiculous shape, your saggy face, your tacky clothes . . . Then reading became a developed form where it became shade. Shade is I don't tell you you're ugly, but I don't have to tell you because you know you're ugly. And that's shade.

Reading and throwing shade are audience-bound practices—the audience exists within the community and as a part of that community. This understanding of audience does not also imply that all members within the community share the same relationship to each other, themselves, or hetero/homonormative cultures, however. When deployed between heterosexuals and queers, reading and throwing shade vanish into violence. When used among queers, reading and throwing shade function as "low pedagogies."[5] In *The Queer Art of Failure*, J. Halberstam offers low theory as "theoretical knowledge that works at many levels at once, as precisely one of these mode of transmission that revels in the detours, twists, and turns through knowing and confusion, and that seeks not to explain but to involve" (2011, 15). Reading and throwing shade are down in the lived experiences of queers, and their low status offers a counterknowledge for agency, openness, temporality, and other concepts that those interested in listening as a rhetorical act will have to contend. A read or thrown shade uses insult to involve others in different ways of knowing and being.

Reading someone to filth or throwing shade cannot be separated from strategies for queer survival. A read can function as a form of "tough love," a love that stings. But precisely because the sting comes from within the community, it functions as a way to toughen each other up against the violence from without. These are forms of defense against a future threat of eradication by a dominant force that does embodied or psychic violence. These are receptive practices that when turned into action carry with them the demand to change, survive, or exist differently. The aid that comes from reading and throwing shade is not found in mimetic reproductions; rather, the aid comes from a refusal to allow others to remain closed to the read or the shade thrown. The persistence of the cultural form of insult refuses to accept a closed stance because reading and throwing shade do not assume that the object of ridicule is always already open. On the contrary, reading and throwing shade seek to pry open closed audiences.

These queer rhetorical practices are a *style* of engagement that is pedagogical as well as inventional.[6] Queers learn to be queers. And in the learning to be(come) queer, it follows that queer teachers exist and have been teaching your children for as far back as that silly cave dweller decided to freshen up the cave with a few paintings here and there. Queers are listening, and how they listen illustrates dynamic responses to the challenge of openness.

Whatever else they may be, these queer practices stomp the runway that divides reception from production. They are forms of stylized listening that play with receptivity, agency, temporality, and accountability in ways that can be instructive for thinking about listening as a rhetorical act. Queer listening practices, such as the ones discussed here, complicate rhetorical listening's cross-cultural negotiation of meaning. Such practices presuppose a different relationship between rhetor and audience that provides insights into the challenge of openness. If queer listening practices are misinterpreted, miss the mark, or otherwise fall flat, that is no indication of a fatalistic flaw in the practices themselves. They give an account of one's self (see Butler 2005), and, through such accounting, demonstrate the collapse of the reception/production binaries that make rhetorical listening a worthwhile project.

When including these rhetorical stylistics into the canon of listening's strategies, I hope to show how the singular rhythms of the texts under consideration circulate as queer listening practices that demonstrate a particular relationship that can be illustrative for those interested in listening's failures. Although it might be difficult to imagine how queer listening practices inform a rhetorical listening that takes openness as a necessary precondition for listening, I ask that we try such imaginings to see where they might take us.

"THE LIBRARY IS OPEN," OR A QUEER LISTENING PEDAGOGY

RuPaul's Drag Race is rich with illustrations of reading. *RuPaul's Drag Race* is a reality competition show where relatively unknown drag queens compete to become America's next drag superstar. On their way to the crown, contestants complete in mini- and maxichallenges and are assessed on their charisma, uniqueness, nerve, and talent. A reoccurring minichallenge throughout the show's ten seasons begins when RuPaul announces "Darlings, in the great tradition of *Paris Is Burning*: Reading is what?" To which the queens respond energetically, "fundamental!" Each queen is then brought to the front and given a pair of ridiculous glasses that they use when "reading" the other queens. On season two of *RuPaul's Drag Race: All Stars* (2016), Phi Phi O'Hara steps to the front and before she begins, says, "This is so hard among friends, which is why this should be easy." And the other queens laugh. Phi Phi continues, "You know what Adore [Delano, another queen] and the value menu have in common? They're both cheap and full of fat." Another contestant, Katya Zamolodchikova, reads Roxxxy Andrews saying, "Roxxxy Andrews, I think about you every day. Especially in the morning. At the bus stop." Katya references Roxxxy's powerful recounting of being abandoned by her mother at a bus stop when she was young. Finally, Alaska Thunderfuck 5000 begins her read of Detox, saying, "Detox. No, really, I mean that. This is actually your intervention. You should really stop this [gestures to Detox's drag]."

When framed as low listening pedagogy, reading functions in noticeable ways. In each case, the reading queen is required to insult, but to do so also requires an understanding of the other queen's vulnerabilities *and* a disregard for the degree to which the read queen wishes to protect these vulnerabilities. Adore's size, Roxxxy's traumatic childhood, and Detox's presumably poor style choices are cracked open. And in the prying open of the cracks is a space for potential transformation and change. What should be kept private is mocked with laughter. Even the intensity of the read, when met with Alyssa Edward's voice over of "y'all some hateful bitches,"[7] is ethereal; it does not stay stuck. Reading is a queer listening practice when the ways in which a queen perceives is used to crack open the other. In the reading exists a demonstration of both receptivity and invention.

Of course, some queers are just bad at reading. When Coco Montrese *tries* to read Alaska Thunderfuck 5000, she says, "Alaska, I'm sure Katya can see you from her backyard." The read fails on so many levels, it is difficult to unpack. Coco alludes to former vice presidential candidate Sarah Palin, who, when asked about Russia during an interview, provided an answer that included "you can actually see Russia from land here in Alaska." Palin was universally mocked for her answer. So, in Coco's read, she is trying to pun on Alaska (a drag queen becomes a state) while indirectly calling Katya (whose drag persona is a Russian acrobat) Russia. But none of it works, because there is no smart crack. Alaska, Katya, and Palin all walk away unscathed, and Coco hears no laughter because she brings no alternative possibility. Coco's inability to get a smart crack illustrates that reading is learned and perfected with practice. If there is any joke to be had, it is that the read so spectacularly misses the mark.

But, it would be a mistake to dismiss reading as mere play or base insult. To be angered by the insult or to dismiss the read is to miss what makes reading and throwing shade low. Reading and throwing shade function pedagogically through insult and laughter and, thus, give value to the low and uncivil. The queer hip-hop artist Ojay Morgan, who performs under the name "Zebra Katz," illustrates the public, pedagogical thrust of reading:

> Schools in I'mma read that bitch
> I'mma write a dissertation to excuse my shit
> When I act out of line and I spit and I kick
> And I rip and I dip and I yah trick
> What bitch you don't like my shit? (Katz 2012)

Like the queens of *Drag Race*, Katz points to both the incivility and pedagogical potential when reading. And while one approach to reading is to hear and experience anger or mean-spiritedness, to stop there is an attempt to elevate a low pedagogy. It is to straighten queer listening into a mode of civility that seeks its eradication.

As Mother Corey notes, throwing shade is an evolution of reading where direct insult becomes unnecessary. Throwing shade is slant insult whereby a person talks about someone indirectly. In *Drag Race*, Detox throws shade at Alyssa Edwards, when they are in the workroom, saying, "It's nice to see that they regrouted the brick. And no I was not talking about you that time." Yes. At this moment, despite protests to the contrary, Detox is throwing shade at Alyssa, and Alyssa states as much with "Oh, she already started, girl. The shade is knee deep already, girl, day one." And though the insult is indirect, the function of throwing shade as a listening practice is similar to that of reading.

The analysis of reading and throwing shade suggests that these queer listening practices share similar intentions with ideologic. A "smart crack" pries open another person and serves to wake them up to a different understanding of the world. When a read doesn't land right, when it falls flat or insult goes to wound, then whoever gets read shatters, closes off to why the crack was necessary in the first place. A read that brings no laughter, thrown shade that recognizes no light, wounds without instruction. When you misread or throw the wrong type of shade, the chance to demonstrate some real love, a queer kind of love, is lost. As such, those reading or throwing shade have to calibrate the ways in which their reads or shade affect others. The calibration of receptivity toward invention with deliberate intentions illustrates a form of queer listening.

Reading and throwing shade, with their embrace of incivility and laughter, open new possibilities for what it means to blur the production/reception binary and thus offer different styles of listening as a rhetorical act. Queers, to borrow from Hélène Cixous, are "stormy" (1976, 878). The laughter they share is tempestuous. This laughter throws participants about, and, according to Diane Davis, "to be possessed by this movement of energy, laughed by a co(s)mic Laughter, is to be thrown into a *petit mal* in which one's consciousness, one's capacity for meaning-making is suspended" (2000, 18). Laughter suspends meaning making and places participants in a state of non-identification. Laughter from a good read or thrown shade creates for others a temporary space of non-identification where the read is asked to reconsider the fixity of their positions, the vulnerabilities, their assuredness. This is a different kind of listening than the one advanced by Ratcliffe. In *Rhetorical Listening*, non-identification is a theoretical space for *rhetors*, a moment for individuals to delay judgment. Reading, on the other hand, pushes others into non-identification.

CLOSING THOUGHTS ON QUEER LISTENING

My analysis of reading and throwing shade is exploratory. What I have hoped to show in this chapter is that queers do listen, and when they listen they do so publicly and in ways that complicate rhetorical listening's need for openness as a precondition of success. When queers listen, they often do so with different strategies for assessing the degree to which others are open to hearing what they have to say. Queer listening changes the methods of ideologic analysis in ways that disallow a closed audience from halting rhetorical negotiation. When situated as a public listening pedagogy that disregards closed postures, reading and throwing shade become resources for taking communities further into negotiation when others strategies imply a moment of rhetorical failure.

In *Rhetorical Listening* Ratcliffe notes how difficult it is for the privileged to listen. My analysis shows that queer listening can function as a public pedagogy that is instructive. What I have tried to detail is how queers listen with the hope that others will explore queer rhetorics as queer *listening* practices. It might mean that new avenues of "quear" analysis can emerge. The portmanteau "quear" comes from queer and ear and signifies a critical commitment to the queer possibilities associated with listening. Quear analysis developed in this chapter reveals that when queers listen, they display a strategic openness that provides cues for how they are receiving messages while also withholding the compelling force of closure.

The queers are listening. However, rather than consider listening queers a threat, it might be that the listening queer has much to instruct us regarding the strategies available for listening rhetorically. The listening queer might drop in or fuck shit up because they are uniquely skilled at hearing what is said and can suffer no fools.

NOTES

1. Those familiar with queer theories might be thinking of Muñoz's (1999) concept of "disidentification" here. However, Ratcliffe is building upon the work of Fuss (1989 and 1995), not Muñoz.
2. Here I am inspired by Muckelbauer's work (2008).
3. In "SNAP! Culture: A Different Kind of 'Reading,'" Johnson notes, "Once signs and symbols permeate the fabric of popular culture, the foundations on which the meanings of the symbols and signs are based become sites of contestation—places where they alternately coalesce and contradict one another" (1995, 138). See Johnson's *Appropriating Blackness* (2003) for a more nuanced understanding of cultural appropriation than can be offered here.
4. For a definition of "kiki," see especially Scissor Sisters TV (2012).
5. By "low" I follow Halberstam in *The Queer Art of Failure* (2011) and the need to explore forgetfulness, stupidity, incivility, and what they might tell us about modes of queer world-making.
6. I follow Freeman's articulation of style. She writes, "style neither transcends nor subsumes culture but pries it open a bit, rearranges or reconstitutes its elements" (2010, xix).
7. Sexism in the drag community is well researched. Stanley's "When We Say 'Out of the Closets!'" (1974) is an early account of sexism and racism in the language of gay communities. As Stanley suggests, the issue is a complicated one.

REFERENCES

Butler, Judith. 2005. *Giving an Account of Oneself*. New York: Fordham University Press.
Cixous, Hélène. 1976. "The Laugh of the Medusa." *Signs: Journal of Women in Culture and Society* 1 (4): 875–93.
Corder, Jim. 1985. "Argument as Emergence, Rhetoric as Love." *Rhetoric Review* 4 (1): 16–32.
Council of Writing Program Administrators, National Council of Teachers of English, and National Writing Project. 2011. *Framework for Success in Postsecondary Writing*. CWPA, NCTE, and NWP.
Crowley, Sharon. 2006. *Toward a Civil Discourse: Rhetoric and Fundamentalism*. Pittsburgh: University of Pittsburg Press.
Davis, D. Diane. 2000. *Breaking Up (at) Totality: The Rhetoric of Laughter*. Carbondale: Southern Illinois University Press.
Freeman, Elizabeth. 2010. *Time Binds: Queer Temporalities, Queer Histories*. Durham: Duke University Press.
Fuss, Diana. 1989. *Essentially Speaking: Feminism, Nature and Difference*. New York: Routledge.
Fuss, Diana. 1995. *Identification Papers*. New York: Routledge.
Halberstam, J. 2011. *The Queer Art of Failure*. Durham: Duke University Press.
Johnson, E. Patrick. 1995. "SNAP! Culture: A Different Kind of 'Reading.'" *Text and Performance Quarterly* 15 (2): 122–42.
Johnson, E. Patrick. 2003. *Appropriating Blackness: Performance and the Politics of Authenticity*. Durham: Duke University Press.

Katz, Zebra. 2012. "Ima Read (Music Video)-Zebra Katz ft. Njena Reddd Foxxx." YouTube. https://www.youtube.com/watch?v=5a7toR0pm1g.

Muckelbauer, John. 2008. *The Future of Invention: Rhetoric, Postmodernism, and the Problem of Change.* New York: SUNY Press.

Muñoz, José Esteban. 1999. *Disidentification: Queers of Color and Performance of Politics.* Minneapolis: University of Minnesota Press.

Paris Is Burning. 1990. Dir. Jennie Livingston. Sundance Institute. DVD.

Ratcliffe, Krista. 2005. *Rhetorical Listening: Identification, Gender, Whiteness.* Carbondale: Southern Illinois University Press.

Royster, Jacqueline Jones. 1996. "When the First Voice You Hear Is Not Your Own." *College Composition and Communication* 47 (1): 29–40.

RuPaul's Drag Race All Stars. 2016. "All Star Talent Show Extravaganza." Episode 2. Dir. Nick Murray. LogoTV. http://www.logotv.com/episodes/oqkn1e/rupauls-all-stars-drag-race-all-star-talent-show-extravaganza-season-2-ep-201.

Scissor Sisters TV. 2012. "Scissor Sisters–Let's Have a Kiki–Instructional Video." YouTube. https://www.youtube.com/watch?v=eGCD4xb-Tr8.

Sedgwick, Eve Kosofsky. 2003. *Touching Feeling: Affect, Pedagogy, Performativity.* Durham: Duke University Press.

Stanley, Julia E. 1974. "When We Say 'Out of the Closets!'" *College English* 36 (3): 385–91.

18

RHETORIC IN DIMNESS

Matthew Heard

PREFACE

I became a licensed foster parent in the State of Texas in 2014. The first
children placed with me were a nine-month-old girl, A, and her two-year-
old brother, J. A year later, the state moved both children away from my
home to a permanent placement with consanguine (blood-related) family. During my time with J&A, I learned to think differently about invention, theory, and rhetorical resourcefulness as I watched both children
respond with resilience to the challenges of their lives. What follows is
an essay written to them—my first "foster kids," J&A.

The form of my chapter responds to Linda Alcoff's argument, following Gayatri Spivak, that instead of writing *for* others, privileged writers
need to learn to write *to* others, leaving space for others to write back
(1992, 23). In writing a personal account *to* J&A, I have risked setting
aside many of the conventions expected of academic essays on theory.
I am grateful for the space to take this risk, as it allows me to make a
leap away from what seems "natural, self-evident, and universal" about
theory making without having a replacement model in mind (Crowley
2010, xi.).

Although personal, my essay is in conversation with the idea of "weak
theory" as described by Kathleen Stewart (via Eve Sedgwick): theory
"that comes unstuck from its own line of thought to follow the objects it
encounters, or becomes undone by its attention to things that don't just
add up" (2008, 72). The inventiveness I encountered in J&A maps well
onto Stewart's discussion of weak theory as a powerful, "supple" way of
forging connections and surviving among the "beaten-up fragments" of
situations in which "things just don't add up" (81). Moved in and out
of multiple homes before their first and second birthdays, J&A did not
have the stability of family or security of place from which to develop
the distance and "wide generality" that characterizes strong theories
(Sedgwick 2003, 134). Instead, they developed an exceptional ability to

DOI: 10.7330/9781607328933.c018

create joy, vitality, and relationship through a "weak" inventiveness that was limited for the most part to their immediate world. I focus on this "weak" invention in my account below because it proved so effective in binding us together as we learned to be a foster family. Although J&A knew nothing of invention in the ancient rhetorical sense of using "systematic procedures for finding arguments appropriate to the rhetorical occasion" (Crowley 1985, 146), they nonetheless created unexpected opportunities for us to *sustain relationality* with one another even when the systematic procedures of the foster care system seemed to push in the opposite direction.

"Dimness" enters as a way of drawing attention to the underlying conditions that make such weak, defiant invention necessary. I offer the term hospitably, as an opening to consider how rhetors such as J&A can come to have powerful, unexpected effects on unstable situations that would seem to afford little space for clear theory making. Foster care can be an experience of dimness for children and parents. So can experiences of trauma (Larson 2018), illness (Santos 2011), disability (Kittay 1999), and poverty (Cushman 1998). These experiences rarely proceed through "bright" academic clarity, with the time and critical distance to rise above the fray and generalize. J&A instead clung to a "nonheroic" inventiveness (Davis 2010, 89), defined not by clearly calculated decisions but by a hopeful, desperate need to survive together. If I have a thesis in my account of J&A below, it is that this defiant, nonheroic, weak invention must be pursued outside of traditional habits of theory making. Rhetoric needs to look for invention in the dimness of struggle and instability. Worth pursuing, such observation is likely to come at a high cost, interrupting the critical distance and clarity that are embedded in the ancient idea of the theorist as "the spectator who is most distant from the scene . . . and whose body is . . . in one sense the least involved in the production" (Crowley 2006, 27). Learning to care for J&A in the midst of the foster care system has taught me that while one can recognize dimness from a distance, learning to navigate it requires something else: a willingness to cling tightly to others, traveling with them through confusion, unknowing, surprise, and, sometimes, loss.

* * *

I got the call that you were coming at 10 a.m. on a Tuesday in April. By then, I had done everything I could to prepare—beds ready, outlets covered, house cleaned. I told other family members that I wasn't nervous, but in reality I was terrified. I had good reasons. You came just a few days after I had completed almost a year of training to be a foster parent. Over the course of many months, I had been prepared to understand that you might be scared, angry, or even violent when you arrived. At the least, you would be disoriented from your abrupt transition; at the most, you would recoil from me and the rest of the world for days or weeks until you felt safer. My preparation ended up making me more fearful than confident. I had stuffed animals ready at the door just in case.

J, you got out of the car first when the CPS car pulled into the driveway late that afternoon. The CPS agent had barely unbuckled your car seat when you shed its straps and tumbled out of the door. You were already running. As soon as you saw me, you bounded over, stretching out your arms for a hug. I was shocked. None of my training had gone over this possibility. I had been taught to respect your need for distance, to keep everything safe and calm. My training even taught me *not* to ask you to call me *daddy* so that our relationship could develop naturally. So, when you flung yourself at me, I found myself looking over at the CPS agent to see if it was OK. From that first moment, you were already challenging the identities we had been given as foster child and foster parent, including the logic that told me you were broken, fragile, and in need of space and distance. I found myself drawn to your enthusiasm. It took less time than I expected to be charmed by your smile. For all my behavioral training as a foster parent and rhetorical training as a scholar of listening and attunement, I was enjoying this change in the script. It had never occurred to me that you could be so happy in the midst of a situation that seemed so fraught with tension and uncertainty. Although I was standing in front of my home, you and A ultimately were the ones offering welcome and hospitality.

You were a bright spot in whatever space you occupied. You leapt from person to person, energetic and smiling, and I learned to expect the rush of footsteps that warned me you were about to launch yourself at me. Despite your brightness, I remember our year together as a year of encompassing *dimness*. I say *dim* not because we were without hope or happiness, but because we struggled constantly that year to adjust to the system we found ourselves within. Foster care has always been a difficult arrangement to manage. Just after you left, a landmark case against the Texas foster care system revealed that it was "broken for Texas's children, who almost uniformly leave State custody more damaged than when they entered" (*MD et al. v. Abbott et al.* 2015, 254). We weren't alone in our experiences of disruption and confusion as a foster family: the case documents tell stories of some children who had over sixteen placements before they were teenagers. And while we liked most of our social care workers and other foster care agents, it was humbling to be at the mercy of a system that was set up to shape your life so powerfully through its standards and regulations. Subject to these rules and limitations, we were never quite sure of a clear way forward.

And so we made our way chaotically, without much planning, hitting a lot of dead ends along the way. Within a week of your arrival, for instance, you were sent back out on weekly visits to spend time with your biological family in a city an hour away. You and A spent many hours strapped into car seats with a random CPS driver, and, more often than not, you would arrive at your destination only to find that no one had shown up. You would then return home again immediately, without the contact that you needed and were promised. It was disheartening, but you usually hopped out of the car with a smile on your face regardless.

We also lived in the shadow of fears that you might be leaving the next month, week, or day. In between family visits, social workers from the state or from our local agency would show up to check on you, leaving behind bits of information about how your case was proceeding and, occasionally, predictions about when you might be taken away and returned "home." One agent might say that family members were going to emerge and lay legal claim on you, while the next social worker to visit would shake her head and say, no, that it looked instead that you might be up for adoption. It was hard to imagine ourselves as a family when I was constantly told not to get too attached so that I wouldn't have such a hard time when I had to let you go.

Although the situation kept changing from moment to moment, your need to be loved was a welcome constant. You ran around, read books, and rode your little scooter. You were not bothered that the plans for your future were swirling around you, never quite in reach. You continued to smile and demand hugs. It was persuasive: faced with either resting on the promises of the foster care system that changed from day to day or being charmed by your mischievous smile into believing that the moment at hand was all that mattered, the choice was easy. We began to bond, and every moment became an education in learning to live well in the uncertainty of what the next moment would bring.

The fact that you invented joy and affection within a system that seemed so poorly designed to foster such relationality was a welcome surprise. For a year before you came, I was learning about you through the 200-page policy manuals I had to read and the hours of mandatory trainings I had to attend with state social workers, child placing agencies, psychiatrists, and attorneys. Together, these measures of preparation gave me a strong, comprehensive theory of *the foster child* and *the foster parent* that mapped out every possible angle of our relationship. One training showed me how to restrain you in case you became violent toward me. Another explained why I needed to spend hours each weekend filling out forms and databases to record your health, attitude, and progress as data for the state to assess. I appreciated the scholarly overtones of this work, which aimed at helping foster parents invent procedures and plans to keep foster children like you safe. But foster care training suffered from the same problem that plagues theory making in general, which is that the wider its scope, the more it loses contact with the objects it defines and explains.

I was consequently unprepared for just how effectively and defiantly your own invention strategies recalibrated the scope of my expectations to focus exclusively on you. You always got the attention that you needed. More often than not, it was through a crazy smile or an attempt to "joke me" (as you would say). But you also learned my commonplaces and quickly used them to get in some extra time with me, watching soccer on TV or stomping around like AT-AT walkers in the living room. And it wasn't just me: you expected reciprocity and responsibility from everyone else as well. Once, on a trip to a large furniture store, I turned around to see you charming a stranger who thought you were lost (you were five feet away), and before I knew it, she was taking your hand and about to follow you in a different direction. We sometimes joke about people who have "never met a stranger," but you took it one step further. In the absence of stable lines defining who could be your family and friends, you treated everyone as a stranger who had a preexisting obligation to care for you. You created relationships out of nothing, forming bonds where none could be expected. Everyone was welcome to enter your world of wonder and joy, and you did not wait (as I did) for the authorities to say OK.

What I would come to understand over the next year of our time together was that you and A had spent nearly all of your existence acclimating to uncertainty and instability. The shaky ground of foster care, which was such a shock to me, was your training ground. You learned to survive in dimness, without clarity. You had little control over the big decisions in your life—who your family would be, where you would live, when (or if) you would eat, where you would sleep. Although you learned to invent joy and cultivate relationships in this setting, you were exposed to a darker side of this unpredictability as well. The first time we stayed in a hotel on the way to a family wedding, you screamed uncontrollably at the hotel room door, and I realized that you were reliving one of those moments of traumatic uncertainty from your past. After that, your usual way of smiling and rushing into everything seemed all the more remarkable.

* * *

A, you were a nine-month-old baby when you first came to stay with us, and my most iconic image of you is from a photograph that shows you clinging tightly to me and staring out beyond the camera, a fierce intensity clearly visible in your eyes. This careful, piercing stare is what many people took away as their first impression of you. Your habit was to watch the world silently, intently, with a slow but perceptive alertness. I only realize now how effective that habit was for your survival. You were a tiny baby, and by taking in every possible angle of a room, you could figure out where you needed to cling to in order to feel safe.

Because you seemed so content when you were being held above the world around you, it took two months for me to realize that you were unable to hear. Somehow, I had missed it. We had all missed it—me and the social workers, doctors, psychiatrists, and other foster parents who all, as caretakers, had failed in our basic responsibility for your care. We missed that you had significant hearing loss. Or, more accurately, we believed in the systematic procedures that gave us confidence in our own theories about your development, to the exclusion of the quiet ways you showed us every day that we were wrong. Theories can sometimes illuminate an idea so brightly that they end up making us miss the little details we should be paying the most attention to. In your case, the more I bought in to what the foster system was telling me—that your silence was a consequence of trauma, or even a sign of cognitive delays stemming from malnutrition—the less attuned I was to how you were keeping me close, closing the distance between us. You were not able to respond to others' assumptions about you through language or clearly reasoned logics, but you kept clinging to me anyway, ensuring that the contact between us would yield the safety and attention you needed.

Fortunately, your foster mother was quicker to understand what was going on than I was. Having spent many nights rocking you to sleep, listening to you breathe in and out, she was intimately attuned to your cries, murmurs, and rumblings in the night. She began to wonder if your symptoms were signs of a present, physical pain rather than remnants of a theoretical response to trauma. And so she treated you as though you were trying to say something to her, whereas I and the other caregivers treated you as an object of our theories: foster child, hearing impaired, developmentally delayed. It took your foster mother sitting attentively in the space beside you, holding you through your crying, watching you breathe, to reveal what you had been communicating all along: that your silence and tentativeness were calls to action and not leftover traces of a damaged psyche. We had read your tentativeness as traumatic, but we never listened for your silence as inventive.

We waited anxiously in the weeks after you had the procedure to put tubes in your ears to see how you would respond. The change was almost immediate. You whipped your head around to noises like the jingle of the dog's collar, which we never knew you hadn't heard. You started babbling and ultimately said your first word ("No!"). You smiled more often and climbed down from the safety of your perch on my hip to play and roughhouse with your brother. Pretty soon you were giving commands to the whole family.

It didn't mean that you stopped being a foster child or immediately overcame your delays in speech or language. But your resilience nonetheless taught us the value of clinging to one another intimately when the procedures of foster care might have directed us otherwise. Whenever I thought about you sitting quietly in my arms, I was reminded that your calm, hesitant disposition was strategic, building trust that would ultimately serve as the basis for our discovery of your hearing loss. All along, you were telling me through your silence and watchfulness that you trusted me, even though I did not understand you.

* * *

We drove to the airport on a bright day in March, knowing we were about to say goodbye and watch you fly away. My thoughts at the time were all sadness and self-pity. I saw us caught up in an epic tragedy: the system had won; our family was breaking up forever. These overtones of tragedy threatened to darken the whole experience. Yet, even in those last moments, you still found ways to surprise me in your responses to yet another turn of events beyond your control. J, you were typically cheerful, sprinting around the lobby to play hide and seek while I made awkward conversation with the CPS workers who had come to escort you away. You didn't seem to wonder about these new rumblings of change. At one point, you came over to tell me, cheerily, "I'm not going to see you again!" You were smiling, as usual, and it was oddly comforting. A, you also comforted me in the way you knew best, turning back into the quiet, clinging little girl who just wanted to sit on my hip and look watchfully at the rest of the world. I held you there again, wondering if it was you or me that needed this contact most. I wished so desperately I could keep you from leaving. One more time, yet again, you were leaving behind a home and family at the behest of a system that was trying, in its systematic way, to make things right for you. You were only toddlers, but it seemed as though you had lived in dimness long enough to have your own resilient ways of shoring yourselves up against interruption and instability. I thought about it after I waved goodbye for the last time and headed back to the airport parking lot: I had hoped to teach you so much about the world, but in the end, I felt like I had leaned on your abilities to remain present and connected even in the face of unprecedented loss.

As terribly difficult as it is to acknowledge now that years have passed without us seeing one another again, your unique ways of showing love made me think differently about the mutability of family and the temporality of home. Even now, these reconfigurations of home and family powerfully shape how I live as a foster parent and as an academic. I know that psychologists and sociologists have theories about how devastating it can be for children to lose their connection to biological parents, and I don't want to minimize the reality of this trauma for you or other foster children. Certainly, we all experienced some of these consequences during our time together. But still, in excess of these challenges, you showed me and so many others how the dimness of foster care could be confronted with a resourcefulness and resilience that left happy and bright memories behind, strange artifacts in a system that was admittedly "broken." You defied identification as the sum of the pathologies and diagnoses that were written in your files. You built family and friends out of the difficult circumstances of your early life, which you did not choose. You invented ways to surround yourself with attention and secure your safety. I hope that you will always recognize these parts of you as worthwhile, positive, sophisticated: through your inventiveness, you sustained relationships with people who even now think about you and care about you. Your dim, defiant, desperate rhetoric passed the most basic test—it kept you alive and it kept you loved.

* * *

I wanted to tell you, J&A, that my experiences with you prepared me to open the door to other foster children who have come into the house since you left. We adopted C last year, and now O is living with us too. Every morning, they walk down the hallway past four pictures—one of each of them, and the other two of you. I hope that by the time you read this, there will be many other pictures in the hallway of children who have spent time in the same rooms where you ran around and played and sat quietly observing the world. They won't ride a scooter as well as you, J, or have A's ability to stare down a whole room with her glance. But they will be safe and as stable as possible, and no doubt they will teach us new things about the world like you did.

AFTERWORD

I will say here for the benefit of those listening in that I believe we are obligated to inhabit dim as well as bright spaces. Many scholars in rhetoric are already shining light on rhetorical practices of dimness. Some have deep experiences with instability and uncertainty themselves, or are living even now without the guarantee of safety. What I find helpful to add from my time together with J&A is the reminder that many of these experiences with uncertainty are unwilled and unchosen. They won't show up in accounts of invention as a systematic procedure, and we won't hear about them through traditional channels of scholarship. But to recall Diane Davis's terms again, we need not wait for "heroic" efforts to turn our attention to rhetoric in dimness (2010, 88). The responsibility to look for the defiant, weak, everyday ways that rhetors such as J&A manage to survive is not the work of heroes. It is our responsibility. We confront a common need for justice, freedom, care, and love. For survival. It may be that heeding this responsibility demands not only strong theories about hospitality and otherness, but also weak theories that sustain hope and relationality in the most improbable of circumstances. I think we find these weak theories by seeking out precarious contact that, as Judith Butler writes, reminds us to look for human inventiveness and response "where we do not expect to find it, in its frailty and at the limits of its capacity to make sense" (2006, 151). The hardest part, I believe, is not thinking about or theorizing what these limits might look like. The hard part is leaning into contact with others and leaping, as I once saw a little two-year-old boy do, without any assurances that someone will be there to catch us.

REFERENCES

Alcoff, Linda. 1992. "The Problem of Speaking for Others." *Cultural Critique* 20 (Winter): 5–32.

Butler, Judith. 2006. *Precarious Life: The Powers of Mourning and Violence*. New York: Verso.

Crowley, Sharon. 1985. "The Evolution of Invention in Current-Traditional Rhetoric: 1850–1970." *Rhetoric Review* 3 (2): 146–62.

Crowley, Sharon. 2006. *Toward a Civil Discourse: Rhetoric and Fundamentalism*. Pittsburgh: University of Pittsburgh Press.

Crowley, Sharon. 2010. *The Methodical Memory: Invention in Current-Traditional Rhetoric*. Repr. ed. Carbondale: Southern Illinois University Press.

Cushman, Ellen. 1998. *The Struggle and the Tools: Oral and Literate Strategies in an Inner City Community*. Albany: SUNY Press.

Davis, Diane. 2010. *Inessential Solidarity: Rhetoric and Foreigner Relations*. Pittsburgh: University of Pittsburgh Press.

Kittay, Eva Feder. 1999. "Not My Way, Sesha, Your Way, Slowly: 'Maternal Thinking' in the Raising of a Child with Profound Intellectual Disabilities." In *Mother Trouble: Legal*

Theorists, Philosophers and Theologians Reflect on Dilemmas of Parenting, ed. Julia Hanisberg and Sara Ruddick, 3–30. New York: Beacon Press.

Larson, Stephanie. 2018. "'Everything Inside Me Was Silenced': (Re)Defining Rape through Visceral Counterpublicity." *Quarterly Journal of Speech* 104 (3): 123–44.

M.D. et al. v. Abbott et al. 2015. Civil Action No. 2:11-CV-84. United States District Court Southern District of Texas. Washington: Government Printing Office.

Santos, Marc. 2011. "How the Internet Saved My Daughter and How Social Media Saved My Family." *Kairos: A Journal of Rhetoric, Technology, and Pedagogy*. Accessed February 13, 2018. http://kairos.technorhetoric.net/15.2/topoi/santos.

Sedgwick, Eve Kosofsky. 2003. *Touching Feeling: Affect, Pedagogy, Performativity*. Durham: Duke University Press.

Stewart, Kathleen. 2008. "Weak Theory in an Unfinished World." *Journal of Folklore Research* 45 (1): 71–82.

Afterword

FEELING AND HISTORIOGRAPHY

Debra Hawhee

In August of 1995, as a wide-eyed and mostly silent new PhD student, I had the great good fortune of a place at the table in Sharon Crowley's History of Composition seminar. Professor Crowley was in the throes of writing *Composition in the University* (1998), and best I can recall, I was jittery with nervousness and excitement. Crowley started the seminar by asking us to introduce ourselves and explain why we were taking the course. My fellow seminarians explained in turn—and with what seemed to me at the time an admirable mixture of practiced eloquence and extreme poise—how their interests in the course stemmed from their work in the writing classroom and a curiosity about the institutional histories of the practices encouraged there, how the subject matter would be foundational for their dissertation, or how they wanted additional training in archival research methods. When my turn came, my insides flipped. I looked down, blushed, said my name, raised my eyes to meet Crowley's, drew a breath, and with a little too much enthusiasm, blurted, "I'm here to work with YOU."

Crowley rolled her eyes.

Work together we did, though. Mostly, like my colleagues in that seminar—including Blake Scott, Kakie Urch, Andy Alexander, the late Summer Smith—I soaked up everything I could. I dove into the archive that I chose (the papers of John C. Hodges, author of *The Harbrace College Handbook*). I read—or really, was consumed by—Michel Foucault's *Discipline and Punish* (1977) for the first time in the class. I was taken in, like so many mid-1990s graduate students, by Foucault's immersive style. I recall opening that book for the first time on an airplane, tearing my eyes from his thick description of drawing and quartering, looking around at the passengers next to and in front of me, and marveling that their breath seemed so steady. My breathing remained uneven as I worked my way through the Hodges archives at the University of Tennessee, Knoxville. Doing history gave me a thrill;

DOI: 10.7330/9781607328933.c019

the pull was undeniable. I was *in*. So much of my approach to scholarly worlds and work started in Crowley's seminar room. I began to develop a feel for doing history.

I want to use the space of this afterword to reflect on feeling, a usefully ambiguous term that pulls toward emotions as much as toward a sensation of touch and toward a kind of bodily knowledge, a habituated mode of engagement. Feeling is front and center in Crowley's book on fundamentalism and rhetoric (2006). Chapter 3, "Belief and Passionate Commitment," presents a dense web of theories and research findings that show how important "depth of feeling" can be for rhetorical processes and the costs of ignoring the visceral in accounts of how arguments burrow, dwell, and even harden within and among individuals (58–101).

Feeling courses through this volume too, especially in the places where writers engage Crowley's work most explicitly, and it positively leaps off the pages when the editors consult her directly. This volume, in short, glimmers with the very best of Crowley, lessons embedded so deeply in her seminar rooms, her writings, and her mentoring—and all of them involve feeling. What Crowley has modeled for so many of us is this: a refusal to conceal feeling with professional propriety, and a willingness to let theory and history exert gravitational pulls on each other, a process I have come to believe depends on a scholarly feeling and commitment.

CANDOR, FEELING, EDGE

Sharon Crowley is as candid as they come, and her candor bristles with feeling. The mentor profile of Crowley in *Women's Ways of Making It in Rhetoric and Composition* draws out this value quite aptly. As Crowley puts it to the editors, "though it sometimes hurts, it sometimes backfires, I try to be honest" (2008, 230). She continues, "I always try to tell [colleagues and graduate students] that institutions are awful places—bitter, nasty, they bring out the worst in people. Don't expect institutions to behave honorably. Don't expect them to have a memory. Don't expect them to appreciate you. I try to tell all those things" (230–32). As these lines indicate, Crowley is most searingly candid when it comes to institutions. I recall one of our many collaborative phone conversations when I told her some story about the egos in my department (I honestly can't recall whether this was at Illinois or Penn State), and howling with laughter she said something like "For a minute there I forgot what Big Ten English departments are like! Thanks for the reminder!" Her edgy delight has been a comfort to me during my time directing graduate studies, especially when colleagues in my office proclaim the importance of their work at sometimes fevered pitches. If a Crowley emoji existed, it would need to combine a grim eye roll with a chortle.

The textbook industry is another institution that brings out Crowley's frankness, and she and I have fought a number of battles together on that front. Once when an editor in charge of the fifth edition of *Ancient Rhetorics for Contemporary Students* (Crowley and Hawhee 2011) informed the two of us via email that the (large corporate) publisher wanted to cut our textbook size by half, Sharon emailed in response that we would simply remove every other word and be done with it.[1] Disciplinary institutions also hold firm in the face of criticism. The most obvious example is how little the universal first-year composition requirement budged during or following the decade Crowley spent arguing against it.

The value of candor edges Crowley's scholarly interventions, infusing the work with feeling. As part of the now-famous Octalog, the first of what would become a foundational series of panel conversations about historiography, Crowley began her "philosophical statement" by observing that she and her seven interlocutors were "physically closer up here than we are intellectually." She then added, "Very interesting, a sort of contrast" ("The Octalog" 1988, 13).

The word "contrast" aptly defines Crowley's relationship with members of her loyal opposition (especially Connors and Berlin). One review essay of Crowley's and Connors's books is fashioned as a compare-contrast essay, but it features far more in the way of contrasts, devised around the notion of "Different Attitudes" (Severino 2000, 645). What results is a sentence like this: "Both authors tell painful stories, but Crowley, who focuses on the 'uneasy' composition-literature relationship and the reasons for her 'uneasy relationship with composition,' tells more of them" (646). The contrasts even turn up in a fine-grained analysis of voice, syntax, and tone: "While Connors hedges and forgives with the passive voice, attributing causality to abstract outside forces ('Composition-rhetoric was forced by cultural pressures to insist more and more strongly on formal and mechanical correctness,' 13), Crowley uses active voice to indict specific agents ('When American rhetoric teachers finished their revision of rhetorical pedagogy in the late 19th century, the only bits of classical invention that remained were the topics,' 35). When Connors discusses misguided and harmful practices, he sighs. When Crowley does, she rails" (651). Railing, or what she (and I) would call polemic, is a specialty of Crowley's; the subtitle of the book in question—"Historical and Polemical Essays"—owns one of controversy's loudest and most charged genres.

That charge is what I'm getting at. Crowley led with feeling, with such captivating and bristly titles as "Let Me Get this Straight" (1994), and "What Shall We Do with the White People?" (2012), and "Reimagining the Writing Scene: Curmudgeonly Remarks about Contending with Words" (1991). This last essay usefully documents Crowley's stance on theory, placing it in service of supporting an imagined view of writing instruction that foregrounds social justice (197). If the word "theory" evokes a view from afar—which I would liken to something like a *vision* of how things might be (so a necessary relation to the future, as Diane Davis's contribution to this volume notes)—Crowley performs theory by wading into the muck of composition's difficult and often conflicting material conditions.

For Crowley, viewing is never antithetical to doing; the two feed and reinforce each other. And theory is something that scholars carry, live, use, *exude*. This is precisely why Crowley seems to be puzzled by—if not resistant to—an interview question asking her to sort out the relationship between poststructuralism and feminism (interview in this collection). Her ruminative answer contains several questions, the first of which is "Who the hell knows?" (a question she repeats). Another is more of an observation formulated as a question: "Feminism sort of becomes part of one's bones, does it not?" (interview in this collection). What Crowley presents here is the way theory works through a kind of inhabiting, which is to say it both inhabits and is inhabited, and never—not if it is to effect change—in a static, unfeeling way.

THE PULL

Crowley's regard for feeling, her embrace of the most charged genres and titles, and her attitude all feed her approach to scholarship and to history in particular.[2] Her candor, care, and commitment to change shape her approach to disciplinary history, demonstrating how history doesn't just use or depend on theory, but how it can challenge and even generate theory. The question of how history can manifest theory is one that has occupied me of late, and this book reminds me of how that seminar with Crowley made its way into my own bones.

History I approach as an act, a deep dive, a plunge into the past, its documents, its lives, its moments, its movements. I learned this in part from working with Crowley. The work of history, to be sure, entails encounters with objects—texts, artifacts, technologies, and the ideas and practices scratched out of those objects. As Crowley put it thirty years ago now in a searing review of James Berlin's *Rhetoric and Reality*, "Sources remain inert until the historian selects and assembles them into a coherent narrative" (1988, 245).[3] And as Sara Ahmed observes, contact with objects impresses on us; it "generates feeling" (2015, 6). History, in this way, can be viewed as an art of compelling—evoking interest, attention, or admiration in a powerfully irresistible way. To start, methodologically, historians attend—okay, I'll say it more provocatively—*should* attend—to that which compels, that which pulls us in.

In a 1994 keynote address at the Rhetoric Society of America conference in Norfolk, Virginia, Crowley used the language of puzzlement to articulate this pull toward what would later become one of *Composition in the University*'s animating questions. "I have long been puzzled about why the pedagogy of taste played such a large role in 19th-century American school rhetoric; in addition to its paradoxical nature, the development of taste seems, on the face of it, an odd project for rhetoric teachers to take on, given its provenance in modern philosophical aesthetics and its pedagogical impulse toward self-improvement rather than civic intervention" (1995, 12). The pull, as Crowley's frame here helps show, is often manifest in such astute observations as "That's weird." Or, put in the form of a research question: "What the—?" Theory, that is, often wells up in questions that, at least initially, bug—if not confound. These are the often not-quite-formulated problems or questions that researchers attuned to the pull will return to, like a child's thumb to a loose upper tooth.

Crowley, of course, turned to other theorists for background to the question, and perhaps to refine or elaborate a problem (Pierre Bourdieu's work on taste seems to have served as a helpful guide in this instance), but to rely exclusively on the theory of others is to miss the opportunity to generate theory anew. Such a move happens through a deep dive into history. And Crowley's findings—(1) "that the pedagogy of taste adumbrated in early 19th-century school rhetoric texts operated according to the principles of discrimination and exclusion" (1998, 12), and (2) that this particular strain of taste meant the "demise of rhetorical education" (36)—grow from her potent combination of history and theory.

I offer this example from the many in Crowley's oeuvre in order to illuminate a conviction I have developed over the past two decades of using history to do theory and vice versa. That conviction can be most plainly stated in this way: if the material does not point the way to a big, broad theoretical commentary (whether it's about pedagogical practices, the discipline of rhetoric, rhetorical practice, political action, communication itself), then it's quite possible that perhaps the material of that particular history itself isn't compelling enough. In other words, to invoke my colleague Hester Blum, who has written on these matters, the justification that "scholars have overlooked" a body of work is insufficient (2012). There may be very good reasons not to study something.

Put more positively, and even more simply: the pull. Pay attention to that. And here I mean both the pull of the scholar toward a puzzling question as well as the pull that theory and history can exert on each other simultaneously. Here I would be remiss not to mention the philosopher-classicist Andrea Wilson Nightingale's work on the cultural context of *theōria*, from which we derive the word "theory." Nightingale points out that the three different ways the word was used in ancient Greece all "involved a detachment from one's homeland, an act of seeing or spectating, and (in many cases) some sort of transformation of the viewer" (2001, 29). The detachment piece relates to the role of the *theōros* as an envoy, someone who would journey to an oracle, take libations and commune there, and then report back. Even the *theōroi* who viewed religious festivals from on high journeyed from their homes to do so and reported back what they witnessed.

A distinction between theory and history may well be found in that very traveling: theory can be built through and even pulled from history; it makes history itself travel.[4] I learned this early on in an osmotic way from Janet Atwill, my first rhetoric teacher, who I think remains one of rhetoric's most brilliant historian-theorists, and with whom I studied ancient rhetoric and contemporary French philosophy more than two decades ago now. Working with Atwill prepared me to encounter Crowley, prepared my intellectual blood and bones to take in the lessons there.

When I say theory makes history travel, I don't necessarily mean time travel, but the ability to get the compelling work of history to range across questions, across subdisciplines or disciplines, to be useful *elsewhere*, to be useful *now*. What I'm talking about here is the very thing Crowley spent her career working on: using the tools of historiography to root out the movements, material forms, and abstract values carried by certain approaches to language, be they nineteenth- and early twentieth-century rhetoric schoolbooks or fundamentalist discourses. It's important not to stop with the rooting out, but to then compel those movements, forms, and values to fold back on current practice. Doing so can upend or extend the discipline's most staunch and enduring theoretical perspectives in a way that jolts the now. As the chapters in this volume demonstrate, Crowley does that jolting, and the work she has inspired here and elsewhere continues to reverberate, to shake things up, to carry forward her explicit findings and implicit scholarly principles.

By way of closing, I want to rewind once more to that first semester I spent with Crowley. I stayed in my apartment over Thanksgiving break to draft my seminar paper on Hodges and the making of his handbook. I gave it to her early in hopes of getting feedback. A week or so later I went to Crowley's office, and she handed me the paper and said, "You get an A for this course as long as you submit this essay for publication." My heart soared! Then she put her forearm on her desk, performed a Crowley forward-lean—along with a gestural equivalent of throat clearing she has where her thumb moves hair away from eyes—leveled her gaze right at me, and said, "One more thing. Not every sentence needs to start with the word 'The.'" My heart leveled off. I had work to do. I absorbed her observation and resolved to do better. Even in such a mundane example, this was quintessential Crowley: telling us, telling us all, in the most direct and specific ways possible, to do better.

Perhaps the best way we can honor her is by listening—and then doing—better, following the pull of history, working to articulate history's implications for the now, and serving as envoys for what we find. None of this can be achieved without attending to professional and scholarly feeling. This volume serves as a guide for just that.

NOTES

1. It bears mentioning here that the large corporation acquired the original publisher of *ARCS*; Sharon is not likely to have signed with the likes of this behemoth.

2. Parts of this section's reflections on the interanimating relationship between history and theory began as my contribution to a Rhetoric Society of America (RSA) supersession, entitled "Theory for (a) Change: Five Manifestos." As organizer of the panel, I chose the manifesto—another of controversy's genres—as our mode, and I populated the panel with women scholars from a variety of theoretical perspectives and disciplinary backgrounds. Sharon Crowley did not attend this RSA, but when a scholar in the audience raised his hand and blurted, "there's something gendered going on here," I could almost hear Crowley cackling from afar.

3. I feel compelled thirty years on to leave space for theories that acknowledge the vibrational aspect of objects, theories that are tantalizingly making their way into reflections on archives. I admire Steedman's (2002) reflections on dust; see Järvensivu and Lummaa (2014) for a pairing of object-oriented ontology with archive photographs.

4. The presentation version of this argument leans on Michele Kennerly's tantalizing explication of *phantasia* and its ability to "jolt" (2010, 287).

REFERENCES

Ahmed, Sara. 2015. *The Cultural Politics of Emotion*. 2nd ed. New York: Routledge.

Blum, Hester. 2012. "Application Advice." *Inside Higher Education*. Accessed April 30, 2012. https://www.insidehighered.com/advice/2012/04/30/essay-how-write-good-applications-jobs-or-grants.

Crowley, Sharon. 1988. "Rev. of Berlin, James A. *Rhetoric and Reality: Writing Instruction in American Colleges, 1900–1985.*" *College Composition and Communication* 39: 245–47.

Crowley, Sharon. 1991. "Reimagining the Writing Scene: Curmudgeonly Remarks about Contending with Words." In *Contending with Words: Composition and Rhetoric in a Postmodern Age,* ed. Patricia Harkin and John Schilb, 189–97. New York: Modern Language Association of America.

Crowley, Sharon. 1994. "Let Me Get This Straight." In *Writing Histories of Rhetoric,* ed. Victor J. Vitanza, 1–19. Carbondale: Southern Illinois University Press.

Crowley, Sharon. 1995. "Biting the Hand That Feeds Us: Nineteenth-Century Uses of a Pedagogy of Taste." In *Rhetoric, Cultural Studies, and Literacy,* ed. John Frederick Reynolds, 11–20. Mahwah, NJ: Lawrence Erlbaum Associates.

Crowley, Sharon. 1998. *Composition in the University.* Pittsburgh: University of Pittsburgh Press.

Crowley, Sharon. 2006. *Toward a Civil Discourse: Rhetoric and Fundamentalisms.* Pittsburgh: University of Pittsburgh Press.

Crowley, Sharon. 2008. "Sharon Crowley." In *Women's Ways of Making It . . . In Rhetoric and Composition,* ed. Michelle Ballif, Diane Davis, and Roxanne Mountford, 217–32. Mahwah, NJ: Erlbaum.

Crowley, Sharon. 2012. "What Shall We Do with the White People?" In *Concord and Controversy: Proceedings of the Rhetoric Society of America,* ed. Antonio de Velasco and Melody Lehn, 9–22. Long Grove, IL: Waveland Press.

Crowley, Sharon, and Debra Hawhee. 2011. *Ancient Rhetorics for Contemporary Students.* 5th ed. With Debra Hawhee. New York: Pearson/Longman.

Foucault, Michel. 1977. *Discipline and Punish: The Birth of the Prison.* Trans. Alan Sheridan. New York: Vintage.

Järvensivu, Paavo, and Karoliina Lummaa. 2014. "Object-Oriented Ontology and Archive Photographs: Towards Ecological Understanding." *Mustarinda: Helsinki Photography Biennial Edition, HPB14.* 76–84.

Kennerly, Michele. 2010. "Getting Carried Away: How Rhetorical Transport Gets Judgment Going." *Rhetoric Society Quarterly* 40 (3): 269–91.

Nightingale, Andrea Wilson. 2001. "On Wandering and Wondering: '*Theōria*' in Greek Philosophy and Culture." *Arion* 9 (2): 23–58.

"The Octalog: The Politics of Historiography." 1988. *Rhetoric Review* 7 (1): 5–49.

Severino, Carol. 2000. "Review: Archivists with Different Attitudes." *College English* 62 (5): 645–53.

Steedman, Carolyn. 2002. *Dust: The Archive and Cultural History.* New Brunswick: Rutgers University Press.

Appendix

SHARON CROWLEY'S
PUBLICATIONS BY YEAR

1972

"A Heideggerian Reading of Contemporary Utopias." *Journal of the Philosophy Club of the University of Northern Colorado* 1: 35–40.

1973

"The Semantics of Sexism." *ETC: A Journal of General Semantics* 23: 407–11.

1975

"How to Stack Firewood so Teachers and Books Aren't Burned by Censors." *Arizona English Bulletin* 17: 64–67.
"Why Teach Writing?" (with George Redman). *College Composition and Communication* 26: 279–81.

1977

"Components of the Composing Process." *College Composition and Communication* 27: 234–40.

1978

"Rev. of New Composition Textbooks." *College Composition and Communication* 29: 82–33.

1979

"Of Gorgias and Grammatology." *College Composition and Communication* 30: 279–84.

1982

"Rev. of Williams, Joseph. *Style: Ten Lessons in Clarity and Grace.*" *Journal of Advanced Composition* 3: 197–201.

1983

"Preparing Your Students for Freshman Composition: On Getting Down the Mountain." *Write, The University of Arizona Writing Program Outreach Newsletter* 3: 4–5.

1984

"Neo-Romanticism and the History of Rhetoric." *Pre/Text* 5: 19–37. "On Post-Structuralism and Compositionists." *Pre/Text* 5: 185–95.
"Response to Robert Connors." *College Composition and Communication* 34: 88–91.

DOI: 10.7330/9781607328933.c020

"Rev. of Horner, Winifred, ed. *Bridging the Gap: Composition and Literature.*" *Rhetoric Review* 3: 105–8.

1985

"The Evolution of Invention in Current-Traditional Rhetoric, 1850–1970." *Rhetoric Review* 4: 146–62.
"Great Expectations: Composition Theory and Practice." *Connecticut English Journal* 16: 99–104.
"Invention in Nineteenth-Century Rhetoric." *College Composition and Communication* 35: 51–60.
"writing and Writing." In *Writing and Reading Differently: Deconstruction and the Teaching of Composition and Literature,* ed. J. Douglas Atkins and Michael L. Johnson, 93–100. Lawrence: Kansas University Press.

1986

"The Current-Traditional Theory of Style: An Informal History." *Rhetoric Society Quarterly* 16: 233–50.
"The Perilous Life and Times of Freshman English." *Freshman English News* 16: 11–16. "Rev. of Horner, Winifred, ed. *The Present State of Scholarship in the History of Rhetoric.*" *College Composition and Communication* 36: 336–38.
"Rhetoric, Literature, and the Dissociation of Invention." *Journal of Advanced Composition* 6: 17–32.

1987

"Derrida, Deconstruction, and Our Scene of Teaching." *Pre/Text* 8: 169–83.
"Method in Nineteenth-Century American Rhetoric." In *Visions of Rhetoric: History, Theory, Criticism,* ed. Charles Kneupper, 58–67. Arlington, TX: Rhetoric Society of America.
"The Teaching of Writing: What Good Is Theory?" *Arizona English Bulletin* 34: 29–33. "The Wyoming Resolution Opposing Unfair Salaries and Working Conditions for Post-Secondary Teachers of Writing" (with Linda Robertson and Frank Lentricchia). *College English* 49: 274–80.

1988

"Octalog: The Politics of Historiography" (with James Berlin, Robert J. Connors, Richard Leo Enos, Susan C. Jarratt, Nan Johnson, James J. Murphy, and Jan Swearingen). *Rhetoric Review* 7: 5–49.
"Rev. of Berlin, James A. *Rhetoric and Reality: Writing Instruction in American Colleges, 1900-1985.*" *College Composition and Communication* 39: 245–47.
"Three Heroines: An Oral History." *Pre/Text* 9: 202–6.

1989

"Linguistics and Composition Instruction, 1950–1980." *Written Communication* 6: 480–505.
"A Plea for the Revival of Sophistry." *Rhetoric Review* 7: 318–34.
"Rev. of Neel, Jasper. *Plato, Derrida, Writing.*" *Rhetoric Review* 7: 392–95.
A Teacher's Introduction to Deconstruction. Urbana: National Council of Teachers of English.

1990

"Jacques Derrida on Teaching and Rhetoric." *ATAC Newsletter* 2: 1–3; rpt. *Journal of Advanced Composition* 10: 393–96.

The Methodical Memory: Invention in Current-Traditional Rhetoric. Carbondale: Southern Illinois University Press.

"On Intention in Student Texts." In *Encountering Student Texts: Interpretive Issues in Reading Student Writing,* ed. Bruce Lawson and Susan Sterr, 99–110. Urbana: National Council of Teachers of English.

"Rev. of Quandahl, Ellen, and Patricia Donahue. *Reclaiming Pedagogy.*" *College Composition and Communication* 41: 344–45.

"Rev. of Warnock, Tilly. *Writing as Critical Action*" (with Tim Peeples). *Journal of Advanced Composition* 10: 434–46.

1991

"Jacques Derrida on Teaching and Rhetoric." In *(Inter)views: Cross-Disciplinary Perspectives of Rhetoric and Literacy,* ed. Gary A. Olson and Irene Gale, 142–44. Carbondale: Southern Illinois University Press.

"A Personal Essay on Freshman English." *Pre/Text* 12: 155–76.

"Re-imagining the Scene of Teaching Writing." In *Contending with Words: Rhetoric and Composition in a Postmodern Age,* ed. Patricia Harkin and John Schilb, 189–97. New York: Modern Language Association.

"Report to the Profession from the Committee on Professional Standards" (primary author, with Linda Robertson, James Slevin, Elizabeth M. Wallace, and Susan Wyche-Smith). *College Composition and Communication* 42: 330–44.

"Rev. of Kitzhaber, Albert R. *Rhetoric in American Colleges, 1850–1900.*" *College Composition and Communication* 42: 514–16.

1992

"Reflections on an Argument That Won't Go Away; or, A Turn of the Ideological Screw." *Quarterly Journal of Speech* 78: 450–65.

"Rev. of Jarratt, Susan C. *Rereading the Sophists: Classical Rhetoric Refigured.*" *Composition Chronicle* 4: 11–2.

1993

Ancient Rhetorics for Contemporary Students, 1st ed. New York: Macmillan.

"A Letter to the Editors." In *Writing Theory and Critical Theory,* ed. John Schilb and John Clifford, 319–26. New York: Modern Language Association.

"Modern Rhetoric and Memory." In *Rhetorical Memory and Delivery: Classical Concepts for Contemporary Composition and Communication,* ed. John Frederick Reynolds, 31–44. Mahwah, NJ: Lawrence Erlbaum.

"Neo-Romanticism and the History of Rhetoric." Rpt. in *Pre/Text: The First Decade,* ed. Victor J. Vitanza, 17–35. Pittsburgh: University of Pittsburgh Press.

1994

Ancient Rhetorics for Contemporary Students, 2nd ed. (with Debra Hawhee). New York: Allyn and Bacon.

"In Memory of James Berlin." *College Composition and Communication* 45: 159–60. "Let Me Get This Straight." In *Writing Histories of Rhetoric,* ed. Victor J. Vitanza, 1–19. Carbondale: Southern Illinois University Press.

"Rev. of Halloran, S. Michael, and Gregory Clark, eds. *Oratorical Culture: Transformations in Nineteenth-Century Rhetoric.*" *Rhetoric Review* 13: 198–200.

"Poststructuralist Composition." In *Encyclopedia of English Studies and Language Arts,* vol. 2, ed. Alan C. Purves, Linda Papa, and Sarah Jordan, 936–37. New York: National Council of Teachers of English and Scholastic.

1995

"Composition's Service Ethic, the Universal Requirement, and the Discourse of Student Need." *Journal of Advanced Composition* 15: 227–39.

"Biting the Hand That Feeds Us: The Uses of Taste in Nineteenth-Century Rhetoric Texts." In *Rhetoric, Cultural Studies, and Literacy*, ed. Fred Reynolds, 11–20. Mahwah, NJ: Lawrence Erlbaum.

1996

"Around 1971: Current-Traditionalism and Process Pedagogy." In *Composition in the Twenty-First Century: Crisis and Change*, ed. Lynn Z. Bloom, Donald A. Daiker, and Edward M. White, 64–74. Carbondale: Southern Illinois University Press.

"Current-Traditional Rhetoric." *Encyclopedia of Rhetoric and Composition*, ed. Theresa Jarnagin Enos, 156–57. New York: Routledge.

"Derrida." *Encyclopedia of Rhetoric and Composition*, ed. Theresa Jarnagin Enos, 177–79. New York: Routledge.

"The Politics of the Universal Requirement: A Response to Edward M. White." *Journal of Basic Writing* 15: 88–91.

"Rev. of France, Alan. *Composition as a Cultural Practice*." *Rhetoric Review* 14: 406–8.

1998

Composition in the University: Historical and Polemical Essays. Pittsburgh: University of Pittsburgh Press.

"Excerpt from 'Early Concerns of CCCC.'" *FORUM: Newsletter of the Non-Tenure-Track Faculty Special Interest Group* in *College Composition and Communication* 50: A12–A14.

"Histories of English, Pedagogy, and Composition." *College Composition and Communication* 49: 109–14.

"Preface." In *Gypsy Academics and Mother-Teachers: Gender, Contingent Labor, and Writing Instruction*, by Eileen E. Schell, vii–xii. Portsmouth, NH: Boynton/Cook, Heinemann.

"Rev. of Connors, Robert J. *Composition-Rhetoric*." *Rhetoric Review* 16: 340–43.

1999

"Afterword: The Material of Rhetoric." In *Rhetorical Bodies*, ed. Jack Selzer and Sharon Crowley, 357–64. Madison: University of Wisconsin Press.

Rhetorical Bodies: Towards a Material Rhetoric, ed. (with Jack Selzer). Madison: University of Wisconsin Press.

"The Universal Requirement in First-Year Composition" (with Kohl M. Glau, Peter Goggin, and John Ramage). *BWe: Basic Writing eJournal* 1: n.p. https://bwe.ccny.cuny.edu/Issue%201.2.html#sharon.

2000

"Rev. of Hinchman, Lewis P., and Sandra K. Hinchman, eds. Memory, Identity, Community: The Idea of Narrative in the Human Sciences." *Philosophy and Rhetoric* 33: 187–91.

"Rev. of Nelson, Cary, and Steven Watt. Academic Keywords: A Devil's Dictionary for Higher Education." *Journal of Advanced Composition* 20: 457–61.

2001

"Abolish or Perish? Managed Labor in Composition: A Roundtable with Sharon Crowley." Ed. Anthony D. Baker. *Workplace: A Journal of Academic Labor*. http://web.archive.org/web/20050107162420/, http://www.fredonia.edu/department/english/simon/workplace/abolishcover.html.

"*Composition in the University* Revisited: Sharon Crowley Responds to Raul Sanchez." *JAC Online.* http://web.archive.org/web/20010303171205/, http://jac.gsu.edu/jac/Revi ewsreviewed/sanchez.htm.

"Judith Butler, Professor of Rhetoric." *Journal of Advanced Composition* 21: 163–67.

"Rev. of Horner, Bruce. *Terms of Work for Composition: A Materialist Critique.*" *College Composition and Communication* 53: 352–56.

"When Ideology Contaminates Theory: The Case of the Man from Weaverville." *Rhetoric Review* 20: 66–91.

2002

"Body Studies in Rhetoric and Composition." In *Composition as Intellectual Work*, ed. Gary P. Olson, 177–87. Southern Illinois University Press.

"How the Professional Lives of WPAs Would Change if FYC Were Elective." In *The Writing Program Administrator's Resource: A Guide to Reflective Institutional Practice*, ed. Stuart C. Brown, Theresa Enos, and Catherine Chaput, 219–30. Mahwah, NJ: Lawrence Erlbaum.

2003

"Composition Is Not Rhetoric." *Rhetoric/Composition: Intersections/Impasses/Differends*, ed. Lisa Coleman and Lorien Goodman, n.p. Spec. issue of *Enculturation* 5. http://www .enculturation.net/5_1/crowley.html.

"Rev. of Alcorn, Marshall. *Changing the Subject in English Class: Discourse and the Construction of Desire.*" *Composition Studies* 21: 143–45.

"Rev. of Sipiora, Phil, and James Baumlin, eds. *Rhetoric and Kairos: Essays in History, Theory, and Practice.*" *Rhetoric Review* 22: 82–5.

2004

Ancient Rhetorics for Contemporary Students. 3rd ed. (with Debra Hawhee). New York: Pearson/Longman.

"Communication Skills: A Brief Rapprochement between Speech and English Rhetoricians." *Rhetoric Society Quarterly* 34: 89–103.

2005

"Rev. of Bousquet, Marc, Tony Scott, and Leo Parascondola, eds. *Tenured Bosses and Disposable Teachers: Writing Instruction in the Managed University.*" *Rhetoric Review* 24: 224–27.

2006

Toward a Civil Discourse: Rhetoric and Fundamentalisms. Pittsburgh: University of Pittsburgh Press.

2007

"Rev. of Cobb, Michael. *God Hates Fags: The Rhetoric of Religious Violence.*" *Journal of Advanced Composition* 27: 819–26.

"Rev. of Steiner, Mark Allen. *The Rhetoric of Operation Rescue: Projecting the Christian Pro-Life Message.*" *Rhetoric Review* 26: 455–59.

"Tolerance and the Christian Right." *Communication and Critical/Cultural Studies* 4: 102–5.

"Two Gentlemen in Wyoming." In *1977: The Cultural Moment in Composition*, ed. Wendy Sharer, Brent Henze, and Jack Selzer, 65. West Lafayette, IN: Parlor Press.

2008

Critical Situations: A Rhetoric for Writing in Communities (with Michael Stancliff). New York: Longman/Pearson.

"Sharon Crowley." In *Women's Ways of Making It . . . In Rhetoric and Composition*, ed. Michelle Ballif, Diane Davis, and Roxanne Mountford, 217–32. Mahwah, NJ: Lawrence Erlbaum.

2009

Ancient Rhetorics for Contemporary Students, 4th ed. (with Debra Hawhee). New York: Pearson /Longman.

"Pure Rhetoric." In *Renewing Rhetoric's Relations to Composition: Essays in Honor of Theresa Jarnagin Enos*, ed. Shane Borrowman, Stuart C. Brown, and Thomas P. Miller, 315–28. New York: Lawrence Erlbaum Associates.

2011

Ancient Rhetorics for Contemporary Students. 5th ed. (with Debra Hawhee). New York: Pearson.

2012

"What Shall We Do with the White People?" In *Concord and Controversy: Proceedings of the Rhetoric Society of America*, ed. Antonio de Velasco and Melody Lehn, 9–22. Long Grove, IL: Waveland Press.

2013

"Afterword: A Reminiscence." In *Theorizing Histories of Rhetoric*, ed. Michelle Ballif, 190–95. Carbondale: Southern Illinois University Press.

2017

Crowley, Sharon, Ryan Skinnell, Judy Holiday, Andrea Alden, and Kendall Gerdes. 2017. "Forty Years and More: Reminiscences with Sharon Crowley." *Composition Forum* 37. http:// compositionforum.com/issue/37/sharon-crowley-interview.php.

CONTRIBUTORS

Andrea Alden is assistant professor in the College of Humanities and Social Sciences at Grand Canyon University, where she teaches undergraduate writing. Her monograph *Disorder in the Court: Morality and Myth in the Insanity Defense* was published by the University of Alabama Press in 2018, and she has also published chapters on community-university partnerships, online "Pro-Ana" communities, and writing centers. Her research focuses primarily on the intersection of the law with medical discourse, with particular attention to mental disability law.

Jason Barrett-Fox is director of composition and assistant professor of rhetoric and writing studies at Weber State University in Ogden, Utah. His research explores the intersections of rhetoric, gender-power, technology, and the new materialisms. His work has appeared in *The American Journal of Semiotics; Rhetoric Review; JAC: A Journal of Rhetoric, Culture, and Politics; Peitho;* and the *Quarterly Journal of Speech,* among other places. His current book project on feminist medial technologies and posthuman historiography is currently under advance contract with Ohio State University Press.

Geoffrey Clegg is assistant professor of English at Midwestern State University in Wichita Falls, TX. He has worked extensively with Jason Barrett-Fox on posthumanist theory and praxis, specifically the posthuman and modern military engagement, and researches the intersections of business communication and disability. Dr. Clegg is a recovering archivist whose dissertation focused on Joanne Cockelreas, one of the early female PhDs who helped shape the composition program at East Texas State University in the early 1970s and '80s.

Kirsti Cole is associate professor of rhetoric, composition, and literature at Minnesota State University. She is the faculty chair of the Teaching Writing Graduate Certificate and Master's of Communication and Composition programs. She has published in *Feminist Media Studies, College English, Harlot,* and *thirdspace* and has chapters in collections focused on stepmothering and digital media, transgressive feminist rhetoric, and the rhetoric of civility. She is the editor of two collections: *Feminist Challenges or Feminist Rhetorics?: Locations, Scholarship, Discourse* (Cambridge Scholars Press, 2014) and *Surviving Sexism in Academia: Feminist Strategies for Leadership* (Routledge, 2017).

Joshua Daniel-Wariya is assistant professor of rhetoric and professional writing at Oklahoma State University, where he also serves as associate director of First-Year Composition. His research focuses on the intersections of digital rhetorics, computer games, and play, especially as those intersections relate to the teaching of writing. His work has previously appeared or is forthcoming in *Computers and Composition, Baseball and Social Class, Bad Ideas about Writing,* and elsewhere.

Diane Davis is professor and chair of rhetoric and writing at the University of Texas–Austin. She is also Kenneth Burke Chair of Rhetoric & Critical Media Philosophy at the European Graduate School in Saas-Fee, Switzerland. Her research and teaching interests include rhetorical theory, critical theory, digital culture, and continental philosophy. She is the author of *Breaking Up [at] Totality: A Rhetoric of Laughter* (Southern Illinois University Press, 2000), *Inessential Solidarity: Rhetoric and Foreigner Relations* (University of Pittsburgh, 2010), and *Women's Ways of Making It in Rhetoric and Composition* (Routledge, 2008, coauthored with Michelle Ballif and Roxanne Mountford). She has edited, as well, *The ÜberReader: Selected Works of Avital Ronell* (University of Illinois Press, 2008) and *Reading Ronell* (University of Illinois Press, 2009). And she coedited, with Michelle Ballif, a special issue of *Philosophy and Rhetoric* (2014), entitled "Extrahuman Rhetorical Relations: Addressing the Animal, the Object, the Dead, and the Divine."

Rebecca Disrud holds an MA in comparative literature and a PhD in English from Indiana University, Bloomington, and is currently coordinator of the Writing Center at the University of Washington, Tacoma. She is working on a project on how circulating new metaphors for writing could transform and diversify university writing centers.

Bre Garrett is assistant professor and the director of composition at the University of West Florida. At UWF, Bre teaches a variety of courses in rhetorical theory, composition peda-gogy, and digital writing. She has published work on embodied composing and rhetorical theory in *The New Work of Composing* and *Computers and Composition*. She has two forth-coming pieces on writing studio curricular design, and she has additional forthcoming chapters that strategize embodied leadership practices in writing program administration. Bre is currently at the beginning stages of a new project, compiling an edited collection on embodied or crip time.

Kendall Gerdes is assistant professor of technical communication and rhetoric at Texas Tech University. Kendall earned her PhD in rhetoric and writing from the University of Texas at Austin, where she was assistant director of the Digital Writing and Research Lab. Her research focuses on gender, ethics, and rhetorical theory, tracing the ways that gender marks and even constitutes the rhetorical structure of address. Kendall's writing has been published in *Philosophy & Rhetoric, Transgender Studies Quarterly, Kairos, QED: A Journal of Queer Worldmaking*, and *Interstitial.*

Catherine C. Gouge is associate professor of English at West Virginia University. Her recent scholarship has appeared in *Rhetoric Society Quarterly*, the *Journal of Technical Writing and Communication*, and the *Journal of Medical Humanities*. Her research interests include the rhetoric of health and medicine, science and technology studies, writing and editing pedagogy, and technical communication.

Debra Hawhee is McCourtney Professor of Civic Deliberation at Penn State University. She is the author of three books, most recently *Rhetoric in Tooth and Claw: Animals, Language, Sensation* (University of Chicago Press, 2016). She is coauthor of *Ancient Rhetoric for Contemporary Students*, in its fifth edition, with Sharon Crowley, who was sole author of the first edition.

Matthew Heard is associate professor of English at the University of North Texas. He is also a licensed foster parent. While his previous research has focused on questions of ethics in intersection with studies of tonality, attunement, and sound, his most recent project looks at ways that ethical and familial identities are contested within the American foster care system. He has published articles in *College English, Composition Forum, JAC, Pedagogy*, and *Philosophy & Rhetoric.*

Joshua C. Hilst is associate professor in the Department of Literacies & Composition at Utah Valley University, as well as the faculty director of the writing center. He obtained his PhD in rhetorics, communication and information Design at Clemson University. He has written on rhetorical theory and composition for *JAC, Enculturation*, and the *Journal of Basic Writing.*

Judy Holiday is associate professor of rhetoric and writing at the University of La Verne. Her research interests focus primarily on issues related to postmodern difference. She has published scholarship in *Rhetoric Review* and *Composition Forum* and has contributed book chapters to *The WPA Outcomes Statement—A Decade Later; Serendipity in Rhetoric, Writing and Literacy Research*; and *What We Wish We'd Known: Negotiating Graduate School*, which she coedited. She is currently working on a monograph about violence as a socially constructed cross-cultural episteme.

David G. Holmes is professor of English, writing, and rhetoric at Pepperdine University. The author of *Revisiting Racialized Voice: African American Ethos in Language and Literature* (Southern Illinois University Press, 2004) and *Where the Sacred and Secular Harmonize: Birmingham Mass Meeting Rhetoric and the Prophetic Legacy of the Civil Rights Movement* (Cascade Books, 2017), he is a frequent presenter at national conferences and has published articles in *Rhetoric Review, College English*, and the *Journal of Black Studies*. His current areas of research include composition pedagogy, rhetorical theory, civil rights rhetoric, and Sidney Poitier's films.

Bruce Horner is Endowed Chair in Rhetoric and Composition at the University of Louisville, where he teaches courses in composition, composition theory and pedagogy, and literacy studies. His recent monographs include *Rewriting Composition: Terms of Exchange* (Southern Illinois, 2016), *Crossing Divides: Exploring Translingual Writing Pedagogies and Programs* (Utah State, 2017, coedited with Laura Tetrault), *Economies of Writing: Revaluations in Rhetoric and Composition* (Utah State, 2017, coedited with Brice Nordquist and Susan Ryan), and *Translinguality, Transmodality, and Difference: Exploring Dispositions and Change in Language and Learning* (Enculturation/Intermezzo, 2015, coauthored with Cynthia L. Selfe and Tim Lockridge).

William B. Lalicker has taught composition and rhetorical theory for over twenty-five years. His research and publications focus on writing program administration, writing pedagogy, translingualism, and intercultural rhetoric. He is a former co-chair of the Council on Basic Writing, and has served frequent stints as a writing program administrator. He is professor of English at West Chester University of Pennsylvania.

Jennifer Lin LeMesurier is assistant professor at Colgate University in the Writing and Rhetoric department. Her extensive dance and performance background has greatly shaped her research trajectory. Her work on the intersections of dance, rhetoric, and writing can be found in *Rhetoric Review* and *College Composition and Communication*. Currently, she is examining the role of bodily rhythms in teaching and learning writing.

James C. McDonald is professor of English at the University of Louisiana at Lafayette, where he has served as Writing Center director, director of first-year composition, and department head. He earned a PhD in English with a concentration in rhetoric at the University of Texas at Austin in 1987. He has published textbooks and articles on rhetorical history, writing centers, and academic labor.

Timothy Oleksiak is an assistant professor of English and the director of the Professional and New Media Writing Program at University of Massachusetts, Boston. This low-femme opera lover prefers he, him, his pronouns and rhetoric. Previous contributions to rhetoric and composition studies appear in *Pre/Text, Composition Studies, Works and Days*, and *Queer Praxis: Questions for LGBTQ Worldmaking*.

Dawn Penich-Thacker teaches composition and gender studies for the Maricopa Colleges in Phoenix, Arizona, as well as political rhetoric and professional writing at Arizona

State University. Her most recent theoretical work was published in *Kairos* and dealt with Burkean identification and identity in online spaces. She studied under Sharon Crowley for her doctoral work on rhetorical subjectivity in the US military.

Ryan Skinnell is assistant professor of rhetoric and writing and assistant writing program administrator at San José State University. He is the author of *Conceding Composition: A Crooked History of Composition's Institutional Fortunes* (Utah State University, 2016), editor of *Faking the News: What Rhetoric Can Teach Us About Donald J. Trump* (Societas, 2018), and coeditor of *What We Wish We'd Known: Negotiating Graduate School* (Fountainhead, 2015). He has published articles in *Composition Studies, Enculturation, JAC, Rhetoric Review, Rhetoric Society Quarterly, WPA: Writing Program Administration,* and edited collections.

J. Blake Scott is professor of writing and rhetoric at the University of Central Florida (UCF), where he was a founding associate chair and director of degree programs for that department. He has published five books, most recently, *Methodologies for the Rhetoric of Health & Medicine* (2017, coedited by Lisa Meloncon), and dozens of peer-reviewed journal articles. With Lisa Meloncon, he is a founding coeditor of the journal *Rhetoric of Health of Medicine (RHM)*.

Victor J. Vitanza is professor of English and founding director of Clemson University's transdisciplinary Rhetorics, Communication, and Information Design PhD program. He is also Jean-François Lyotard Professor of Media and Communications at the European Graduate School in Saas-Fee, Switzerland. He has published extensively in rhetoric, philosophy, literature, art, and cinematography, including three monographs: *Negation, Subjectivity, and The History of Rhetoric* (SUNY, 1996), *Sexual Violence in Western Thought and Writing* (Palgrave, 2011), and *Chaste Cinematics* (Punctum, 2015). He is also the founding editor of *PRE/TEXT: A Journal of Rhetorical Theory*.

Susan Wyche received her PhD in rhetoric and composition from the University of Washington in 1986. She received tenure at Washington State University, where she served several years as the director of writing, and also at California State University, Monterey Bay, where she founded the University Writing Program. Midcareer, needing a change of pace, she trained in the University of California–Berkeley Garden Designer program, and spent ten years creating sustainable landscapes on the West Coast. In 2007, after moving to Maui and seeing the impact of the recession on the construction trade, she returned to academe as assistant for special projects to the chancellor at University of Hawai'i Maui College. Today she is director of the Grants Office for the UH Community College System, in the Office of the Vice President.

INDEX